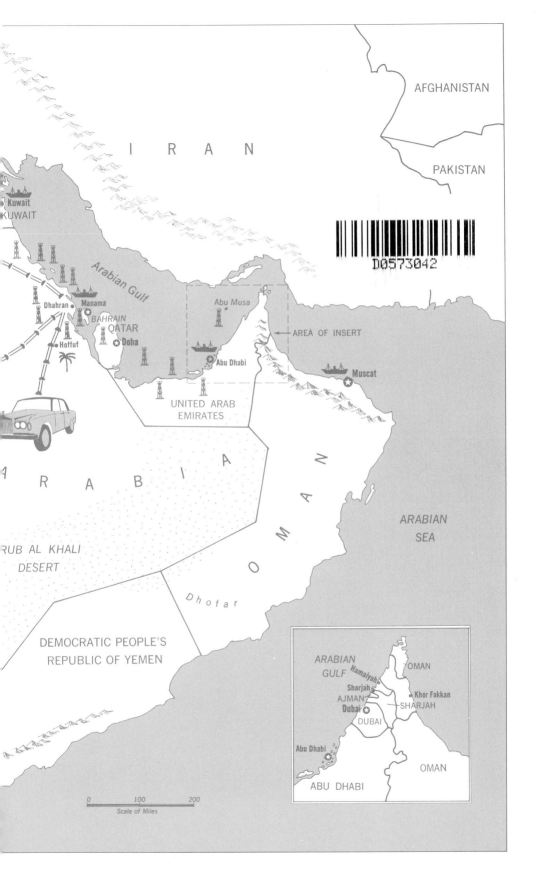

AFGHANISTAN

PAKISTAN

I R A N

Kuwait
KUWAIT

Arabian Gulf

Dhahran • Manama
BAHRAIN
QATAR
Hoffuf
Doha

Abu Musa

AREA OF INSERT

Muscat

Abu Dhabi

UNITED ARAB
EMIRATES

A R A B I A

O M A N

ARABIAN
SEA

RUB AL KHALI
DESERT

Dhofar

DEMOCRATIC PEOPLE'S
REPUBLIC OF YEMEN

D0573042

ARABIAN
GULF

Hamaiyah
Sharjah
AJMAN
Dubai

OMAN

Khor Fakkan
SHARJAH

DUBAI

Abu Dhabi

OMAN

ABU DHABI

0   100   200
Scale of Miles

$UPER-WEALTH

THE SECRET LIVES
OF THE OIL SHEIKHS

$UPER-WEALTH

THE SECRET LIVES OF THE OIL SHEIKHS

by **LINDA BLANDFORD**

WILLIAM MORROW AND COMPANY, INC.
NEW YORK   1977

Published in the United States in 1977.

Copyright © 1976,1977 by Linda Blandford

Published in Great Britain in 1976 under the title *Oil Sheikhs*.

Printed in the United States of America.

1   2   3   4   5   6   7   8   9   10

Library of Congress Cataloging in Publication Data

Blandford, Linda.
    Super-wealth.

       1. Wealth—Arab countries.   2. Capitalists and financiers—Arab countries.   3. Millionaires.   I. Title.
HC498.9.W4B58   301.44′1   76-45099
ISBN 0-688-03135-8

BOOK DESIGN   CARL WEISS

ACKNOWLEDGMENTS

I HAVE NO DIFFICULTY IN DECIDING HOW TO START THIS PAGE OF acknowledgments. Susan Mary Richards worked with me on the project almost from the start. There were many people she met in Arabia, and her meticulous reporting contributed to many of my chapters. I have valued her support all along the way. Without her there would have been a book, but it would not have been the same book.

I doubt that I would have finished the book without the encouragement of Christopher Falkus and Shelley Singer, Lois Wallace, Carol Hill, George Seddon, Pearson Phillips, Tony Smith, Stephen Montefiore, and Mrs. E. Pendlebury. I would also like to thank Andrew Barrow, who helped me with research in London.

That I started it at all is due to Larry Hughes of William Morrow, whose idea it was, to Giles Gordon, who persuaded me to do it, and to the *London Observer*, who gave me leave of absence at short notice.

Many people helped me in New York, London, and the Arab countries I visited. They are too numerous to name and I know that most of them would rather I did not. I am grateful to them all.

I am especially grateful to my parents. I understood their concern; I appreciated their interest.

The book is dedicated to my husband, Lynn Harrell—with love and thanks for his songs without words.

LB

New York

CONTENTS

PART I / GREAT SHEIKHS—"WHAT THE MIRROR REFLECTS . . ."

1	/	HOT MADNESS	13
2	/	THE BLACK SHEIKHS OF THE FAMILY	23
3	/	THE NAME OF THE GAME	35

PART II / SAUDI ARABIA—"FIRST STEP THROUGH THE LOOKING GLASS . . ."

4	/	A TOWN CALLED ALICE-IN-WONDERLAND	47
5	/	A PRIDE OF PRINCES	59
6	/	PITY THE POOR PRINCESSES	72
7	/	MONEY AND MIDDLEMEN	79
8	/	THE RISE OF THE MERITOCRATS	91
9	/	BANKING ON A WAR HORSE	109
10	/	A MODERN BABEL	122
11	/	THE CLOSED BOOKS	133
12	/	THE FILM STRIP	149
13	/	COMINGS AND GOINGS	159

PART III / BAHRAIN—"A GLIMPSE OF THE FUTURE . . ."

14 / PLAYING HAPPY FAMILIES   *173*

15 / "WE'RE NOT RICH, YOU KNOW"   *185*

16 / JADED PIECES   *198*

PART IV / KUWAIT—"PEERING INSIDE, AFRAID TO LOOK OUT . . ."

17 / THE MEN WHO CAME IN FROM THE COLD   *211*

18 / SHOPPING AROUND THE SNOBS   *220*

19 / NO EXIT   *231*

20 / RACING AROUND WITH A ROYAL   *247*

21 / WATCHING THE HERITAGE GO BY   *258*

22 / THE LONER   *267*

PART V / QATAR—"A PIECE OF A THING . . ."

23 / NUTTY PRESENT, DOTTY PAST   *275*

PART VI / ABU DHABI, DUBAI, AND SHARJAH— "MORE PIECES OF THINGS . . ."

24 / ROYAL FLUSH   *289*

25 / THE DAY DISASTER STRUCK   *303*

26 / GOOD-BYE TO ALL THAT   *312*

$UPER-WEALTH

THE SECRET LIVES
OF THE OIL SHEIKHS

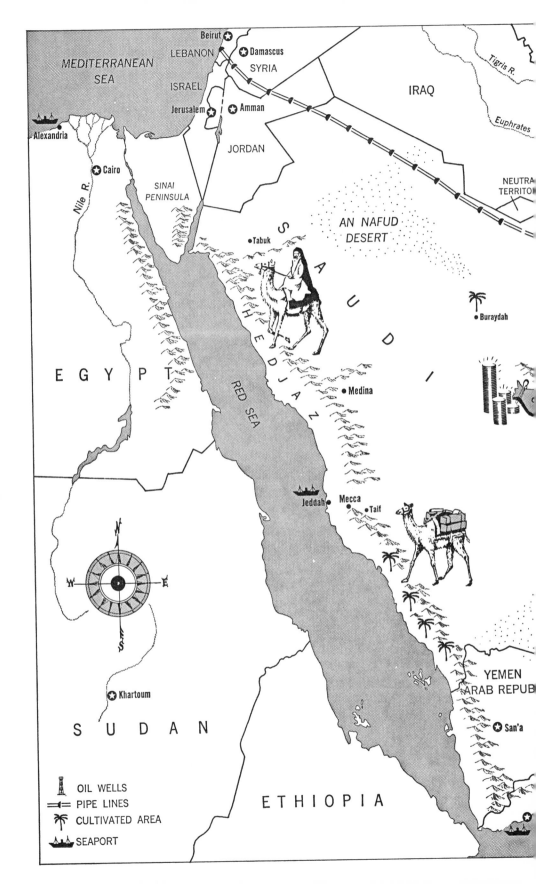

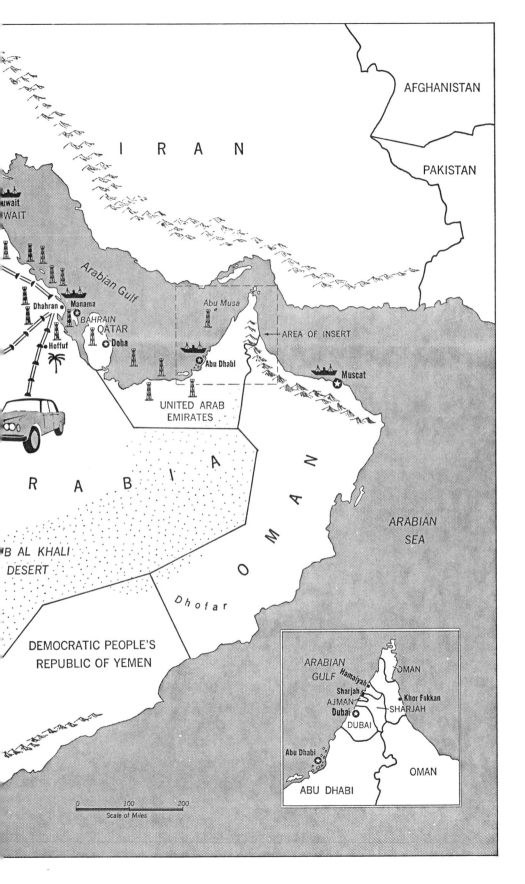

AFGHANISTAN

PAKISTAN

IRAN

uwait
WAIT

Arabian Gulf

Dhahran Manama
         BAHRAIN QATAR
Hoffuf   Doha

Abu Musa

AREA OF INSERT

Abu Dhabi

Muscat

UNITED ARAB
EMIRATES

R A B I A

O M A N

ARABIAN
SEA

B AL KHALI
DESERT

Dhofar

DEMOCRATIC PEOPLE'S
REPUBLIC OF YEMEN

ARABIAN
GULF   Hamaiyah   OMAN

        Sharjah   Khor Fakkan
AJMAN   SHARJAH
Dubai

        DUBAI

Abu Dhabi

OMAN

ABU DHABI

0   100   200
     Scale of Miles

PART

GREAT SHEIKHS—

"WHAT THE

MIRROR REFLECTS . . ."

CHAPTER

1

HOT MADNESS

THE SEA IS DAZZLING. IT'S WARM, TEEMING WITH FISH. I'M LYING half in the water, half on the beach, lazily waiting for the speedboat to zip past with the bronzed, muscular man up on a mono-ski behind it, turning and dodging like a professional.

I'm completely relaxed; it's the perfect holiday. I'm staying with friends in their beachhouse and tonight we'll run a movie on the terrace after dinner. *Emanuelle*'s playing somewhere in town. We're in for an historical epic here. As the sun works on my tan I remember weekends like this on Paradise Island in the Bahamas, on the Costa Smeralda in Sardinia.

Three days later I'm in a hotel room in the same seaside town howling with fear and loneliness. Something has gone wrong. I don't know what it is. You never know what it is here. But I sense it. Atmospheres in this place run through your body like quicksilver. I have visions of being found "accidentally drowned." Maybe They (whoever *They* are) have found out that I'm Jewish. To get here at all, I've had to "prove" that I'm not.

I'm in a country that you'll never find in a holiday brochure. They don't allow tourists anywhere near it. At times it's awe-inspiring. But then there are the other times. . . . I'm in Saudi Arabia, the richest oil kingdom in the world, a vast

13

desert land with salt water on two sides but none (or next to none) to drink. It's choking on its oil wealth and its crazy madness is choking me as it does most Westerners who come here. It has the same compulsive attraction and intensity as Hollywood in the 1930s. Like Hollywood then, it has nothing to do with whatever else is going on in the world.

Where did it all start? A few years ago, say ten, hardly anyone had even heard of Faisal ibn Abdul Aziz except a handful of dry scholars, diplomats, or bankers, maybe. But in 1974 *Time* Magazine ran a cover story on this man who ruled Saudi Arabia with the total power of an absolute monarch and named King Faisal its "Man of the Year." Three months later he was shot dead by his own nephew, a thirty-year-old ex-University of California at Berkeley student prince who had his head chopped off publicly by way of reward.

King Faisal's assassination had about the same impact on the Western world as President Kennedy's. Would there be another Mideast war? Or would the death of the man who wanted so much to pray in Jerusalem before he died (not that he prayed there when it was in Arab hands that anyone can remember) make it more of an area of conciliation than an arena of conflict? Diplomats feared a Socialist revolution, another oil embargo (like 1973) with gas stations in the States running dry again. It was a false alarm, but the shivers of fear managed to cross half the world to us here.

It was about this time that people started to notice an influx of strange men in long white sheets descending into low limousines around Lexington Avenue after a rush through their favorite New York store, Bloomingdale's. Arab fever hit the U.S., and as Beirut crumbled in the summer of '75 more and more white-sheeted sheikhs moved over to the West for their months of summer vacation.

If one had to pinpoint a moment when New Yorkers woke up to this phenomenon, it was the day that some extraordinary news leaked from the Olympic Tower. Saudi Arabian multimillionaire Adnan Khashoggi, well known in the arms-buying trade and to congressional hearings for his giant-sized commissions from Lockheed and Northrop, had bought the apartment below his new multimillion-dollar apartment—to catch any drips from his glass-sided swimming pool under construction? If one had to do the same for London (most of which was up for sale then and moving only into Arab hands), it was the day when airing mattresses appeared over the windowsills of a $750,000 mansion opposite that of Douglas Fairbanks, Jr., and next door to an outraged Conservative Member of Parliament who telephoned to ask his new neighbors to tidy up the offending windowsills. The family of Sheikh Zayed of Abu Dhabi (not the kind of name normally associated with this fashionable patch of London) had moved in.

That summer of '75 anyone who hailed from an oil-producing country in the Mideast automatically became a "sheikh." That at least was one word we could latch onto. Arabs have peculiar, unpronounceable names punctuated with ibn and al and all very confusing. Sheikh was snappier; menservants of rich Arabs spotted on Fifty-seventh Street were "sheikhs." Iranians were "sheikhs." And sheikhs meant spending, diamonds, "men in pimpomobiles," as one American businessman very thick with Arabs put it. He meant men with money to burn looking for women to buy. (Just let his Arab friends hear that; it's an image they hate.)

They seemed so alien to us. They came from countries hardly anyone had even heard of. Saudi Arabia, yes. But Qatar? In fact, they came from very few countries indeed. These oil-rich sheikhs come from a handful of countries with two basic things in common: they're the seven with almost feudal autocratic rulers plus so much wealth and so few people that they have large petrodollar surpluses. We're talking about Saudi Arabia, Bahrain (the first to bring in oil, the first to be running out), Kuwait, Qatar, and three sheikhdoms from a part of the world that was once known as the Pirate Coast and is now more respectably titled the Federation of the United Arab Emirates—Abu Dhabi, Dubai, and Sharjah.

These are the countries that give rise to the stereotype of the oil-rich Arab getting down from the camel and into the Cadillac, off-loading his wealth around the world. Another country helps—Oman. Its ruler, a classical-music freak, got an organ builder to combine work on a half-million-dollar contract for London's St. Paul's Cathedral with the construction of a walnut, mahogany, and rosewood job with seven hundred pipes for a corner of his palace drawing room. The ruler also found himself a world-famous organist to take home to play it. Alas for the ruler of Oman, he's had Communist guerrillas threatening his musical peace and not enough oil to make many of his subjects rich. So Oman doesn't count, but bear it in mind.

The Magnificent Seven have a couple more things in common. They all have cultures and traditions rooted in the desert; however they live now, the source of it all for them is the wandering past of the nomadic Bedouins. Enter the first contradiction (and there will be plenty more, rest assured). The man the Arabs revere, the Prophet whom the one God, Allah, chose to make the final and divine revelation (the Koran), the founder of their religion of Islam, was no desert Bedouin. Prophet Mohammed was an orphan from the trading town of Mecca in the country that is now Saudi Arabia. He married an older and richer merchant's widow and his ensuing success in business gave him the leisure to discover his mystical qualities.

Next contradiction. Iranians aren't oil sheikhs. Iranians aren't even Arab. They're Muslim, but they couldn't be more different from the peoples of the Seven in the massive peninsula facing them across the Gulf (to the Arabs, it's the Arabian Gulf, to the Iranians, it's the Persian Gulf). Persians, or Iranians as they're now called, have a wholly different culture. Most of the really choice Mideast sales through dealers like Sotheby Parke-Bernet over the last six years have been to Iranians. They have centuries of conditioning to appreciate and judge paintings, ceramics, furniture, possessions. What could the desert Arabs have? Their ancestors certainly didn't set up shop in a tent in the middle of a sandy wasteland and worry about where to hang the ancestral heirlooms on the goatskin walls.

Today there are more fundamental reasons why Iran doesn't

count. It has a population of 35 million people and it's running into the red. It's cutting back on projects (not arms, but more dispensable items), not out of fear of change but out of fear of running out of small change. A country that large, in Mideast terms, can't be rich by Saudi standards. It isn't as badly off as poor old Egypt, of course, with as many people but no oil, but Iran is another neo-feudal dictatorship. And the police network involved in controlling all those millions of people doesn't come cheap. Saudi Arabia, by our standards, is as much of a police state. But it's easier to grease the onionskins of watchfulness when you're only coping with 3.5 million Saudis. The Saudis will say officially that they have 7, yea even 8, million—forget it. Everyone's very confused about population figures in Arabia. It's what's called "a politically sensitive issue" (why will become apparent later).

So, Iranians aren't sheikhs. Now for the next killer. Most of the Arabs in the Magnificent Seven aren't sheikhs either. In Saudi Arabia sheikh is a special title (it means "old man," which doesn't sound like much of a compliment, admittedly) given to honor a distinguished man or the head of a large family. It's nothing much; anyone from the royal family is his Highness the prince. In the other six countries all royals and only royals are sheikhs (and let's face it, we're not talking about the Romanoffs or Hapsburgs, we're talking about members of a "royal" family that happen to rule a few thousand people on some valuable real estate, that's all). The rest are commoners, albeit mostly plain common rich. But to the West all oil Arabs are oil sheikhs, a new breed that seems to be overrunning our world and buying up a big chunk of it.

That's how it looks from our side. But I wanted to know how it looks to the new pirates of today, if that's what they are. I wanted to clamber into the walled gardens of Arabia and find out what life feels like to the men and, particularly, the women who are trying to get by on those oil millions. I don't know what I expected to find—Rudolph Valentino, tents, harems, erotic mysteries lived out in settings that Cecil B. De Mille would have been proud to call his own? There wasn't much time to expect anything, actually. The sheer logistical problems of getting there took care of that; the task of squeezing a visa out of the Saudis nearly killed the project in the beginning. The tea and charm I enjoyed during endless hours of small talk at their embassy were delightful, but they've never let in a woman unknown to them before—let alone for the time and with the freedom they gave me. It wasn't until the day before I was due to leave that the Foreign Office in Saudi Arabia got on the phone and gave an okay. Allah knows why they said yes. No one who knew anything about the place thought they would.

What's more, the Saudis paid. I didn't ask them to. I was a guest, and hospitality is part of their tradition. In the desert in the old days they offered the traveler coffee, food, a bed, and wouldn't murder him for three days. After that he was on his own. For weeks I was given hotel rooms, cars, and generosity such as I have met nowhere else in the world. It's as well. American businessmen have gone broke before now spending thousands of dollars to stay in Arabia waiting for deals. I reckon I've cost the countries I visited about $20,000 (it seems fair to admit it, and I told them all along I'm only a nosy journalist, not a sycophant). To start with, Gulf Air gave me $2,000 worth of tickets. To my relief (since I promised in return to tell the truth), traveling with them was easier than with many Western airlines, despite horrendous warnings from other Arabian Gulf know-it-alls about planeloads of passengers being kicked off to make room for a sheikh who has taken it into his head to borrow the machine to go visit a relative or something for the day.

It's a weird, disorienting part of the world for a newcomer. Even down to the coast, it's miles of sand. Sometimes beautiful, breathtaking, orange sand dunes. More often boring, dusty, scrubby stuff. It's hot. Even in "winter" it's hot. In summer the heat and humidity burn the brain, scorch the temper, and soak the skin in seconds. There's nothing romantic about the desert if you get stuck in it. But they don't have to have desert

anymore. They layer it with concrete, decorate it with buildings that are straight off Park Avenue. In Kuwait, for instance,
they bought (and I mean bought) in the architects of the Sea-
gram Building on Park Avenue to put up a little something
to house their very own aid-giving agency. As a result, from a
white castle that would do justice to Walt Disney's idea of
fairyland, the Kuwaitis now dole out millions to the less fortunate nations of the Mideast that haven't got those valuable
black lakes under their sands. No sooner had the Kuwaitis
heard who had won the Australians' Sydney Opera House
design competition, than they got him in right away. Give us
a new parliament building, they said. Why not? They can
afford the best.

But you can't import, buy in, money-no-object, other peoples'
styles and cultures without some strange juxtapositions. Some
of them work. Arabs like finger food; they enjoy eating with
their hands (who was going to cart a sackful of best silver
cutlery around the desert?), so now they have Kentucky Fried
Chicken houses and they're coining money. But the rest of it?
It reminds me of one place more than any other: in the late
1960s I went to report from what was then the Congo (now
Africanized into Zaïre). It was a period of reconstruction after
a bloody civil war. No one in Europe cared about the reconstruction; they preferred to remember the outrages of the war—
Africans going in to fight, high on magic and drugs; nuns being
raped; mercenaries on both sides. It made the Congolese bitter
and wary of foreigners (the Arabs don't like *their* image much
either). And then there was Kinshasa, the capital city built
by the previous owners (the Belgians) in true old-fashioned
style—wide, tree-lined boulevards, stately white buildings; it
had the imagination and elegance of Europe at its best. And
next to nothing worked, and none of it had anything to do
with the hungry, savage green jungle surrounding it or the
people living in it. Substitute desert for jungle and there's the
same feeling of strangeness, incongruity, madness, and fascina-
tion in Arabia. In one generation people have moved from

mud cities to Beverly Hills mansions and gardens. And this in countries where water is the greatest luxury and green the greatest status symbol.

Well-kept green is an even greater luxury. Their desert past never taught these Arabs about upkeep, and many's the rich man who has planted a garden in Arabia, didn't read the back of the packet, and never thought to ask if these things need aftercare. To keep up some of the gardens I saw takes an army of horticultural commandos. There's oil, there's money, but virtually no fresh water that isn't man-made. I saw diamonds such as I've never seen in my life hanging casually around the necks of women in Saudi Arabia, and yet one admitted that the highlight of her week was the one hot bath that was all her mansion's reservoir could run to at present.

Saudi Arabia is the heartland of the peninsula. It's where Prophet Mohammed was born and his military-minded evangelism took root. It hogs three-quarters of the peninsula, most of the oil, and has the strictest Muslim sect (Wahhabism) there is. And what does Saudi Arabia remind me of? Nassau in the heyday of the '60s. There's the same international riffraff rolling in to get rich. There's even the same smell of laundered money in the evening air when you go to dinner in some of those mansions with their green, green gardens.

The 1960s threw up their own cult figures: Bernie Cornfeld of IOS, for instance. He made a goodly portion of his fortune selling the "people's capitalism" down the Gulf (before he was blacklisted). Where is he in the 1970s? Charged with cheating on his phone bill, leading a quieter life, and making pocket money by renting his London house to a family from Qatar for some thousand dollars a week during the summer of '75.

Then there were Roman Polanski and Sharon Tate. Let's just say that in the 1970s I ran into many of the same people who hung around the totem poles of the mad 1960s in Arabia. Judy Gatowski, for example. I walked into a hotel suite in Abu Dhabi (a place practically no one had heard of when Charles Manson's murders were hogging the limelight) and I met Judy again for the first time since 1968. I last saw her in the snobbish, Italian ski resort of Cortina celebrating Christmas with her husband in Roman and Sharon Polanski's chalet, with carols trilling on the record player and gifts all around. Judy's film-producer husband and Roman were good friends. Here she is in the 1970s with her friend, who's a Lebanese journalist with an open shirt, a very hairy chest, and a habit of dropping in on the ruler of Abu Dhabi late at night. Her friend, Bassam, and the Abu Dhabians are also good friends. The phone rang in Bassam's suite. Judy answered it. Who should be on the other end? Judy's estranged producer husband, discussing with Bassam the possibility of coming down to Abu Dhabi to see the ruler. Finance for a new movie project, mentioned Judy.

There were other familiar faces in Arabia. Mostly men on the make. The Arabs are where the 1970s are at for those who always seemed to gravitate toward money in the 1960s. Where you get a honey pot, you get the wasps. And as I shake off the drips still clinging to me from the honey pots of Arabia, I remember many people. This book is about people. Some of them seemed mad to me at first because I didn't understand how different are our ways of being and thinking. Others were mad. But then they're living through the greatest change to hit their private world since the birth of Prophet Mohammed in A.D. 571. They live literally in two different eras. I visited them in 1975 and 1396. We have our calendar; they have theirs. It doesn't date from the year of Mohammed's birth (that would be too easy). It dates from the year he fled the hostile merchants of Mecca (who didn't like his ideas of giving up too many sybaritic pleasures here on earth in return for promises of paradise later) and found refuge in the rival city of Medina some miles up the camel route.

Maybe this book won't make much sense to you. Don't expect simple patterns as we travel together through Arabia and across the Western world with the oil sheikhs. There aren't any. You can't iron out and put into tidy, logical piles countries like these.

Even the names look crazy to us. Phonetically I've made them as easy as possible, only there are so few first names to go around that nearly everyone is called the same thing. I can offer only one rule: a man has his own first name, the name of his father, and his family name. So, King Faisal was Faisal, the son of (ibn) Abdul Aziz, of the family of (al) Saud. And just in case you've missed the point of how rarely you can see the point—King Faisal called his father King Abdul Aziz (it was the man's name, after all), the Saudis called him King Abdul Aziz (there's even a street named after him in Jiddah— it's the main street: King Abdul Aziz Street). The whole world knew him as King Ibn Saud. Just mad, that's all.

CHAPTER

2

THE BLACK SHEIKHS OF THE FAMILY

KING SAUD OF SAUDI ARABIA HAD FORTY SONS AND A BAD IMAGE.
He went in for gold-plated Cadillacs, watches for visitors, concubines, and morphine. He was fired from his job in 1963 to
make way for his younger brother, Faisal, and died in exile in
1969. The image lingers on.

A favorite habit of young King Saud bloods has long been
crashing expensive automobiles. Residents of Kensington
Court, a quiet square in London opposite the royal park, are
at any moment likely to be startled by any one of three Lamborghinis frequently bearing wounds imposed by their royal
owner—Prince Turqui, son of Saud, twenty-three years old.

One day at London airport last summer a tall, skinny youth
delicately arranged in white by Yves St. Laurent, hung around
with gold chains, slim black briefcase in one hand, tiny black
handbag in another, emerges among the tourists off the flight
from Spain.

Waiting by the plane is the British Airport Authority's top
people greeter. "Your car is waiting downstairs, your Highness" (a long black limousine with a disgruntled driver called
Harry. "The trouble with Arabs is that they always keep
you waiting. They never let you know whether you're wanted").

"Your Highness had a good journey, I hope." His Highness

Prince Turqui is whisked off to the VIP lounge, where his passport is taken away for stamping and airport flunkies produce his plastic, rope-bound suitcase. There are some gaps in his Highness's kit of status symbols.

His Highness complains. He isn't at all well. He's in great pain. After three weeks in Prince Alfonso Hohenlohe's almost exclusive Marbella Club (he went for a weekend) he has returned with a bad back and a temperature. He talks vaguely about water-skiing accidents and the bumping of a high-powered speedboat. He does, however, perk up a little when he opens his briefcase on the way into London. It's full of photographs. He's had a party. "It cost me twelve thousand dollars, but it was the party of the season. Everyone said so. Everyone was there. People keep telling me that I have to get to know the right people, and I have. Look at her." (He points to an overripe, well-endowed blonde.) "She's a princess." Which princess? "I don't remember—a princess. That's a contessa." Which contessa? "A contessa," he says impatiently, hurrying on to show off a baron from Austria. No, he can't remember his name either, but the baron has invited him to a beer-drinking festival in Munich and, by the way, wouldn't mind discussing a business proposition with Turqui.

The car pulls up in front of his new apartment. It's an alleged real estate coup. A friend found it, he explains. Asking price, $180,000. His friend went to see the agent for a quiet chat and came back advising him to offer $165,000 in ready cash. The prince went to the bank, drew out the bills, waved them in front of the agent's nose, and bingo, the apartment was his within three days. Turqui doesn't like waiting for what he wants. Even so, a real estate expert might question whether there's $165,000 worth of apartment upstairs on the second floor.

The long converted mansion block corridor is covered in plush red velvet wallpaper (of a style familiar from Indian restaurants). It's a modern decorator's delight. It didn't take Turqui long to find out that young, trendy Arabs in London go for the sci-fi, satin-chrome, and glitter look and that the decor kings of swinging Arab pads are the Zarach brothers. They specialize in custom-built knickknacks: a ten-foot-high brass palm tree incorporating ostrich eggs ($7,000), white leather-covered bed with obligatory built-in hi-fi ($4,000), a set of steel-framed, suede-covered chairs ($460 each), and miles of mirrors on walls, doors, and ceilings in case the owners haven't caught sight of themselves for a second or two.

Zarach's men have left their mark of chrome and glass on Turqui's place with squishy sofas, chrome chairs, electronic toys—and a pile of bills. He pushes them aside (into the garbage pail). Later will do.

It's time for Turqui to summon a few friends. He doesn't like being lonely, and his Afghan hound is boarded out. First to arrive is his "very best friend," David Fu Tong, big burly son of a Liverpool Chinese restaurant owner from around the corner. While Turqui's off tending his ailing back, David holds forth on all he's done to bring the royal up to the mark. "When I first met him he was down in a real dive of a disco all the time. I didn't know he was a prince, did I? I just thought he was an ordinary bloke like me. Anyway, I got to know him and as soon as I found out what he was I said, 'Turqui, listen, you can't go around with girls like they have here. Not you. Rich and royal and everything.' I said, 'You have to get to know the right people.' He needed a real friend like me to tell him straight.

"Anyway, I got Turqui going to better discos. But I still say he's got to get to know the right girls. He could know anyone. But he just won't bother. I've said to him time and again, 'If you want to take out a really classy chick you have to have patience. They don't go with you just like that.' But Turqui, if he wants something, he has to have it right away."

Next to arrive: Michel, an Iranian friend who was in Marbella with Turqui. He has an interesting credit-card business proposition he's excited about discussing. On second thought, apart from a warmup reminder, he decides that it can wait on the royal back, now getting worse by the second. Michel brings in tow an Austrian model he's brought back from Marbella.

On goes the soul music at maximum volume. Out come the photographs. "You've really made it this time, Turqui, they really liked you." Alfred, the chauffeur, is bringing more photographs back in the Lamborghini which he's driving home overland.

The model isn't happy. Michel's put her in a cheap hotel in a grayer part of town and she hasn't got enough to do and Turqui promised to come earlier. The doorbell buzzes somehow over the deafening rock. It's David's wife, Marion, a sample-offer-sized blonde with dark glasses. She's a croupier in a gambling casino ("I've been working the clubs since I was sixteen although my mother didn't like it much to start with. But I get on with the customers real well and we're having a wonderful season"). Marion's very concerned about Turqui's poor back and his temperature, and her small son, apparently, has missed him a lot. "He thinks the world of you, Turqui. He's always asking when you'll be home."

The evening jives on. It's eleven o'clock. Turqui makes another call. Half an hour later the buzzer goes. "You're going to meet my wife now. She's a really educated lady. And my children, they're the best." She appears. Princess Khalthoum is twenty-four, she's wearing a cheap red nylon top and black, washable long skirt. Khalthoum. In this crazy, noise-infested room (particularly now that Sara, three, and Saud, eighteen months, are racing around screaming), her Highness is a monument of calm dignity. Every now and again the couple exchange quiet words in Arabic. For a moment all the acting and pretense drop away and Turqui seems real. Then he's distracted and the show goes on.

Khalthoum smiles now and again. She examines the photographs of That Party and nods approval. It's as if it's the most natural thing in the world for her to be summoned halfway through the night (from where isn't yet clear) and then be dismissed half an hour later (to where still isn't clear) when their children begin to demand too much of the available spotlight. Turqui does not like to be upstaged.

David is dispatched to get food. Turqui is in a predicament.

He doesn't like eating out in restaurants much; although he'll sit for hours in Tramp, the discotheque where Ryan O'Neal conducted many of his close, darkly lit "friendships." ("You'll never see Turqui actually dancing," contributes Michel, "or even talking. He just sits there and the girls kind of close in on him. After all, with all that gold and jewelry hanging around him, he's obviously something special, isn't he?") Turqui doesn't want a live-in cook or valet. His cleaning lady, Connie, turns up each day with her grumbles and her small son and manages all right. But he does like to eat at home.

Not, of course, in the dining room with its vast oval table covered with curtain-matching fabric that looks like a country garden. He likes to eat at home around the kitchen table without anyone going to the bother of cooking. So David goes off to the Mideastern restaurant nearby and returns with an army's ration of second-rate food. David, a domesticated, willing sort of guy, busies himself getting it ready, while wife Marion sits in the living room glued to the round, plastic-domed television through her dark glasses and the model sighs heavily, listening to the heavy rock. At two in the morning the party sits down for a cozy supper, involving much tomato catsup spilled over his Highness's white attire. It's beneath his dignity to notice it.

At three in the morning the music still rocks on, and I stagger home to sleep. At three the next afternoon Princess Khalthoum is waking up. It's the religious month of Ramadan when faithful Muslims can't eat or drink from dawn to dusk. Khalthoum fasts (unlike her husband) and rises late to kill the hungry daylight hours. Her Highness is staying in a flaking, formerly grand roominghouse a few streets away from Turqui's hangout. Her second-floor front balcony has become a noted landmark for local shopkeepers, much impressed by the size of her bra cups hanging out to dry.

Khalthoum lives in Saudi Arabia, in the city of Riyadh. She's used to not seeing much of Turqui. They were married four years ago and he left for Texas two weeks later for a three-year air force pilot's course that he never quite completed. He left her behind, pregnant. She saw him again for a while, hence young Saud, and she has been summoned to London to be with her husband. She arrived two months ago and spent the first month in a suite in the Intercontinental Hotel, the newest prime stopping-place for visiting Arabs. It's graced by many because of the manager, veteran hotelier Max Blouet, known to them from his, and their, years at the Georges V in Paris (Arabs haven't quite got over the shock of the London Hilton: its lobby was torn apart by the Irish bombers in September). But the delights of M. Blouet were lost on Khalthoum shut into a suite with two young children, so Turqui took this humble, two-bedroom, sparsely furnished apartment for her. He wouldn't know how shabby it is. He hasn't seen it for himself.

The television is on permanently. Cheap plastic toys litter the floor. Saud is sitting on a potty demolishing a plate of French fries. He and his sister display all the spontaneous warmth of children brought up in a protected environment; their surroundings are lost on them. The Ethiopian servant girl glides around, noiselessly picking up the debris of two children confined to an apartment all day long. Yesterday they did go to the park. Today they'll stay in. Outside the sun shines gloriously.

Eventually Princess Khalthoum makes a lazy entrance, concerned at keeping me waiting. Behind the passive acceptance is a perpetual sadness. "Of course I mind that I'm not with Turqui. I'm sad all the time. But what can I do? I'll say one thing. He," she points to Saud, "won't grow up like that. Turqui and I grew up together as children in the same house. My sister was married to his father" (I can't even begin to tackle that one). "We were like Saud and Sara then, and now . . ." Her face shuts again. The moment of confiding is over.

While her husband spends his energies in his (as yet) unrealized ambition to be an international businessman (chicken farms, credit cards, jeans factory, and the like) Princess Khal-

thoum lives in Riyadh and goes to the university. She's studying psychology.

Meanwhile, five minutes' walk away, in the splendor of his
new, multibedroom London home, Turqui has taken to his
bed. The doctor has been summoned to attend him. His illness
is unfortunately timed. The model, fed up with Michel and
her cheap hotel, has moved in. Turqui has relegated her to
the smallest guest room. She is still sighing. David has discovered a few puzzles in the Marbella Club bill. He's planning
to fly out to Spain with Turqui to help him sort the matter
out. Only right now Turqui is unable to move. After talk of
strained muscles and speedboats, his Highness's trouble is revealed. He has a boil on his royal bottom.

The gathering pus on Turqui's rump runs up considerable
bills before he's fit enough to fly back to Marbella with the
ever-constant David. London medics love it when Arabs become ill. Become ill? When they so much as feel a twinge Arabs
run to that Old-World stretch of London's Harley Street where
specialists in black jackets with gold watch chains offer a most
reassuring and warm bedside manner to their Arab patients.

It's the one service area where the impoverished English
can still feel complacent. Arabs get nervous at the efficient,
busy, clinical approach of successful American doctors. So few
British can afford private medicine anymore that the consultants there have all the time in the world to pore over the
coughs, gallstones, slipped disks and toothaches that fly in
daily for their attention from Arabia. If they have a warm
bedside manner in the office, the doctors are even more
obliging when it comes to providing a warm bed in a costly
private clinic (cheap by American standards at $200 a day;
aspirin, etc., extra, naturally). They have enough takers—
Arabs are hypochondriacs of the first order.

As a tribute to this financial support, London has built an
institution unique anywhere in the world, geared totally for
what they call "Muslim" patients—the Wellington Hospital,

named after one of the nation's great warrior heroes, the Duke
of Wellington. The clinic was founded in 1974 by a shipping
company that realized there was money to be made in using
its experience for people suffering the rigors of travel, in tending those travelers oppressed by illness. Arab travelers.

There the normally gun-wary British seem to turn a blind
eye to bodyguards; one of the Saudi King's brothers showed
up with eight. But it's the small touches that go down so well:
the Château Mouton Rothschild '64 at fifty-five dollars a bottle.
The special closed-circuit television channel devoted to Arabic
programs. And in case one of the full-time staff of Arabic in-
terpreters isn't available, there's the miraculous floating X-ray
table that allows a radiographer to move a patient by pushing
a button (quite an advance for the British, who prefer "diag-
nostic instincts" to machinery) instead of trying to mime the
message "Would you please move your ass over a bit."

There's a waiting list for the Wellington's deluxe suites,
and its medical director, Dr. Arthur Levin, is fast becoming
something of an Arab folk hero. Dr. Levin is a Jew. "What's
so strange about our going to a Jew?" asked one grateful Arab
ex-patient. "Eight centuries ago when you were dying in
ditches and we Arabs were the ones with the medical skills,
our leader's personal physician was Maimonides the Jew."
Ouch.

Even the dentists are in on the act. Many Arabs have terrible, terrible teeth. A daughter of a top diplomat in London
turned up in a dentist's chair with sixty-four decayed surfaces
in her mouth. And Arabs always want attention *Now*—and
that means extra fees. In the summer of '75 an internationally
fashionable dentist (renowned for capping film stars' teeth)
found a busy Kuwaiti in his office requiring the carving of a
whole set of custom-built, best porcelain-capped teeth. The
Kuwaiti was so pressed for time that he hired a Rolls-Royce
to drive across the country with a set of impressions of his
teeth to the dentist's best mechanic. The Rolls waited for the
new gleaming dentures and then rushed them back to London
the same day.

Over the odd glass of sherry the physicians marvel at their luck. One sportsman and eye specialist has trained his secretary to offer the tactful hint that a large gift token from his favorite fishing-tackle shop wouldn't come amiss. But one less well-prepared surgeon is a trifle stumped at present. He can't work out what to do with his new racehorse—an unexpected gift from an Arab patient now minus an appendix. If an Arab doesn't need his tonsils out soon, the surgeon won't be able to afford to feed the beast.

British doctors handle the Arabs well because they combine authority with that edge of creeping humility, parodied in countless movies by the English "gentleman's gentleman." Every Arab somehow walks out of his British doctor's waiting room feeling like a million dollars (having left several hundred behind).

An Arab may be a hero to his doctor; no Arab is a hero to his chauffeur. The limousine trade has doubled in a year in London thanks to the oil spenders. Dick Roberts, forty-seven, with a soft, pinkish skin and an utterly forgettable face, has benefited nicely, thank you. He makes a thousand dollars a week with a good Arab. A hundred dollars for the car, plus tip (sometimes as much again), plus rakeoffs from whatever his hirer may buy.

Roberts spent twenty years in the army before taking to chauffeuring. He likes the uniform and a sense of knowing his place. In August, 1975, one of his grateful customers gave him five thousand dollars to buy a five-year-old limousine. Now he's in business on his own. To him it's a skilled profession.

"Now you have to understand what Arabs you're talking about," he starts, tugging cheerfully on his pipe. "Most of the ones you see, they're just the big shots' servants. And even they've more money to spend than most American big shots. Sex and gambling's what they want. Gambling's easy. I belong to the large clubs myself and I just slip them in. Wads of money, they've got. When it comes to sex, that's different.

"If they're low types, I take them to one of those sauna joints. Well, it's no more a sauna than you've got in here. The sauna's ten dollars, then for six the masseuse will go topless and for another ten she'll give light relief, if you know what I mean. If they're something higher up, I take them to places with hostesses. Then it's a couple of bottles of champagne at twenty-five dollars each with the girls they pick out and if they want any more, it's negotiable. Some of them don't want to bother with all that, in which case I'll pick up a girl from the streets. It's thirty dollars to go back with him, sex in the car is ten (lucky I've got a big car) and her place is twenty.

"I know them all. After all, I've been driving long enough. Now that's the servants and that's what most people think of when they say Arabs. If they're secretaries or something, they'll want a girl from an escort agency and they'll send me to pick a good one and bring her back. Blond and big boobs is what they go for. It's a change, isn't it? Cheap stuff is thirty dollars (plus my cut from the agency, of course) and the rest is negotiable. There's broad-minded girls and there's straight ones. I make sure I pick the broad-minded ones. My gentlemen don't like it if they're not cooperative."

Dick confesses that many hookers won't go with Arabs. They say they're rough, go for kookiness too much and it's not worth it even when being overpaid. "They're the real low servants. I say it's the girls' fault for not knowing the difference. There's rough English too, isn't there?

"Then there's the tops, the sheikhs. They want complete secrecy. That's where my little book comes in handy. I know a few good girls, a hundred fifty dollars a trick for Americans, several hundred for Arabs. I'll take them up to the room and the servant says, 'Right in there,' and the girl will go into a pitch-black room (a sheikh likes the curtains drawn so she can't recognize him after), get undressed, and ten minutes later—out. Some of my gentlemen go through three or four a day like that.

"I had one who actually got me to take him to a girl's flat. Well, he had to, his wife was in the hotel. He said, 'Dick, you'd better make sure you can trust her.' It was just me and him, not even his bodyguard. He was there for three hours; he even talked to her, that's unusual. She got thousands out of him that time.

"Sometimes they take them out to dinner, but that's rare. If they do, they'll tag along behind in another car so it looks like they're with some of the entourage. One of my gentlemen went with this girl who gets at least two thousand dollars, looks so good she could be royal herself, and I'm told she doesn't even screw. She's just there for decoration. I don't understand it. Still, it's not my place to ask. You can't with Arabs, you see. With anyone else, if you get him a girl you can say afterward, 'Well, how did it go, sir?' Not an Arab. You'd never drive him again."

Dick's a bachelor. He lives with his mother. Looking after women who aren't his mom is a treat for him.

"What a scream. They come down with their veils and all that, carrying these vanity cases, stuffed with hundred-dollar bills so you couldn't squeeze in a matchstick. The bodyguard always comes too. He's usually 'carrying,' but the police must turn a blind eye. Guns aren't allowed here. As soon as we're around the corner from the hotel, off come the veils, particularly with the young ones. First stop is always Marks and Spencer. They don't speak English, these women, so I go in to make sure they don't get taken. Well, money's just paper to them, they don't understand change. They'll buy every shape, size, and color they can. Never spend less than five hundred dollars each. They're so used to someone else paying that sometimes I have to catch them before they walk out of the shop without handing over the bills. Nasty business a while ago. Some Arab's wife, diplomat he was and all, got caught for shoplifting in Marks and Spencer, and their embassy closed for two weeks because they were so bloody furious.

"Next day we're back at Marks and Spencer and then it's more parcels to go up to the room. And you know what's the funniest sight of all? All the old women sitting around taking off every St. Michael label that Marks puts in from every damn thing they've bought. Well, they have to, don't they? Marks and Spencer is owned by that Jewish lot that give all the money they get from the Arabs to Israel. Funny, I call it."

Roberts has three good moments: when an Arab wins a pile gambling and hands over a cut, if he wants jewelry and Dick can get in there first and fix his commission, and then there's his real dream. His limousine prince of that summer of '75 was the one driven by his friend Mike. Mike spent two months driving a Saudi Arabian prince around in his brand-new $30,000 Rolls-Royce Corniche. On the day his Highness left, Mike drove him to the airport, checked him in, and asked what he was to do with the car. "Keep it," came the answer. To the prince it was a gesture in keeping with his culture: showing generosity to those who serve well. To chauffeurs everywhere as word traveled it was something to hope for as gas for their ten-miles-per-gallon cars looked ready for another price hike.

To the gaping airline staff it merely confirmed the image of Arabs as idiots with too much money.

3

THE NAME OF THE GAME

WHEN THEY COME TO THE GREEN FELT OF THE GAMING TABLES Arabs bring unlimited amounts of money. They're obsessive gamblers but desperate about security. Press leaks are their nightmare.

Las Vegas frightens them. The pace is too fast, the gaming rooms too crowded—they feel exposed and at the mercy of gossip columnists. The French Riviera used to be fairly pleasant until the story splashed over the Paris press that Crown Prince Fahd of Saudi Arabia had dropped $500,000 in a casino there. The South of France paid a high price for that deplorable lapse—in the summer of '75 Monte Carlo was notable for the absence of regulars from Saudi Arabia.

All of which makes Victor Lownes a happy man. Lownes is the boss of Playboy Clubs in Britain, the ones with the gambling licenses. This American Anglophile, slow-talking, quick-thinking veteran of the rich night scene, sips soda water in the restaurant of the Playboy Club in London. Brown-louvered shutters block the daylight from those paunchy eyes that have seen it all. "Arabs don't care how much they lose. We've had the best quality ever this summer." The gambling freaks roll in to throw money across his tables—mostly Arab.

Gaming tables that flourished in the 1960s on American and

Jewish money are licking their wounds. The Americans have temporarily run out of money and the big Jewish losers have learned better. Lownes has the contented look of a man who is one throw ahead.

At the Clermont Club, his other establishment around the corner in Berkeley Square, Lownes cleared out the aristocratic titled in-crowd who used to sit downstairs, eating and playing backgammon among themselves. He introduced a fleet of limousines to ferry restless customers from the Playboy to the Clermont. Now it's the Arabs who eat there. It's the Arabs who gamble.

He's had a frantic season. He flies to the U.S. for two weeks every month to help sort out Hugh Hefner's troubled Bunny empire. But he still keeps his London territory in good order. His organization is so smooth that he even manages to get away to spend weekends at his ample country manor, which is used during the day as a croupiers' school for Bunnies. He knows there will be no mistakes in his absence.

Lownes's security in his clubs is tight. Wherever Arabs gamble security has to be tight. Important Arabs are never addressed by name. Clubs know which ones to bankroll for credit (some London gaming clubs will go up to $2 million for the right Arabs). They make sure that no press stories get out that might frighten the pigeons away.

The press is the enemy; the journalists have forged an unusual alliance. They've gotten together with the girls known in certain London circles as the Mayfair Mercenaries. They're not hookers; they're career girls—men are their specialty. They're looking for rich ones to live with, richer ones to marry. The Mayfair Mercs cluster around Berkeley Square where most of the gaming clubs are. They meet for lunch at Morton's, get taken for dinner to Annabel's, go gambling at the Clermont. They're not so much the butterflies of London's society as its moths. Long, slender girls with pepped-up tans and pepped-up cars, who come at some time of the day to Berkeley Square to signal to men with long fat bank accounts. Arabs now have the fattest bank accounts. The Mayfair Mercs spent the 1960s hunting property magnates and mutual-fund million-aires. The 1970s see them fluttering around the Arabs.

Misunderstandings soon arise. Most Arabs can't see the difference between the Mayfair Mercs, just back from someone's yacht in the South of France or someone's estate in the north of Scotland, and the outright streetwalkers from around the corner in Piccadilly. The men take them out, throw them a bit of jewelry or a week in Paris, and then dump them fast and brutally. And when the Mayfair Mercs get spiteful they grouse to their traditional enemies, the gossip columnists. Suddenly princes with strange names are finding their extravagances splashed around the daily press. It makes good reading for everyone but Arabs. Now when they want girls those in the know stick to nameless pickups who take the money and don't make trouble. And when they want to relax they stick to gaming clubs. It's safer. All they can lose is their money. They trust the men who run the clubs. They trust Victor Lownes most of all.

Perfectionist Lownes is sipping his soda. He scrawls an angry note to the house manager; there are no fresh limes. That's how careful he is about detail. His face breaks into what passes for a smile as his gaming manager, Bernie Mulhurne, comes up. "Seen the figures then, Victor?" In the month of August, 1975, according to Bernie, the Playboy Club cleared $4 million profit on its gaming tables. Victor mulls over the $4 million for a moment and then turns his mind to a new calculation.

Eighteen months ago Graff, the up-and-coming jewelry store, rented a $3,000-a-year showcase in the Playboy. Now they want to open a separate branch on the premises. The store will be squeezed into the second-floor hallway. For this space, eight by four feet, Graff, it seems, is offering $100,000 a year rent for five years.

"Not bad," muses gaming manager Bernie on hearing the news. "Not bad. But not necessarily good. If a man wins twenty thousand dollars, he can do three things with it. He can keep it, he can stay at the tables and lose it, or we can get another shot at it tomorrow. But if he goes to the counter and buys an item for his wife or girlfriend, Victor, that's dead money, we'll be locked out of it."

"Where do our people go to buy now, Bernie?" asks Victor, as if he doesn't know.

"They go to the Hilton jeweler, Victor, but he's closed at night."

Las Vegas has shops, Victor points out. They do good business. So do the tables. Why shouldn't Playboy? "If we have a store, a woman might say, 'Let's go to the Playboy tonight,' instead of bitching, 'Not the Playboy again.'" Victor and Bernie finally agree in principle that it's worth pursuing the deal. Victor will continue negotiating.

Laurence Graff, sharp, friendly, thirty-eight, is a guy from the wrong side of the tracks who's worked his way up in the jewelry trade. His new store, in one of the smartest sections of London, is a sumptuous setting of Muzak, smoked glass, potted plants, and suede sofas. Its atmosphere is more akin to a hairdresser's than a craftsman's showcase. At this moment he's selling jewelry to a fat, slouchy Arab. Well, to the Arab's wife, actually. The Arab gets bored and goes out for a walk. No one would look at him twice, let alone recognize Prince Abdullah, brother of the Saudi King, himself king of the military.

When you talk about jewelry and you talk about Arabs in London, more and more Graff's name is bound to crop up. Graff, his fair hair deliciously styled to flop just right, has the warm personality of a cab driver who's made good. He greets Prince Abdullah's fat, blank-faced wife. "Hello, how's yer heart? It's grown bigger since last week." The princess's heart-shaped $300,000 diamond drop (last week's bauble) hangs on her heaving bosom. She gives Graff a big smile. Only later in Saudi Arabia will I find out why his relaxed attention gets such a grateful response.

Graff doesn't push. He's building slowly for the future. He sends a man regularly to Saudi Arabia and on around the six countries along the Gulf. He doesn't go himself. He's Jewish. In the store that's irrelevant. He, the princess, and the prince (who's back, having been bored with his walk) swap the chat of friends.

Graff goes downstairs to order tea and talk as he rummages through his safe. "Anyone who tells you the Arabs are stupid has never done business with them. Not in areas they know, anyway. A fourteen-year-old boy from Bahrain spotted a flaw in a seemingly perfect stone last week quicker than most jewelers could. And if you try selling the Arabs gaudy, flashy settings, you might as well shut up shop. They look for value. The second they think you're driving too hard a bargain they lose trust in you; they don't say a word. They vanish. I'm more careful to be absolutely straight with an Arab than with the most experienced European dealer."

Oh yes, Arabs know about jewelry. And when they don't, they pick the men they'll allow to buy for them very carefully indeed. One New York free-lance jeweler was asked to start a collection for some Saudis. Graff found out that the Saudi Arabian consul had been checking him out. "When I got a call from someone in California telling me the Saudis had been on to him, boy, I knew they were efficient. I'd thought my clients were hanging back because they couldn't get round to making a decision."

The Arabs are sniffing Graff out right now. And he knows it. They don't waste money buying good stuff for floozies. For them the jangling gold chains (three hundred dollars a piece) will do. The good stuff stays in the family. And it's the family business Graff's after. Prince Abdullah's, for instance. Graff bolts upstairs—fantastic news. Prince Abdullah has expressed an interest in some emeralds. As I leave, the Muzak is piping "The Impossible Dream."

That's how the Arabs buy jewels in the West. What's really interesting is to see how they react to the eager beavers who come to see them at home in Arabia. Everyone in the gems trade knows that at least six thousand Arabs in the Magnificent

Seven oil-rich states spend well over $500,000 every year buying jewelry. It's the biggest market there is.

Switch forward with me now a few months to Kuwait. It's November. I've just arrived at the Kuwait Sheraton Hotel. So too has the traveling circus from Tiffany, in New York. The troupe from Fifth Avenue have already "done" Saudi Arabia when they breeze into the Sheraton and take a suite, seven single rooms and an overkill of security men, who cause alarm by charging huge meals to the Tiffany account. Tiffany is going on show in the Blue Room.

The Sheraton Hotel's Blue Room is something of a world-famous institution. The '73 oil embargo was signed around a table here. So too was the Kuwaiti government's $17.5 million purchase of the uninhabited Kiawah Island off the coast of South Carolina. Here the Kuwaitis announced their plans to spend $200 million decorating the island as a vacation paradise with a $4 million luxury liner, *Catalina*, to ferry visitors across from the mainland. The Blue Room has seen some big deals. In the off season it's The Venue for visiting accessory salesmen.

Henry B. Platt ("Just call me Harry"), the great-great-grandson of founder Charles L. Tiffany, is handing out copies of *"The Tiffany Touch*—the fabulous, fascinating story of the world's most famous jewelry store and its glittering clientele." He's also adding style to the swimming pool patio, deepening his Palm Springs-based tan on his fiftyish-year-old bachelor body.

"We've waited a long, long time before coming here. We've waited to be sure that they were ready for us. You know, I'm not just in the jewelry business, I'm really a student of international affairs. I always make a great point of finding out everything about a country before I go there; and they're always so impressed by that. We had a wonderful time in Saudi Arabia. I was in every royal palace. I met princesses. I went to so many parties. Not that this is an entirely new area for us, of course. We've sold in New York to King Faisal and to his father, King Saud, who was ruler before him." Hard as it is to interrupt Harry's flow, I can't help feeling that this slight reconstruction of the Saudi royal family tree wouldn't go down well in palaces where everyone remembers the bitter rivalry between the two brothers, Saud and Faisal.

"Faisal's *father* Saud?" I query.

"Oh yes, his father. I know the families well, you see." His clean blue eyes sweep the patio for the pool boy. He needs a drink.

"We've had a great success here. Sheikha Badria, who is one of the royal family, graciously opened the exhibition for us. And she has even invited us to her palace for dinner. I do believe we're the first Europeans ever to go to dinner with her. We've sold a lot here. Of course I can't tell you to whom because we're very discreet. I mean, I never mention names. When Christina Onassis, who's a very good friend of mine as it happens, used to come into Tiffany, or even Jackie, who's also a very good friend of mine, I would never dream of telling anyone. There's someone else I could mention who rings up all the papers every time Christina walks in." Harry turns himself over with care; it's time to toast the other side.

"It's our policy in New York, of course, never to discount our prices. As a matter of fact it's one of the things we're known for. But I say, 'When in Rome do as the Romans do,' so in very special cases we offer a slight discount here."

The Blue Room is small and square; it's on the mezzanine floor opposite the hotel's mosque (a built-in Muslim chapel for the earth-weary). After Harry's poolside commentary I wander up to see how business is going.

A chic young sheikha is examining the wares. She decides on a few trinkets. She starts to haggle. Of course she does; this is Kuwait. She wouldn't do it in New York. When she hits the 15 percent ceiling, Bruce Cummings, a clean-cut East Coaster, starts to fidget. "We have a very special reputation," he elucidates. "Our quoted price system guarantees the same standard of top-class workmanship in all our designs, and they're of the finest quality, too." At this point the sheikha cuts him off and switches to Arabic. She opens negotiations with the smartly dressed society Kuwaiti woman "borrowed" by Tiffany to get Sheikha Badria for the opening. Bruce Cummings is taken off for a quiet word. A price is agreed to everyone's satisfaction.

Just as well Harry isn't at coffee next morning with three members of one of Kuwait's oldest families—the al Ghanims. As the Mellons are to Pittsburgh, the al Ghanims are to Kuwait. "Tiffany is just like the others," one high-flyer complains. "They all think they're bringing us something new. But Tiffany doesn't even realize that they've been sending me their catalog from New York for fifteen years. I swear a salesman at the opening thought it was the first time I'd seen such jewelry. We've had Boucheron in our home, Bulgari of Rome three times, and my husband has bought me large collections of diamonds. In our safety-deposit box in Europe we have a priceless wedding necklace made in India for my grandmother studded with rubies and diamonds. So don't talk to me about 'new.' But the thing I really can't take is the way all Westerners treat us as a 'new market.' I prefer to be approached as an individual."

I return to find Harry back at the pool, working on his tan again in the Kuwaiti winter sun, welcoming as ever. "When you think it over, Tiffany is the obvious choice for this place. It's exciting for them that we come from New York." He lowers his voice confidentially. "You know, Harry Winston is a Jew. That's all right in New York, but I don't think it would be all right here, with these people."

Didn't anyone ever mention to Harry B. Platt that King Faisal used to go to Harry Winston too? He even bought his favorite wife's engagement ring, a vast, rectangular blue-white diamond baguette, from him. What was Platt doing at all those Saudi parties not to notice Winston jewelry all around him? In the week before Tiffany hit Saudi Arabia, gossip had it that Harry Winston's man sold over $1.5 million worth of jewelry between Jeddah and Riyadh, the country's two main cities. Word came out at a level where gossip isn't wrong about such matters. Harry continues brightly. "I won't go out of my way to tell anyone how successful this trip has been when I go home. It would hurt the feelings of the people here." It wouldn't do him much good in New York.

Over dinner at Sheikha Badria's after the departure of Tiffany someone did mention the total sales figure of the Fifth Avenue happy band. It was not impressive. It might have been wrong, of course, but they do know about money in Kuwait. They have a very special reputation for it.

They also have a very special reputation for liking to buy in secret. The Blue Room exhibition might not have netted any whoppers, but I wouldn't put it past the Kuwaitis to nip on the next plane to New York and make straight for Tiffany. They'd rather miss out on the discount in return for having Fifth Avenue privacy the way they'd like it. You never know where you are in Arabia. You simply never know—until you get on the inside.

PART

SAUDI ARABIA—

"FIRST STEP THROUGH

THE LOOKING GLASS . . ."

CHAPTER

4

A TOWN CALLED ALICE-IN-WONDERLAND

SOME BANKERS AND MOST SAUDIS WILL TELL YOU THAT SAUDI
Arabia is really wised up about money. Not yet it isn't—it
wants to be, but it's still too much of a child determined to
have all the toys the adults have and be able to afford them.
For adults, read the West. Saudi Arabia envies Western technology and it wants it all—fast; good, bad, or indifferent. So
millions of dollars' worth of contracts are up for grabs, and
every huckster and businessman in the world who's chasing
money passes through Riyadh at some time right now.

Only one thing is certain in this ferocious desert land. It
isn't about to go broke. Old King Saud, with such pet extravagances as his $50 million al Naseryyah Palace complex
(separate palaces for his four wives, thirty-two mansions for
concubines and thirty-seven palaces for select princes), almost
managed to bankrupt the place. But that was before tight-fisted
King Faisal took over and long before oil prices rocketed.

They say King Faisal found $100 left in his state coffer when
his brother got the boot. This royal kingdom's revenues for
1975–76 add up to $30,603,000,000 to go around precious few
Saudis. The government's just banned contraceptives in an
attempt to boost the number; they'll have to wait a while for
the millions they need to be born, let alone grow up. Mean-

while rich women are merely adding the Pill to their shopping lists for their trips abroad.

Riyadh, bang in the middle of this barren, empty, frightening country, is Saudi Arabia's Washington—the center of government and growing every day. Now forget that comparison because Riyadh is tension-charcoaled daily under the desert sun. Nothing is predictable. Has some unseen Dr. Pavlov run wild here? Tempers flare like dry tinder. Something intangible and inexplicable sends gooseflesh across one's spirit. The place only looks like a modern city, more correctly a modern building site.

The hotel lobbies (such few as exist) throng with businessmen, nerves, and expense accounts stretched to breaking point, baffled by this entirely alien culture. Today is an average day in the lobby of the Al Yamama Hotel. Walter Faulds, an old Africa hand and architect, is doing his daily newspaper crossword over a cup of undrinkable tea. He's been in Riyadh for three weeks. Fortunately, he doesn't yet know that he's doomed to be here for another three weeks. Faulds is waiting.

His British firm is about to sign (everyone's always about to sign) a design deal for part of Saudi Arabia's new Olympic Stadium. Not that Riyadh could house the Olympics. No Communist countries for starters (it's a toss-up who the Saudis hate more—Communists or Zionists. Most of the time they think they're the same thing plotting together). Women competing? Never. But the Saudis want the best Olympic Stadium in the world, so that's what they're going to have. All of this leaves Faulds, with his rapidly graying hair and suede shoes, waiting with pained resignation for Prince Faisal ibn Fahd. The young prince, son of the Crown Prince, possesses (in his capacity as director of youth welfare) the crucial signature Faulds needs on his contract.

The whereabouts of Prince Faisal is a mystery. His office says he isn't there now. He might be there tomorrow. But *Bukra, in shaa' Allah* (tomorrow, God willing) is a well-known password. God might not be willing tomorrow. He very often isn't. And Prince Faisal's office staff have been saying that for the last three weeks. Faulds waits, along with all the lobby captives.

The lobby men are the concubines of the 1970s, shut away in purdah at the pleasure of their Arabian masters. Everyone's terrified of quitting the hotel in case That Call comes. Around one table near Faulds huddles a group pushing bulletproof Cadillacs. At another there's an Egyptian psychiatrist playing anxiously with his worry beads. He's here to set up a psychiatric unit at the $200 million (that's only the check for the first stage) King Faisal Medical City up the road. ("A psychiatric unit in Riyadh?" says a government official in horror. "Nonsense, it doesn't exist. We don't need psychiatry; we have Islam." Doesn't exist? The Egyptian is real enough.) He's waiting on the Medical City's executive director, Jack F. Frayer, an ex-football player from Macon, Georgia ("where ah have the prettiest Herefords you-all ever saw"). And in case that doesn't work, Maharishi Mahesh Yogi, who shot out of obscurity by the Ganges when the Beatles embraced him in the 1960s, has a rep in town trying to sell the Saudi Education Ministry on transcendental-meditation programs.

Bill Lear has flown in to find financing for his newest jet. But that tidbit's lost on the engineers whispering in another corner. They're worried sick that their foundations for a new university haven't allowed for sand erosion. This *is* the desert. It's merely decorated with high-rise buildings. Another multi-disciplined architect from Texas is nonchalantly covering his attempts to eavesdrop on their worries. He's designing a flashy villa for the cousin of a minor prince whose brother is a minister. Perhaps the villa will lead to an office and shopping complex. The fellow from Dallas is slowly going nuts; he admits it himself. But if he leaves and cuts himself out of the game, he'll never be able to deal himself back in.

For the operators, it's about as easy as watching a film backward and upside-down. Everyone has his contact. Every businessman waiting for That Call is about to make millions.

Some do. More never find out whether their contact has a contact with the right contact or not. The game beats them and they go home.

At odd moments during the day and evening deadpan Saudis drop in to watch the survivors. They ought to be charged an entrance fee; most of them treat it like a trip to the zoo to inspect the chimps. They usually get amusement somewhere. Westerners can't distinguish a taxi driver from a big tribal chief. National dress (that white sheet, a *thobe,* with the table-cloth headdress) is a great equalizer. Better-informed lobby hands extract sadistic delight at seeing a newcomer oozing charm at a Saudi known to have no more power to arrange anything than the doorman. Probably less.

At least the doorman can arrange women. A black bundle may tap late at night on the bedroom door of a man who's had the sense to befriend the doorman. There are few other diversions—no movies or theaters. But there is Mike, the hotel manager. Mike is a Palestinian who was raised in the States and just arrived in Saudi. This back-slapping teeth-flasher is having to learn how to handle his *thobe.* He's not a delicate man, so I soon know how difficult he's finding it to piss without spotting his long white frock as he holds it above his waist in the john.

The lobby also knows that Mike has a friendly supply of Scotch that he shares, except on days when the hotel's owner, a tall, dignified Saudi, puts in an appearance. But Mike's worth a few giggles. His moonlighting is something else. He reads the late-night news in English on Saudi television—or rather stutters it, trying hard to keep his unaccustomed headdress from falling off. It's the one guaranteed comedy show of the day. As an encore he rushes back to the Al Yamama to ask the lobby how he did. Lousy.

Usually at about this time the patient Mr. Faulds has a last cup of cocoa, folds his newspaper, and retires to get his strength together for another day's waiting. But tonight his boss, Ian Fraser, is flying in. Fraser, a big, cheerful man, arrives in a naval blazer and white moccasins, just the thing for Newport, Rhode Island. This linchpin of the international set brings news at last of the elusive young Prince Faisal. He's finally been tracked down. He's doing as well as can be expected in a London hotel suite, where he's officially ill. Not too ill, though, to have been seen wining, dining, and dancing at Annabel's nightclub. It's hard for the men playing the waiting game in Riyadh.

By comparison, life for a visiting Western woman is a cinch because at least the rules are clear. You have to be untouchable, that's all. Before the journey began, one scholarly Arabist offered some advice: "The only way you'll get round that part of the world, my dear, is on your back." It's the one way not to travel. Too limited a view.

I size that one up at Dhahran airport. This center of the oil-producing region on the east coast is the window through which foreigners swarm en route for Riyadh (international airlines can't land in the capital—an understandable attempt to keep foreign contamination at bay). It's limp hot in the terminal. I feel like an idiot standing around in a long nightdress (where else can you buy a long-sleeved, high-necked, demure cotton frock in fall, except a lingerie department). In all my years as a journalist, I've never had to dress up like something out of "Hansel and Gretel." I feel an even bigger dope when I find out that an okay on an airline route on Saudia, the national airline, doesn't mean a seat on the plane. It's the okay to fight for one.

Normally I'd be in there with the crowd, trying at least. But Saudi Arabia clamps invisible handcuffs on a woman. I know I'll lose that way before I start. The only other woman in sight is bundled motionless, inside what looks like a black laundry bag, guarding the ladies' room.

But what's this? A Saudi, toting an impressive crocodile overnight case and heavy gold watch, emerges from the "lynch mob" attacking the check-in counter to find out if I'm in need of help. He disappears, promising a seat. There's something about this man in his impeccable Western suit (made in Taiwan two days ago) that makes me certain he'll deliver. A nearby Britisher drawls knowingly: "There'll be a high price for that favor."

Wrong. There's no price. The Saudi gets the seat, shepherds his flock onto the plane and across the desert to Riyadh, and hands me over to the Head of Passenger Relations, leaving stern orders for Pepsi and cake. He refuses to give his name but offers instead a small, stiff nod. "You're a guest in our country. I hope you have a pleasant stay with us."

Saudis in Riyadh aren't used to having women flapping about on their own. Until they are, the few that get in are privileged creatures—providing they observe the rules. These include such clauses as: sit in the back of the car automatically unless invited up front. Remember at all times to be as sexless as Snow White and shut off any signals that may be misread as an invitation. Don't allow Mike the Manager through the bedroom door at two in the morning when he arrives with Scotch to offer avuncular advice on how to deal with men. Don't be offended if he then badmouths you around the lobby. No one will believe that any woman in her right mind would have a man in her room here. Everyone works on the assumption that rooms and phones are bugged. Paranoia is a disease that goes with Riyadh's claustrophobia as malaria goes with swamps.

A Western woman here is safe, suffocatingly safe. I am by no means helpless by nature. But here I am wafting around in this nightie, not allowed to walk out of the hotel alone, treated like a china doll. I've covered civil wars, been beaten up in Nigeria and I don't remember crying: terrified, yes, but tears? No. Arabia is the only place that has reduced me to that. I'm not ashamed to admit it (hell, I see a Western *man* crying for the same reason here). You're not a person here, you're playing a part all the time—everyone is. The Saudi obsession with form, ritual, outward appearances, and pretense creates raging inner tensions.

Eventually I know I'll either blow my stack (as I've seen men do in final exasperation—out, they're finished. Saudis don't like displays of temper), or something. That something is a flood of tears—my only form of release—over the bedroom basin. I have to tell you this because what happens next is important: there's a timid knock on my door. The room-service man, good Arab that he is, is desperately concerned that I am unhappy in Saudi. He wants to send for the manager to translate (oh no, not him!) because he can't bear that I'm upset. Can you imagine that in an American hotel? Maybe now you're beginning to get the picture of artificial craziness combined with overpowering warmth.

There can, of course, still be misunderstandings of a trickier nature. It's eleven at night. The phone rings. A high court official has finished work and he's prepared to talk. In the lobby the piped rock 'n' roll blares across a conversation centered around royal matters while contract hunters stare curiously. "I think," says the official, his face inscrutable, "that if you don't mind, we'll go around to the house of some friends to talk."

Nothing unusual in that. Once inside the cemented circle of power in Riyadh, you're led around all manner of strangers' homes at all hours to find tea, coffee, and unquestioning hospitality. This time, the house is in a dark, unlit back street. The friend opens the door, greets the man from the court and closes the door behind us, leading the way into the living room.

By now accustomed to the Saudi habit of giving away as much as a Chinese poker player, I register no surprise at the illegal *Playboy* magazines stacked in the bookshelves and nude centerfolds adorning the walls. They add an almost homey look to the slinky room with its discotheque-style lighting, low sofas, and stash of Akai stereo equipment and bottles of Scotch.

My predicament: to walk out would be an automatic indictment if I was found running around the streets of Riyadh at night (a woman is always wrong here; she doesn't get the benefit of the doubt). To ask immediately to be driven back to the hotel would lead to a confrontation. What if he refuses? The friend has disappeared and the court official is oiling himself with whisky. He tells me the villa's rented by a group of married men as their communal "bachelor pad" (prostitutes, mainly Egyptian, and a river of cooperative stewardesses keep it well supplied). But I'm in the capital of a people whose tribal, desert traditions haven't all been cashed in for petro-dollars. There's a way out if I keep calm.

"Do you mind being here with me?" leers my host meaning-fully.

Mind? I'm scared stiff. But I say pleasantly, "Not at all. I'm a guest in your country and so I know you will not harm me. I am under your protection."

I now have him in a complete moral dilemma. As a Saudi challenged with this age-old appeal in the desert, he's incapable of infringing his sense of honor. As a man, he's dying to jump on me. He blusters away for a time because he is about to lose face and that's one of the worst disasters an Arab man can suffer. He even begs me to stay the night locking myself in one room while he sleeps in another—so that his friend won't know what's happened. I turn down this invitation. "The hotel will worry for me."

In the end the Saudi in him wins through and he weaves his way toward the door, out to the car, and drives me back to the hotel. I totter into the lobby, shaking with relief. "Did you have a productive time?" asks the cozy Mr. Faulds as we share our late-night cup of cocoa. "It's been boring here as usual. How I wish something, anything, unexpected would happen."

A couple of days later a leading Saudi government official drops me off at the hotel after a more conventional business meeting followed by lunch at his home. It's not my first visit to his family, and I'm interested to hear an American's com-ment as the car roars away. "That man has everything. He's educated, bright, rich, and successful. It has all dropped into his lap."

But has it? Follow that man home, out of the public eye, and you find another Riyadh. The black oil spurting from under-ground is not as simple a blessing as the biblical manna float-ing down from heaven. Behind the high walls of Saudi homes there are casualties. That man's wife is one. How could it be otherwise? I know how hard I find it living up to the Saudi view of women—treasure or tramp. There's nothing between.

She sits in her living room hooked on cigarettes and tranquilizers. She's in her late twenties, shrinking, wasting away, her face pale and pasty. Her long slender legs hang listlessly below her short Paris couture skirt and skinny T-shirt. In some ways life was easier for her mother. There were slaves then (slavery was abolished officially only in 1962) but a wife still had work. No California-style kitchens a generation ago, no air conditioning, no schooling abroad or glimpses of an alternative life to the prison of the women's quarters.

The daughter has lost and gained from progress. Several times a week she covers her face with a mask of makeup, slides into long gowns, mechanically arranges the jewels that label her the possession of a multimillionaire—and they go out together; that's avant garde for Riyadh. They go out to sit within the four walls of friends. Walls can be a haven; they can feel like a coffin.

"My father arranged our marriage when I was sixteen. I remember our honeymoon, sitting on the plane with this stranger and I didn't know how to begin talking to him. I didn't know the first thing about contraception, so I had four children in four years. How could I take care of a child? I was a child myself.

"Now I've grown up. I'm not a child any longer, but he won't see that. You think I don't know that my husband suffers too? I've stretched out and longed for him to see that I'm not the stupid child he married, that he can trust me, confide in me, let me share some of his worries. He doesn't want me to grow up.

"I went to a European boarding school with normal girls. Do you know how hard it has been for me to adjust? Women can't drive here, so I can't leave the house without a driver for the car. When I do go out I have to put on a long black cloak and cover my face. I suffocate. I know other women say it'll disappear one day. But what about now? It's now that the veil suffocates me, now that I am humiliated."

I understand only too well. One weekend I'm invited away

by another family. With great embarrassment they ask if I'd mind covering my face. If I were fair, everyone would recognize me as a European. Because I'm dark, they fear people who know their family will take me for an Arab—an unveiled Arab woman would dishonor them in the eyes of others. It is an eerie experience. I do suffocate, but what's worse is the way that *I,* I don't exist to the people around me who see the black anonymity of a person who isn't there because she can't be seen.

How can this woman's husband begin to understand this humiliation? Or see that he lets her out of the country to a freedom she can't handle and then brings her back to a constriction she can't bear. "Here I rule my house, that's all. I decide what food must be cooked when he telephones at noon from the office to say he's bringing ten men home for lunch. I arrange for the meal to be served while I disappear through another door in the kitchen so that no men can see me. Has time really brought more freedom? It's brought the freedom of tickets to Europe or the States. If I want to go away I only have to ask. And what do I do there? I go shopping, sit in a hotel room and daren't go out because there's always someone from Riyadh who might see me and tell his family.

"He's unfaithful. There isn't a husband in Saudi Arabia who isn't unfaithful. Not here, of course; here they're angels. And hypocrites. I mind, but what can I do about it? We don't discuss it because we don't discuss anything that matters. Every now and again I scream at him and believe me, I have a tongue like a serpent, I know it. He wouldn't hit me. He couldn't. To do that would be to admit that I'm another adult human being, not a child."

This woman isn't unusual, but I can't name her. To make her unhappiness public or that of other women who talk openly to me would dishonor the family. That's the real crime; a family's honor is its life raft in this society. So this depressed woman sits at home and everyone around her pays the price for her confusion. Her husband is, as she says herself, a good man.

"I love that woman. My father showed me many photographs of suitable girls when it was time for me to get married but I chose her myself—I wanted her. And now she can hurt me more than anyone. But what do you want me to do? I give her jewels, she shrugs. I give her thousands of dollars to buy clothes from London and New York. She complains because she can't wear them in Riyadh except at home. 'Then why buy short skirts?' I ask. Why must she remind herself every day of what she can't do?

"I work all day and it isn't easy. It's one decision after another and government life is one long fight. Must I fight at home every night? She says I don't talk to her. When am I supposed to talk to her? It's part of our way of life to have an open house with friends walking in at any time. I can't lock our door against them to make time to talk to her. And I don't want to. What else is there that matters in life but your friends and your family?

"I don't believe in her covering her face but I wouldn't bring shame on my family by letting her be seen unveiled in daylight. But at night, if we're going by car to friends, I don't even ask that of her. I just ask her to put on her cloak and a thin chiffon scarf over her hair. Don't women wear headscarves in your country? Is that a terrible sacrifice? Ten years ago I couldn't have driven with her sitting beside me in the car, let alone without a veil. I couldn't have let her go to Europe for the summer to get away from the heat. Why won't she see how things have changed for the better?

"Work? Of course she can't work. Why should she need to? We don't need the money and our families wouldn't like it. Sometimes I think it *was* better in the past." At this moment his face looks like that of a sad old man, and he's only in his early thirties. "Life is getting too complicated. I'm afraid of what's happening to all of us."

One of his friends is building a $3 million villa in Riyadh. Every weekend he goes out to inspect his site. It will have soft beige terrazzo floors, many courtyards, a swimming pool, a "bachelor" room downstairs for his male friends, a boudoir to take morning coffee with his wife. There are hidden gardens and waterfalls glimpsed through the windows.

This will be the first home of his own. He and his wife started in a large family compound with all his brothers and cousins and their families. Now they share a house with just one brother's family. The next step is the house on the hill— one man, one wife, and three children.

He grew up in a mud mansion teeming with people and the protective warmth of a traditional Saudi extended family. This empty marble house will seem like a mausoleum to him. Every Saudi multiplying his millions asks himself at some time—is the change worth it? In those lonely moments of doubt that foreigners don't witness, few answer yes.

CHAPTER

A PRIDE OF PRINCES

ONCE UPON A TIME IT DID INDEED SEEM VERY SIMPLE. WHEN King Ibn Saud agreed to the first oil concession with the Americans for 35,000 gold sovereigns in 1935, the sale was his to make. He had conquered a kingdom and, to make sure nobody forgot it, he named it after his own family. He left behind a few other souvenirs. Opposite the small shops selling plastic toys and gaudy women's panties in Riyadh's equivalent to Fifth Avenue, there's an old mud fortress. On one side, stuck into the wall, is a remnant of a sword. It was left there at dawn one day in 1901 when Ibn Saud took the fortress and town from his enemies of another tribe. It was his first major victory—he was twenty-one years old and had ridden with a band of only forty men across the wasteland of the Empty Quarter to do it.

The battles had only begun. But Ibn Saud's policy toward his enemies (neatly summed up by one diplomat as "kick 'em in the teeth, then marry into the family") has left behind more troublesome souvenirs. Rather a lot of al Saud. When Ibn Saud's son Faisal came to the throne there were about three thousand al Saud princes. Today, with *his* brother, King Khaled, ruling the country there are twice as many. It's no wonder that the local nickname for the al Saud is "The Factory"—they turn out new models like Detroit on a super-bonanza day.

There are many princes whom even prominent Saudis have never met. There are many they've never heard of. Some years ago one such prince, Musad, was better known in Cairo (for certain costly personal eccentricities) than in Riyadh. He made the French newspapers when he was found dancing naked in a Paris fountain brandishing a sword, and King Ibn Saud didn't appreciate the joke at all so he brought him home to comfortable house arrest. Faisal gave Musad money later to buy a house in Beirut and shove off. But in 1975 Musad's name was globally circulated. It was his son who shot Faisal and mislaid his head to an executioner's sword.

Musad's is not a name to conjure with in Riyadh today. But then few Saudis ever talk much about princes, and when they do it's in hallowed terms. The royals are gods here.

This is the tale of three "godlike" princes. All they have in common is what all Saudi princes have in common. From the moment they were old enough to understand anything, they understood that they were very special beings. Prince Abdullah ibn Faisal *is* special—he's a leader who hasn't put progress before people.

It's part of the Bedouin tradition, left over from those days in the tents, that any man has access to his ruler and members of the ruler's family. No one could imagine an Appalachian farmer going along to the White House, barging in on the President and grumbling about the state of his fences. But this is Saudi, and the equivalent still does happen here. It won't for long; once government becomes more formal, fewer and fewer poor Saudis will be allowed into the offices of the great—all those multimillion-dollar buildings will probaby frighten them off anyway.

I don't understand how fundamental this change will be until I go to lunch with Prince Abdullah ibn Faisal al Saud.

Prince Abdullah is the eldest of Faisal's sons. He is one of the few important old-style princes left. By the time he was born his sixteen-year-old father had fought in desert wars, traveled to Europe and seen the grave-scarred battlefields of Flanders. Abdullah was raised in desert ways and brought up in Riyadh when it was a walled-in mud city.

Today he lives in a small villa on the edge of town. There are no armed guards; any ragged Saudi can walk in. Abdullah used to have a palace until he separated from his first (and then, only) wife. He gave it to her fully furnished, and she sold it to King Khaled for $16.5 million. Abdullah has his offices (many of them) scattered all around the place. That's another leftover from the time when a man could pitch his tent in the desert and not stay put too long. Another contradiction: although his home is open to all (men, not women, naturally), he doesn't entertain formally. To be invited to lunch is a signal honor. But no one has warned me that Prince Abdullah is the only one of Faisal's sons you would recognize on sight. The likeness is uncanny, and I can't conceal my shock.

"It's my curse," he says with moving sadness. "I see this face that was his every day when I look in the mirror. When he died the beating of my heart ceased. Did you ever hear of a man living with an unbeating heart?" The roomful of men fall silent. Some of them he knows personally; some he doesn't. Here you don't write your congressman, you walk in to see the prince—to see one like Abdullah you still walk into his home. Some men have come to greet him out of respect. Some to seek his advice: they want to marry off a daughter, need money, a job, they don't know what to do with a grant of land. He listens to each gravely; of course, he'll help. A servant enters with a letter and tries to kiss his hand. Prince Abdullah snatches it away angrily but allows him to kiss his forehead instead. He's not that kind of prince.

When he smiles he displays a perfect set of dentures. As a young man a quack took out all his own teeth as a cure for some illness. His generation was too busy to send boys abroad to study (as all his own sons have done), neither were they used to traveling to the West to cure every headache.

He has inherited his grandfather's love of practical jokes (no, I never thought of King Ibn Saud having a sense of humor either). He soon launches into a few of his favorites. There was the time he was so fed up with some friends who were always pestering him to take them up to the King's palace for lunch that he arranged a picnic sixty miles out in the desert. "We'll meet you there," he promised. The friends tortured their Maserati over the sands to the rendezvous—no one and nothing. They got back to town at midnight and never asked Abdullah for an invitation again. Then there was one joke played against Abdullah in a hotel suite in Cairo—a friend got a woman with a sexy, alluring voice to telephone Abdullah and arrange to meet him. She described herself to make certain that it suited the royal taste—the bust of Jane Russell, the eyes of Marilyn Monroe, the walk of Lana Turner. He dressed himself up, went rushing over to meet this peach—to find a hag of about fifty-five. Laughs all around.

Prince Abdullah's affability is deceptive. King Ibn Saud thought so much of him that he nicknamed him "half the world," and his grandfather also made him the country's first Minister of Health in 1952 to prove it. He was an outstanding administrator but left the government under King Saud and never went back. He prefers business: he has the Saudi agencies for Sony and BMW, and owns a pipe factory that actually exports in this country where every port and airport is clogged with imports. He's building Saudi's first auto-assembly plant—for General Motors. He's got a head for business, and being the King's son helped to get him off the ground.

His greatest treasure is displayed in the middle of his *majlis* (the Saudi word for a male reception room). It's a gold-trimmed model of his oil tanker, *Mecca*, just launched in Japan. It's the first truly Saudi tanker. But why, in the middle of a world recession, with nearly four hundred supertankers laid up idle in waters all over the place, go to the expense of building a new one? The Saudi pride rides majestically across the bows of business sense. "I want it Saudi. I want it good. I don't want something secondhand."

We go to lunch and, to my surprise, a bunch of T-shirted soccer players arrive. Abdullah explains that he was converted t› the game after the '48 Olympics and helped to sponsor the country's national team. He writes poetry on the side, and the legendary Egyptian singer, Umm Khalthoum, recorded three of his songs. In Arab terms that's like Leonard Bernstein recording a symphony by a Kennedy.

Abdullah eats only boiled meats and yogurt (they look disgusting but he isn't offended when I refuse). The rest of the table is piled high with spicy Mideastern fare—roast lamb, rice, meatballs, chicken. He usually eats in about ten minutes, but as a sign of appreciation for unaccustomed female company, he lingers for over an hour talking, telling stories—mostly against himself.

On his wrist is a heavy watch. It cost thirty dollars. It was a first-anniversary present from his new, second wife (not eating with us, of course). His tale of his new marriage starts with his explanation that he had been alone for many years after he left his first wife. "I asked two young girls for their hand. Both said no. Very wise. After all, look at me. I'm fifty-five years old and people call me uncle now." He hates that. "One of my cousins at teachers' training college told me of a classmate, a beautiful Bedouin called Safwa. This girl had already rejected many handsome young men because she said that young men play around and she wanted an old one she could trust. I didn't do this thing through other people. I went straight to the girl's house and said, 'I am old, you can trust me, and I want to marry you.' She told me that she didn't love me but that she would. Very honest. I asked her father and we had the religious ceremony that day. After all, for Prince Abdullah to visit her house without marriage would spoil her reputation.

"I took her out for a drive every day for three months. She lived at her father's house, and I promised her that if at the end of those months she didn't want me, I would divorce her immediately. Not once in that time did I touch her, you understand. At the end of it I asked her again, and she said yes and came to be my wife, my real wife."

That was two years ago and now Safwa has given birth to Abdullah's only daughter. He has seven sons by his first wife (one of whom was killed in a shooting accident) and this daughter gives him unconcealed delight. He shyly takes a picture of his wife out of a brown pocketbook to show; male guests aren't even allowed to peek. "Every time I go out of the house I say to my wife, 'You are the stupidest girl in the world. You must be—you married me.' "

The afternoon sun is calling Prince Abdullah to the unseen Bedouin princess and to the black nothing of siesta time. "I hate to eat anything more than I need, and even more I hate to sleep. I love the night, when I can read and listen to music until dawn. I think there will be a long time ahead to be bored." In the long time ahead men will only remember that there were once Arab princes like Abdullah ibn Faisal.

The second prince is another Abdullah (I warned you that there aren't many first names to go around). It was in the summer of 1975 that this Prince Abdullah entered the life of a former British professional soccer player turned coach. George Smith was twiddling his thumbs at home in the north of England when the telephone rang. A foreign voice claiming to be Prince Abdul Aziz ibn Nasr al Saud told Smith that he was telephoning from Riyadh and that his older brother, Prince Abdullah, would like to hear from him at the Carlton Tower Hotel in London. "I thought it was one of my mates taking the piss, so I told him to bugger off." The patient prince phoned again (no mean feat from Riyadh).

This time, out of sheer curiosity, Smith rang the London hotel. A Prince Abdullah was certainly staying there and indeed waiting eagerly for Smith's call. He offered a contract, worth $20,000 a year (good money for a British coach, plus heaps of extras, all tax-free), to manage the Prince's soccer team, Hilal, an amateur affair in Riyadh. (Anyone wondering whether it would not have been easier, let alone cheaper, for Prince Abdullah to lift the telephone for himself in London has not yet absorbed the illogicality of things Saudi.)

Smith zoomed off to Riyadh only to find that the players didn't like being coached. They preferred the simple satisfaction of banging the ball in the net. Smith yelled and cursed at them (soccer is an international four-letter language), ran them up and down the field, and wouldn't let them back into their air-conditioned dressing rooms until they had some better idea of the game. Hilal won their first match of the season.

"He's a hell of a guy, my prince," says Smith, dangling his toes in a swimming pool, toasting his balding head. "He's a real soccer man." Prince Abdullah ibn Nasr is the son of King Ibn Saud's twentieth son, Nasr, sometime governor of Riyadh, now semi-retired. Nasr's been spending an unfortunate amount of time in the hospital.

His eldest son, Abdullah, pursues a healthier, outdoor life. He's patron of Hilal for a start. The "amateur" players live in expensive houses and drive expensive cars, but it's Prince Abdullah's very own team and he's a generous man.

He's also one of the country's toughest, most experienced falconers. He's to be found every fall afternoon taking the air in the backyard of his Riyadh palace, sitting under his tent next to a garage housing a fleet of cars, sipping tea, reclining in a plastic deckchair. For company he has his regular pals and sixteen hooded fierce falcons (average cost: three thousand dollars).

It takes time to get past his gate guards. They answer any stranger with a friendly "No, he no in." Being courteous Arabs, they don't like to challenge my right to visit. Prince Abdullah ibn Nasr, the hardy desert falconer and football fanatic, is a skinny, pale, thirty-four-year-old who looks as though the first puff of wind would send him blowing away in his fine cotton *thobe*. His handshake is as firm as a dead crab's.

The prince has a bad time at Hilal games. His royal awareness forbids him to cheer his team (although there was one never-to-be-forgotten occasion when his self-control broke and he actually waved an arm after a goal). But at the end of each game he's so tense with excitement that he runs with sweat and his knees shake.

His falcons are trained as hard as his footballers. He's training his newest himself—Habdan, a prize from Pakistan. "Habdan is the most beautiful bird in the country, look at its coloring, look at its eyes." Unhooded, Habdan is about as beautiful as Frankenstein. Prince Abdullah is holding Habdan on one wrist with his hand protected by a glove—somehow the ungrateful bird is managing to scratch his Highness's long, delicate ungloved hand to ribbons. His Highness doesn't deign to notice. "This is a bird of strength and of courage. It could fly one hundred and fifty miles a day and still down another bird."

Habdan has his suede bonnet fixed tenderly back over his head. It's Mansour's turn. Mansour is the prince's favorite—it's a Hur falcon, a type that's easy to train and not as temperamental as the fast, tougher Shaihan kind of falcon that's liable to pick and choose whether it feels like hunting today. Prince Abdullah has a superb Shaihan called Najla, but Najla's been sent to the seaside for a holiday. It's good for his nerves. His feathers are a bit shaggy and Riyadh makes him tense. The sea air might induce him to trade in the old for a new, faster plumage. Every December, Prince Abdullah goes out into the Saudi desert to hunt, with his falcons, converted trucks, and his personal falcon groom, Magaad, who's been with Abdullah for twenty years.

It's teatime, so Magaad brings on the raw meat. One by one he lifts the birds off the pedestals and takes off their hoods. Still tied to his arm, they tear apart the flesh that he holds in his other hand. Being chained to a pedestal most of the year must be a rotten life for a falcon—small wonder that they don't always come back once they get out into the desert during the hunting season. Prince Abdullah lost two of his best birds last year. There's a custom that if someone else finds your falcon, he keeps it unless you figure out who's got it within a year, in which case you can get it back. Prince Abdullah hasn't found out who picked up his falcons, and he didn't find anyone else's either. So last year was something of a loss.

The raw meat has been devoured. With this gruesome spectacle over, Prince Abdullah goes along to the concrete hut on the other side of the garage to see how his wife is enjoying her afternoon in there. Through the door of the room stares a delicate creature, flowing in traditional silken robes. She's Abdullah's only wife. "I have the best; I don't need others." If she's such a prize, wouldn't he be proud to let others see her? He looks surprised. *"I* can see her; that's what matters."

His palace, built eight years ago for several million dollars, stands empty. It has the bare, temporary look of owners who prefer to be elsewhere. Prince Abdullah's off somewhere else right now; to one of those enigmatic business meetings royals go in for. He walks away, swaying slightly backward.

"My prince," says George Smith, the burly English soccer coach. "I knew when I met him that we were going to get along. He walked downstairs in the Carlton Tower Hotel wearing a sky blue suit, with that gorgeous wife of his bursting out of her skintight black and red trouser suit and I said to myself straight away: 'Whhhhooooaaa. That's one hell of a geezer.' "

Some princes, like Abdullah ibn Nasr, occupy no special role in their country. They're part of the scenery. Others do. All of King Faisal's eight sons, for example. Captain Bandar (Prince Bandar ibn Faisal al Saud) of the Saudi Arabian Royal Air Force, according to his superiors, is a brilliant officer—when he turns up for duty. He may not, depending on what other royal duties he has. But periodically he makes an impressive contribution.

Periodically he also makes a contribution to the night life of London that is impressive enough to make Warren Beatty seem like a stand-in. I had been warned off Bandar in London.

Prince Bandar has arranged to carry me off to the desert. Naturally, having absorbed Saudi imprecision, I don't expect it to materialize. Lo and behold, a driver turns up. I feel so safe in this city that I follow without so much as asking who sent him. Not for nothing do the Saudis boast they have the lowest crime rate in the world. (At a price, but nothing is for free: I do not accept one thoughtful Saudi's invitation to a public execution.) About an hour down the road, shooting along the highway, I have a few misgivings. The driver is one of those silent types. The car turns off, bumping across the undulating dunes. It's scorching hot and we're in the middle of nowhere. Hello, I think, trouble. Wrong again.

We arrive at a sort of goatskin and wool four-room tent encampment. There's a large living area with exquisite Persian rugs on the floor, a larger room set aside where servants can be seen busying themselves, and two other rooms with their walls (can tents have walls?) firmly closed. At first I can see nothing but sand to the horizon.

Then in the distance a tall figure appears striding across the dunes. The effect of the total silence (after the raucous abuse of Riyadh's traffic), the shimmering heat haze, and the lone man with flowing robes and lofty bearing is straight out of Omar Sharif's arrival in *Lawrence of Arabia* (minus camel). Prince Bandar's language on arrival is not. He's minus his silver-spangled dune buggy that broke down some miles away.

The irritated princeling disappears into one of the other tent rooms, where a valet has laid out a change of clothes. He reappears in a white, Western-style suit. He's stunningly handsome with an impressive body that snakes onto the floor rugs, props itself carelessly against some cushions. Whatever he does the rest of the time, today Bandar has decided to play the role of the perfect gentleman; serious, considerate, aware of being his father's son: "My father never told us what to do. We were always given a choice but we knew what he expected of us."

He talks for hours, easily, sincerely, in English perfected by a private tutor at Princeton and salted a bit in air force messes in Britain. His servants pad around offering a banquet (rice and lamb again, it's always rice and lamb—but delicious, and mountains of the stuff). Bandar does point out in passing that it's better, and there's a lot more of it than Queen Elizabeth's kitchens could rustle up when she had him to lunch at Buckingham Palace.

He talks of his brothers with such respect and affection that it takes some time to realize that they're not all full brothers. I knew that Prince Abdullah ibn Faisal (that first Abdullah) was by one of King Faisal's earlier wives, but I thought the other seven were all the sons of Queen Iffat: Faisal's favorite wife and companion for forty years. Few Saudis even know the name of the present King's only wife (say *queen* here and everyone still assumes you must mean Iffat). So no one remembers now that Faisal had another long-standing spouse, Haya, at the same time as Iffat. According to Koranic law Faisal had to spend one night each in turn with Iffat and Haya. (All wives must be treated equally in *all* ways.) The story goes that one night he got to Haya's, after two nights of absence, to find her bedroom door barred against him—he divorced her and never saw her again. It's hard for a Western woman to understand how Iffat and Haya worked together for thirty years to make their children grow into one solid clump—but despite Faisal's unforgiving pride after that divorce in 1940, Iffat went on seeing Haya, and still does.

Whatever The Factory (the al Saud) looks like from outside, tidy and unified, the surviving sons of the kingdom's founder, Ibn Saud, struggle together in an atmosphere of rampant politicking between one power-seeking group and another. Bandar makes no bones about his regret at his uncles' carryings-on. "I look at some of my father's brothers and I don't understand how they can fight among themselves. We of Faisal were brought up to be close and trust one another."

They of Faisal were also brought up to have only one wife— Queen Iffat's doing. As tied as he is to his indulgent mother's apron strings, Bandar has tried marriage—to a first cousin. "We of Faisal," he starts again, "were brought up to understand that a man should have only one wife. It was different in the old days. Marrying several was a way of uniting tribes and offering protection to women who would otherwise have no home but their father's. It's still better than casting them off and leaving them divorced and stranded as they do in America." Bandar's now divorced from his cousin. He lives for the present in an apartment (rather garishly decorated) in the family compound opposite Queen Iffat's palace. He's building a one-room bachelor villa with swimming pool to have more privacy. Prince Bandar may be discreet but the palace guards still clock him in and out.

Western toys such as Maseratis, Lamborghinis, and Ferraris

may pass through Bandar's speed-hungry hands like grains of sand, but women slip through much more swiftly. And yet, under all his sophistication, Bandar ibn Faisal is just another conservative Arab. We're lying on a rug, which a servant has considerately laid out for us on top of a sand dune, watching the sunset. He's wearing no shirt under that white jacket. He knows exactly how sexy he is but he wouldn't dream of touching me because I'm an honored guest and I wouldn't dare let him or I wouldn't see him or another prince for dust. So we're discussing a girl I know in London who went out with a Saudi (she's a good-looking, intelligent, independent blonde from a well-connected, well-heeled family) and she really liked the man. So she went to bed with him. She woke up the morning after to find no Saudi and one thousand dollars under her pillow. Bandar thinks it serves her right for sleeping with a man who isn't her husband. He means it; at this moment anyway.

He's suffered his own minor humiliations. There was the day he was driving his mother along the French Riviera. He parked his Maserati while she went shopping, and a passerby gave him the nod. "You Italian gigolos have a good time." Even now he can't see the funny side of the story. "You think that's amusing? Are you stupid?" I manage not to laugh at his fury about the episode at a hotel in Cannes. "An American woman came up to me in the lobby and propositioned me right to my face. I explained that I was with five women already. [His mother and sisters.] 'You can manage another,' she said. Do you wonder that I hate the idea of introducing European ways into my country." No comment.

By midnight, we've moved back onto the rugs in the tent, and there's another feast. "Would you like a shower to freshen up?" asks Bandar. How do you get water for a shower in the desert? "Turn on the taps." But of course. He shows me into the other tent—a bathroom fully equipped with shower, john, basin, and bidet. I come back to find Bandar's hangers-on, two Lebanese brothers. One's a car mechanic, the other a sycophant. "Bandar's my friend," states the sycophant. "He has taken me in and I love him as a brother. Believe me, I'm not getting any money out of it." Bandar raises an eyebrow. It stops that conversation dead.

At 3 A.M. the rugs are rolled up, the pump is turned off in the bathroom, and we set off. "Most of what you've heard about me isn't true," he skids across the dunes, punishing yet another car. "Do you know how many Prince Bandars there are in London? Last time I was there I found a bill in my apartment for a statue in solid gold that some Prince Bandar had sent to an actress. You English are so carried away by your own fantasies about us that some shops hand over goods worth a fortune to any Arab who calls himself a prince."

The Western-playboy set has one image of Bandar. Another sticks in my mind. It isn't the way we end up at the Lebanese brothers' home to find the woman Bandar calls "his secret love"—their mother, a cross, blond, middle-aged lady, covered in blankets and poodles, who berates him for not showing up for dinner when he promises. While she's laying it into him the phone rings. It's a girl who knows that the Lebanese know Bandar. Could they fix her a date? Bandar nods, apparently meaning "right now," and it's arranged.

It isn't that. It's the way, as the night hugs the desert before we ride back into Riyadh, he talks of his Lightening fighter-pilot days during the war with Yemen. "Do you know what they made me do after the raids, after it was all over? The commanding officers made us go down into the countryside and see what we had done. There were Yemenis who had been holed up in caves with no chance. The stench sickened me. You can't do that to a human being and then expect him to be a soldier. I'm a professional air force man, but I don't believe in the military [this from the son of the king who spent more on guns than his wastrel brother did on palaces]. I don't believe in wasting millions on weapons and keeping the best men in our country, those we need so desperately, under arms. What a waste, what a world." Indeed.

CHAPTER

6

PITY THE POOR PRINCESSES

SAUDI ARABIA'S PRINCESSES ARE ALMOST THE LAST FAIRYTALE creatures left on earth. Sad, pathetic beings for the most part. They're shut away in palaces, soaked in luxury and loneliness. Officially it's as if they don't exist. "King Saud," says the British Foreign Office's royal family tree, "was the second King of Saudi Arabia; more than forty sons (and many daughters) survive him."

Most princesses are doomed to a lifetime in parentheses. They wake in their gilded cages around noon, perhaps later, go for tea with other princesses and then wait for their royal husbands, who probably eat with the men anyway.

Princesses exist to marry cousins and produce princes (and more unlisted princesses). Slaves and wet nurses looked after their mothers' children. Nannies take care of theirs. That's progress. If Saudi folk talk of princes in hallowed terms, they don't talk of princesses at all. Now and again a mention of one will flicker across a conversation. But slowly, very slowly, these sleeping beauties are stirring.

The house isn't big. By commuters' standards it's not even impressive. Inside, a mixture of old and modern furniture stands awkwardly on deep-piled white carpet. None of it matches very well, but there's a good feeling. Family snapshots help. One in particular stands out: a moving color photograph, more like an icon, of an old man praying. It's King Faisal.

This is the home of his daughter, Princess Lateefa. Her name in Arabic means "gentle." It suits her. She's gentle and plump, with the look of one who's been told for as long as she can remember that she isn't pretty. Not like her younger sister Lulua. You can see in an instant the generation gap that Saudi's rapid development has compressed to a few years. Lateefa was once sent to school in London. Conservatives in the family objected to this experiment. She was brought back after a month and reared at home. Tonight she's wearing an aging, black lace evening gown and a diamond and ruby pendant more like a fraternity plaque.

Lulua was a few vital years younger. She was allowed to go to a Swiss boarding school and on to a French finishing outfit. Her English is superb, her French fluent. She's elegantly draped in Yves St. Laurent decorated only with a languid air of boredom. She doesn't see much of her husband and hasn't much patience with her children.

Lateefa has a genuine warmth that starts to show the moment her only son, ten, a small replica of his father, creeps into the dining room to say goodnight. There are only four of us for dinner (no flunkies, no footmen, no guards): Lulua, myself, Lateefa, and her husband—another distant al Saud, Abdul Aziz al Thuniyan, mayor of Riyadh since his father-in-law appointed him to the job ten years ago at the age of twenty-six. King Faisal brought him up as his own son after his parents died. He and Lateefa have been close for as long as they can remember. Unusually, they still are.

Later Lateefa and I tiptoe into her son's bedroom to make sure all is well, and then she shows me around her home: the one guest room, the serenely plain master bedroom with rare silk screens hanging above the double bed. It's downstairs that the furniture and accessories don't match too well. I begin to understand why. The Arabs are in a cultural fix. When the oil barons of Texas made money, they knew whose taste they wanted to emulate, that of old money. They wanted to live like the Brahmins of the East Coast, moving in one another's wood-paneled drawing rooms. It took a generation or two to get it right, but at least they had a blueprint for the homes that were the flagships of their newfound wealth. When America first grew rich it had the European civilization that had spawned it offering a style to copy, a style that suited it. Lateefa's father lived most of his life in the desert or in mud palaces. Is it any wonder that the pictures on her walls (which probably cost a fortune) look like the results of a zip around a five-and-ten?

Over dinner and afterward on the terrace overlooking the floodlit swimming pool Lateefa opens up even more. Not that she says much while her sophisticated sister and high-powered husband (B.A. from Cairo, Ph.D. from the London School of Economics) discuss the intricacies of urbanology. But every now and again a smile lights her whole face, and when she opens her mouth it's because she has something to say.

Lulua gets onto the thorny question of the image foreigners harbor of Saudi Arabia. "The first question they always ask me is, 'Do you live in a tent?' I ask you. Do I look as though I live in a tent?" Hardly. But her ancestors did.

"Perhaps," contributes Lateefa timidly, "it's because they don't know much about us." Lulua complains at length about the way Western newspapers emphasize the fact that thieves lose their right hand here. "They never bother to mention that it needs two witnesses to catch the thief in the act, or that the hand is severed only after the third conviction." It's Lateefa who asks me how many one-handed men I've seen and then asks her husband how many choppings there have been recently. "Two in three years in Riyadh," he answers. (As mayor he should know: I assume he doesn't lie.)

And this gentle princess has in her own way made a contribution to the status of her cousins in Riyadh. With her mother, Queen Iffat, and older sister, Sara, she founded the capital's first women's club: The Saudi Progress Society ("In the name of Allah, the kind and most merciful"). She's now actively involved in it and its main patron.

A charitable institution in which princesses change orphans' diapers, make and sell embroidered doilies, and run a hair-dressing service might not sound much of an earth-shattering advance. But in Riyadh, where women never enter restaurants or hotels, have no social life outside one another's palaces, it was a huge step forward for Faisal's daughter to become something of a public figure.

Princess Lateefa looks after her son herself. She would prob-ably love to be able to have more children. Most other prin-cesses don't see their numerous offspring from one day to the next, but then they don't have to. If their kids are lucky, they find their way to an unusual phenomenon in Riyadh—her name is Vickie Caldwell. Vickie sees more of many of them than do their mothers.

Along a bumpy, unpaved road outside Riyadh, there's an arena with a racing camel tethered by the entrance and forty-seven stunning Arab horses stabled inside around two riding rings. This is Miss Vickie's backyard, where chauffeurs and nannies deliver royal children each day to train under the long, leggy blond horsewoman from Texas.

Officially, Vickie Caldwell doesn't exist. She came here on an American aid teaching program thirteen years ago and stayed. The stable sort of happened. She can't run a riding school; co-education? You're joking. She can't run a business—as a woman that's not allowed either. A lawyer (now in the Cabinet) pre-sented her with the typically Saudi way out: "Vickie, you live in a house, you have a backyard, you keep horses as pets, and some of your friends' children stop by to ride them."

She has very royal "friends." These small children demand a lot of themselves, have no fear, and absolutely no feeling for the horses they ride. And these aren't docile ponies; they're temperamental Arabs. Princess Bandri sits astride a beast of fifteen and one half hands. Already, at three years old, she never considers that there's some living creature that won't obey her will.

Nearby, Princess Haifa, a few years older, is in trouble. Her stallion is determined to throw her. "Keep calm, Haifa! It's your own fault; you weren't concentrating," yells Vickie through her megaphone. "Show him you mean business." Slowly the groom edges toward the animal and seizes the reins. Haifa pushes him away. By the time she can be bullied off her horse, her brother, Khaled, is bubbling with excitement. These are the children of King Faisal's most impressive son of all, Foreign Minister Prince Saud. Their uncle Prince Khaled has sent his young namesake a staggering racehorse as a present. The horse is called Queen of the Wind.

Haifa runs around trying to get sugar lumps from the stable kitchen. Only her brother hands them over. I ask her wouldn't she like a present too? She looks puzzled. "Boys have racehorses, not girls." Conditioning starts earlier than riding lessons.

Sitting on the sidelines, chattering among themselves, are a group of well-dressed European women. They're nannies. Fiona is a no-nonsense import from England who tries to run her nursery with old-fashioned strictness. Annette, an Australian, is a more affectionate, brassy type. While the children study in the mornings, the nannies meet by one of the palace swimming pools. They travel with their charges; it means deluxe holidays all over the world. But they're still paid semiservants, a fact not lost on these imperious royal children.

"Does their mother ever play with them?" I ask one nanny. "Play with them? We haven't seen her for three days. She's either sleeping or off to someone else's palace. Still, at least my princess is better than some. She doesn't spend the day high on drugs like others we know. They have a miserable life for all their money. I wouldn't be a princess if you paid me."

Princess Fawzia wouldn't *not* be one for anything. She's wanted to be a princess ever since she was a middle-class Egyptian kid playing make-believe with dolls. Fawzia made it to princess when she married one of the King's brothers, Prince Fawaz, governor of the district of Mecca.

A dinner party is underway at a beachhouse in Jeddah (hold on for why this can happen in Jeddah but not Riyadh—that's another explanation in itself). The host, one of Jeddah's richest merchants in this rich-merchant port, has provided a buffet table loaded with delicacies and an equally generous supply of alcohol. There's a hush over the sea next to the floodlit swimming pool.

This is an Occasion. All of top-drawer Jeddah will be here, but that's nothing. Prince Fawaz and Princess Fawzia are coming, and they very, very rarely go to commoners' parties. The excuse for this outing is a farewell for the new Ambassador to Washington. But what could be an idyllic evening turns out to be appalling. The mere presence of royalty injects it with stiff formality.

Prince Fawaz with his drooping eyes, drooping moustache, drooping shoulders, clutches his tumbler of Scotch for dear life. He's as limp as a stale stalk of celery. It's hard to see where he once got the backbone to go over to Nasser's Socialist Egypt for two years during the height of the Cairo-Riyadh feud. Still, that's in the past. Fawaz is an example of how smoothly The Factory reabsorbs its black sheep; Egypt was just a lapse, that's all.

Fawaz clings for support tonight to his whisky (which as governor he's ultimately responsible for confiscating and destroying) and to the one leftover from his Egyptian lapse—his forceful wife. Princess Fawzia is royal enough for them both. Living her part to the hilt, she sweeps into the room rustling white chiffon, wearing a crown of rich black hair, offering a large white hand with one emerald rock on her little finger. Her carriage is superb; her smile demolishingly gracious. She's nearly six feet tall, an unnerving manifestation of royalty owing more to Madame de Pompadour than the image of passive Saudi princesses. When the couple finally go at two in the morning (no one can leave before them), she bequeaths the memory of great, powerful shoulders supporting a pair of magnificently royal breasts.

Princess Fawzia's breasts never pass unnoticed. It's afternoon; she's receiving a few women at home, another singular honor. There's a long wait in her Louis Quinze drawing room (what else?). It's a stage set for a star. For once the antiques aren't repro but real. The bric-a-brac is "purfect" for this Versailles-style sailing ship of a woman. There are eighteenth-century enamel boxes on the tables, silver goblets for the guests' orange juice. It's as if someone masterminded the background for how a royal should live. The mistakes are small but significant. The slightly shiny wallpaper would better suit an enchanting bathroom. The silver vases bloom with red roses, natch—but plastic roses.

Princess Fawzia makes another of her stupendous entrances. She's really good at them. Conversation revolves around her ample bosom. Most princesses have an obsession with things medical. Fawzia carries it a stage further. She has the confidence of the very grand who never so much as doubt that intimate details about her breasts will fascinate the drawing room. They have been felt and kneaded by some of the finest consultants in the West.

It needs money to maintain this exotic royal life-style, but Fawaz is not only prince but governor of Mecca. This is boom time. He actually has to work five hours a day, when not so long ago two would suffice. But work means deals means money although the petty cash and affairs of state seem far away from the drawing room of Princess Fawzia and her monologue about her breasts. For once she doesn't have a sister-in-waiting for company. Fawzia can't have children (she can't have everything), and her adopted son is abroad on holiday. Not one of her visitors would dare suggest to this Junoesque statue with her marble skin and royal bearing that she drop over for a meal if she's lonely. She's graciousness itself, but loneliness is the price she must occasionally pay for drawing an absolute line between royalty and commoners.

I'm never to see the like of Fawzia again during the journey. It's a mixed blessing. Nowhere else is unreal in quite the same way, nowhere else flooded with money in quite the same way as Saudi Arabia. That's what makes it so compelling.

7

MONEY AND MIDDLEMEN

THE AL SAUD GET FIRST SHOT AT ALL THAT MONEY. NOT FOR nothing is the country their "company store" and every prince a shareholder. Just how rich the princes get depends on what they decide to do with their lives. Some are only stinking rich; they drop out, draw their pocket money and do nothing. Others do nothing, but they own land and have the sense to find business managers to capitalize on it for them. Some princes go into business secretly; others go into it openly. Others go into government, and some go into everything at once. As a result it's hard to work out who's making how much, let alone for whom and from whom, but one thing's for sure: the sharpest al Saud aren't merely stinking rich—they ooze millions.

Less ambitious princes hire out their names to foreign businessmen to help them win contracts; such hiring fees come heavy around here. Other more go-ahead types actively use their names to get to see some powerful relative themselves and do the winning in person. That's how you get the unconventional situation (to Western eyes) of one of the King's brothers threatening to sue a major British corporation—he's after his $1,250,000 unpaid commission on an arms deal made with his government. Well, when you boil it down, the deal was made with his brother, the Minister of Defense.

The arms business in Saudi Arabia is something else. It's

worth a fortune to anyone who gets into it. And the princes got into it first. They've been helped by all that mutually suspicious, interfamily strife. There's a key saying in Arabia (the most important to remember, along with that more hopeful thought about God being willing tomorrow, *Bukra, in shaa'-Allah*). It goes: "I against my brother, my brother and I against my cousins, my cousins and I against the world."

After Faisal's death, when they were taking their time to set a date to execute his assassin (doubtless they had a few questions to ask him first), there was a very bad period in Riyadh when everyone wondered whether The Factory would hold together. Of course it did—and everything settled down under the new King. A few itchy-fingered princes left out by Faisal were given some new slices of government cake and everyone went back to business as usual.

It's very neat; until you know what "business as usual" means. Khaled is the King; his half-brother, Fahd, is Crown Prince, now emerging as strong man and a reformed character (to the regret of casinos everywhere). The Crown Prince's full brother is Minister of Defense in charge of the regular armed forces of well-paid volunteers. But the King's full brother runs the National Guard, a crack force drawn from tribesmen whose fierce desert loyalties run thick in their veins. The regular forces and the National Guard are kept so separate that neither knows what arms the other is getting from where or when. The government watches its outside enemies. The army watches the country. The National Guard watches the army. The middlemen commoners do well by selling arms to both, the princes don't do too badly, and even the generals aren't forgotten.

The Saudis get sore at the West's attitude to the big commissions and payoffs involved in selling arms here (although they've felt much better since it's come out that various European countries have been up to the same lark). The West calls the Saudi arms deals corrupt. The Saudis don't like that; they see commissions as "fees for services rendered" and payoffs as a traditional part of patronage. Noblesse oblige? Here noblesse always feels obliged to give to others and sometimes feels obliged to take a rakeoff itself.

Whatever statements his Majesty King Khaled's government makes in public, in reality no one makes money (well, hardly anyone) without the consent of some royal faction. Every powerful businessman in Riyadh, the center of government, has been drawn into the royal web or he wouldn't be successful. That's how the company store operates.

Being in business, even the company-store business, simply doesn't mean the same thing to the Saudis as it does to us. Prophet Mohammed was a businessman, after all. He gave it a very good name. It's everything to many Arabs: their lover, their joy, their inspiration, their game, their way of being with people and of talking to them. It's not simply an obsession with making money, a passion that's seen as narrow and unattractive through our eyes. Business is an honorable profession to the Saudis, so why should the royals be exempt? It's merely a little unfortunate if sometimes their private and public interests overlap.

Arms are a question of national security, yes. They're also just another form of business, the national sport that's about the only area where Saudis can legitimately scheme and plot. And anyone still drawing breath over recent American congressional hearings into the Saudi arms trade should bear in mind a tale told of King Ibn Saud:

A man needed a contractor to deliver a consignment of one hundred cooling fans. He invited bids for the job and was delighted to find one 50 percent lower than the rest. He accepted it, and in due course a donkey and cart arrived carrying one hundred ladies' fans. The fuming businessman took this swindle to King Ibn Saud to Get Justice Done. The King said the deal was fine; fans he'd said and fans he'd got. It wasn't sharp practice, merely ingenious. It doesn't matter if it's only another Saudi tale; the point is—they tell it. And of course the resourceful fan salesman wasn't a Westerner; he was a Saudi.

Adnan Khashoggi (whose Northrop and Lockheed commissions alone came to several hundred million dollars) couldn't have made it to first base without the knowledge of the Minister of Defense. Khashoggi has also been a great buddy of the minister's full brother, Crown Prince Fahd; Regine's nightclub in Paris was a favorite haunt of the tubby twosome before Faisal's death.

But Adnan Khashoggi, known as AK to all and sundry, is only one of a myriad of middlemen. There are many others whose interests are as big, diverse, and intriguing as Khashoggi's—but the West hasn't focused on them. By now most people know about AK, with his private, unmarked Boeing 727 jet with its six TV sets and gold-plated bathroom, his close links to certain European party-givers with their coteries of available women. They might even recognize his much publicized South of France-based yacht, *Mahomedia,* with beauty parlor, electric elevator, telex, movie theater, and a mass of safes and strongrooms.

Few people would look twice at Ghassan Shaker going into the Fifth Avenue Olympic Tower Building in New York, where he has an unlisted office with its deep-buttoned, burgundy leather sofas, on the ninth floor; driving his Mini (occasionally his Rolls) around London, where he has an apartment in Grosvenor Square opposite the American Embassy (but stays at the Dorchester for convenience). No one would notice his arrival at Geneva airport to visit his three brighteyed kids at their boarding school, or even wonder who he was if they saw him with them at Disneyland recently—the trip to Los Angeles was his children's reward for passing their exams that quarter.

Ghassan Shaker arranged one of the most controversial military deals of '75: the recruitment of former members of the U.S. Special Forces and other Vietnam War veterans by a private contractor, Vinnell Corporation of Los Angeles. Their brief: to train Saudi National Guard troops to protect the oilfields. It was a deal that set off alarm bells. Was this a straight mercenary outfit or a "spooks" setup? And if so, who was spying on whom? Who were the Saudis protecting the oilfields from—

America, Iran, Israel, internal sabotage? Ghassan Shaker's name was mentioned in Congress at that time; but there's been no newspaper publicity about him since. That's no coincidence; once Arabs like Khashoggi or Shaker start hitting the headlines you know they might be on the way out, and he certainly isn't. Secrecy is desired for its own sake; not because it's (necessarily) hiding anything.

I get to like Ghassan in Riyadh. Without saying a word, he somehow lets me know that he sympathizes with the spectacle of a Western woman covering her head completely with a black chiffon scarf (by now I've been reduced to that to make life easier; it saves the hostile stares). Shaker is thirty-nine, grandson of an officer in the Ottoman army (the Turks' Ottoman Empire stretched over Arabia for centuries until the 1914–18 war), a graduate of St. John's College, Cambridge, where he studied law and English literature. He's something of a sport; besides playing cricket, soccer, and tennis for his university, he made his name as a freshman when he stuffed a potato up the exhaust of Princess Margaret's car. Shaker's enormously smooth, with a husky, velvet voice that, should he run short of other things to do, would make detergent commercials sound like exercises in erotica.

This is the man who arranged Vinnell's contract for a $4.5 million fee that a Congressman, already used to Saudi customs, called "suspiciously large." Sitting in his black-cushioned office, offering endless cups of sweetened tea and bitter cardamom coffee (the local brew that tastes like no coffee you've ever had), he genuinely seems not to understand what the fuss was about. "There's nothing evil or wrong in taking a commission for your services on deals like this. Ultimately, all arms arrangements are made between governments. I've arranged dozens of much bigger contracts before and as far as Vinnell is concerned I've spent eight years helping to establish it here. It's not my fault that it came up in Saudi Arabia and the American press has such a phobia about our country that there was a ridiculous fuss. God has bestowed on this country fantastic wealth, and I like to think I'm serving my country and my God."

To listen to the Saudis, who bring Him into the conversation rather a lot, Allah has a very keen nose for business. But don't confuse a man like Shaker with Richard Nixon having Billy Graham home publicly to the White House to pray and then going on with life and Watergate. Most Saudis don't yet see a contradiction between what they believe in and what they do. Islam cuts deeply into their being; they haven't grasped that if they're not careful, they may soon be serving two gods— Allah and Mammon. It often sounds outrageous to me to hear Allah join us as we chat abut deals; many Saudis don't understand why I react as I do. This country is still founded on religion, a demanding, exacting religion. Apparently there couldn't be an arms business if Allah hadn't had it in mind.

Shaker is divorced from his first wife; he hasn't remarried. He travels the world with his Italian girlfriend but wouldn't dream of bringing her here to Riyadh. It's not out of fear of offending his patrons and friends; it's out of respect. For Shaker has very powerful patrons, and he's far more influential than he appears. He's the only Saudi to hold an official position in a foreign government (he's adviser to the Sultan of Oman) so that his agency businesses are the least part of his significance— although he has under his aegis in Saudi such companies as Reynolds Tobacco, Middle East Airlines, Air France, etc., etc.

The son of a self-made millionaire, Shaker is a self-made multimillionaire: "I started from zilch, really. My father lent me his surname and that was my only capital." You have to be well in with the al Saud to handle Shaker's business deals, and he is; in Riyadh he drops in on some of the most important princes there are. But he does it openly; he'll tell you he's off to see the Foreign Minister, Prince Saud, at home, and the Foreign Minister's staff speak warmly of Shaker.

Shaker doesn't talk so warmly of foreigners: "Believe me, I feel shame as an Arab when I see the way some of us behave in London. But I have no respect whatsoever for some Westerners when they come here and don't bother to learn the ways of the country. For instance, in the Arab world you never cross your legs and put the sole of your shoe in a man's face—it's an insult. If anyone comes into the room you get up. You'd be astonished how these small things have a bearing. Westerners come here with no respect for our customs, so they have no right to point fingers at Arabs who go to their countries and behave like wild animals." I'm not surprised the Foreign Minister's staff go for Shaker as they do. As an independent middleman he's able to say quietly what most of them would probably love to shout if only they weren't diplomats.

But there are some middlemen whose names you don't ever mention in the offices of the princes they serve.

The only way to show how devious most businesses are in Riyadh is to tell the curious tale of a prince, a luncheon party, and how I made a boo-boo by mentioning the luncheon in the prince's office. The prince holds one of the biggest jobs in Riyadh, and he's promised to see me. This is a real promise; after a while you do get to know the difference. Unfortunately, he's forever off to the airport to greet some foreign head of state, but to pass the time a Saudi fixer I've met takes me to lunch with the prince's business manager.

The Saudi fixer I'll have to call Mohammed. He would be in danger if I named him—the Saudis aren't going to like my telling this tale anyway. Mohammed started life guarding his village's flock of sheep. He now owns a flock of limousines and an intricate web of companies. I couldn't even begin to guess how he evolved from shepherd to one of Riyadh's big-time wheeler-dealers.

Our host I'll call Abdullah. He's an unprepossessing man with an unprepossessing home. It's a strange party; some American executives are here who are trying to lean on Abdullah to get the prince to okay a huge program they have in mind. The twinkly-eyed Mohammed acts as interpreter (our host doesn't speak a word of English). We all sit on the floor, trying hard to enjoy the traditional Arab feast—a sheep whose teeth grin macabrely on its platter. The Americans shower oily compliments on the host through Mohammed. Not a business word crosses the sheep's teeth, but the specter of money hangs over us all. Host Abdullah unexpectedly turns his glittering eyes toward me (one of the first ever females at his table). "What did you expect before you arrived in our country?"

Since I don't want anything out of Abdullah and have long since decided that Saudis enjoy honesty (in small doses), I reply: "Grim-faced, frightening men with no sense of humor. Have you ever seen a photograph in a Western newspaper of a smiling Saudi?" My American fellow guests glare in silent anger. Abdullah chews this over with another bit of sheep. Then he asks if I would like to see his wife. That's something; an old-fashioned Saudi like Abdullah never mentions his wife in front of foreign men.

In the outhouse, crouched over huge cooking pots, is Mrs. Abdullah—she's exquisitely beautiful. Her husband calls out for his troop of children and without a word, leads the way upstairs. He points to a vicious-looking wooden truncheon hanging on his bedroom door. Through an English-speaking daughter he communicates the fact that it's for beating his children. It's feasible. He has an unflinching, brutal face and a bark for a voice. Then his children can't keep up the charade. Peals of laughter. Abdullah rocks with mirth. "How could I ever hit a child of mine? Look at them. What do you think I am—a monster?" Yes, to be frank.

But this monster has been abruptly transformed into a human being. The man with his guard down will never be seen by his other guests downstairs, by now beside themselves with worry. I understand their worry. Abdullah handles millions of dollars' worth of investments and businesses for the prince he "works" for. These businesses operate in areas in which the prince has power to grant contracts. Of course some of the contracts come Abdullah's way—it's the Saudi princes' way of lining their own pockets without being too crass about it. As a result Abdullah, in his unprepossessing home, is no pauper himself.

The boo-boo is that I don't realize just how unofficial a channel Abdullah is for the prince's own money-making interests until after I try to leave a thank-you letter for him in the prince's official government office. There's a ghastly silence. The prince's *chef de cabinet* in clipped tones professes never to have heard of him. I never do meet this prince. I do have a bad time keeping away from the American fellow guests. They've heard about my mistake. They're convinced it'll sink them; guilt by association. That's how important princes can be in Riyadh.

It's not only the local and foreign businessmen who approach princes as though they're treading on eggshells. The diplomats of the world (the ones that are allowed in, that is—no Communists, of course) have to run rings around themselves these days trying to sweet-talk the Saudis. Their contortions are sometimes even funnier (to an outsider) than the miserable wheeler-dealers who are only after a few millions' worth of contracts. In business it's mainly Americans who are the hapless victims of Saudi whims. That's largely because the Americans are the ones whose companies can afford to bankroll them to wait it out in this costly marketplace.

But diplomatically, Americans are in the strongest position of all. This government is propping up the regime in Saudi Arabia—perhaps propping up is overdoing it, but both countries have the same interests at heart. Whatever Saudi princes say in public for the benefit of the rest of the restless Arab world, in private they admit how much they need America. That's why, for all their hot air, they have swallowed American support for Israel (nicknamed "America's 52nd precinct"—the cop shop where Yanks can keep an eye on the rumbling Mideast). America has the largest military presence in Saudi, helping the al Saud to stay in business. The last thing the State Department wants is a bunch of nationalistic Lefties running this country, which has the world's largest oil reserves. And the more intelligent al Saud have cottoned on long ago to the fact that absolute monarchy is hardly the political fashion of today. Oh yes, Saudi and American diplomats are pretty thick.

No, today it's the poorer, lesser governments of the Western world that have to make a play for Saudi attention. They're like small-time starlets in Hollywood dancing round big-time producers. Come with me into a secret world in London known to its inmates as the "Palazzo" and you'll get the idea. Behind blackened walls, reached through a great square Italianate courtyard, the servants of her Majesty's Government's Foreign Office are at work. In a dingy, high-ceilinged room, its walls covered with tattered maps and esoteric family trees, the men on the Middle East desk are in the nearest they get to a flap.

Crown Prince Fahd has let it be known that he might consider making his first "official visit" to Britain. With the intricacies of an army HQ planning a major offensive, diplomats in shirt sleeves hang over their paper-laden desks plotting success. Robin Kealey, a fresh-faced Arabist is blocking out huge charts trying to juggle government ministers' time for mini-Cabinet meetings with their honored guest. If he agrees to come, that is.

There's a hitch. The Queen's cousin, the duke of Gloucester, has been provisionally booked to greet HRH at the airport ("It's hard getting royals on such short notice") and escort him to his government-booked and paid-for floor of Claridge's Hotel. But word has come from Our Man in Saudi Arabia that there will be no Crown Prince alighting on the tarmac at Heathrow unless Prime Minister Harold Wilson is there to say hello in person.

Impasse. Wilson wants the visit to go well, as one of his swan songs before retiring. (The British pound is in poor health, and his voters are blaming most of their problems on the Arabs and their "bleeding oil.") But Wilson sends word via his man in Downing Street that he doesn't drive to airports for lesser fish than heads of state. Kealey makes a stiffening cup of coffee and decides against sending alarming messages off to the ambassador, who's already been sending pointed messages of his own about how well the Americans do it all. Maybe Wilson will come around. He does, but not until a few hair-raising days before the visit. Snap. Crown Prince Fahd doesn't confirm that he'll show up until a day or so before either.

The Prime Minister, the Chancellor of the Exchequer, the governor of the Bank of England are all giving intimate lunch and dinner parties with ten or twenty senior government ministers and a few bankers from the City of London. It's called in Foreign Office jargon a "cultivating Prince Fahd" visit. There won't be any floodlit football matches or opera galas. ("He's known to enjoy gambling slightly but that's not the kind of thing you can include in an official program.") But her Majesty's servants are sparing no effort to make his Highness feel sufficiently well cultivated. Even the Queen's doing her stuff. She's having Crown Prince Fahd to lunch at the palace before he leaves. Not that that will impress him much. The guest palace in Riyadh (old King Saud's $50 million dwelling, recently redecorated for a few more million) is a mighty impressive affair run by Iain Cameron, a graduate from some of the best hotels in the West.

The point of all this Foreign Office fuss is a crucial morning meeting in the Chancellor's second-floor Treasury office, with its impressive paintings and two marble fireplaces. In this hushed sanctum the Chancellor of the nation's fast emptying purse hopes for "useful exchanges" with Saudi's new strong man over the long rosewood-topped conference table. On the agenda for the meeting some official stripling had typed "reduction of sterling investments." A wiser, more experienced senior has tactfully inked out "reduction" and written in "retention." The whole campaign is geared to the hope that before he leaves Crown Prince Fahd will sign something called an Anglo-Saudi memorandum on Economic Cooperation—in plain words, he'll promise to cough up some cash.

I'm in Riyadh when the visit finally comes off. I learn from arriving Londoners that Wilson not only presented himself at the airport——he even kissed the royal hand. I scan the Saudi television set for news of this momentous visit. To Britain that is. (Not to Prince Fahd, he only left London a few weeks ago after a long private holiday at his stone portal house there—rather like an expensive prison.)

After all that effort in the Palazzo, Fahd's first official visit to England warrants a few seconds right at the end of the Saudi news broadcast.

There was a vintage London joke circulating at this time:

The Prime Minister's private secretary comes into his boss's office.

"Excuse me, sir, but the Pope and an oil sheikh are waiting to see you."

"Oh dear," frowns the PM, "who should I see first?"

"May I suggest the Pope first, sir? You only have to kiss his ring."

CHAPTER

8

THE RISE OF THE MERITOCRATS

I GRAB FOR A NEWSPAPER IN RIYADH ON 9 SHAWAL 1396 (TO THE Saudis; October 14, 1975, to us). At last, the announcement of the newest and largest Cabinet in the history of the Saudi kingdom. For a moment I almost think the princes are being overrun by the hoi polloi. Out of twenty-five ministers, only seven highnesses. What? The moment passes as I study the other new ministers, those with the even more unfamiliar names. They all have links somewhere with the al Saud.

Two, for instance, are of the al Sheikh family. That doesn't sound like anything much except more confusion at first. To the Saudis, being an al Sheikh more than tops Americans being able to trace their line back to George Washington. It's not just being in the *Social Register;* it's being indelibly printed in it. No bad marriages could wipe an al Sheikh off the Social Register of Saudi Arabia. This family is directly descended from al Wahhab (sorry about the names, the Saudis can't make ours out either). Al Wahhab was an austere, puritanical preacher and wandering scholar of the eighteenth century, who didn't have much luck until he ran into a minor tribal leader with control of an oasis and guns. What a combination—water, shot, and religion. The two men got together and between them they overran the country. Wahhab gave his name to Wahhabism, the

91

Saudis' own Islamic sect, and the minor tribal leader was an al Saud. That's where it all started.

So here we are, a couple of centuries later, and there they are with two al Sheikhs in the Cabinet. They fill two of the most important jobs: Higher Education, for one; Agriculture and Water is the other. Bearing in mind the fortune the Saudis spend importing food and skilled labor and on producing, finding, even buying water, the al Sheikhs are sitting on two major ministries.

And those other ministers? They nearly all come from merchant families made rich by swimming within the tentacles of the al Saud octopus. No outsiders here. Slowly, though, middle-class (by Saudi standards) lads are being hand-picked by the al Saud and groomed for stardom.

The first to be put under contract, of course, was the only Saudi that anyone will ever have heard of—assuming they've ever heard of anyone from Arabia—Zaki Yamani, Minister of Petroleum and Oil Resources. He's the man *Time* labeled "Yamani or Your Life" during the '73 embargo, when his face and name were on every television set, every front page for months. He's Saudi's Mr. Oil, now almost a global piece of media property. Thousands of column inches report his every statement; foreign-affairs men pore over his every word with the dedication of code breakers. Does he mean that the West should have all the oil it wants? Does he want to hike the prices up, bring them down, or keep them steady? Will he cut back on production? Will he this, will he that—and the irony is that Sheikh Ahmed Zaki Yamani can't move an inch on his own initiative without the King or Crown Prince's go-ahead. Yamani is a commoner, so back in the old days (the 1960s), he could be dandled before the Western media in a way that was then considered undignified for royalty. He was a puppet; not the string-puller. But every now and again he will pull a string or two of his own behind the scenes.

I suspect that Zaki Yamani pulled a string to get me into Saudi Arabia. He was one of my main targets for the letters of intent that I scattered like confetti around the top men of Arabia when I was still knocking hard on that invisible door they have in those invisible walls. There was one sentence that would sting Yamani in particular: "In the West, there is an urgent need to overcome the simple, even caricatured images of the Arab world." He still hasn't forgotten the time during his globe-trotting, oil-crisis days when an American paper reported that he travels with his own army of belly dancers, gourmet chef, and servants. Zaki Yamani travels with his kids (sometimes), his new wife (less often), but in the hectic early 1970s, the only man he traveled with was his right hand, *chef de cabinet* Ibrahim Obaid.

Shortly after my letter gets to Yamani in Riyadh a telex bolts into my office in London from Obaid. He's arriving next week and he wants to see me. Obaid is a grave, slightly vain man (in contrast to Yamani, who is very vain). He has dark hair, a dark beard, which he strokes often, and we spend long almost silent hours together in his hotel suite while he tries to figure me out and I give up trying to figure him out. I can't figure out what he's waiting for me to say. I don't yet grasp that he can't figure out what I'm waiting for *him* to say. I still don't know that in his country you're not an individual, you're a type, to be put in a clearly labeled jar of jam. There are two types—men jam and women jam. In my innocence, I'm still trying to talk to him like one human being to another. Well, our silent conversation obviously wins him around.

He invites me to lunch with his wife, Souad, and then one evening, an even larger jump up the ladder of approval, he invites me to their apartment. Their apartment? What's the hotel suite for? An office, as it happens. But I doubt if his wife has ever asked him. Take in this one: Souad and I are waiting in the hotel one afternoon after lunch for her husband to join us (he's buzzed off somewhere for half an hour); Souad has with her her nine-month-old son, who's making an extraordinarily un-inhibited noise in the lobby. I suggest that she go and collect the key to Obaid's suite and we go upstairs where baby Ahmed can get out of his stroller and make a noise in peace. Souad's sophis-tication drops away. She blushes and I realize that she won't under any circumstances take her husband's key without his permission. She'd rather endure that frosty look from the front-office staff. I'm consumed with curiosity to see the apartment. I've already spent hours with Obaid and neither of us has so much as mentioned Yamani's name. Come to think of it, it's very odd that Obaid's here at all. Normally, every appointment with Yamani is fixed by Obaid, he's never away from the minister's side. And at this moment there's a vital OPEC conference going on in Vienna, where the oil-producing nations are deciding whether to put up the price by 10 percent (the Saudis' figure) or 35 percent (favored by the Iranians, running out of spare cash). There isn't a major Western newspaper that doesn't have an overkill of reporters covering the conference.

It so happens that a few hours ago Yamani stormed out of the Vienna conference room and flew to London for the night. All over London, journalists are trying to find Obaid because the rumor's spreading that *he*'s in town too. What's Obaid doing? He's having a good laugh at the discussions I'm having with Souad about what clothes I should take to Riyadh. His mother is chipping in too; she's a natural scene-stealer. It's the first time she has ever left Saudi Arabia, she doesn't speak any English, and she's here for a month with rheumatism—she goes for physiotherapy every day. We may not share a language of words, but I get on with her from the start. She notices that my teacup is empty. She reproaches her son in Arabic who reproaches his wife in Arabic who apologizes to me in English and refills it. Obaid's hotel suite isn't big; the apartment might have been designed for dwarfs. But there's always room for tea-kettles and coffeepots—the Arab symbols of hospitality.

No one mentions Yamani, no one mentions OPEC, even though the television is on and it's the main story of the week. Obaid's seemingly more interested in whether baby son Ahmed will finally get drowsy enough for bed and also whether the baby-sitter will arrive before his merchant-banker friend and wife. Tonight's going to be an evening on the town. Miss Ward, a silvery-haired trained nurse turned doctor's receptionist, enters timidly. She's here to mind Ahmed. Miss Ward is diverted by Obaid from her discreet path toward the nursery.

"Come, join us. Sit down; may we offer you a drink?"

"Oh no, really. Well, perhaps a cup of tea."

"Please may I ask your first name?" Obaid.

"Christine," Miss Ward's rather embarrassed answer. From that moment Christine is one of the family. ("Oh dear, I wish I could find somewhere to hide. I've never been treated like this before and I feel so conspicuous.")

"I'm so glad you're English, Christine," Obaid says. "I wouldn't like to trust Ahmed to a foreigner."

There follows a long discussion about the merits of screaming versus nursing on demand and then Christine, too, is drawn into the problem of what I should wear in Riyadh. What I should wear? I still don't have a visa and here's Yamani's right-hand man who won't even discuss the subject.

In the middle of this the merchant banker and his wife turn up. The wife, one of those particularly proper English types, is all done up for a party. If she's slightly surprised at being introduced to a baby-sitter, Miss Ward, as "our very good friend Christine" (being familiar with servants is *not* the English way), the banker's wife doesn't show it.

Somehow we all find places to perch while Obaid distributes photographs taken at a beach party in Saudi given in Teddy Kennedy's honor. Miss Ward is now completely overcome. Mrs. Obaid, Sr., who has obviously seen these photographs before, still can't remember what a Kennedy is and has to have it explained again.

When Miss Ward is nervous, she has a habit of gently patting her neat hair; by now it's received a battering. She'd give anything to wrest baby Ahmed from his father's arms (Obaid won't put his son down; this is the first but not the last time I pick up on how physically affectionate Saudi men are with their children). Obaid doesn't notice Miss Ward's concern, but the banker does notice the time. They have a table booked at Annabel's nightclub, and it's time to move on.

Miss Ward's final wide-eyed look is reserved for Obaid's elderly mother. With Ahmed more or less settled, Mrs. Obaid, Jr., wrapped up exotically for a night among the rich and famous, Mrs. Obaid, Sr., ties a head scarf on firmly and puts on her coat. She's firmly escorted out by Yamani's right-hand man to join his friends at Annabel's for a spot of dinner-dancing. Miss Ward is stunned. "I don't know any of my English employers who would actually take their mother out to a place like Annabel's unless she's used to that sort of thing. I don't understand them, I simply don't."

She doesn't understand. Here I am, having been summoned by telex, having spent hours now, quite pleasantly, with Yamani's man surely sent to sniff me out, and he hasn't said a word about the small matter of a visa. I'm late for a dinner party elsewhere; Obaid finds a taxi for me. Just as I get in, he says quietly: "I'll look forward to seeing you in Riyadh, Linda. So will the minister. We'll arrange whatever is necessary." That's brinkmanship.

A couple of months later on 9 Shawal 1396, Obaid comes to pick me up at my hotel in Riyadh. He looks different in national dress. In a Western suit he's impressive; in his *thobe* he looks rather scruffy. But he's still the same grave, slightly vain Obaid. He's like a letter from home. By now I'm so confused that anyone, anything, familiar is reassuring. That's not the only reason I'm relieved to see him. I've been calling Zaki Yamani's office every day, and every day they say Obaid isn't in Riyadh. But I know he is. I've already seen him for lunch—Souad is still in London—and he's taken me to his brother's home (who's also abroad) for lunch. There's nowhere else for us to go. Obaid wouldn't dare compromise himself, let alone me, by eating with me in public, so we have to steal into his brother's house to be able to sit and talk. We talk about everything—except Yamani.

This evening he senses that I'm feeling the need to touch or feel something I can recognize from that former life back in Europe. I'm going through an identity crisis, to put it mildly. He doesn't put it any way at all. He takes me to his brother's home and without a word puts on a videotape of the Boston Symphony Orchestra playing Mahler (he knows how much I enjoy classical music). I don't know if he likes it or if he's bored stiff; he wouldn't show me either way. That's the measure of the courtesy and the silences of the Saudis. Slowly I'm learning that you can't be with these people by any standards I understand. In all these hours I spend "illicitly" with Obaid he doesn't so much as shake my hand good-bye. There's no physical contact and only unspoken mental contact.

That's only half of his consideration. Obaid has an important official banquet to go to. I'd never guess from his calm exterior. He allows the familiar music to work on me; offers a cold drink and when he senses, correctly as usual, that I feel better, he drives me back to the hotel. I ask him why I can't get hold of him at Yamani's office. He doesn't answer. I needn't have wasted my breath. Direct questions rarely get direct answers, if they get any at all. As I'm getting out of the car at the hotel Obaid says quietly, so quietly that I almost miss it, "Call the ministry tomorrow. Ask for Sheikh Yamani's office. His Excellency is waiting to see you."

His Excellency Sheikh Ahmed Zaki Yamani works on the ground floor of his ministry. It's marble and white and would be very tidy except for the armed soldiers littering the corridors. His anteroom is crowded with some of the top people of Saudi who've been waiting to see him—the head of the Western section of the Foreign Office and I have the most interesting chat about the differences between labor unions in the States and in Britain, and it passes the hours. At nine o'clock I'm shown into the largest office I've seen anywhere in Riyadh. Behind the desk is a gray-faced, ashen man, almost dropping with fatigue—and on top of that he's got the flu. I look at him; he looks at me. Those famous eyes are not exaggerated by the newspaper reports. He's attractive, all right.

His voice is like one of those records they used to sell to put you to sleep—it's so soothing that if I'm not careful, I'll drop off, and I don't trust him not to then put me through a third-degree interrogation. He takes his time to see that I'm not going to relax that far and that I'm not remotely interested in the intricacies of oil. He smiles even more broadly. "I think I'm going to take you to my home and later my wife and I will take you to a party. You'll feel easy there; it won't be your first." Yamani and I have seen each other before.

Yamani is one of "The Group." It's the substitute for the tribal and family security blankets he had to leave behind in his native Hejaz (the coastal strip, another world away from this desert-locked government capital) when King Faisal picked him out and made him oil minister at thirty-one. We drive to his home, or rather he drives me home. He lives in a suite in the side of my hotel; it's his permanent and only home in Riyadh. It has its own entrance, a side door in a completely dark alleyway surrounded by trees. I'm surprised. "Aren't you worried about security? Any nut could easily take a shot at you here." Sure it's tactless, Yamani was by Faisal's side when he was killed, but he shrugs: "Allah decides our fate. It's not for me to worry. I hate the soldiers at the ministry. I will not live with them here."

How things change. A month later Yamani is one of the ten oil ministers kidnapped by the Palestinians at another of those Vienna OPEC meetings. Three people are killed, and he is held prisoner on board a plane for days afterward. He comes to America a few months later to, hopefully, complete negotiations for the 100 percent takeover of American oil interests in Saudi. He won't come until he's assured that the 1,100 acres of the Panama City Bay Point Yacht and Country Club in Florida will be crisscrossed by plain and uniformed police with shotguns and walkie-talkies. Now abroad, he's security-conscious and less fatalistic.

But there's no armed guard outside his Riyadh home—Allah is more reliable in Saudi Arabia, Yamani feels safe here—physically. Emotionally, he's not doing so well. He's never been terribly close to the brother of his hero and father-figure, King Faisal. Now the atmosphere between Yamani and Crown Prince Fahd is common gossip in Riyadh.

Yamani opens his front door and calls out to his wife. His new wife. Meritocrats spiraling upward here run into the same problem as their Western counterparts; they outgrow their first wives. Yamani married his old one when he was a lonely student at Columbia in New York; they've been separated for nine years. They're not divorced (she'd lose out financially) but he spent a long time alone before he remarried. He's been lonely—cooking (he has aspirations to being a gourmet chef), writing poetry, studying the Koran fills the time, but cuddling his disgusting snuffly black Pomeranians hardly amounts to a relationship.

That's in Riyadh. In the West his life is different. All those thousands of television interviews and newspaper profiles showing him as a dashing playboy with flatteringly cut suits and hairstyles. That famous night recently when they kept Harrods open late especially for him (an honor London's famous department store has hitherto condescended to bestow only on the Queen). In half an hour Yamani spent $70,000 working through a (for him) trifling shopping list. He came out and ordered his chauffeur to hire a van for the cumbersome parcels and assorted boxes that he wanted to take on his flight with him. The chauffeur explained that the hour was somewhat late to hire a truck. He was smartly ordered to stop one in the streets and persuade its driver to oblige. Shortly afterward Yamani glided out smoothly to London airport in his limousine—with a coal-delivery truck bearing his booty following behind.

It does not stagger me in Riyadh to hear from one of Yamani's few close friends that this global celebrity is totally mixed up as an individual. He feels safe only in Saudi, but his experiences in the West are fast turning him into an outsider even with The Group. Yamani's friends were and are very fond of his first wife. As often happens in "divorces" they take exception to the fact that at forty-five she's alone and he's with a much newer model. A young girl of twenty-four, a former biology student he picked out in Beirut—Tammam. The new Mrs. Yamani is something else again.

I don't learn much about her at our first encounter. She hangs back, simpering shyly. She's dressed to kill; beautiful, smothered with makeup and eager to be off to the party after Zaki's had a short rest. When he's ready Tammam gathers her black cloak (managing *not* to put it on as ostentatiously as a woman puts on her first mink coat), winds a suspicion of black chiffon around her hair, and her husband drives us away.

To explain the even greater shock of what happens next, it's worth another short diversion. The Ministry of Information is sponsoring a glossy, coffee-table full-color illustrated book titled *The Kingdom of Saudi Arabia.* The photographs showing women were ripped out of the dummy in a massive committee censorship jag until there was only one left—of a woman heavily veiled à la laundry bag. In this tense religious capital I rarely glimpse women on the streets. Somehow I still assume that under the black ugliness lurks more ugliness. Perhaps the few unveiled women I've seen at home so far are exceptional? I've spent several evenings with The Group by now, but the experience still comes as a shock.

We walk into the living room of a small house. It glitters with beautiful women. It hurts my eyes to see them all at once. They're decked out in the brightest evening robes Europe can invent. There's hardly a woman who isn't ravishingly made up. Were it not for the men's *thobes* and headdresses, I could be anywhere in the world that rich, overdressed women gather . . . until the atmosphere gets through to me.

Mixed gatherings are new to Riyadh. It's like being with teenagers at dancing class. There's the same shyness, the edginess of not knowing how to act with the Opposite Sex. It's so infectious that after a few of these parties I find it almost impossible to talk with men myself. When one man comes over to where I'm sitting I feel ashamed—almost as if I'm doing something dirty in the act of conversation. The undercurrent of sex permeates such gatherings by the very absence of its acknowledgment.

With maybe forty people here, the place gets hot despite air conditioning. But this is Riyadh. Necks are high, sleeves are long. A woman wearing a woolen three-piece from Paris won't take off her long-sleeved cardigan; her tank top below is sleeveless. It's like Victorian England where the mere sight of an ankle bred fantasies and desire.

Every arriving couple goes around shaking hands stiffly. (Both men and women get up to go through their greetings. The bobbing up and down is tiring to say the least.) When I say stiffly, I mean it. A woman who has just returned from three years in Beirut, from a nightmare of bloodshed, is greeted by the other women she grew up with as if they'd never met.

There are great bowls full of cigarette packs—every brand imaginable. It's offensive to smoke your own. In the West you're offered peanuts; here you're offered nicotine poisoning. By this time I'm on five packs a day myself (from one at home), so I'm not complaining. Women sit, talk, and chain-smoke together. A foursome for bridge is made up in another room; mental relaxation for some, a way of avoiding desegregated chitchat for others.

What kind of people belong to The Group? Top people, very top people. A peaceful-looking man sits on a couch puffing away at his pipe. He's General Zuhair, the air force brass who, with another general now "retired," were known to Northrop's headquarters as Trumpet and Geranium in coded messages sent between Riyadh and Century City concerning some $450,000 private arrangements over fighter plane contracts. He's such a friendly, unaffected man. Dr. Hasham Abdul Ghaffar joins us; he ran a lucrative dental clinic until he became Deputy Minister for Health. Then his partner ran it, and he split the profit with him fifty-fifty. But he hasn't been made minister in the new shuffle; his nose is out of joint, says his wife, so he's going back to drill richly in his dental retreat.

Hasham's married to Sharifa (a title) Fatma Mandili. Women don't change their names when they get married here (they've learned to for foreigners; staying in European hotels has taught them about that). "Of course not," says one. "Your name is your identity, your personality. Why should you lose it?"

Fatma is a stunning Jackie Onassis type, the first woman university teacher in Riyadh, the first woman radio broadcaster, and a Hashemite. The Hashemites were the ruling family of Hejaz in the west before the al Saud kicked them out in 1926. As a consolation prize the European colonials gave them the thrones of Iraq and Jordan. The King of Iraq got chopped in a revolution; King Hussein still clings. That makes Fatma pretty royal, you'd think. Not here it doesn't—she's the wrong royalty. Here she's just a commoner from a good family. Fatma's studying for a master's degree in Beirut and produces a red leather-bound volume of her thesis, "The Arab Element in Tennyson." It sums up everything: this woman bedecked for a ball when in fact it's a few friends having supper together as they do several times a week, poring over this most Victorian of British poets while Arab music deafens us from the speakers in the corner.

It's interesting to note what people mention first when they talk of Sharifa Fatma; some say, "She's a Hashemite" in tones of envy; family names count for so much. Men usually say, "She's the man of the family," thereby explaining away her "unfeminine" unconcealed intelligence. Others dig at the way she hogged Teddy Kennedy's attention when he was in town.

While dutifully reading Fatma's thesis, I keep a careful eye on Zaki and Tammam Yamani. He's sitting on the floor, as usual, the only man with his headdress off. His short, graying hair sways in time to the sinuous music. He's playing belote (a card game favored by old ladies in faded novels) with Tammam. No wonder she's not one of the group's favorites—she's about as self-effacing as Bianca Jagger.

Almira Nazer *is* one of their favorites—although she's another of the new wives brought in by an older meritocrat made good. She's twenty-five, has long chestnut hair, the face of a fifteen-year-old, and is no swank. The doe-eyed Yamani has competition. He's no longer the only teacher's pet; his excellency

Hisham Nazer is juggling for top billing with the al Saud. Nazer, Ph.D. from Stanford, California, is the confident (his enemies say conceited), resourceful Minister of Planning, who produced the 663-page script for the next $142 billion, five-year epic, subtitled "In the name of God the merciful and compassionate."

God was jolly merciful last time. The five-year plan before this didn't get more than 18 percent of its future shock into existence. If Nazer's achieves that, it will still radically change the country. It means importing foreigners wholesale to work this jolting change. How can you do that and at the same time realize the plan's stated number-one development goal: "to maintain the religious and moral values of Islam"?

To look at Nazer leaning back in a chair, watching Almira with pride and talking easily to friends, you wouldn't think he has a care on his mind. But I've seen Nazer in his office too; I can appreciate the contrast of his working and private life.

His Excellency Hisham Nazer works in another pristine ministry, a prototype of tomorrow's Riyadh. No desert Bedouin could wander in here to gossip or moan. Nazer's so businesslike that he's even abolished the serving of tea and coffee. Every other office in Riyadh is as welcoming and flowing with liquid as an old-time, small-town drugstore. After these offices Nazer's comes as a dousing of cold water, and on top of that his conversation is as speedy as a dumdum bullet.

Few visiting Westerners, their contracts at the mercy of his five-year plan, have the faintest clue how it came into being. Having read bits of it, I'm staggered at the monumental ambition of it all. Nazer hardly lacks assurance for the task. He bears the mark for me of the former head boy at Victoria College, Cairo, the British boarding school in Egypt that raised future ministers, kings, and presidents on a life of cold showers at 6:30 A.M., team spirit, and canings for wearing brown shoes with the gray school uniform (Nazer still remembers the day he got whacked. He knew as a small boy that he was going to make it to this rosewood desk at the top. "I had a hunch that it would be this way." He should be content; his face, the receding forehead above the jutting chin, is creased with worry.

Don't think a great deal of thought hasn't gone into the chiseling of Nazer's weighty tome. For months before it was written he organized dinner parties in the secrecy of Riyadh homes. Various young men from ministries and business, thinkers, idealists, cynics, working royals got together over the rice and lamb to chew over their country's future. At first they met weekly. Toward the end almost daily. The Georgetown clique of Riyadh were trying to work out where they wanted the country to go. Outsiders were flown in—from America, Europe, Egypt.

At the end of all this Hisham Nazer offered the Cabinet four possible plans. "Naturally they rejected the first three and accepted the most difficult, the most complicated, and the most challenging," says Nazer with resignation, "but even if it's only a dream isn't it worth having dreams?" They also chose the most frightening to Saudis. How much change can you absorb overnight? It even frightens Nazer. (Fortunately, after all that effort, the Saudi government let it be known in March, 1976, that it was unofficially abandoning the plan—not for lack of cash, for sensible lack of nerve.)

"Don't you think I don't know that we're in danger of losing a tremendous heritage," says Nazer. "Our family unity is our heritage and the strength of our religion. People ask me why an important ministry like this stops for prayertime. I say, 'Coffee's out,' but if it will take us a few more years to make progress if we pray, that's fine."

He's on thin ice when he talks about family unity—what with that discarded first wife and his second young one, Almira. He picked her himself when she was a medical student at Cairo University. After they married, she stayed on in Cairo for two years to qualify, with Nazer's willing permission (he's one of the rare Saudi men that feminists might approve of—no question of her quitting her career for his sake). Now she has a small son, and their house is one of the few in Riyadh that could make *House and Garden*.

With his polished, delightful wife and his own lovely, husky voice and American-style vitality, Nazer's destined for a starring role in his country's attempt to make itself liked abroad. Hisham does his duty with goodwill trips, but he gets discouraged. "I've studied in the States; I know how hard it is for our people to understand your culture. But sometimes I don't think anyone in the West wants to bother to *try* to understand ours." His attitude hardens every time he goes off and comes back to his office to find letters from people he met abroad. They're not thanking him or expressing interest in seeing him again; they're just offering to sell him real estate in Switzerland or their family heirlooms.

It's no wonder that Nazer needs the relaxation of evenings with The Group. It's not much relaxation for me; it's the nearest he'll get to it in Riyadh.

By now, at The Group's supper party, it's time to eat. I've never seen so much food. The Arab idea of a "little supper" makes the most jumbo-sized American portions look like aid relief for the starving. Here's a whole sheep, chicken, vegetables, meatballs—enough for a few hundred. Almira Nazer, wafting pink chiffon, her gentle voice chatting over the buffet plates, looks tired. That's not surprising. She's the only working woman in the room. Every morning at seven she reports to a local hospital where she's employed as a pediatrician. We don't eat until eleven; it's now way after midnight. Hisham and Almira Nazer exchange a quick glance; he nods to the door. He makes a point of saying, "Sorry, we'll have to go. I have a working wife, you know."

The Yamanis are back on the floor playing belote. They don't leave until much later. By now Yamani doesn't look drawn with fatigue; he's half dead—but he doesn't have a working wife. We arrange for me to spend the day with Tammam.

The day with Tammam doesn't start early. It doesn't start until the afternoon, when Tammam wakes up. The public

Zaki Yamani, the world's apparent oil sorcerer, is everyone's property. The clue to the private Yamani is the black-eyed smug-puss, Tammam. At home she's the queen of her court. She always has some companion at her beck and call. It may be her older sister, Johara, a psychology student, whom she's bossing around. It may be an intriguing Frenchwoman of a certain age who's come to stay. To say Tammam's like Anne Boleyn at Henry VIII's court would be an exaggeration. To say she's like a pop star who's had one hit and is big in Hamburg would not.

Tammam can't make up her mind how to fill her time today. The bookshelves offer astrology, history, explicit picturebooks on sex techniques, philosophy, Gaylord Hauser. Tammam doesn't feel like reading. The videotape shelves offer everything from Muhammad Ali's latest fight to *There's a Girl in My Soup*. Tammam doesn't feel like a movie. She wouldn't think of going shopping, not in Riyadh. Tammam's very sniffy about where she shops, and the city's provincial stores aren't her mark. No, Tammam feels like giving me the benefit of her advice.

"I'm quite modern, I want you to know that. I think a girl should get to know a boy, have coffee with him or something. But no more than that, you know what I mean?" It's one of her favorite expressions. Tamman knows exactly what she means. "Every man, however educated he is, wants a virgin for a wife. And it's not difficult to hold a man—for an Arab woman, that is. I think you Western women have forgotten how to do it.

"I have a friend who is very pretty, but she went to school in America and stopped using makeup. Her husband came to me one day and asked me to show her how to do it. She doesn't look like a woman without it, really. You know what I mean? And I see you don't use makeup either for that matter."

The day passes under Tammam's tutelage. At nine she goes to make herself ready for her master. It takes an hour; her dressing room table has an armory of scent bottles and beauty products. The makeup, the canary-colored evening dress, the hair carefully curled down to her waist seems to me overdone for a quiet supper at home with her husband. But, as Tammam has pointed out, "An Arab woman knows instinctively how to do the right thing."

The Minister of Petroleum and Mineral Resources finally staggers in—he's beat. Tammam has now switched roles—she's Lolita. She robs Zaki of his headdress, sits him on the floor and plays belote. The young temptress goes through an ABC of seduction with this forty-five-year-old man with his soft eyes and soft paunch. She flirts outrageously, giggles, cheats with much smacking of cards and lips to trap his attention. It's almost a pity to have to interrupt it for supper—another feast.

While Zaki is offering to chart my horoscope (he's a Cancer and an expert on the subject) I'm working out how to ask him what the hell's happened to his *chef de cabinet*, Ibrahim Obaid (the one who led me to Yamani in the first place). He gives me an opening. "Who do you think arranged your visa?" he asks, in such a way as to suggest it might have been Zaki himself.

"Ibrahim Obaid?" I answer innocently.

He withdraws and doesn't say a word to me until we're nearly finished eating. (It takes weeks for me to find out that Obaid resigned because he didn't get a ministry of his own, it's said, and was no longer working for Zaki all the time his office was saying I should call back tomorrow when he might be in. That's Saudi Arabia.)

"How would you feel if you suddenly found you had to live here?" Zaki starts again.

"As an expatriate? I don't think I'd like to be a stranger in a strange land anywhere." Zaki shrugs impatiently at the way I've dodged his question. So few people ever ask anything directly, I feel I've insulted him. I enjoy the man too much; I answer honestly, "I would suffocate."

Zaki smiles. He's content. Tammam jumps in, says that I'm not very good at explaining myself, and then rushes him off

for more belote. Early in the morning, when they're still playing together like small, happy children, I leave them to their
double bed in the shabby hotel suite.

Tammam has one philosophy about life—it's a woman's job
to please her man. "Now listen to me. You're older than I am,
and I don't mean to be unkind, but you evidently haven't been
able to hold a man so far. Just remember that every man, no
matter how big he is in the world, he's a child. You know what
I mean? Not a child to cry or anything, but he needs warmth,
love, affection and that means that when he comes home from
the office he must find you cheerful and beautiful. That's how
you make sure that he will always come back." And the last
devastating thrust. "Then you'll be able to get anything you
want from him."

9

BANKING ON A WAR HORSE

THERE WERE OTHER COMMONERS ONCE WITH GREAT POWER. They helped Ibn Saud to found and then run his domain. They came from abroad, bringing the education the desert Arabs lacked. Some of them stayed. One is today's eminence grise, King Khaled's only official adviser, Dr. Rashad Pharaoan, once Syrian, now Saudi.

In a green villa in Riyadh two old foxhole buddies are chewing the fat. They've got forty years of shared memories. Once they went to war with Ibn Saud (somewhere safe in the back lines), now they both have white hair and statesmen's bearing. There comes a point in some men's lives when they've become so important that they stop moving their heads—they merely incline an ear. Both Dr. Rashad Pharaoan and his pal, Dr. Medhat al Ared, Saudi Ambassador to the UN in Geneva, reached that point many years ago.

Pharaoan, mandarin and medicine man (retired), sees more of King Khaled than any commoner and most princes. I'm here alone with Pharaoan and al Ared by accident. Pharaoan invited me to dinner on the phone the other day, and I make a point of arriving tonight bang on time. When I knock on his door he looks happy to see me but puzzled. After a while he explains why; he was waiting dinner for me *last* night. Terrific start. But he isn't in the least put out. "Would you like to join us? We're only talking." You bet I would. But he still looks puzzled. Finally he confesses that he can't believe I'd want to waste an evening with two old men. I must want something; a favor, an introduction. Why don't I tell him right away and he'll see to it? It takes me a while to believe he means it; Saudi men aren't normally given to humility. Pharaoan can't see that he's interesting in himself.

He's far more interesting than the King's arrogant young interpreter who'd been boring me to death for two hours before I came on to Pharaoan's. This spoiled brat of thirty-plus, who looks vaguely like Laurence Harvey (if you call that handsome), was told by Joan Kennedy when she was here a few months ago that he should be in movies. Now he's even more full of himself.

Poor dear, as royal interpreter he had to travel back across the desert on his Majesty's caravan from the court's summer quarters in Taif, a green hillside resort on the west coast. The experience has almost destroyed him; he doesn't know how he'll recover. His aristocratic features curl with distaste as he describes the journey. "I'm worn out. We had to wake up at dawn and wash in a tub of cold water. Ugh, that cold water. Then I couldn't get out of the tub for the scorpions. At night I was so scared I couldn't sleep a wink. Ten days in the desert is awful. Nothing but heat, flies, and boredom, and what do you think they did all day? Nothing, absolutely nothing. They just sat around and talked about the old days."

Now I'm listening to Pharaoan describe the same journey to al Ared. Traveling across the desert with the King and his brothers is Pharaoan's idea of a good time. It needs stamina; even in October the sun beats mercilessly. Only six months ago this adviser was in a Cleveland hospital having open-heart surgery after a coronary and here he is, his beard trembling with pleasure, telling Medhat of his trip with the court.

"It was splendid. There's nothing like the peace and the stillness of the desert. Word passed around that the King was coming and the tribesmen came from miles around to see him. We sat up all night remembering how it used to be. Nothing like now, of course. Now we travel with about three hundred cars, what with all the court officials, the princes' servants, telephone operators, cooks, and those generators humming all day."

Dr. al Ared nods understandingly, his eyes moistening with nostalgia behind his thick spectacles. These two men have stitched, patched, and advised three generations of al Saud kings (excluding Saud, whom neither would serve). When al Ared came here it wasn't even a country yet. Ten years later he was joined by an old comrade from Damascus University—Pharaoan, who had escaped from Syria after being condemned to death for resistance work by the French, then in charge of the place.

In 1948 King Ibn Saud appointed Pharaoan as Ambassador to France. The French refused to accept him as he was still officially under sentence of execution. Ibn Saud threatened to break diplomatic relations. Pharaoan went to Paris; he still gets a kick out of that twist of fate.

The personal physician turned royal adviser and, along the way, grew rich. But passing an evening in this empty house, puffing on his cigar with al Ared is a real treat to him. For me, too, but for one problem—I'm not hungry (it's a relief to miss out on one of those gigantic meals for a change), but I'm dying for a cigarette. Out of respect I can't smoke in front of Pharaoan—I'm a woman, it would be a terrible gaffe. Thank heavens he doesn't notice how his cigar smoke is getting to me.

The two men smile at each other and remember the days when Pharaoan delivered royal babies and slept at the bottom of their beds when they were ill. Al Ared recalls his first operation—it was on the floor. "When I operated on a table I thought that was progress." After going around the King Faisal Medical City with all its electronic wonders, meeting these two is like coming across a record shelf where there are old 78s in bare brown covers. And yet. Pharaoan's name opens all the Riyadh doors that matter.

We're waiting for Mme. Pharaoan who's flying home from Taif via Paris; intercontinental travel at this level of wealth counts for as much as a subway ride. The Pharaoans have been married for thirty-seven years. Rashad sent home for a wife soon after his escape from Syria. The family shipped out a sixteen-year-old cousin, Jameeda, born in Syria but raised and educated in Jerusalem, then under British mandate but with at least some facilities. She came to a town with no schools, electricity, telephones, or airplanes, and not much water.

Pharaoan keeps looking at his watch. To divert him, al Ared reminds him of the time he shared a tent with H. St. John Philby—the ex-British politico, explorer, Arabist, and father of the notorious double agent Kim (now a retired KGB officer in Moscow). St. John Philby had converted to Islam and was entitled to some more wives; pretty useful since his English one, Dora, didn't much dig hanging around the desert with her husband's hero-King, Ibn Saud.

Ibn Saud ordered al Ared to find Philby a new Saudi wife. "You chose well," recalls Pharaoan, "she was a fine girl and she gave him a good son. The son teaches at Riyadh University, you know."

Before I can get my mind around the oddity of finding out that the half-brother of the British diplomat who betrayed both his own country and America to the Russians is alive and well and teaching in Riyadh, the door bursts open. A black figure enters; the indomitable Madame Pharaoan is back. She throws off her veil; what an astounding sight. A young-looking blonde rushes across the room, and Rashad winds his arms around her, his face almost breaking up with pleasure. I can appreciate what a rare show of affection this is; normally Saudi couples don't even touch in front of other people. Madame, mother of five, grandmother of several, is not what I expect.

Next morning Rashad goes off to the King and Jameeda settles down to plates of sticky cakes, a long chat with me, and the telephone. It rings all the time. Mme. Pharaoan is very popular; probably because she's one of those women who makes the best of everything and has no time for moaning. Most Saudi women fall into two categories: *nebish* and *mezzo nebish*. The air conditioning breaks down in most homes and there's histrionics. It breaks down here and Jameeda beams at me. "Isn't that good? Now we can open the windows and talk without that noise."

One moment she talks of her daughter living in Paris, the next of flying to Rome in a few days for a cousin's wedding, and then about the time, years ago, when Ibn Saud was wounded in battle and Rashad rushed off to treat him. He came back many hours later. The wound wasn't much, but Ibn Saud had been reading to him the chapter of each of the thirty-six scars on his body, an anatomical history book of his conquest of Saudi Arabia.

Jameeda tells me that her son Raith will talk to me too. If she says so, he will. Raith Pharaoan is, in many ways, far more interesting than the Adnan Khashoggi legend that most of the Western press has focused on lately. Raith has the money and the international deals (his empire straddles the Mideast and across the Atlantic; insurance, shipping, petrochemicals, arms, you name it). He has the requisite private jet, but he has a blanket of security around him.

Every summer all the Pharaoans go to Raith's villa in the hills above Cannes. No one hears about it. They don't want publicity and they do want secrecy; apart from anything else, Raith has children and fears kidnappings. In the winter all the Pharaoans go skiing in Megève. They give parties for certain friends but gossip columnists don't get to hear about them. No one reads of their gatherings as they do of Khashoggi's caviar fling for fifty in Gstaad.

The Saudis are now using Khashoggi's willingness to endure publicity and his "popularity" with Western newspapermen as a decoy. They would dump him if it suited them. Already in some fields he's a figure of the past. Not in the West, but here where it counts, where the big money is. If you read any well-informed profiles of Khashoggi in which he's had a chance to contribute some information, notice the way there's always mention of his houses in Riyadh or Jeddah. Mention those to certain top Saudis and watch the flicker of amusement. To them he's based outside the country; his father (who was another personal physician to Ibn Saud) is also out, almost permanently in London.

There's one reliable trump in the Saudis' hand: their names. Newspaper readers couldn't keep up with them even if Western newsmen could get them right. Khashoggi is one they almost know. Reams of reporting of congressional hearings have seen to that. It might blow his cover as an arms broker, but he does draw the flak away from the inner circle still barely known in the West. And if they ever think Khashoggi goes too far, the Saudis can let him know.

If he wants to allow himself to be persuaded to fly around with an NBC film crew including Caroline Kennedy on board as a researcher, exposing his importance and his proximity to attractive women on American television screens—that's fine. But when he wanted to break into the world of movies and hired Anthony Quinn to star in a multimillion-dollar production, shot in both English and Arabic, about Prophet Mohammed, scripted by Harry *(Battle for Anzio)* Craig, that was different. Filming was already under way in Morocco when word went from King Faisal to King Hassan; word went to Khashoggi. The film set went quiet.

Raith Pharaoan has to be another kind of operator; his father sees the King every day, after all. We're sitting on a terrace in Jeddah. Behind us there's another of those parties going on where the country's fat cats purr at each other. Pharaoan, baby-faced, friendly (because I mention that his mother, a major shareholder in his corporations apart from anything else, told me he would be), looks like an important man's secretary.

I'd hate to be on the wrong side of a negotiating table from Pharaoan. He's filling me in on a meeting early in '75 at the Hotel Pierre in New York. James T. Barnes, Sr., chairman of the Bank of the Commonwealth in Michigan, is there to see lawyers from ex-Secretary of the Treasury John Connally's law firm in Texas. The lawyers and Barnes have been negotiating a multimillion-dollar takeover for his shareholding in the Detroit bank. A nameless Mideast client is involved. In the anonymous comfort of the hotel suite, James T. Barnes, Sr., is about to meet the man who's buying him out: Raith Pharaoan. It's a deal Pharaoan has spent months planning down to the smallest detail; it slips through smoothly.

At about the same time as that Hotel Pierre meeting, Khashoggi has been thwarted in his attempt to acquire his third bank, the First National of San Jose. It isn't as if he's buying Wall Street, after all, but there's still a national stink. Democratic representative Fortney H. Stark, who sold him a bank in Walnut Creek, publicly announces that he wishes he hadn't done so. Most of the opposition is gathering around the disclosures that are coming forth about Khashoggi's arms commissions. Get down to the nitty-gritty—and it might have gathered anyway. Arms or no arms he's Arab.

Pharaoan doesn't hide his regret at the way Khashoggi handled the affair. "He should have withdrawn his offer in San Jose the second he realized there was local opposition. Suppose he'd pulled out, I reckon the people in the town would have got worried that he'd seen the bank's financial position and decided it was unsound. The board would probably have ended up begging him to buy it. He might have got it cheaper that way too."

Pharaoan got his bank in Detroit exactly as he'd planned it. "I wanted an American bank in the center of an industrial city, not a small town. Saudi Arabia's buying into technology and industry, not tennis clubs. A small-town bank without enough capital assets wouldn't have been the right vehicle for me. It had to be a bank with one major shareholding and not too high a percentage of Jewish money on deposit in case of a run after the takeover. My lawyers went through every bank in the States that could be up for sale. I went through their list, found four that met my particular specifications and settled on the Commonwealth."

Some Jews withdrew their money, now it's flowing in again. Jewish employees weren't fired (the first question everyone in America raised when the takeover became public news) and no orders were given against hiring them. The only change made on Pharaoan's insistence was that the bank had to move into the black areas of the city. "First, it's a public service. You can't refuse black people banking facilities. The board argued against it on a question of security. I said, 'Buy security guards but open those branches.' It's not altruism. Blacks work; those branches will make money."

Nothing flames American paranoia like news of Arabs taking over banks. As a kitchen is to a home, its bank is to a community. But nothing provokes Saudi paranoia like the resulting snarls of protest organized by local merchants, usually Jewish. It's a vicious circle.

Every time the Saudis try explaining themselves to America at large they make matters worse. No sooner had the new Saudi Ambassador to Washington presented his credentials than he got dumped with the potential scandal that there was a "no Jews" clause in a $25 million highway-building contract his country was discussing with the state of California. How did he get out of it? By issuing a statement that anyone, even blacks and women (whatever next?), could come and work in his country, unless he/she adhered to Zionism.

It's riddle time, folks: when is a Jew not a Jew? Answer: when he's a Zionist. But how are you going to find out and who is going to judge who's a "good Jew" and who's a "bad Jew"? The American press worries away like a dog with a bone at the question of whether Saudis get Jews pushed out of companies they're dealing with. But behind this concern lies the crunch question: have the Saudis really got it in for all Jews?

I'm in Saudi as a "proven" Christian; it isn't true. I grew up in an Orthodox Jewish home. Yes, I *do* have a nasty shiver when a perfectly intelligent, Western-educated Saudi tells me in all seriousness that every practicing Jew has to drink the blood of a Muslim once a year. But this is only one man. And Jews have told me equally seriously that every Arab wants to slit the throat of every Jewish woman and child in the world. They're both nonsense. But there's always been that kind of nonsense. It's nothing like the pogroms in Russia or the hideous happenings in Nazi Germany. It's more like the situation in 1815 when the ship carrying Napoleon into exile on St. Helena anchored off the coast of Britain. Hundreds of people went out in small boats —to see Napoleon's horns. The English had been cut off from France for a whole generation, so of course there were some who believed tales like that.

Saudi Arabia's in a filthy position. Officially it's in a state of war with Israel. (How much did America trust the Japanese living here during the last world war?) And I do meet some Saudis for whom only the extermination of Israel will do. I do meet a few Saudis who because of Israel now have it in for Jews, period. But there's one vital difference here from any anti-Jewish feeling I've known or heard about: Saudis and Jews are much more alike emotionally and culturally than Saudis and Westerners. That's what leaves me so confused, so horrified at the things people from both sides (Jews and Saudis) say to me.

I stay with Saudis who are astonished that I, a "cold Britisher," am so at ease with their noisy families. Of course I am but how can I tell them that every night is Passover night to me here? Of course I'm at ease with the strong Yiddisher mommas of Saudi Arabia, the enveloping warmth of their homes, the undercurrents. It's what I grew up with.

There are moments when I'm instinctively afraid of being surrounded by so many Arabs. I've unconsciously absorbed fear; three Mideast wars have seen to that. But I'd rather have the overt, angry, hurt anti-Semitism of some Saudis than the understated, sarcastic anti-Semitism of some of the British Establishment.

I meet only the elite of Saudi; when I run into a Jew-hater I know it. It's out front. I can remember enough dinner parties I've been to in London when someone has made a remark about a man with an obviously Jewish name and then without actually putting prejudice into words (that's bad manners, after all), dropped poison on him in a way I can't pin down or challenge (that's bad manners too).

When it comes to the average Saudi attitude to Jews, you

couldn't find a better example than the Saudi Ambassador to Washington, when he's "off duty." He heads a family corporation that has the agency for Harry Winston in his country and has nieces, nephews, and cousins who all went to school abroad and are sophisticated. They can and do distinguish between Israelis and Jews. That's what makes this story even more upsetting:

The Alirezas were exceptionally close to King Faisal. The day he was killed they were in London together. Their shock and sorrow left them stunned. That evening they gathered in a small Italian restaurant for dinner. As they were leaving one of the ambassador's nieces, Hoda, asked her husband whether they could buy some of the oranges decorating the ceiling, to take back to their flat. A large party of Americans had been sitting at the next table. As Hoda put up her hand to the oranges, one woman yelled out, fortissimo, "Go ahead, enjoy them. You know where they come from, dear, they come from Israel." This wasn't the first time Hoda had been on the receiving end of remarks in public from Jews hearing her speak Arabic. Normally she would turn icily away.

This was the wrong moment: she took down an orange, slung it in the woman's face as hard as she could, and shouted back, "You want to enjoy the Israeli orange? Why don't you catch it?"

I have become very close to Hoda in Saudi Arabia, as I have to many other women. I see how burned up she gets as she tells this story. That's how hatred festers; it's the sadness and the threat of the Mideast.

They even follow me home from Arabia. A strange collection of visitors wind up at my home: there's the Saudi with a crucial government position who doesn't believe I'm writing a book at all. He's heard that I went to his country to spy for Israel.

At first I laugh. "Come on, what was I supposed to be finding out? You and I talked for hours when I stayed with your family. Did I once ask you about your job?"

"No, but they have departments that study us psychologically."

Then there's the Saudi who believes I'm writing it but that

I'm sponsored by a Zionist organization. Taking courage in both hands, I tell him I'm Jewish but that I'm not employed in the Zionist cause.

"Why didn't you tell us, why did you lie?"

"I wouldn't have got a visa, and you know it."

"My government won't like it. Didn't you realize that if we found out we'd suspect you of spying?"

"No. But tell me straight. Does my being Jewish make a difference to you personally if I'm not associated with Israel, although I have been there?" (Another sin by Saudi standards.)

"To me? No, Linda, your being Jewish makes no difference to me, I swear." I know it's true; he keeps in touch and his concern is only for what'll happen to me when his government starts checking me out. As a Saudi, if he'd minded, he would simply have disappeared.

The final story came from CIA contacts in the area. The Saudis used to allow Jews in; they still do *if* there's no fuss made, *if* it's handled discreetly, and *if* they trust the personnel concerned. But a while back several Jews in Aramco were thought to have direct links with Israeli intelligence. They left, and the Saudi and American governments hushed it up. There's been a nervous "no Jews need apply" ever since.

Can you really wonder at the Saudis' bitterness? Without their backing, that Egyptian-Israeli first tottering step toward peace would never have come off. President Sadat wouldn't have dared make an agreement without Saudi behind him; much of the Arab world around still hasn't forgiven him and never will. And every time Saudis look at the American press, the only coverage they see their country getting is about bribes and how they attack Jews.

Unless they're forced to (by pressure from Palestinians, publicity, who knows?) most Saudi businessmen would rather not operate a Jewish boycott. Raith Pharaoan certainly doesn't want to. "Fire Jewish employees from the bank in Detroit?" He laughs. "I'd lose some of my best staff."

But the Pharaoan family have under their umbrella a most

amusing example of the insecurity working the other way around. I discover Ghazzam Pharaoan, Raith's cousin, by accident.

My teeth need cleaning. After all those cigarettes, they're as furry as a small bear. Friends direct me to the only decent dentist in town. The entrance nearly puts me off, it's like an old block in the West Seventies of New York, with roaches running up and down the hallway. Upstairs is this snazzy dental clinic—orange-and-white color scheme, deep-pile carpet, the very latest equipment. A beautiful black nurse from California restores my teeth and charges me fifteen dollars. I'm pleasantly relieved; the daughter of my friend is having orthodontia here, her bill is nearing thirty-five hundred dollars, and work's hardly started. On the way out the name clicks—Pharaoan.

That night at a party a flat, cheerful, booming voice behind me starts to make my ears tingle. Among the elegantly rolled "r's" and precisely molded vowels of top Saudis who've grown up almost bilingual, is this unmistakably English accent. I turn around to see a young man with the appearance of a medical intern and the confidence of a Saudi. It's most confusing. No foreigner behaves like this here (it's impolitic) but no Arab dresses like this either. He's got a mop of untidy curls, no jacket, and an open-necked shirt with three buttons undone. He beards the room with his happy-go-lucky manner and hairy chest as if it were a burger joint full of his friends.

Around him swish the long dresses (both men's and women's), and he has in tow a pretty little blond girl in a pantsuit. This is Ghazzam Pharaoan with his girlfriend who teaches at the American school. Ghazzam grew up in England—he was only three when his Arab father and English mother moved there. In those days he was just another London kid with nothing Arab about him but his name and his relations, who dropped by now and again. After he went through dental school he was doing rather well, earning seven thousand dollars a year—not bad money for Britain.

His peaceful, middle-class English life was interrupted by the '73 October War. "I've never thought of myself as Arab in my life, but when the war happened, the Arab in me leaped right out. I suddenly found that I was incensed by the pro-Israeli stand of the English press. That took me aback. And it so happened that my cousin Raith was in London then. I went to see him at the Hilton Hotel, and there he was, the same age as me, with his own suite and people at his beck and call. I was thinking, 'Hey, that could have been me,' when Raith asked me why I didn't come to Saudi Arabia. I left London there and then."

In a slack time like the summer, when everyone goes west, he clears $10,000 a month. If he's busy, he makes nearer $15,000 —all tax-free. He has two dentists and seven technicians working under him and gets away every weekend. He has a reputation for being a terrific fisherman in the family.

His English wife couldn't take the country, divorced him, and left. In the end he'll have to marry the American or break up; "dating's" not for a man in his position. Ghazzam plays at fighting the obligations incumbent on a Pharaoan, but he knows he only gets away with his outrageous (for Saudis) behavior because of the name.

The nearest he came to a close scrape was the time "Uncle" Rashad Pharaoan sent a friend along to join him, another fishing enthusiast. Chaos. "I just managed to get out of it. The only things I've ever caught were a shark by mistake and a barracuda swimming the wrong way with its mouth open. I don't fish—I say that so's I don't have to spend every weekend with the family. It's hard being a full-time Pharaoan, believe me." It's made easier by the vital fact that Ghazzam doesn't live in Riyadh. He lives in Jeddah, which is just cosmopolitan enough for him to get by.

CHAPTER

10

A MODERN BABEL

IT'S NOT POLITE TO TALK ABOUT OIL IN SAUDI ARABIA, JUST AS IT wasn't to discuss coal in the drawing rooms of Victorian England. The stuff comes out of the ground in the east, where Aramco laid the foundations of American suburbia. It underpins the capital of Riyadh, where concrete flattens the desert. But for sheer wealth it's Jeddah that counts. In this major commercial center on the Red Sea a plot of land that cost $700 two years ago has just changed hands for $200,000.

Nor is it polite to reminisce in company about the 1920s: the fanatical al Saud troops took Taif and then got carried away with rape, murder, and looting before Ibn Saud arrived to quiet them down. And then there was a two-year siege of Jeddah before that fell. Still, that was all fifty years ago, and it's another "politically sensitive" issue.

When I heard about Jeddah in coöp-happy Riyadh it sounded like San Francisco. "Ah, but wait until you see Jeddah," people would say wistfully. Yes, it's different. It's got a few hundred thousand more people, for a start. It's no use asking how many more than Riyadh; it's one of those things no one knows. For once this vagueness is excusable. This port is the last call before Mecca, birthplace of Prophet Mohammed, the hotline to Allah. Hundreds of thousands of Muslim pilgrims from all over the world arrive in Jeddah every year on their way to Mecca, fifty-five miles up the highway. Many stay on, poor, possibly diseased, sleeping rough. The pilgrimage, or Haj, is the season for burglaries; there were five hundred last year, a scandalously high crime rate incomprehensible for the Saudis.

Jeddah is an ancient port. Foreigners have poured in for the Haj and merchants have set out to trade for centuries. In the Nejd, Arabs boast of their pure blood. Hejazis have always married foreigners from all corners of the Muslim world, and besides that the Ottoman Empire left behind a trail of Turkish blood—yet another "politically sensitive" issue.

Jeddah's the only city in the world that houses foreign embassies and isn't a capital. The Foreign Ministry, more of a wedding cake than a building, is a copy of the Hejaz railway station in Damascus, built by the Turks. It overlooks one of the best and one of the worst views in Saudi—the sparkling sea that delights me after desert-bound Riyadh, and the road between, packed with cars and dangerous drivers.

As an Arab remarked, "Saudis drive their cars as they drove their camels. They look neither left nor right and they beat them until they go faster." They couldn't look left or right if they wanted to: they're blinkered by their headdresses. Add to this the natural exuberance of Jeddah, and the traffic's a disaster —that is, unless you're a pedestrian. If a driver kills a pedestrian, at best the law will get him with a $10,000 fine. At worst the family kicks up a fuss, insists that he has to pay blood money, and a foreigner can get stuck in prison until the price is agreed. It's a driver's hell; a pedestrian's paradise. I just put up my hand and cars screech to a halt to let me cross (especially if it's a foreign driver who takes me for an Arab).

A really troublesome family can be a ghastly headache for a pedestrian-slaying foreigner (and it's not hard to be one; the roads are anarchic). At least it's not as bad as the story I heard one Western businessman relating to a newcomer, from all his experience of four days in Jeddah: According to this "authority," if a foreigner kills an Arab, he has to lie down in the road and let someone run him over. Ridiculous. Most stories you hear like that are nonsense. Er, nearly most stories. Well, that one is anyway.

The stories about how much money's made in Jeddah certainly aren't ridiculous. It's very obviously the government's money center. You can sense the hidden world inside the Saudi Arabian Monetary Authority (SAMA) in the middle of town. It's from here that orders go out to Aramco telling them into which foreign banks to pay the oil revenues. Then huge amounts are checked into current accounts in chosen clearinghouses like Chase Manhattan, Morgan Guaranty, Citibank. Moments later exact instructions arrive from SAMA directing dollars, converting sterling in the City of London's clearinghouses, moving millions. Result: a disproportionate number of banking gnomes from America, Britain, and Switzerland standing around in the Kandara Palace—an institution, not a mere hotel.

Its scruffy grandeur reigns over Jeddah life. There's no postal delivery service, only unreliable P.O. box numbers. The Kandara acts as *poste restante* for a large part of the city. Nearly all Saudis who matter in Jeddah (men, that is) will spend some time in the lobby here during the week.

I arrive in my long dress from Riyadh, looking silly again. There are so many foreign women in Jeddah that it's back to short skirts. A top man from the Union Bank of Switzerland is sipping coffee with his team, waiting to go to SAMA; his bank is an official adviser. A big noise from Credit Suisse, White Weld, another SAMA regular, is bullying the switchboard operator to get him London in four minutes. Some chance.

My one consolation is the sight of the spare figure of the son of the former British Prime Minister, Sir Alec Douglas-Home. His offspring, David, a merchant banker from London, is slumped in an armchair looking just like a man with a firm reservation but no hotel room. He is.

During the oil-embargo days after the October War, David Douglas-Home was pilloried in the press as an "Arab-lover." Over nine hundred Americans went to the trouble of writing him letters of abuse for putting together a loan for the Arabs (it was for Abu Dhabi, hardly a front-line fighter in the Israeli struggle). Those correspondents should see him now. He's sent his right-hand man, Rupert (son of former British Defence Minister, Lord Carrington), off to do battle with the switchboard and find a bed, somewhere, anywhere in town. Unlike the lowlier fixers, the men who are completely trusted don't feel the need to sweeten up every Arab around. "Fred," he calls out to the waiter, "bring me a drink."

Douglas-Home is fed up with Jeddah. "You couldn't do business here if you were a romantic Arab-lover. You'd go out of your mind. Nothing works. Not the telephones, not the hotels, the roads are abominable. It's collapsing around us."

He's here to see a client who's a "diversified concrete king." "Every time he does a deal he turns over twenty to thirty million dollars." Douglas-Home strolls into a beauty shop; the owner is his client's brother, Saleem. The youngest brother is at the register, "wetting his fingers in business," explains Saleem.

Douglas-Home stands around, hands in his pockets, with the air of an Ivy League law professor. His aristocratic hauteur goes down well with the Saudis; they understand it. He feels sad at what's happening now that the cowboys have ridden in. "Two years ago the place was deserted. Now look at it, a shambles."

He's right, of course. This San Francisco of Saudi Arabia doesn't work. It's rumored there's a garbage-removal service; most people rely on stray goats. "It's the west today," is the kind of scrap I overhear at coffee mornings. It doesn't mean the wind. It means the telephones of the entire western section of town have been unplugged or cut through with an ax by workmen. A quarter of Jeddah's phones are out of order at any one time.

The princely merchants have found a way around the problem of international calls (six days to get New York? Four days to London?). They know all the international operators at the central exchange personally. The telephone men bring their problems to them (money problems usually). The merchants solve them and, by coincidence, they get their calls abroad at once. As big, as sprawling as it is, inner Jeddah still works on a

personal basis. I asked one such merchant prince, whose investments are now in Luxembourg- and Lichtenstein-based companies, why he doesn't operate from Europe or New York
permanently.

"I couldn't bear to walk in a street where I didn't see people
I knew. I'll never forget staying in a Paris apartment once when
an old lady died. When they came to take her away, no one in
the whole block knew who she was or remembered talking to
her. That couldn't happen here. I'd rather put up with a telephone system that is, I admit, useless. But please don't quote
me by name. I mustn't be heard criticizing the government."
Saudis can be real boot-lickers.

Until the apparatus of a modern commercial center arrives
(the telex only got going in 1973—security reasons) Jeddah re-
lies on the oldest form of communication known to man—word
of mouth. Getting an invitation to someone, making an appointment is an adventure. It means sending information via
any intermediaries who might be in contact with other intermediaries. As a result everyone in Jeddah expects everyone else
to turn up for something at any time. It may be yesterday's
lunch today or tomorrow's dinner party the day after.

It also means there's twice as much traffic on the roads as
there need be. Everyone's sending notes with his driver to
everyone else. Outings are further complicated by the fact that
there are no street names or numbers and, unlike Riyadh, no
visible town planning. Directions for dinner go something like
this: "Tell the driver to go to the school. I don't know its name;
it's the boys' school. Take the second turn, go over a hill—but
mind the oil drums—look for a yellow gate, then count seven
more. You'll know if it's the right one, because I'll have a man
standing there."

It turns out there are several boys' schools in the area, the
oil drums are a mound of building rubble, the gate's turned
brown in the sun, and every entrance has a whole crowd standing in it. That's assuming the driver hasn't chickened out of
the rutted, craterous mud tracks that lead off the new highway
to the expensive residential areas.

So how and why does anyone bother to do business in this city where communications approximate those of a medieval town? Because, answer the bankers, well briefed on SAMA's accounts, there's nowhere else (Abu Dhabi and Kuwait included) where the profits are as big. Big? The chief assistant to one government prince is dismayed at the sums involved. Five years ago this foreign Arab (who picked up his prince while eking out a living as a Paris pimp) would take a cut of $30,000 to get his boss's signature on a contract for a foreigner. Now he thinks twice about doing it unless it's worth $250,000 to him. I know. He told me this most seriously over coffee.

And why go out to dinner when every drive is a fight past the twin monsters of logistics and directions? Because when you've finally arrived, haggard and neurotic, the people of Jeddah make up for it by being the most generous, hospitable, and outgoing there are anywhere.

There's a group in Riyadh, there are groups in Jeddah. At the very top there's only The Group. Ma'moon and Lita Tamer are part of it. They're having a soirée. Ma'moon owns the biggest chain of pharmacies and beauty parlors in Jeddah. One look at his house and I know that he makes money.

Of course he does; all women are covered in costly warpaint and drenched in the most expensive scents in the world. As I go around the room shaking hands with everyone (yes, they bob up and down here, too), I feel like a dog let loose in the park. I go from one interesting sniff to another—only instead of trees, poodles, and trouser legs, I'm sniffing Joy, L'air du Temps, and Calèche.

The house is elegant, which isn't unusual for Jeddah, and that's the first difference from Riyadh. One woman and I swap notes on a decorator we both know in London. It turns out that he landed a job for a cousin of hers doing his house in the capital. "It's a small world," we both say on cue. It turns out to be even smaller. I've heard the decorator anguishing over this particular client: "Any interior decorator would just die on the job, dear. My client brought in tea urns, brass tables, lanterns, cushions, the lot. He put a model of the Eiffel Tower next to an exquisite fifth-century B.C. piece of bronze I found him. He even had his name in Arabic produced as a neon sign to swing over the bar. I ask you? He completely messed up my design concept."

His anguish got back to Arabia long before I arrived. It's messed up any chance that decorator has of any future design concepts here; Arabs are touchy. But of course, everything he said was true. I've seen houses like that in Riyadh. To his client the bronze and the Eiffel Tower were equally appealing to the eye. I don't see houses like that in Jeddah. When I say the Tamers' house is elegant, it means it's so unobtrusive, I can't even describe it. The tones are discreet, the sofas low and comfortable, the picture windows in the split-level drawing room look out over the lushly landscaped swimming pool. In Jeddah the million-dollar look means restraint. They've long outgrown vulgarity.

Compared to those stiff Riyadh parties with barely desegregated men and women suffering from prickly awareness of each other, this could be New York. The women are all decked out—but in thin-strapped dresses, sometimes cut short to emphasize their chic and daring. The better the Jeddah name, the less flamboyant, the plainer the material, the finer the cut. Only the blue-white rocks betray the accumulated wealth in the room. The women are iced with multikarat diamond rings, necklaces, and bracelets. None of it's insured; no one would dare burgle the names in this room—it's more than their life's worth, let alone their right hand. The jewelry's kept at home in boxes, but it doesn't travel abroad. The owners have learned that sometimes foreigners don't have quite the same respect for other people's property as the well-trained Saudis. Needless to say the crime rate in New York horrifies them ("I hardly dare leave our apartment on Fifth Avenue").

The whisky flows unselfconsciously. No one's surprised, as they are in Riyadh, that I don't drink alcohol. Because it's taken so much for granted here, it doesn't have the same obsessive attraction. There are no knots of women or men tied together. Everyone mixes freely. There's the same polished, flirtatious ribbing that goes on wherever the international rich meet.

In one corner I listen to some surprisingly well-informed dirt-digging about who's sleeping with whom in London society. But this is Jeddah, so flirtatious gossip can't stretch to who's doing what to whom here. Not much in fact. The Group's too small. They need each other too much.

One woman holds forth to me at length on how the new rich from the small Gulf states are ruining London.

"Claridge's is still all right; they haven't discovered that yet, and we always go to the Dorchester. But have you been to the Grosvenor House recently? It's humiliating. Those Gulf women sit in the lobby, masked and veiled from head to foot, surrounded by half-dressed children. But that's not the half of it. I'm told when they've gone, the bedrooms have to be redecorated. They look as if the locusts have been through. Those people have never used a toilet or a chair in their lives . . ."

I break away to another corner where more serious talk is going on. Medical talk. Outside of a convalescent home I've never met so many people who talk so much about their doctors. For women it's often a way of alleviating boredom. The men's passion for their health is harder to plumb. "It's simple," confides one woman with catty delight. "Once they've been rejected by three stewardesses in a row they become venerable and then the only grope they're likely to get is in a doctor's office."

What separates this party from any of the snowy gatherings in St. Moritz in the 1960s or the upper crust, black-tie affairs in New York isn't the white *thobes* and headdresses of the men. It's the staggering warmth of the people. Once you've been accepted there's a flood of invitations, all genuine. None of the "you must come over and see us sometime" variety. Come to stay, come for the weekend, come any time.

But after a while with The Group I see another glaring difference from Riyadh. Look around the room at any Jeddah party. There are some Saudi men married to Saudi-born women, mostly first cousins. Because these women live right at the top, they've grown used to going out with their husbands; they've long since dropped the veil proper. But this is an uneasy existence. They're following the life-style their husbands want them to lead. But there's still her family and his in the background, observing rigid, traditional ideas of what's honorable. Few of these Saudi women would dare to smoke in front of their family elders; none would drink.

Then look at the wives of the other Saudi men here. Most of them are foreign. Lita Tamer, sloe-eyed, lovely, is Christian. Jeddah respects her for holding to her religion, but in this country where people go on and on about Saudi for the Saudis and all that pure-blood stuff, Lita Tamer is Greek.

Burly Abdullah "Ali" Alireza, Ambassador to Washington, is holding the floor with his own brand of switch-on instant charm. The Alirezas are one of the top families, bankers to Ibn Saud right from the start. But I frequently hear them called "nonorigin." It's a polite way of suggesting they're not the Saudi equivalent of good WASPs. That's because generations ago they came from Persia, where they'd gone generations before that from Jeddah. Dammit, the Alireza family was trading with Egypt from Arabia before the Prophet was born—and that's "nonorigin"?

Ali's first wife was American. His second, Jugette, exotic, with a vivacious face, is Jeddah's leading socialite. Her friends are nice enough not to refer to her first marriage to an American pilot (to an Alireza as socially acceptable as 1900s Beacon Hill marrying Irish).

But Jugette's daughter of that marriage, Monica, is a constant reminder, as she stands quietly in a corner watching the party go by. And on top of all that—Jugette is Lebanese. Never mind, their marriage is one of Jeddah's successes. But then she can lead pretty much the life she wants here. Her restrictions are her luxuries. What, she can't drive? Why should she want to with a driver permanently on call? What, she can't work? She's far too busy being social.

Jugette had a fit when her husband's appointment to Washington came through—floods of tears at the very thought of it. Far from leading the free, Western-style life she was used to, it now means acting out the kind of life that a Saudi woman is *supposed* to live. She's representing Saudi womanhood abroad, so it's good-bye to Jeddah's intimate parties where men and women meet with a peck on the cheek, the arm around the shoulder. It means staying upstairs at home in Washington while her husband gives male dinners and goes off to receptions alone.

They may be called Saudi now, but most of these wives were born Egyptian, Jordanian, or Lebanese. The West may lump them all together as Arabs but Saudis can tell them apart. It's the way out for Saudi men who are too cosmopolitan, too worldly, to buy the complete emotional package called "the Saudi way of life." They don't marry "out" to find a woman who's educated: Zaki Yamani wasn't the first to send his daughter to a California campus. Saudi men marry foreigners to escape the goldfish bowl and the awful problem of what a Saudi-born wife can and cannot do. One family's expectations are enough. Two families impose an unbearable weight.

The man who chooses an Egyptian, Lebanese, or even European wife might have to fight like hell to get his father to accept her, but after he comes around, the son can make his own way of life. His wife isn't torn by conflicting loyalties. It makes no sense; the whole kingdom is structured around a superpatriotic ideal, and here are more and more Jeddah men deliberately choosing foreign wives. It's the result of having a country founded on unrealistic (today) religious ideals. Nowhere else in the world is there the same discrepancy between how things are meant to be (separate development for women, no liquor, etc.) and how they are, except possibly in Russia.

So here I am in this country, clinging to these ideals like an unsure virgin clinging to her nightdress. There was a right old palaver in Riyadh when a certain London newspaper report came through. Gracious, the new Saudi Minister for Industry (note: a German wife) "showed a readiness to enjoy certain local customs such as a stiff Bloody Mary." And at every party in Jeddah, everyone drinks openly. When I go home what do the Saudis imagine that I'm going to say? That I saw consumed only large quantities of Coca-Cola (correction: Kaki-Cola, Coke's on the black list)? The answer, unfortunately, is Yes.

Dinner's served on the terrace around the pool. I share one of the sidewalk-café tables with Abdul Aziz Suleimann. He's forty, compactly built, jet-black beard, jet-hard eyes, boss of a trading empire turning over several hundred million dollars a year. They don't come more Saudi than Abdul Aziz. He's Nejdi, his father was King Ibn Saud's first Finance Minister and the man who signed the historic Saudi-American oil agreement for the King in 1933.

Abdul Aziz is just back from New York, where he's negotiating to build new Intercontinental Hotels in Jeddah, Dhahran, Jubail, and Cairo. I'm interested that even this bundle of nervous energy finds the pace of New York disturbing, that even he prefers the snail's crawl of London. But it's late and time to go. Abdul Aziz's wife comes over. She's intelligent and fashionable but the point is that she's Lebanese.

As we swish out of the circular Tamer drive onto those muddy tracks we pass the Suleimanns' five-acre estate with its twenty-room palace and four guesthouses. There's an equally muddy confusion in my mind about what being Saudi is going to mean after the country's been walloped by more oil millions and more foreign wives. And how, for heaven's sake, do the Saudi-born women feel about it all? They stand apart at The Group's relaxed parties. They mix as politely as well-trained children going through their party pieces, but behind the painted scarlet smiles—nothing. Unless you knew otherwise, you'd dismiss them as charming, mindless trinkets. Saudi women are a closed book.

CHAPTER

11

THE CLOSED BOOKS

IT'S BESIDE THE POINT TO SAUDI OFFICIALDOM THAT IT MAKES NO
sense (not as far as manpower, let alone human happiness is
concerned) to keep one sex locked in a box in their country,
while the rest of the world capers around believing in a different way of life. The government's afraid that if it lets up
one set of tight controls and officially says good-bye to one part
of their religious ideal, anything could happen.

I've fallen into Saudi society: businessmen on the outer rims
of influence, insiders, royals, princesses, and cameos worthy of
Oscars for best-supporting-actor roles. I've seen how most men
adjust to the double lives they lead at home and abroad. But
there's always that closed book—the women.

Their husbands can't explain to me what makes them tick;
they don't know themselves. One woman can't help me to
understand another. I start to think that the only open, un-
guarded wives are those imprisoned in the past—uneducated,
untraveled, unquestioning. They live in rabbit warrens of
women and children (more than one woman introduced a close
friend saying, "Our children have the same father"). They
make lots of noise, grow fat, and don't know what their husbands do when they're not in bed with them.

Then one day the threads of the educated women that I've met and got to know better begin to weave together. Many of them are beginning to wonder who they are and what they want from life. Education has given them the tools to search inside themselves. Again, I can't identify them, but what sets them apart in this country where no one asks direct questions is that these women do. Just as I want to fathom and understand their existence, they want me to explain mine.

"What's it like being divorced and not going back to your family? Does it make you feel ashamed? Aren't you ever frightened of dying alone?" asks one. Divorce has no public stigma here, but it's unthinkable for a woman not to return to her father (or her brother). And wanting to live alone, even wanting to be alone, is a state of mind that few Saudis can grasp. The Bedouin culture is too deeply rooted inside them. To be alone to a desert nomad means death. Outside the patch of shared life there's nothing—no water, food, or shelter. The sick are left alone in the desert; to die.

Now there's a new generation of women discovering about being alone. Servants do the work; children go to school. Many of them plug the gaps with sisters, friends, tea parties. Others use the experience to look inside themselves and to look hard at their husbands who, in their frenzy of money making, don't have time for self-examination.

When I first met Aisha I thought she was hard and brittle. She was at one of those table-laden tea parties where everybody shouts at one another at once and it's considered antisocial to move your chair out of the circle for a confiding chat. Women's parties fall into two categories. There are the boisterous ones like a girls' basketball team in the locker room after a game. At these, women bellow across the room, their raucous voices curiously at variance with their studied "femininity." At one such gathering I can't stand it any longer and pull myself closer to the next woman—to hear something, anything, of what she's saying. Everyone, but everyone, stops talking and eating, and stares at me until I push myself back again. I might have thrust my hand down her tea gown to judge by their reaction. And then there are the others; at these, women dress up, even dance, for one another, flatter and flirt, and the lesbian undercurrent sends waves of tension down the back of my neck. I meet Aisha at one of these. Here and at dinner parties later she seems another of those beautifully bound, closed books. She has everything: money, powerful husband, children.

One day I see her alone and we talk for hours. "I would give anything to leave my husband, but he'll take the children and never let me see them again. He can under our law. I hate him and at the same time I know it's not his fault. I simply cannot stand our life together anymore.

"I was a virgin when we married and I expected him to teach me things. Nothing. The first night he rolled on me, and two minutes later it was over. It's been the same for twelve years. I found out quite early on that he was going with other women, three, four times a week. And me—once a fortnight, once a month.

"He can't make love to me because I'm his wife. Can you imagine? His father drilled into him the idea that a wife's a man's most precious possession, the mother of his children, to be honored in every way. To him what he does to me in bed dishonors me. You Westerners think that Arab men are great lovers. Ah yes, they talk a lot about it and they pride themselves on being strong as horses, but most of them believe that a woman is there to serve a man—is that being a great lover?

"I found out there were psychiatrists in the West who specialize in problems like ours. We could go to one in America and no one here would know. He wouldn't hear of it. I begged him to let me be his wife and his prostitute too. He wouldn't even discuss it. So I read books and saw blue films; after all he's my husband. Wanting him to make love to me isn't a crime. One night I did something to him that I read about. It's the only time he's ever hit me. Then he cried, he was so horrified at himself and at me.

"It's still the same. And I've nothing in my life but him and the children. Would you believe that he finds a way for his girlfriends to see me? He says he wouldn't dishonor me by letting them think I'm ugly. Whose honor is he worrying about —his or mine?"

Many women are as sexually frustrated as Aisha. It's another of those Saudi contradictions; most Arab men believe that if you leave a man and a woman in a room together they (probably she, because she's weaker-willed) will rip their clothes off. That's the reasoning behind the segregation. At the same time they believe that men take pleasure from a woman physically, they don't give it. It's still true of some of the most educated men who've had more open, giving relationships at college in the U.S. Western women are one thing; their own are another.

Education has caused nearly as many problems for Saudi women as it's solved. Girls' education has been as emotional an issue in Saudi Arabia as busing in Boston. When the first girls' school opened in the 1960s King Faisal had to call out the National Guard. So, to appease the country's conservatives, schoolgirls spend half their time studying the Koran.

Nadia's not the kind of woman I would have expected to question her government's wisdom, but she's frightened that so much Islamic tuition is exposing her daughter to things she isn't ready for. "It's all right for some girls, they learn parrot-fashion. My daughter's intelligent, she thinks about things. The Koran says that a man and a woman must wash immediately after intercourse. My daughter came home from school one day very upset and asked me if we wash because what we do is dirty. What could I say? I told her, 'No, it's because it's more hygienic to wash.' To her, garbage is unhygienic, open sewers are unhygienic. At ten she's already convinced that if our religion says you must wash after love then the act itself must be dirty."

Nadia takes a long time to get the next words out. For a Saudi woman to admit to adultery needs a great deal of trust. A husband's honor is totally invested in his wife's purity. If she loses it and it becomes public knowledge, his honor's completely wiped out. The civilized Saudis no longer stone women to death for adultery—the family tries to hush it up, the husband accepts it (usually with bitterness) for the sake of not losing face. But if it gets out, his family may well make him divorce the wife, whether he wants to or not. So Nadia stumbles over her words:

"It does something to you when you both get up as soon as it's finished and go to the bathroom. I'll never forget the first time I made love to a European and he stayed there and held me. I felt closer to him than I ever had to my husband just because of that." Nadia goes to Europe alone, pretends to be Italian, and picks up men. She wants sex, affection, and she knows the risk she's running if she gets found out.

Sex matters, because there's so little else to think about or do. After marriage a woman's freedom is completely in the hands of her husband. Suppose she wants to work—she needs a letter of agreement from him to get a job. And even the most understanding of Saudi husbands has a cutoff point that leaves his wife stranded in frustration.

I'm staying with a couple who are unusually close. They're first cousins and grew up together. He tries hard to give her as free a life as possible, right out to the limits of what their traditional and prominent family can tolerate. She travels, goes out with him in Saudi, he discusses business with her (that's rare) but we've just come to *his* cutoff point. He and his wife spent a month together in London. She came home ten days ago because of the children and he got back yesterday. He's puffed up with pride; he's got a surprise for her. It's a $170,000 apartment in London; he saw it last week and bought it on the spot. She's furious and won't talk to him. He's bewildered and, not for the first time, I find myself caught in this curious man-woman confrontation that I'm not used to or prepared for.

The husband takes me aside. For a moment it's almost as if I'm one of the men. "You're a Westerner, you're independent —does that mean you wouldn't be delighted if your husband presented you with such a gift? Tell me, why isn't she happy? Don't you think she's being childish?"

Every fiber of me is tuned to his wife's fury. Of course she's angry; of course I think she's right. I try to explain in idiot's language: an intelligent wife like his might have liked to choose the apartment with him. It hadn't occurred to him, and it's his right to buy what he sees fit. It's nothing to do with his wife unless he decides it should be. He dismisses me sulkily and sends me back to the women, where I belong.

I feel for him: he's as disappointed as a small boy whose mother tells him to go out to play and then yells at him for bringing her his prize worm from the garden. I feel for her: she's as hurt as a small girl whose father decides she's grownup enough to have her own allowance and then tells her she's too silly to spend it properly. I feel for them both. Few Saudis are alone (their home either has relatives living in it, next door to it, or dropping in on it) long enough to make up these mis-understandings in a hurry. And the crazy thing is she wants this apartment. Why? That's the knockout: "Because in London, we'd be able to stay in watching television and I could sit between his knees and he'd hold my hand. That would mean very much to me. In all the years we've been married he's never once sat holding my hand at home here. We must think of his family and mine; someone's always with us. In London, yes, in Saudi, no." Create a situation so hidebound with rules and rights that a couple can't work out their own relationship as individuals and they must get stuck somewhere between adult and child.

Inevitably, some of the women trapped between the old and the new become bitches. They use their education as a tool to dominate their children. There've always been ambitious women here; they were locked away from the world, but they gained the power denied to *them* through their sons. Some worked negatively, some positively.

The most famous, the woman no one will talk about (you don't talk about royal women, remember?) is Princess Hassa al Sudeiry. One young woman who knew her well finally filled me in on Hassa's remarkable marital career.

She married her first cousin, King Ibn Saud, but they had no children so two years later he divorced her and palmed her off on one of his spare brothers. She gave birth to a son. The brother obligingly divorced Hassa and returned her to Ibn Saud. They remarried and she had seven sons and two daughters by him. She was the only one of Ibn Saud's countless wives to bring up her children herself.

She may have been uneducated but she dedicated her whole life to her sons, forging them together by sheer will power. They're known to diplomats everywhere as "The Sudeiry Seven," the pillars of the kingdom, Crown Prince Fahd and his full brothers. To the end of her life, Hassa drove through Riyadh rounding up her adult sons if they didn't appear at her table. No wonder they're close today.

Women who won't fight for themselves will nearly always fight for their children. Tasnim has always accepted her husband's dictates as law. But much against his will, she's forced him to send their sons abroad to school. Saudi women aren't allowed into, or anywhere near, boys' schools. They can't go and talk things over with the teachers—the teachers are men. Fathers are usually too busy to go and wouldn't know what to look for anyway when their wives sense trouble. It's not uncommon for a boy to start losing weight and dreading school. His mother can rarely get out of him what's wrong. The moment a boy's old enough to know his mother is "second class" and must "be protected," his instincts usually hold out against confiding in her.

It happened to Tasnim. She hates the emptiness of the house when her children are away and feels bitter that it's necessary. "People from your country envy us. They say we're so rich. We're not rich. We can't even educate our own children here properly yet. Learning is wealth. We're people of the Book, not of the moneychangers. How could I stand by watching both my sons so unhappy when I couldn't even talk over the simplest things with their teachers—did they need more help with this, should they be doing more homework? I'm prepared to wait for the changes that make my life hard. But I'm not prepared to sacrifice my children's future." It's creating new problems for her, small, hurtful ones. When her sons lived in Saudi, they accepted her veil without question; everyone's mother goes veiled. Now when they come home from school abroad, they notice her veil as they never have before. They react by ignoring her when they're traveling together. Tasnim talks to them; they stare straight through the black nothing before them. Each contradiction creates new conflicts, pushes Tasnim further into herself.

In public this woman looks like any other Jeddah trinket. But she's searching for herself, uncertain and alone. She wrote this poem for her husband:

> There is so much beauty
> Hidden in me
> Close your eyes and reach within
> Beyond that mask
> Beyond that skin
> There is so much beauty
> You could share with me.
> If you let me take you by the hand
> And see through my eyes
> You might understand
> I can sing with the wind
> Yet bleed with each and every wound.

I was there the day she finally steeled herself to read it to him. "Yes dear," he said tolerantly. "Very nice." I could have screamed for her. She said nothing. The book closed again.

The casualties aren't all among Saudi women There are Western ones too. Not so much among the wives. By the time a Western woman has gone through the struggles involved in marrying a Saudi (one British woman had had two children before her Saudi husband could summon courage to tell his family back home about her), she's prepared for the difficulties. The casualties are among girls like Nancy.

I get to talking to her at the airline office, and we go for coffee. She's waiting for a flight home to England In the way that you sometimes do abroad, Nancy unburdens herself to me, a stranger. She's quit her job nursing at a hospital in Jeddah. She liked the work, the pay was marvelous, but she didn't realize how different Saudi Arabia is.

"One day a young Saudi came into the outpatient department. He was literally tall, dark, and terribly handsome. He also spoke super English. I'd only arrived a few weeks before and I was very lonely. I didn't know what I was doing here and I longed for home.

"Then suddenly here was this guy who'd been educated in England. He's read the *Daily Mail* and shopped in Harrods. It was my world. He also made me laugh. I wasn't busy so we sat and talked, and when he asked me out I accepted. Naturally I liked him; he was the first decent person I'd met in weeks.

"One of the other nurses flew at me when she found out. She told me I was crazy. 'If you're going to go in for that kind of thing, why have you been putting off all those other men?' You get propositions all the time in my job, you see; you get used to it. I told her she was like all the rest, cynical. I also thought she was a bit jealous.

"Ahmad gave me a marvelous evening; he was so unlike the English men I'd been out with. Everything he said was so passionate. We started going out together, visiting friends of his. I've never felt so attracted to anyone in my life. It wasn't only that. He didn't seem to have anyone else to talk to. He had a wife. But I wouldn't have called her a wife. She seemed more like a mistress. He never talked to her, never spent any time with her, never took her to visit his European friends. He took me."

She keeps pushing the bangs out of her eyes. She has that white, papery look about her face that people get when they're about to crack. It seems she's the daughter of a country doctor. She qualified in London and stayed on there to nurse. She sang madrigals, went to concerts and on walking holidays in Wales. She answered an advertisement for nurses in Saudi Arabia one day when she was fed up. "Pure escapism; I never thought it would come to anything." Her parents were horrified. Her friends made cracks about her coming back with an oil sheikh.

"Ahmad's wife didn't seem real to me. He was unhappy, and I wanted to make him happier. He was miserable at work as well. He used to turn up after work fuming at the humiliation of being at everyone's beck and call the whole time. He used to say that at thirty-five he felt he was being treated like a child.

"Of course we wanted to sleep together after a while. He did from the start. But it was one thing wanting to. Where could we go? I was in the hostel, and all he had was his home. In the end we told some old friends of his, a German couple, and they said we could use their house.

"No one's ever made love to me like Ahmad. It was fantastic. He was very strong and passionate. But looking back I knew something was wrong. I had the queerest feeling that this was some kind of performance for him. He kept asking if it was good and he used words that must have come straight out of a European brothel. He got very angry when I wouldn't masturbate in front of him—he said it excited him. I've never seen anyone so angry. I was frightened of him. But then he changed again, and I forgot about it.

"Anyway, the German couple couldn't keep their mouths shut. They told someone, and it was all over the place in no time. Ahmad dropped me like a brick. He never got in touch with me again. I didn't understand it at first. Now I do. You see, deep down, I was like someone out of a brothel to him. And he was scared of his wife. The worst moment came when his brother came to see me. He warned me not to try to see Ahmad or get money out of him. And I thought I'd had a love affair . . ."

Nurses on contract have three options. They're sensible and find European boyfriends. They keep to themselves, save money, and go home. Or they see Arab men. And that the Saudis hate; they put guards along the roads near the hostels where they can. Every nurse who sleeps with Saudi men, let alone takes money from them, confirms them in their opinion that all Western women are up for grabs. Another contribution to the mutual fund of distrust.

But in case I've given the impression that Saudi men are all lecherous monsters, I'd like you to listen to this man. He's nearly forty, has a high government position, travels constantly and is still single. "I want to be married more than you can believe. Not just to solve my sexual problems, although they're not easy—I don't like using stewardesses or nurses, the women whose bodies are available. So when I come to Saudi Arabia, I switch off sexually. I block it. How do they say: 'sublimate'?

"But where will I find a wife? I want a companion. I'm too old to settle for a woman whose only ability is that she can give me children. What's worse—to be married to an empty head and live without caring for her or to live alone in a hotel as I do? We work here from early morning until one and then all afternoon and at night until ten or eleven. Don't you think I'd work better if I was married, if I had a woman I could talk to?

"There are several of us like this in the ministry. We believe in what we're doing, and Prince Saud, our minister, is one of the finest men in the country. You say there are women who would understand, who are interesting. How am I to meet them? I'm too old to let my family arrange it or rely on my sisters' reports from their tea parties. No Saudi woman can show herself to a man who isn't her husband, so what do I do?

"I would marry a foreigner, but what kind of foreigners do we meet? Seriously, what kind of women go out with Arabs in New York or London? I need a Western woman who's looking over my shoulder at our money less than I need an empty-headed Saudi. Suppose I met a respectable woman abroad.

We'd have dinner together for a few days and then I'd have to leave. Months later I'd be back; that's no use. I'm alone and it's a cold life. Find me a wife, I'll be grateful to you. As it is, men like me, we smoke a lot, we work a lot, we spend our time together. We're trying to build something. Not everyone's out for himself, you know. Some of us work like hell and we don't have private businesses, we don't have 'extras.' We do it because we believe in Saudi Arabia."

He's such a super man; my matchmaking instincts go into overdrive. I've met so many women in Saudi who are desperate to meet a man like him, but he'll never know about them. There's nothing I can do. Advertise? Broadcast? Drop hints? Not on your life. He's also a casualty. And I believe him completely when he says, "Working for our country takes all the hours, all the energy of everyone in the foreign service. If I won't settle for second best for my country, how can I settle for second best for myself?"

I see him at a party before I leave. He's charming, polite—totally impersonal. He gives nothing away.

There's another closed book in Saudi Arabia. This one you don't even hear about and, if you have any sense, you certainly don't seek it out. It's the secret world of security. I don't want to know about it but I can't help myself; I come across it by accident.

Some weeks after I leave Saudi I meet a man in Kuwait. He's sent by another who takes four days deciding whether or not he can trust me. Abdul Aziz Muammar stumbles in on me and spends two hours trying to make me tell him about Saudi. He is desperate to talk. His eyes half unseeing, his brain barely comprehending, he has the look of an animal that has just fought its way out of a cage.

Muammar has spent twelve years in solitary confinement in a prison in Hofuf in Saudi Arabia. King Khaled let him out, and now the Saudis are paying to send him to the finest eye specialist in Boston. The darkness has left him half blinded.

He says that he was kept in chains; those who are in the know confirm that it is likely. His crime? That, no one knows. He says he was never told himself. In King Saud's time Muammar was leading the good life as Saudi ambassador in Berne. Faisal took power, recalled Muammar, had him arrested, imprisoned without trial. He was released without warning when Faisal died. He sits in my room wearing a faded suit against the incongruous luxury of a Sheraton hotel. There's nothing I can do for him; nothing I can tell. We've come out of two separate Saudi Arabias.

Muammar says there were about seventy prisoners like him in Hofuf. And that was only one of the country's jails. When people who are interested in the country find out that I saw him so soon after his release they react. They want to know about him, where he is now. I can't say. The man crossed my life without warning. He disappeared from it, leaving only the memory of his pain. The years taken from Muammar are the other closed side of Saudi Arabia. Its security works secretly, efficiently, and incomprehensibly.

No one says or does anything to frighten me in Saudi Arabia, but I feel threatened constantly because security is so much part of the way of life here. On one level, it means that newspapers from abroad arrive on bookstands a mass of tiny holes, like lace. An army of censors goes through each one like silkworms in mulberry bushes. They cut out everything objectionable, like the word *Israel,* any obviously adverse comment, and endless other surprises.

In September '75 the British Embassy staff in Jeddah sat around mystified; they were trying to reason out why twenty-eight hundred copies of an inoffensive (yea, toadying) London *Times* supplement on Saudi Arabia, puffed out with advertisements, had ended up on a government bonfire. It took a Saudi official to point out to me the most probable boo-boo: an overenthusiastic education correspondent, helpfully trying to show that Saudis aren't all that different from the rest of the world, had written a story headlined: MIXED CLASSES AT SCHOOLS

PROMISED IN TWO YEARS. Nonsense. But even if it was a possibility, saying it out loud almost guarantees that it can't happen—that's Saudi for you.

On a more serious level, security runs the gamut from snatching men like Muammar, to carefully screening laborers from abroad who might foment political unrest. Men from the Yemen have the rawest deal. They come over the border from the impoverished republic to the south (no, not the Communist one, the other one) to build roads and mansions for the Saudis. Among them are bound to be Left-wing political agitators. The Cabinet has been so worried by it that they recently persuaded the Religious Research Unit (made up of the ultraconservative Wahhabi leaders) to allow them to order women's photographs to appear on passports. You can't imagine what a show-stopper this is for the Saudis—it means that male officials will have to unveil strange women, to match the faces with the passport snaps. Wow. Why did the religious leaders agree to this horrendous change? Because the Saudis knew that troublemakers were slipping in with Yemeni laborers disguised as women under black cloaks and veils.

It's safer not to know any details of the networks of paid informers, the men who do the dirty work, the all-seeing eyes, and I don't. But I do know that if any Yemenis come under suspicion, they're deported at once—and that's getting off lightly. The system is all part of keeping Saudi Arabia for the Saudis, safe and secure in its status quo—and the oil flowing to the West.

Now the ultimate Saudi contradiction must surely be the fact that the head of intelligence and national-security affairs hasn't a drop of Saudi blood in his veins. It's one of those more exquisite ironies that you might find hard to swallow. But no, it's true. Kamal Adham, the man who heads the intelligence system, is half Turkish and half Albanian. How did he get to this exalted position? An unbeatable combination of natural intelligence and nepotism.

Adham is the adored half-brother of Queen Iffat, the adored favorite wife of Faisal. During King Faisal's time Kamal Adham was as close to the throne as anyone. When Khaled acceded, Adham's enemies waited gleefully for him to fall; far from it. He had grown far too powerful under his brother-in-law's rule for King Khaled or Crown Prince Fahd to cream him now, even supposing they wanted to.

Queen Iffat also was "nonorigin"—Saudi by descent, Turkish by birth. She returned to her native country in 1933, unveiled (the reforming leader Atatürk had ripped the veils off Turkish women), and went to petition Prince Faisal for the return of her family property. Faisal took a look at her—which is more than he got of his former wives before the wedding night— and married her. It infuriated King Ibn Saud who, for years, nursed the grudge of her Turkish upbringing against Iffat. (No, that's not mentioned in polite company these days either.) Kamal Adham, Iffat's half-brother, came to join her as a boy; she brought him up as her own son. Are you still surprised at his position today? And there's nothing Saudi about Kamal Adham except his adopted nationality—least of all his personality.

He's secretive, shadowy, moves around the world almost without disturbing the air. To the merely curious, he's as accessible as was Howard Hughes. He travels not just on government business; he controls an intricate financial empire and manages a hefty chunk of the private fortune of his dead brother-in-law's family. King Faisal had austere tastes and thrifty habits; he died rich. Very, very rich.

Adham's wells of power bear deepest down through the connection he made with Egypt when, as the most trusted of Faisal's servants, he was the go-between for the country's reconciliation with Cairo after years of feuding. King Saud once wasted $4 million trying to have Nasser bumped off. Nasser almost certainly returned the compliment to brother Faisal.

Today Adham is still Saudi's Mr. Egypt, in close contact with President Sadat, channeling millions to him for arms and aid. Adham has an organization of his own in Saudi that can bypass officialdom. If anyone runs into trouble in Riyadh or Jeddah, Kamal Adham would be the man to go to—he has the power to make decisions and the sophistication to weigh the decisions he's making. Anyone with a less than clear conscience should stay away from his X-ray eyes.

But there's another Adham, "a proper gentleman," as a friend puts it. He's the top of Jeddah's top group. When he's at home he entertains. There are no invitations; you're either in or out. At home he's a character that only Hollywood or Saudi could have created.

12

THE FILM STRIP

KAMAL ADHAM LIVES BEHIND WALLS THAT SEEM TO STRETCH forever. His garden is the next signal of his position: jungly trees, flowering plants, and spotlit greenery everywhere. This in a climate that's steamy hot in winter, humid hell in summer. Third giveaway: Adham's driver dozes over the wheel of a Rolls in front of the door. Anything might happen; a call may come at any time.

I walk into his house; the next James Bond producer could do worse than borrow this spooky, sophisticated set for a location site. It's the only time I feel relieved at being able to hide inside the one smart dress from my suitcase. It's intimidating; there are marble floors, white walls, beautiful carpets, and chinoiserie. It isn't splashed about the place as a proof of wealth. There are stunning museum pieces without the museum atmosphere, not a lapse anywhere.

In the large, low rooms The Group wander around, starting at the bar. It's the usual crowd, caressing their whiskies, talking quietly among themselves. But all the time everyone is aware of the presence of the round, blue-eyed Buddha in repose in front of his videotape set. Adham spends most of the evening glued to it.

The house, a mixture of exotic and calm, is an extension of

Adham himself. He has a way of manipulating his acolytes. Every now and again they approach tentatively, drawn into talking at him. He takes it in and gives back nothing, just that gentle, all-knowing smile. Every now and again he addresses a question at someone. It sounds like a riddle from an oriental sage; it may be nothing more complicated than a question about a recent trip abroad.

The complex and active mind of this guardian of Saudi Arabia seems bored by his groupies. And yet he's pleased to have their presence. Most of them perform a service for him in one way or another. Under the grandeur and charm I sense in him the Turkey where he was born. It was a sick, dying old lion watching its empire disintegrate. Turkey was rampant with cunning, treachery, decadence; at the same time there was learning and a passion for reform.

At first I stay away from him, trying to get some measure of the man. Most Saudis are still naïve enough to confuse modern Western journalists with traditional Arab poets, who come to eat at the great man's table. After dinner the poet would return the hospitality by composing a eulogy in his host's honor. He'd concentrate on the heroic qualities and ignore the shortcomings. Adham is far too subtle, far too aware to think that's how I see my function. I know it from his first shrewd glance; but he's calculating how far I've come here with an open mind. There is a court poet here tonight; but one of the finer brands. Kanaan ("I'm named after Canaan, it flowed with milk and honey") al Khatib was King Faisal's *homme de lettres*, there to praise the heroes and overlook the warts. His heart is worthy of his name and, noticeably, he's one man in the room Adham's mere presence doesn't cut down to size. Is there anything this adorable old man in his seventies hasn't done? Al Khatib taught five British ambassadors to the Mideast at Beirut University before going into the oil-exploration business. He lost seven friends in three plane crashes; he was the only survivor of one and saw some of his closest friends burned to death.

He prefers to remember the good days. Like the night he

met Paul Getty at a cocktail party in Paris, and Getty persuaded him to be his representative in Jeddah. He quit that job when Aristotle Onassis passed by and enlisted his help. The Greek was working out an agreement with Saudi Arabia to control the country's entire oil shipments. That deal collapsed unexpectedly; it was undermined by the CIA egged on by the worried oil companies.

Nevertheless, al Khatib enjoyed working for Onassis, nearly as much as working for the Texan oil billionaire, H. L. Hunt. But while he was enjoying that job an order came from the Saudi court: Return and work for Faisal. He stayed by the King's side until his death. Once a year he composed a poem for the Haj to be recited in Mecca, and he spent many months in London minding Queen Iffat while she was having a hysterectomy. ("She had two of her daughters with her and they were always dying to go out. They danced me off my feet." Impossible, he's still too full of energy.) Al Khatib read and translated Western newspaper clippings for King Faisal and compiled reading lists for him. "I came across him reading Karl Marx one day. Not my idea; he said he had to understand the man's inferiority complex."

At this point I feel Adham's eyes boring into me. He gestures for me to join him on the sofa. He's made his decision one way or the other. It seems favorable; he starts talking about his nephew, Prince Saudi ibn Faisal, the country's thirty-six-year-old Minister of Foreign Affairs. He's the one son of King Faisal who's making an imprint on Saudi power; and Adham is close to him.

When I ask anyone else in Saudi Arabia why Prince Saud made his debut on American television sporting smart Western clothes instead of the all-important national dress, I get any amount of evasive answers. Only Adham has the confidence to tell me the truth.

Some time before, an in-group had sat down with Adham and examined Prince Saud as a "marketable commodity." With his Princeton command of English, his economics and oil-affairs background (he was Petroleum Minister Zaki Yamani's second in command before taking up foreign matters), he seemed a good bet to overcome the image of Saudis as hawk-eyed predators in white sheets. Yamani had been used as an experiment. He appeared at OPEC press conferences in a suit, he looked "normal" to Westerners, they trusted him. Having put the commoner's toe in the water, time was right for a royal dip.

Cover Prince Saud's dark features with a headdress and he looks as much of a Chicago heavy as his father. Leave his head uncovered, get him a good haircut, allow his stylish sense of Western dress to come through—and he makes an impact. Adham, smart as a whip, sees slowly but surely that the plan is working.

He asks if I saw Prince Saud's TV debut on "Meet the Press," the hard-hitting interview program. "No, I've only heard about it." He'll give me a treat and run through the videotape of it. The acolytes, who talk and cluster around the drawing rooms during Adham's customary feast of movies, instinctively know to fall silent in admiration.

Indeed, Prince Saud is a TV natural. He knows when to make the solemn, carefully worded reply, when to bite back, when to allow a personal show of emotion or humor to seep through. The Saudis could well be backing a winner: at last the Saudis are learning to stop bleating that the devil (Zionism) has the best tune. They've found one of their own. Prince Saud easily wins "Meet the Press" on points.

Adham sits silent afterward, savoring his nephew's celluloid success. Al Khatib dances around the room in his black silk *thobe,* tailored in Hong Kong. He's praising the prince with the same fervor with which he once recited one of his poems before a crowd of fifty-four thousand at a state affair in Algeria.

When al Khatib's flow of adulation finally runs dry Adham continues. He fills me in on the background of Prince Saud's appearance at the opening of the last United Nations General Assembly. Nearly a bad moment there. Adham and Saud were ironing the English speech in a Waldorf-Astoria suite. Someone remembered in the nick of time that Saudi Arabia had led the battle to get Arabic recognized as an official UN language. The political ramifications were obvious.

Prince Saud addressed the UN in Arabic, to the inevitable boredom of the press corps. Adham was disappointed; in English, Saud's charisma could have been irresistible. Never mind; there's time.

Slowly I become aware of resentment rolling across the room toward me. The attendants feel I've had more than my share of the Buddha. I retreat, regroup, and look around the room. It isn't polite to glue myself to one guest, so I can't go back to al Khatib. Where's Fouad Rizk? This Lebanese smoothie is now so rich that his arrival at Adham's anonymous apartment suite of offices in London is treated like a holy visitation. Fortunately, he's not in sight; here he's a creepy hand-kisser, watching Adham with an anxious attention that reminds me of an ambitious office boy. And Philippe Trad? He's a solid, humorless, neckless bull and another of Adham's small fry who seems so important away from The Presence. He's playing bartender.

Eavesdropping is far more fun. "Where's Kanan living these days? Oh, the Kandara. He's rented his house, hasn't he? But then who wouldn't. I rented one of mine to an embassy six months ago for fifty thousand dollars a year and now I wish I hadn't. I could get seventy thousand for it easily today." That's how fast rents are going up in Jeddah.

On I go. "I feel sorry for Mohammed; that huge yacht of his in the Creek and no one, absolutely no one will go near it. Well, it's such a bother. I'd rather sit around the pool. And do you suppose he's ever *sold* a Stutz? He's given *four* already to King Khaled's son." Mohammed Ashmawi has the Rolls and Stutz agencies. Stutz, Elvis Presley's favorite, is the world's most expensive car ($50,000 in America, heaven knows what here), gold-trimmed, mink-rugged. These Saudis think it's showing off.

No one talks about problems in the abstract. It's all money, possessions, swapped anecdotes, children, and, inevitably, doctors. Beirut is being ravaged. There's hardly a person in the room who doesn't know someone who's been killed. It's passed off with: "Isn't it dreadful? How many died today?" It's a wariness of talking politics; it's also a reflection of a society where people are brought up not to ask questions. Business is where they shine; all that Levantine intrigue is perfectly safe.

At one o'clock it's time to move into the stately dining room. Adham's "at homes" are a new development instigated by his wife. She was once a great beauty; now she's an attentive, sad-eyed hostess. For years Nadia Adham was left alone night after night while her husband went off to visit the men. A few years ago she suggested that he bring his friends and their wives to the house.

It means catering in style for a multitude: ten or sixty may turn up. It means staying up until three, four in the morning while her husband wastes his stamina running one bad movie after another. It means having some of his entourage, whose company Nadia Adham would surely not seek out otherwise. But it's brought her husband back home.

He treats her with the greatest respect. She treats his guests with the greatest kindness. "Good-bye, I do hope you enjoyed yourself," she says as I leave. Far more than she must have. As the door shuts behind me the sound of another movie fades away.

The movie king of Jeddah is Mohammed Ashmawi. He lends films. You can't imagine how important that makes him to The Group's social life. It's as if he controlled the biggest stash of cigarettes in a POW camp.

I see more movies in a week in Jeddah than in a year, maybe two, at home. Everyone's into video. They don't bother with their local TV station; they gobble up cassettes at the rate of two or three a day. That's where Mohammed comes in. He doesn't have a large collection of movies; he has a library of them.

"Oh, no, not *Serpico* again. Ring Mohammed, see what's new over there." I have by now heard so much about Mohammed that I can't resist a visit—his forlorn yacht parked in the Creek, shunned by The Group, the four Stutz cars gracing that royal garage, all those telephone calls begging for new movies. So far I've only glimpsed him at parties, he's an Adham regular.

By the time his phone directions have, as usual, taken in a gasoline station and a set of traffic lights, one permanently green, the other red (typical Jeddah), we both give up. He sends his car for me, or rather one of his cars. The fur-lined navy Lincoln parks outside his house next to his Bentley, his Rolls, his Stutz, his Ferrari, and his "Cadirolls" (a long sleek mongrel of dubious ancestry).

It's four in the afternoon. I've left one lunch party, to find Ashmawi sitting down for lunch with his children (his German wife Elfrida is delivering again in Munich) and an unspecified stewardess. I get the feeling that this isn't the best moment to arrive. But nothing will satisfy Mohammed Ashmawi's hospitality until I join in yet another lamb feast.

His son Ahmed, twelve, and daughter, Neveen, nine, have discovered Harvey's basket overlooked in the juggernaut loads of furniture and packing cases that have arrived from Munich. Mohammed's wife has been looting department stores. With the ports so clogged up that there's a three-month unloading delay, he couldn't ship the stuff. He flew it in. That's not an expense to worry Mohammed. Harvey is outside with the baggage, locked in his basket. He's glad to be allowed out at last to stretch his tiny legs.

Harvey's a chihuahua. A nasty, twisted-looking thing that once had an accident down a flight of stairs. I wouldn't blame the person who kicked him. Nor, from the expression on his face, would Mohammed. Like most Arab men, he shrinks at the thought of a dog in the house. But it's "the thing" for women to have now. I keep finding these small ferocious creatures glaring at their mistresses' husbands. A glare by proxy, so to speak. The Koran has rules about dogs. No dogs; they're unclean.

Yes, but Muslim men are forbidden to wear gold, too, and

Mohammed has a gold watch on one wrist and gold cufflinks on both. Nobody seems to have one gold watch in Jeddah; they have a wardrobe of them. The men with a troublesome Koranic conscience settle for a wardrobe of platinum watches instead. But considering how little sense of time there is around Jeddah, watches are hardly functional utilities here. They seem to fill some ceremonial niche.

Mohammed, however, is getting very conscious of the passing minutes. He's an attractive man; there's no getting away from the fact, and the admiring stewardess isn't trying to. He's forty, smooth as easy-spread margarine, and can hardly rely on a couple of car agencies and a lending library of movies for a living. He doesn't; he isn't just a service center for the jet set, doling out cars and films. He plays up to the role all right, but he's another of those entrepreneurial conjurers whose tricks are many and mysterious.

Jeddah airport is one of his many launching pads. He refuels half the aircraft landing there ("over a million gallons a day during the Haj"). He only refuels half because he has the Shell concession and someone else has the other half for Mobil. A million gallons a day isn't bad, and that's only one of his outlets. They shell out enough for him to have homes in Munich and Beirut and four houses in Jeddah. Four? "My mother lives in one, my sisters live in one, you're in the third now, and then there's my favorite. It's a comfortable little house where I can turn off the telephone when I don't want to be disturbed."

The telephone in this brocaded, tasseled Vienna 1930s house does ring, however. It's someone else after *Jaws*. (*Jaws* was showing here simultaneously with New York—who knows how Jeddah's Group got a copy?) Mohammed promises to look and gets up swishing his *thobe* with the finesse of an expert. Don't be misled into the notion that a long dress makes a sissy out of a man. It turns male deportment into an art of self-presentation.

Mohammed pops over to see what's on the shelves of the library. The Group's famous Jeddah film library has a house of its own. A sexy secretary-receptionist, who would look at home on Madison Avenue, sits at her desk by the entrance, answering the phone, keeping the catalogs of incoming cassettes and outgoing borrowings. It's a full-time job.

After the chaos of the house, with Harvey scooting under the refrigerator, and the chaos of the yard where the swimming pool will be once Elfrida's loot has been unpacked, the library is organized as systematically as a college archive.

Jaws isn't in. There are six unedited versions of *Deep Throat* doing the rounds of Jeddah at the moment; but not from Mohammed. His shelves stock more wholesome entertainment. These are for family gatherings.

Another of those ubiquitous Saudi contradictions: I'm watching one of Mohammed's films after dinner with friends. It's a harmless, action-packed thriller with blood spilling everywhere. So far, so good. Nothing wrong with gratuitous violence. Dissolve to a naked woman climbing onto a battered man to offer solace. Grandma in the back row of the sofas yells into the darkness: "Cover your eyes everyone; you mustn't watch." We spring to attention.

In Mohammed's library there's a prominently displayed notice: Please return films in four days. Does everyone obey the rules? The secretary turns her eyes to the ceiling. "I only wish they would." I ask if he charges a lending fee. I choke on the words as soon as they're out. "Charge my friends?" His gray hair and smiling brown face turn to frost. The moment passes when I remember that he's another old boy of Victoria College, Cairo (along with those other tycoons, ministers, presidents, and kings hardened by 6:30 A.M. cold showers) and hurl that into the conversation as a coverup.

Surprise. The car salesman's patter grinds to a halt and Mohammed tells me of his time as a proper English preppie at a school set in a greensward in rural Hampshire. From there he went to another snobbish English private school, and from there I assumed he went on to a university. Back with a bump to the unexpected that I'm always expecting: "University? I didn't think it necessary. I took a course in shorthand and typing instead."

By now this ex-stenographer-typist is more than ready for a nap. He's sending me away in a Rolls this time ("last year I sold seventy"). I look longingly at the Stutz Blackhawk. "No, the Rolls for you. The Stutz is too ostentatious, it's more of a toy, really. Another time, though." Of course, there's always another time with The Group, if not in Jeddah, in New York or London.

The Rolls carries me off to a birthday party with some more friends. As a "treat" there's another movie. A Robert Redford opus. Mohammed's naturally.

CHAPTER

13

COMINGS AND GOINGS

AFTER JEDDAH YOU REALIZE HOW SIMPLE IT IS IN THE WEST TO guess about wealth; who has it and, usually, where it comes from. Here there are no recognizable clues. If a banker so much as breathes particulars of the money he has on deposit from these secretive people, he'll have lost their millions. No one's in any particular business, either. The age of the specialist hasn't dawned here; specialists are what you hire from abroad on short contract.

Possessions are no guide. The Saudis spend a fortune to live passably well in Jeddah. Inflation runs higher than 50 percent. That's why those London apartments go for such high prices; that's nothing compared to Jeddah. One man shows me the plans for his new villa: five bedrooms, five bathrooms. It sounds large, but he has to keep his mother, sister, wife, and four kids. Six months ago he made a deal with the builder, and it was going to cost him $200,000 before he got around to buying a stick of furniture. Now the estimate's over $300,000 and rising daily.

Mohammed Ashmawi lives in a home that would suit a surburban doctor in his sixties. How much he's worth is anybody's guess. There's no exchange control here, no band of IRS men with their detailed tax returns, no taxes for that matter.

So a man works for the government; it doesn't mean a thing. I'm with a low-grade government official; so low-grade that I don't like to watch him pay the bill for the Kandara's over-priced coffee. Then he reaches into a pocket for a handkerchief (he has a cold and many homeopathic remedies for it) and out tumble a three-karat canary-yellow diamond, an even larger blue-white marquise, and a good five-karat solitaire. He's a bit of a diamond dealer. He, too, is having trouble with builders. No, they're not building a house for him to live in; he's seen to that already. They're working on a few plots of land in Jeddah and Medina that King Faisal gave him. Anyone hanging around the court for long enough gets something for his services. And anyone in government can get to hang around the court sometime. When he gets through cursing the builders he starts on the cost of food. It's just like home. Two years ago a whole sheep, essential for those hospitable soirées, cost $20. Now it costs $100. When he starts on the problem of finding a reliable plumber it has an even more familiar ring to it.

The only place the Saudis do well is in the domestic quarters, where other Arabs do the dirty work. The Saudis treat their servants without a trace of snotty standoffishness; they feel as responsible for them as they do for their families. And they're as mean as hell with their paychecks. A gardener gets $125 a *month,* a cleaner gets $70, cooks come more expensive at $220, but those all-important drivers now command the impressive salary of $275 a month. Although they're foreigners, mostly Yemeni, a certain money militancy has entered the ranks of the sought-after men behind the wheels. Where would the women be without them?

But even knowing how much it all costs doesn't help you place a Saudi. There's no class structure as we know it here; just rich, very rich, and at the top there's the very rich close to the Right Ear. What can you tell from a man's long white national dress?

In the West you can weigh the cut of a man's suit, the material, perhaps his club tie. National dress is only a negative giveaway. It doesn't tell you if a man's rich, but you know he's poor if he turns up in the afternoon wearing the same *thobe* he wore in the morning. Everyone else changes several times a day. Even those expensive watches and cufflinks don't necessarily tell you anything. They may be something he couldn't resist in Cartier's last week; they could equally well be a gift from some higher being.

But the wealth is there, all right. It's what brings home the young men who have tasted the freedom of the West at universities in America and Britain. They know they'll be able to pick up enough money in Jeddah to buy their way into the high life, or the highbrow, whenever they want.

Some young men come back and kick a bit at first. I'm in a family living room with a new Ph.D. of twenty-five who's making rude noises about the gangsters shooting it out on the video. "I don't watch rubbish; Buñuel and Bergman are more my thing." He sniffs with disgust at the latest Harold Robbins his mother's digging into. "I'm reading an interesting book about Libya by Ruth First." But isn't she a Communist? If so, he couldn't be caught reading her. "Oh, is she? I had no idea. I'd better throw it away." He's learning.

Umm Khalthoum, then the Beach Boys, go onto the hi-fi. "I don't know how they can put up with that noise." What does he like? "I'm into chamber music mostly, but I do enjoy a good performance of Mozart, his *Eroica* symphony."

As he sits hankering for his Western newspapers ("Oh for the sight of the *Village Voice*"), he's indulging in that Saudi weakness; playing another role. It's those small mistakes that give it away again. (*Mozart's Eroica?* Come now.)

While all this is going on, his family is worrying needlessly about his future. Sooner rather than later he'll settle down, learn to make money and, relinquishing his last gesture of defiance, marry the first cousin already earmarked for him. Or he'll hold out and marry a foreigner, but they'll patch it up somehow. This boy wanted to come home.

Salim ibn Ladin didn't plan on coming home in a hurry.

He was having a marvelous time with friends he'd made at his coeducational private school in England. He was chasing around talking about becoming a doctor and doing some female anatomical research on the way. That was 1966; he was the son of the largest construction tycoon in Saudi Arabia and enjoying in London the proceeds of the palaces and roads his father built in Saudi.

Ibn Ladin, Sr., died in a plane crash. Salim came back to take over the firm and play surrogate father to his fifty-two younger brothers and sisters, one of whom wasn't born yet, two of whom he'd never met.

Nobody in his right mind would take Salim for a multimillionaire. He's Peter Pan, who looks about seventeen, is thirty-six, and lies through his teeth about his age. "Everyone has one fear. Mine's the fear of growing old."

He's sitting in a deck chair in his in-laws' cozy house on the Creek, an inlet from the Red Sea. He's wearing a swimsuit, and there isn't a hair on his youthful body or an ounce of spare flesh. He looks like any young man from Gimbel's shirt department having a day out by the shore.

A house at the Creek, however modest, is one reliable signpost to wealth. The Creek's a special place indeed. It's not only the water, the beauty of it, it's the exclusivity. For love or money you can't buy into the Creek. A large chunk is owned by the King's older brother, who has a fortresslike place of his own and keeps the rest as a public beach—although no Saudi who's anybody would be caught on it. Crown Prince Fahd owns a chunk, naturally. It's another well-guarded fortress.

What's left firmly belongs to a few families; top families. Ibn Ladin takes the Creek for granted. Everyone he wants to know has a beachhouse here. He's drooling over his baby daughter and being unexpectedly smashing to his wife, Sheikha (Sheikha Sheikha)—a frail but intense girl with deep pits under her eyes.

Sheikh Salim (as he's now called as boss of both the family and its business) didn't want to come home at all. He couldn't have been less interested in being a merchant prince. It wasn't his fault that he was the oldest son of a man who started life as a semiskilled bricklayer and died at the age of forty-seven, leaving an empire with five thousand employees.

It wasn't money that pulled Salim back to Jeddah. It was that Saudi conditioning that forced the responsibility on him. "I decide what schools my family go to, how much money they should have to spend. I even have to decide who my sisters can marry. My father was a great man—he couldn't read or write to the day he died—but in his own way he was a genius. He was very religious, worked fifteen to seventeen hours a day, and he never had a holiday in his life. I'm nothing compared to him, nor will I ever be. I don't want to be a slave to money or work. I like having a good time."

He gets by. He spends at least six months abroad, not always hunting new contracts. When his father died King Faisal put the family business under the control of a board of trustees, and he has younger brothers, who tower over him, to keep things going.

When he's at home he plays with his four private planes. "It's so peaceful up there; you look down on the whole world and you're as free as a bird. Why should my father's crash stop me flying? In our religion we believe it happens the way it's meant to. I'm even teaching my wife to fly. She can't drive, but there's no law to stop a woman from flying."

And he stays away from the office as much as possible, doing most of his business on the phone from his bed. One night I'm in the office with him when a bevy of Americans arrive from the airport, dazed by jet lag. The expressions on their faces when they finally meet the man they've hotfooted it halfway around the world to see make the irrelevant Salim even merrier. They have to swallow their pride at being confronted with this sprout of a man. Trustees or not, Sheikh Salim counts.

He doesn't take much more sense of solemnity along with him to the Dutch ambassador's celebrated Monday musical evenings, high point of Jeddah's cultural life. Salim's regular offering is a cherubic rendering of "Where'er You Walk." They're lucky to get off with that. He usually turns up at official receptions with his harmonica, which stunned one bunch of American corporation presidents hosting a banquet in his honor in the U.S. He gave a turn on his mouth organ instead of a speech. He doesn't like to take life seriously.

Sometimes his high jinks are even appreciated. A little while ago he arrived in Cairo to find no room at the five-star inn. Even a multimillionaire's temper tantrums wouldn't have budged that situation; but they're not Salim's style.

"If I play the French national anthem to you on my harmonica," he asked the surprised hotel manager, M. de la Porte, "will you give me a room?"

"That's a funny way to get a room," said M. de la Porte.

"It's the only way left," answered the pragmatic Salim. He played the "Marseillaise" and slept well that night.

But if you catch him in a fleeting, serious moment, he admits with sadness and humility that all that he has left to accomplish in the world is to make good marriages for a few more sisters, and satisfy his burning desire to own a Battle of Britain Spitfire. "We, the younger generation, we are nothing and we have nothing to be particularly proud of. It was given to us. Maybe when I'm dead, my son might say, 'You know, Salim wasn't such a bad guy.' That's all I deserve. It was the old guys who made what we have today."

His father helped to build this country. His money gave Salim ibn Ladin a taste for what it could buy. He's aware that men like him will come home for the money, but they'll change the country that draws them back, because they're softies compared to the old-style pioneers—and it's probably just as well.

If I have to explain to anyone why I feel so drawn back to Saudi Arabia, I know that it has something to do with one particular old-style family, the Alirezas, and all they represent.

On the left-hand side of the Mecca Road spinning out of Jeddah there's a particularly forbidding pair of gates. They open (rarely) onto a long, tree-lined drive leading to a wide turnaround with an island in the middle facing a large mansion smelling mustily of its history. It's a reminder of the 1920s when there were only four cars in Jeddah and one belonged to the Alirezas. The house stands empty now; it belongs to Mohammed, the family's stern disciplinarian and head. He's off being Ambassador to Paris.

Behind that stands another not quite so large affair. That one will soon be empty too; it belongs to Mohammed's brother, Abdullah "Ali" Alireza, now Ambassador to Washington. Scattered around the two mansions are a collection of other houses, which have been built over the years as the Alireza family expanded. Faisal, Ambassador Ali's half-American son by his first wife, lives in a California-style bungalow with his all-American wife, Bryony, and their two children. Faisal's soft guitar music wafts out of the front door as servants go back and forth between the homes.

This is the scene of that uniquely Saudi institution: the family compound. It's the base for a whole clan of brothers, cousins, uncles, and their offspring. No matter that some of the families living here are half American, that the whole family still bears that "nonorigin" label from their generations spent in Persia. *Plus royaliste que le roi:* the Alirezas are more Saudi than the most pure-bred Nejdi. Their compound is the outward, visible structure of that binding magnetism that brings home those foreign-educated young Saudis for whom money and obligation would not be enough. There are few such compounds left.

Early in the morning the steam heat of Jeddah gives me the lazy, languorous feeling I've always associated with Southern plantations, *Gone with the Wind,* and all. There's no one else up but servants (many of them former slaves), silently going about their business. About ten the families stir, mingling over any one of a variety of breakfast tables.

I go over to Hayat's. She's the wife of Paris Mohammed, looking after Washington Abdullah's grandchildren, in someone else's house for a few months, while their mother's in London (that's an extended family for you). Hayat speaks an English all of her own; a combination of flailing arms, flashing eyes, and a vocabulary picked up from four years spent watching TV in a New York apartment that she never left. At sixteen, Shereen, her eldest daughter, married a plastic surgeon and went to America while he finished his studies. She had one child after another; Hayat dropped everything and flew to New York to take care of them. She did the same for her second daughter, Hoda. She's that kind of mother.

Today we're off to the Alireza compound in the Creek. It's something that happens every weekend and it still takes two and a half hours to get everyone mobilized. There are problems. Hayat, hair awry, is panicking as usual, until she's reassured that the food *did* go off with the servants hours ago and that cleaning instructions *were* sent too ("I can't have my family finding an untidy house") and that trucks full of desalinated water *will* be delivered there shortly. In all this babble of excitement Fahd, twenty-eight, is looking unusually surly and threatening not to go. There's a rumor that the generator has broken down. What, no hot showers after swimming?

It's an unpromising start, but at last we're off—past the airport, past the cement factory, out past the staked-out plots of real estate, down to the Creek. This cluster of Alireza houses (fenced off of course) is centered around a large, terraced waterside residence under the trusteeship of Sheikh Ahmed, white-haired, dignified, acting head of the Alireza clan in the absence of cousins Ali and Mohammed. In their absence he's also minding the family firm. The Alirezas aren't the richest merchant princes in Jeddah, but they're "old money." They had it centuries ago, long before oil. Today there's a high-rise building going up in the center of Jeddah to house their multifarious interests.

Their entrepreneurial emporium stocks insurance, shipping (four 8,500-tonners), agencies like ITT—and Harry Winston. While we frolic at the Creek this weekend a $3 million diamond-and-emerald rope lies smoldering in Sheikh Ahmed's office safe. It'll be sold by next weekend.

Doing business with the West is no novelty to the Alirezas. In the 1930s another Mohammed Alireza ran a pearl empire stretching from Bombay to his shop in the Faubourg St. Honoré, in Paris, and his suite in Claridge's, in London, that in its time attracted the world's top jewelry dealers. Then came the Depression; the pearl trade crashed with it, but not the Alirezas.

What is remarkable is that throughout all these cosmopolitan dealings and three generations now educated abroad, the Alirezas as a clan have preserved their intense traditional family life. Ambassador "Ali" Alireza seems something of the odd man out—but that's because of a slight reserve in the atmosphere between his Lebanese second wife, Jugette, and his half-American children. Families like this are so close and warm that the slightest reserve stands out.

For the rest, their closeness is extraordinary. One of the family's other Abdullahs, a thirty-three-year-old, high up in government, was sent as a boy to Winston Churchill's old school, Harrow, the sausage machine for English gentlemen. He went on from there to Fitzwilliam College, Cambridge, and then to Berkeley. Friends say that when he came home he scrubbed his voice clean of any upper-crusty tones to help him fit back in. But today he's a conservative Saudi (of the best sort) through and through. He holds to the old values, to caring for his family and friends, to keeping almost the same standards abroad as at home (whether wintering at the family chalet in Évian-les-Bains, or summering in their villa in Cannes and suite in London).

At the Alirezas' over the weekend there's only family (and honorary family); no business entertaining here. There's a babble of children and a multitude of adults, all of whom respond with the same immediate physical affection to whichever child happens along. It's taken for granted that children scream and shout and get away with murder. But when they're told to do something, they respond without question. It's easy to see why so many first cousins marry in a family like this. It's not because it's arranged for them; when these kids grow up

the only members of the opposite sex that they'll ever remember being free and happy with are the cousins of their
childhood. Two of Ambassador "Ali's" half-American children
married Alireza first cousins—despite their mother's initial opposition.

The kids make all the noise they want, and we do whatever
we feel like. I go thrashing in the sea in a discreet coverall
one-piece swimsuit (no question of a bikini). But I'm free at
last. A procession of women go in to swim later, modestly clinging to their wraps until they reach the water's edge. Swimming
in front of men, even family, is still somewhat risqué; the
Alireza women only do it in the comfort of a flock. Motherly
Hayat reveals herself as a demon at backgammon, thrashing
whoever takes her on. She favors a flamboyant game with a
lot of clacking of men on the wooden board and frequent ex-
plosions of triumph. She wouldn't get along well in the Clermont Club but she's marvelous to watch here.

At night there's the inevitable film, projected against a
screen painted on the wall. It's three in the morning before
I get to bed, not lapped to sleep by the noise of the waves, but
drummed into it by the throb of the air conditioning.

At dawn a hardy few chug off on a fishing trip before the
sun gets hot. The rest of the clan don't stir until much later.
It'll be another relaxed day, punctuated by four mealtimes
(lamb and rice, of course, delicious salads and chocolate cakes
—every meal's more tempting than the last) and five prayer-
times.

The Alirezas are religious enough for praying to be personal
and unselfconscious. At odd times, not necessarily simultaneously, they go off and fetch their own mat, kneel in (I suppose)
the direction of Mecca, and pray. It's a personal, unspoken
commitment to the one God, in words that Muslims have re-
peated for centuries.

One woman doesn't pray all day. I ask her why not. "I can't.
I'm having a period," she says matter-of-factly. It's a stabbing
reminder of how the Koran, the foundation of their life and
kingdom, stresses the lowlier status of women. It's a status that

in Hayat's case has been intensified by some deep personal tragedies. Sitting here, her face full of animation and fun, she betrays no bitterness toward the past. But in the past Hayat was the only wife of Mohammed, the stern pillar of the family, who's absent in Paris. In the 1950s, Mohammed took another wife, Hamsa. Unlike many other Saudi women of that era, Hayat couldn't face sharing her husband. She preferred the pain of living apart. Not very far apart; she stayed in one house in the Mecca Road compound with her children by Mohammed, watching him and Hamsa, who lived next door with theirs.

Hayat's oldest son died slowly of leukemia in an American hospital two years ago. One day he felt better. He got out of bed, took his wife (the daughter of Washington's "Ali"; yes, his first cousin), one of his sisters, and his nurse out to lunch. He died the next day. And then there was the car crash in Paris. Amabassador Mohammed decided to take some of his family off to Deauville. He ran the car into a tree. Second wife, Hamsa, sitting up front, was killed instantly. The wife of Hayat's second son had her neck broken. An adopted daughter's skull cracked open, and Hamsa's youngest daughter, physically unharmed, saw it all.

You can't begin to understand anything about Saudi Arabia until you appreciate the force that keeps an old-fashioned family like the Alirezas together. It's so strong that after the accident it was Hayat, the discarded first wife, who laid out and washed the body of her successor, Hamsa.

PART

BAHRAIN—

"A GLIMPSE

OF THE FUTURE . . ."

14

PLAYING HAPPY FAMILIES

SHEIKHA MARYAM IS HOT. DROPLETS ESCAPE FROM HER SHORT, lustrous hair. Last week she decided that it was time for winter (a short cold spell that interrupts Bahrain's perennial steambath). Her summer clothes were packed away and thirty-year-old Maryam is wearing the latest Paris layered look. She could be the picture of elegance if only she wasn't so hot that when she finally discards her mauve Chanel-style jacket, wet stains creep from under her purple silky armpits.

Even an al Khalifa sheikha can't dictate to the weather in Bahrain. It may be time for winter in Maryam's mind, but outside it's still boiling. As the al Saud are to Saudi Arabia, the al Khalifa are to Bahrain, give or take a few differences. The size of the place is one; Saudi has gorged three-quarters of the Arabian peninsula. Bahrain amounts to a scattering of islands with one main one the size of Guam and a population the size of Austin, Texas.

But Bahrain is al Khalifa land, ruled by the family since 1783 when they swept out of Arabia, down the Gulf shore and over the eighteen-mile stretch of water to push the Persians off Bahrain and divide up the richest date gardens among themselves. Sheikha Maryam is married to her mother's aunt's son (a common family knot), Sheikh Isa ibn Mohammed. Since there are al Khalifa Isas all over the island, you have to get the ibn Mohammed right or you may end up visiting any number of other Isas.

Maryam and Isa don't live in a palace. They have a typically al Khalifa, comfy, two-story house, the decoration of which can best be summed up by mention of the Louis Quinze telephone.

They live in the suburb of Rifaa, the al Khalifa housing development where the family pile together about nine miles outside the capital of Manama. The focal point of Rifaa is the roundabout in the road outside the ruler's palace (he's another Isa and it definitely is a palace). Tubby topiary ponies trot on top of a neatly trimmed hedge around a ring of clipped green grass. The family's terribly proud of its leafy bit of highway sculpture, but it doesn't see how apt it is: the al Khalifas look like short, friendly ponies. There are some with big heads, some with saggy middles, and sleek economy-sized ones like Maryam.

She's in a quandary. Guests are coming for tea, there's not time to unpack the summer clothes, so she'll have to grin and bear it. No, grin isn't the right word. Maryam smiles. Anything larger would bare her only bad feature, a set of distinctly ponylike gums.

The manservant, dressed in white trousers and jacket, is getting the tea cart shipshape. It's a work of art in itself. A gilt cocktail cart by birth, it's now arranged with organdy-decorated plates of cakes, china cups, and a silver tea service. The only thing that doesn't rise to this *Ladies' Home Journal* standard of afternoon entertaining is the manservant's bare feet. He doesn't go in for shoes.

All this is in honor of Isa and Maryam's architect and his wife. They're bringing over the final drawings of an extension. By the time everyone has done justice to the cakes, Maryam and Isa have scrapped the idea of an extension in favor of gutting the house entirely and adding a new wing. Fortunately, there's a spare al Khalifa roof to occupy somewhere while the two years' building goes on here. And fortunately there's no lack of available funds.

Maryam begins conversations with the Bahraini slogan, "We're not rich, you know." You might even believe her. The furnishings reflect more of a yearning for elegance than its achievement. But not her clothes; little numbers she picks up in London—and Paris—and San Francisco—and Rio de Janeiro—and then there was that time on holiday in Barbados. She was sunning herself on the beach, and an American came up to find out where she hailed from. "I told her Bahrain. She was all over me. 'So you're the wife of an oil sheikh. I've never met a real live one.' It was nearly as bad as the time in New York when I went to change a few thousand dollars in the bank and the cashier asked me how I get on with my husband's other wives."

Few of the al Khalifas bother with several wives now. Trouble ahead. They still stick to marrying family, and inbreeding isn't the best thing for blood stock. In the old days number one wife would be a first cousin, but there'd be a foreigner or two among the next batch. Since they didn't hang onto these outsiders very long, the stock so far (apart from minor hereditary diseases like diabetes) has been bright and lively.

Sheikh Isa ibn Mohammed, Maryam's attentive husband, is a good example. He's an able al Khalifa, so he's been drafted into government to be moved around desks wherever he's most needed. It seems a waste of a qualified petrochemical engineer, but then engineers can be hired. Al Khalifas have to run the place. And no one is quite sure how many there are. A house-to-house count two years ago numbered them at three thousand in all. "To tell you the truth, I was surprised. I thought we were at least five thousand."

Once the maid has found something cooler for her to wear, Maryam's week perks up. She doesn't do very much, but she's happy looking after her two young sons. "I don't want any more children. My mother had ten, but in those days they didn't know how not to have them. I must say, though, it did give us friends to play with."

One of her friends, sister Sheikha (Sheikha Sheikha, you understand) drops by. She's Bahrain's Marisa Berenson, married with two children and taking a law degree by mail. "Poor Sheika," says Maryam, pouring a consoling cup of coffee, "she always has her nose in a book. Imagine, I have two sisters and a brother studying law and my father was a judge. My mother and I sometimes go mad listening to them. We housewives have almost nothing to talk about."

She and Sheikha have something important to talk about today. Maryam's youngest, aged four, might be getting spoiled. "Salman's going car-mad. He consulted me the other day about whether he should have a Lamborghini or a Ferrari. What can I do with him? I blame my nephew; he should never have given Salman a ride in his new Lamborghini. Now the boy thinks everyone has to have one." The nephew's twenty.

Isa ibn Mohammed comes home from the office. He's thirty-seven, comely, quick-witted, gentle, and very hungry. We go in to lunch, joined by Isa's mother, who lives with them and does the cooking. ("I can hardly boil an egg," Maryam.) This couple, veterans of some of the world's most select watering places and cuisines, sit down to—that's right—more lamb and rice. Maryam daintily uses her knife and fork. Her husband and mother-in-law forage with their fingers in the dishes, making a satisfying mess and a great deal of noise.

"If you're going to Kuwait," Maryam makes herself heard above the din, "you must go and see my best friend, the ruler's daughter. Mind you, she doesn't have much style. The first time I went to stay with her in Kuwait, I jumped into the swimming pool before anyone could warn me. Can you believe it, it was full of *sea*water. I said to her, 'How can you be so stingy? Your father's the ruler and you don't even have fresh water in your swimming pool.'"

I never thought it would come to this back in '67. I was spending a nervous time then in Aden at the tip of southern Arabia while the British army was signing off a colonial past with a certain ignominy. Soldiers were being sniped at, grenades lobbed, booby traps laid, and a security handout at the military base began, "The terrorists who carry out attacks are not noted for their courage." Neither was I. So the arrival on the scene of Sheikh Isa, ruler of Bahrain, had the romantic relief of Errol Flynn in the next to the last reel.

He presided over a regimental boxing match, and word soon got around that after handing out the army's cups to the winners, he presented his own consolation prizes to the losers—cars all around. When I finally got out of the Aden hellhole to Bahrain on the way home it felt as though I had arrived in a safe corner that would be forever Britain.

Since then Aden has gone Communist (the People's Democratic Republic of Yemen), the British have pulled out of Bahrain, too, and the ruler's lucky if he figures as an "also ran," as the new oil superstars farther down the Gulf race onto the world stage.

Al Khalifas like Maryam and Isa ibn Mohammed have settled down to nice, ordinary lives, trying in vain to keep up with the royals next door, and it all seems yawn-makingly dull. Only people who never have to go near the place still harbor the old glittering image of yesterday's Bahrain. A British newspaper recently ran a cartoon of Bahrain's busiest marketplace in Manama; it featured fat, gruesome-looking Arabs standing around, all wearing national dress, many carrying daggers at their waists. The only woman was a wretch heavily veiled in black. What a farce.

The marketplace of Manama is about as exotic as Broadway in August. It's full of European "ladies" with frizzy permanents, shapeless striped dresses, sensible sandals, and shopping bags. The distinguished international fixers that you find in Saudi Arabia give way here to low-grade mechanics and soldiers from the ranks who stayed on after independence for the good life they could never afford in Britain, for the cheap over-the-counter liquor and cigarettes.

The few Bahraini men to be seen in national dress (and many don't bother with it) aren't loitering with lascivious intent or murder on their minds. They're going about their everyday business and they haven't been near a dagger since they last saw one displayed on some collector's mantelpiece. The main attraction of the center of Manama is the post office. It's the only place in the Gulf where mail arrives from Europe without fail, sometimes in two days.

And here's the next letdown for those clingers to long-gone memories. The post office is almost entirely staffed by Bahraini women. The only apparent difference between them and the women behind American counters is that here they take time to be pleasant. Bahraini girls in mini-skirts and jeans work alongside men in offices, and when the day is over they climb into their own cars and drive themselves home.

Why is life so different for women here than in Saudi? Take any answer you like: it's an island, and you know what they say about islands (all that open sea and stuff). It never caught Saudi Arabia's fanatical Wahhabi disease; being stuck out in the water was like being in an isolation ward as far as that particular Islamic epidemic was concerned. It's never been locked away from the rest of the world as Saudi was (is?). And you can't have much in the way of deep-rooted, desert traditions on an island this size—nomads wouldn't have very far to wander, enduring the elements, braving hardships, in a place that's only thirty miles long.

And if all that wasn't going to make Bahrain something of a cultural hodgepodge, the British took care of the rest. Nowhere has the British character been so hard at work chiseling down the natural quality of a people within its "sphere of influence" as it has in Bahrain. If Saudi Arabia is the most Arab of Arab countries, in the sense of Islamic and desert traditions, Bahrain is the least. So, on the surface, its women lead the most normal of lives.

At first all this normality hits me hard. Coming straight from Jeddah, it's like entering a decompression chamber. There's that helpless feeling on the first day when someone suggests that I take a taxi to a strange place. For a moment I've forgotten how. I go on being "an Arab woman" until the silliness of it dawns on me and I wake up to my former self. That's on the credit side. On the debit side, I've been looking forward to

Bahrain for all those date groves, rambling gardens, green, green, green I've been hearing so much about. Green to anyone from Saudi: brown, brown, brown to anyone who's seen the Berkshires or Kentucky.

Still, it is a very *tidy* place. That's another legacy from the British. They inherited quite a lot from them, come to think of it: movie houses (the first opened in 1937) and, more important, driving tests. You can't believe the way Bahrainis drive. It's the same way they live: slowly and safely with both hands clutching the wheel. Notice the traffic lights; they work. If they're red, the obedient drivers stop. Notice the curbs, painted white, the pedestrian crossings, the alert traffic police.

That's what happens when you grow up. Bahrain's an adult country now, having to work for a living. In the 1930s, it enjoyed a brief reign as the richest teenager in the Gulf when its oil came in before anyone else's. During this time the crafty ruler acquired a considerable tract of land in Kuwait in return for loans to his impoverished fellow emir. It wasn't worth much then, but it makes the present ruler the landlord of the Kuwait Hilton, the American Embassy, and twenty of the smartest villas in town.

Just as well. Bahrain's own meager oil reserves are running out. Its main source of income comes from refining Saudi oil piped across the sea. It's a big comedown for an island that once strutted confidently under the protection of the British military, when that still meant something. That had its drawbacks, mind you. It meant getting stuck with a lot of bored army wives too snobbish to make pets of native sheikhs. But the sheikhs, their appetites whetted, took to flying in curvacious bunnies from European rabbit hutches. Today the army wives have been superceded by not-so-stuck-up wives of limp-shouldered British technicians, an array of stewardesses, some "resting," others with Gulf Air. But many of the sheikhs have taken to staying home with their families these days.

You don't have to spend very long with any family in Bahrain before the question of That Causeway comes up. Saudi Arabia is offering to pay for a highway to stride across their watery divide. It's a connection viewed with concern by both sides. The Saudis worry that their strict Wahhabis will zoom across at weekends to make whoopee with stewardesses and alcohol. The last thing these suburban-hearted Bahrainis relish is the prospect of becoming the garbage dump for Saudi repressions.

Like suburbanites everywhere, they've got personal garbage of their own to cope with behind those walls of respectability. There are over eight thousand certified alcoholics in Bahrain. It's typical of them to publish the figures. Ask Saudi officials how many alcoholics there are in the country and they'll say there aren't any because there isn't any alcohol. Bahrainis are too realistic to try the old-fashioned double-talk anymore.

Even before the al Khalifas the island had accommodated whole waves of conquerors (Portuguese, Persians, Omanis, Saudi Wahhabis) and shrugged them off again afterward. When the slave trade was on, Bahraini sea captains were in on it too. Before the Japanese came up with a cultured alternative Bahraini divers brought up the best pearls (Catherine the Great sported some of them). When the oil came they led the way in playboys and Cadillacs. Now respectability is the order of the day. At least that's what it seems on the outside. And on the inside? There are blue movies served as the last course at some select mixed dinner parties. Only I'm surprised; to the Bahrainis it's a nice way to round off an evening with friends.

Happily married couples go away for the weekend; not always together. Each drives off through the traffic to the countryside (all of five miles away); the rich wife is going to her "bustan," a gardenhouse by the sea. The husband is off to his. He's having a stag party; rutting on the menu, but not obligatory.

It's all discreetly handled, in the same way that they neither parade nor deny their private family shootouts.

Take Sheikha Dana for example. On the day her husband was doing the honors at Bahrain airport when the Anglo-French Concorde flew in supersonically fifteen minutes ahead of schedule on its much publicized inaugural trip, Sheikha Dana wasn't there handing out bouquets. Her husband, Sheikh Isa ibn Abdullah al Khalifa might have the crucial job of Director of Civil Aviation, but Sheikha Dana was clearing out the horse stalls as usual.

Sheikha Dana lives in the middle of nowhere, if there's room for nowhere in Bahrain. She's protected by salukis, six of them, that greet a visitor with paws on the fence and a hell of an unfriendly racket. The only other living things in sight are a bunch of sleek, leggy Arabs: the horses. Sheikha Dana wanders out to call off the dogs.

She's wearing her customary jeans and shirt with a jaunty red gingham cowboy hat. She looks about forty; she has the tough, sexy appeal of a woman who deserves flattery from men. When she takes off her hat, long blond hair tumbles onto her shoulders. Sheikha Dana is the Scandinavian who landed a Bahraini oil sheikh when the al Khalifa didn't go in for that sort of thing, not that they've changed much.

Her story is romantic enough. Dana's Swedish father worked in the Ukraine under the Tsarist regime. He married a Russian, and they both fled to Scandinavia after the Revolution. Their half-Russian, half-Swedish daughter hit the University of California in the late 1950s. "A Swedish girl in Hollywood in those days was really quite a sensation. They all thought I'd be modern and free."

A fellow student, an Arab, asked Dana to teach him Russian. "God knows why. He thought if he knew Arabic it would be easy to learn Russian."

His Russian didn't improve much but a year later they were engaged. After they married and Dana had her first child Isa ibn Abdullah went home "to see what he could do about the family and all that." Nothing.

Dana ended up living alone in Beirut with her daughter; the al Khalifa under the weaselly eye of old ruler Salman had decided to make an example of Isa. "They confiscated his lands" (a considerable blow to Isa; as the ruler's first cousin, he owned desirable slices of Bahrain). "They confiscated his passport, they even confiscated his name, he was just left with Isa ibn Abdullah, not even al Khalifa."

Isa resorted to cunning. Dana was living on nothing; he

reckoned the only way to squeeze his family for money was by divorcing her. "Through the mail I got a page torn out of a schoolbook. It said 'I divorce you' three times, signed with the al Khalifa seal and a check for eighteen hundred dollars. Isa put in another letter telling me what he was doing."

What was he doing? Marking time, hoping his family would come around. No way. He went back to Dana, annulling the divorce, and tried job hunting around the Mideast. The al Khalifa had got in before him; word went out that Isa ibn Abdullah was an outcast. No one would give him a job. Finally an English headmaster in Beirut took pity on him and offered him a teaching post. "Even before he had time to collect his first pay check, he got a telegram from home welcoming him back and forgiving him. It was brilliant on their part; at first they thought he'd give up and come running home. When he didn't they changed their tune."

But did true love win out in the end? Not on your life. This is Bahrain, not bedtime stories. Dana and Isa moved to the east coast of Saudi Arabia and he commuted to work on the island; she wasn't included in the "royal pardon." Then, for everyone's peace of mind, she was settled somewhere farther off, in Cairo. "They were difficult years for me. On top of the problems of being alone with two children, there were all the complications of being a foreigner alone in Egypt in Nasser's day." She's recounting this without a shred of self-pity in her deep, disturbing voice and periwinkle blue eyes. "One day a poor boy came to the door and asked me for some baksheesh for having put a tap on my telephone. What could I do? It was so funny, I just gave him the money."

Her daughter's American passport caused additional trouble when the Egyptians started throwing out Americans. "One evening they came for her. There was a knock on the door; I opened it up just a crack and suddenly there was this foot in the door. I didn't know just how large a foot could be. They took her out of bed. I followed them to the police station and only by some miracle managed to get her out."

Finally Isa ibn Abdullah struck a bargain with his family.

Not a bargain to every woman's taste, but then Dana wasn't given much choice. Isa promised to take an al Khalifa second wife and in return Dana would be allowed to come to Bahrain. She arrived with the stallions she had been breeding in Cairo. It was as well she had them along for company. She arrived to find Isa off to London for a year's course, taking his al Khalifa wife along. "I had a hard time, I tell you. The family were watching me like hawks, only waiting for me to put a foot wrong. But by the end of the year I had passed their test."

Ruler Salman had died; his son, the new ruler Isa, was altogether different. His new Highness appreciated Dana's flair for horses and decided to let her into his stables. She didn't become the royal groom or get paid for wielding a set of royal horse brushes on the muddy beasts, you understand. She's much grander than that; she *is* an al Khalifa, after all. She sort of nosed around inspecting what he had in the way of stock and was appalled at what she saw. For centuries Bahrain had the best pearls in the Gulf; it was also supposed to have the finest, purest Arabs. The ruler's stock bore as much resemblance to fine, pure, well-tended Arabs as a wagon of dented food cans bears to a properly stocked supermarket shelf. "There was chaos in the royal stables." Dana is still shocked at the memory. "Those that were kept under the eye of his Highness were too fat, and the rest, much of the finest Arab stock in the country, were being totally neglected. They were nothing but bags of bones." The grooms weren't "naturals" with horses; their only wish was to please his Highness.

The ruler didn't give her responsibility for running the stables, nothing as official as that; he shrewdly allowed her to indulge her breeding passion on his Arabs. Sheikha Dana dedicated herself to nurturing the stock; putting the purest stallions to stand at stud and getting them to service what was left of the purest mares. As a result ruler Isa's Arabs are once again the finest in the Gulf.

She's tackling the salukis, too. They're the only dogs Muslims are supposed to keep. "It's because they don't smell," says Dana, pushing furry coats into close sniffing distance. They don't.

What with improving the salukis and breeding the Arabs, she doesn't have time for much else. "Isa lives with his al Khalifa wife, and I suppose we've been effectively separated for about ten years. Although he comes to see me here every day, he lives there. But we get on so well now it's funny. We vaguely discussed the question of divorce once, but it wouldn't work because he wouldn't be able to come to the house anymore."

Sheikha Dana's daughter is away at college in the U.S., her son boards at a private school in England. She lives alone in a small bungalow covered in bougainvillea and exuberant yellow flowers. Only her husband (and one or two of the other al Khalifa who have made a point of keeping in touch) comes and visits. The English vet can't set foot in the house when he pays his calls, even though it's in a deserted country spot. The gardener would talk. Occasionally she and her husband entertain old European friends who pass through Bahrain. The friends, understandably, find it embarrassing when Isa proudly presents Dana as if to say, "Look how well she has survived."

Excursions into the capital open her up to Bahraini directness, so she keeps to the bungalow. She once ventured into a flower shop in Manama and the Bahraini girl assistant asked who her husband was.

"Isa ibn Abdullah."

"An Arab. What's his surname?"

"Al Khalifa."

"So you're *that* Dana. You're not sleeping with your husband anymore I hear. How do you manage?"

"Yes, I am that Dana," came the proud reply. "Yes, my husband lives in a separate house. But whatever passes between us is, I hope, our own affair."

In Sheikha Dana's bungalow there is a private display of photographs. There's an old family portrait of her father's Swedish family. There's a picture of Dana's two children when they were young. And there's a photograph of a fragile blonde and a startlingly handsome Arab. It was taken soon after Sheikh Isa ibn Abdullah al Khalifa had married Sheikha Dana. Radiant newlyweds.

CHAPTER

15

"WE'RE NOT RICH, YOU KNOW"

IN SAUDI ARABIA THE AL SAUD ARE ALL POWERFUL, AND THEY'RE richer than the richest of their subjects. For even the biggest merchants there, safety means conformity. That's why when you've met one Saudi-based multimillionaire you've met the lot, give or take a private jet or two. Not so Bahrain.

There aren't all that many multimillionaires to begin with, and the al Khalifa are always running into money troubles. They got used to the British keeping their housekeeping in (relative) order and doling out allowances when they ran short. As a result, half a dozen merchants support the finances of the al Khalifa dynasty. It makes for amusingly delicate relationships between the royals and their local sugar daddies. The al Khalifa are autocratic rulers, up to a point, and they're chummy with their friendly rich merchants, up to a point. Need glues them together. The rulers need the merchants and the merchants sure as hell need the al Khalifa—for better or worse, they stand between them and socialism.

This mutual-support system gives the merchants freedom to develop their own individuality. Living in such a small space makes them tolerant of one another. They can go too far, though. Even the Yateem family had a nasty moment when their son slipped away to England to marry an al Khalifa girl.

And the Yateems are right at the top; the ruler has regularly dipped into their pockets when he's been in a fix. But taking away a royal brood mare is much worse than taking in a Nordic blonde.

Are there any rich left in Bahrain? Of those six thousand Arabs in the peninsula who spend $500,000 a year on jewelry, six are from Bahrain. They are the same families who support the al Khalifa. Not that you'll see the wealth hanging around their necks; it's not done here. What they buy is probably locked away in safety vaults in foreign banks, along with most of their money. There are still a few rich left; how much of their wealth is still on the island with them is something else again.

The Yateems are rich; the Kanoos possibly richer. "It's only a matter of a few millions here or there, but for my money I'd take the Kanoos any day," as one merchant banker put it over one too many drinks. General Motors, Goodyear, Champion Spark Plugs, English Electric, Kelvin Marine, Toyota, Wimpey —the Kanoos' interests go on and on. Not for nothing is this the only Bahraini family that Khalifa ladies regularly visit with for coffee mornings.

Maryam Kanoo's home is a cut above most. This means that it's everyman's idea of the dream holiday villa in Naples (Florida, not Italy). The furnishings are fey Arabia toned down to Ideal Home proportions. Mrs. Kanoo is tidy-looking, like the country's roads. She's big, clean, wearing a nicely made tangerine-colored dress. There's a gaggle of Kanoos present. They all have the same face, not unlike a friendly anteater's, with long, dark hair.

The only way you can judge Kanoo wealth from their home is by noticing what's *not* here. It's more negative distinctions; no peeling wallpaper, no lifting tiles, no warping doors. But notice who *are* here: the al Khalifa are present in force, including no less a personage than the ruler's wife, Sheikha Hasa, with her sister, her daughter, and a spare daughter-in-law. To call this a coffee morning is a typically Bahraini understatement. The board is groaning with stuffed pancakes, meatballs, cheesecakes, tartlets, cinnamon squares, almond mounds, poppy-seed bonbons—and it's only an hour or two till lunch.

Someone's dwarf tomato plants are doing well this year: "Can my man bring you some? And I wouldn't mind a couple of your rose cuttings, the one by the door."

"You know, when I first got married I used to do all my gardening myself. But it's no good, the heat's too much for me. But at last I've found a Pakistani I can really trust."

Who would expect to find horticultural freaks in a place like this? But here they are. It's another of those British legacies, a hankering for rural cottage gardens. If they're not swapping plants, they're chatting about the problems of foreign domestics. At least there's no language barrier. Bahrainis and Pakistanis learned from the same colonial British grammarbooks.

Talk of tea roses is gently but insistently interrupted by the latest visiting peddler. Marina Volochine, a Russian who got out by marrying a Greek diplomat, is trying to interest gardeners' corner in silver-covered, jewel-embedded Korans, "a very special gift for your husband."

It's strange that Europeans, raised on the idea of pushing Bibles out to all and sundry, took so long to wake up to the killing to be made pushing Korans. In the summer of '75 one of the richest bookdealers in the world, H. P. Kraus of New York (included in his list: a $2 million Gutenberg Bible) bought forty-four loose hand-written leaves of a tenth-century Koran at a Sotheby's auction for a mere $2,400. Word went around, and only then did the speculators realize that there was a new vein to mine.

Marina's coffee-morning Korans aren't rare old editions; their attraction is in her handmade covers. But her Korans simply aren't moving. It's not that she doesn't know how to sell. She hits just the right note of threadbare breeding so familiar in Russian emigrés. She'll set them up but she won't outshine; she's the wife of a diplomat, after all. Her problem isn't one of language, either: one esoteric group she charms in Russian, the next in French, and she tries her luck in English on the row of al Khalifas (they do tend to clump together). The problem: her work is too subdued; she's used silver where gold would do, an amethyst where an emerald would go so prettily.

The waiting game, Bahrain-style, is underway. Everyone's waiting to see what everyone else thinks. It's an agonized moment for Marina. Everyone's delightful, polite, but noncommittal. The moment breaks. Someone says that someone heard that Nevine was thinking of buying a Marina piece. And what's more, Nevine's mother had declared it to be *charmant*. Ah, Nevine . . . that's all right. The Korans start moving.

Who is this paragon of taste? It turns out that Nevine is a more prize variety of Alireza. Yes, there's another clan of Alirezas in Bahrain. But unlike their Saudi cousins, these Alirezas are not in the first league, more of a reserve, one might say. The Alirezas in Jeddah have a hint of "nonorigin" as it's tactfully put, around their name. But they're too powerful and respected for that Persian connection to matter.

The Alirezas in Bahrain live on a knife edge. Here Iran is a *threat;* it only dropped its claim to owning this country in 1970 (and that was after some secret international dealings). Hailing from Persia is a liability here. People will forget it if you marry a well-born Egyptian like Nevine. Nevine Maghrabi is Abdullah Alireza's wife. That makes Abdullah socially acceptable. People don't forget the taint of Persia if you revert and marry from the Iranian mainland as elder brother Mohammed Alireza did. What makes it worse is that Mohammed is the family honeypot; he's got the warmth, charm, and spontaneous affection of the Jeddah clan. But watch the reaction at the mention of Alirezas. Frown. "They're not typical. They speak Persian at home, you know. What do you want to spend time with *them* for?" I say that it's Nevine I'm going to see. "Oh, you mean Nevine. That's all right, that's good."

Nevine's front door is opened by the most spectacular man. He's massively tall, pitch-black, majestic, and big-bellied. This major domo is dressed from head to foot in an emerald green caftan trimmed with gold. His white headdress completes the dazzling effect.

It's a very small house for such a big man. But after all those other houses I can hardly believe my eyes. French eighteenth-century furniture of the finest quality and exactly the right silver knickknacks. No fakes here. Nevine's mother understands that you don't put whipped cream on truffles.

Nevine's mother is a proper lady. She's here to supervise the forthcoming birth of her latest grandchild, just as she was here to supervise the birth of Nevine's house. "When I got married," says the heavily pregnant mistress of all this, "I swore I was going to live in an entirely modern house, I longed to get away from all that French stuff I'd known from childhood. But after three weeks I telephoned Cairo in desperation: 'Mama come.'" Mama flew in with the paneling, furniture, and all. Mme. Maghrabi is the darling of Bahraini drawing rooms. ("Isn't she perfect?" breathes *le tout* Bahrain.)

A bit too perfect for my taste, certainly a bit overpowering. But Madame is what fixes Nevine's retiring husband, Abdullah, fine of form and face, on the right side of the Gulf. Nevine herself is sweet, distinguished-looking, but no pusher.

It's time for lunch. There are three cut-crystal glasses by each place at the table. When it's been established that I don't drink, the wineglasses (for red and for white) are taken away. The Alirezas don't drink either, but they didn't want me to feel that I couldn't. It's the only meal of such sophistication I'm served in Arabia. The vichyssoise ("Mama's recipe") is terrific, and the chives are fresh. The presentation of the *canard à l'orange* ("Nevine's specialty") is ritzy and restrained. The meal may be Europe; the conversation is Bahrain. Sitting opposite me is discontented Samira, Abdullah's niece. Samira, twenty-four, single, dumpy, and aggressive, has been giving trouble. Nevine, in her sweet, winning way, is trying to get through to her. Samira has come straight over from the boutique she runs in the middle of Manama. She wears blue jeans, T-shirt, and a rebellious look. Running a boutique isn't the issue. It's a chic thing to do: Yateems do it, even al Khalifas do it (though royals don't work, naturally).

Briefly, this is the situation: a girl from Samira's background can run a business, a car, work in her own shop, but she has to be home by dark, isn't ever allowed out alone with a man, and is expected to stay in every night with the family. No one is suggesting that Samira's dating. (Unthinkable.) But she's kicking at the restrictions. This takes the eccentric form of staying late at work to avoid going home. For several nights now she hasn't closed the shop until after seven. "I mean it's not safe in Manama at night. Any man can walk through the door," explains Nevine gently. Samira glowers her way through the meal. Lunch is finally over; the family debate will go on.

You might think that none of the great merchant families could be more different than the Kanoos and the Alirezas—that is until you meet the Fakhroos. They've done all the usual things; brought slaves from East Africa; shipped spice and wood from India, and changed at the right time to those money-spinning agencies. Ahmed Yussef Fakhroo, one of the grand men of Bahrain, is devoted to the ruler. "He's one of the finest men in the world," he says with tears in his eyes, shuffling his carpet slippers. He catches the glazed look and pulls himself up proudly. "I can see you don't believe that. But of course you wouldn't know that I don't need to praise him. I am not dependent on him." I know that only too well; it's the other way around.

But Ahmed Yussef is the last of a line. Not one of his eleven children will go into the family business. They've gone professional: a teacher, civil servant, engineer, architect. This is what happens with time to the entrepreneurial empires. "He's both proud and disapproving," says his architect son, Abdurrachman. "He's like a father whose child is caught driving at the age of ten. It may be wrong, but it's clever." Abdurrachman, curly-headed, spilling over with indignation at the world, rails loudly against his country's inefficiency and the suppression of free speech.

(The Bahrainis experimented with a National Assembly to let off steam. So much steam burst into the hot air that Saudi Arabia got the jitters and leaned on the ruler. The fractious, mainly Left-wing Assembly was dissolved in '75. No one's seen any ballot boxes lying around for the next.)

Free speech? In Saudi Arabia, Abdurrachman couldn't talk the way he does here against the government. And even the Fakhroos have embarrassments they don't talk about. The father may be secretly satisfied with his sons, who refuse to run after money. He makes no mention of the two Fakhroo cousins who were last heard of studying at the university in Beirut. Later they joined the Dhofari rebels, the Communist-backed guerrillas fighting against the Sultan of Oman farther down the Gulf. They haven't been seen since. That's even worse than pinching an al Khalifa girl; that's not simple bad manners, it's dangerous.

But for the time being the top families tolerate their little differences, overlook one another's little failures, and pull together, doing business as they always have. They support the al Khalifa financially and each other socially.

Nowhere else around here but Bahrain would you find the wives of the ruling family and merchant princes grouped around a bed in the maternity ward of the local hospital. Nevine has had her baby. Everyone's sent flowers, and Nevine looks wonderful. There's another reason this scene couldn't happen anywhere else in the Gulf. Bahrainis trust their hospitals. Everyone else, everywhere else, who can afford it flies to Europe to deliver.

Bahrain was the first to deliver oil. It will be the first to run out of it. So don't be misled into thinking the disproportionate number of bankers you see flying in from Europe and America are here for the island's pickings. The Bahrainis are bidding to become the offshore banking center of the 1970s (more respectable, they say, than the Bahamas or the Cayman Islands). To induce the bankers into luxury, streamlined offices in Manama, the government takes a paltry license fee of $24,000 a year from each offshore operation that promises to keep its books in Bahrain and make its deals elsewhere. That's not a hard one to keep. All the big deals are farther down the Gulf.

Bahrain has much to offer—that postal service, virtually instant telephone calls abroad, and a pleasant enough social life if you're "in." Bahrain is the only place anywhere around that isn't crazy in some way. And it *does* work in its suburban way, despite the setback of a day that will rankle forever in the history of the local fire brigade: The Day the Bank Caught Fire.

It happens soon after I arrive. At 7:30 in the morning the electrical system in the two-story Chase Manhattan Building goes haywire. The building in the town center goes up in flames. The Manama fire brigade trundles down in its vintage red engines to put out the blaze. No *Towering Inferno* heroics here; the firemen are so keen to keep away from the heat that their hoses don't even make it to the flames. They call out all the firemen from the airport; the $10 million airport has to close. Chase Manhattan burns on. In desperation they call in the oil company's fabled modern firefighting team from the other end of the island. Up they roar, raring to go. What a pity; their hoses are punctured.

It takes half a day for the police to think of shutting off the road to clear the maze of fascinated onlookers and those slow-moving cars. It takes twenty-four hours to soak the bank's building into blackened submission. "Isn't it typical," mopes one Bahraini businessman. "Here we are trying to convince half the world that this is the perfect service center for the Gulf, and we can't even cope with a little fire."

But it's not that unfortunate lapse in the fire brigade's efficiency that disturbs bankers in their know-it-all penthouses in the West. It's the creeping rumors about those black sheep who've imbibed Marx or plunged into the Socialist Baa'thist party.

The Jeremiahs have been predicting the downfall of the al Khalifa for years. It's not generally known, but it's hardly surprising in the circumstances, that Bahrain has the tightest security system in the whole area; another British legacy. It's Ian Stewart MacWalter Henderson's job to make sure it works; he's one of those colonial, hard-headed, understated types, who won his colors as Superintendent of Police in Kenya during the Mau Mau's fight for independence.

One of his jobs there was to walk into terrorist-infested jungle. If he got his head blown off, the high-powered British negotiators in his wake would know that the Mau Mau didn't like talking that day. He survived with no less than two George medals and even a "mention in despatches." Henderson leads an inconspicuous life in Bahrain, but he's keeping a weather eye out. When an American secretary was raped last year (a rare occurrence) his network of informants unearthed the villain in two days. And if, as a result of his beady-eyed surveillance, a few locals have gone off "on vacation" to a small Bahraini island, at least it's all in the cause of the status quo. Iran, the Aryan colossus across the Gulf, and Saudi Arabia and the mainland behind also keep a weather eye out—another Cuba isn't their idea of fun.

It isn't the bankers' idea of fun, either, which is why they're being rather cautious about setting up shop here. The ones that do keep more closely in touch with each other than you'd expect.

There's a narrow, bumpy, unpaved street in the middle of Manama with a little corner store where old men sit on benches outside arguing and gossiping. Go up the street and on the right is a tall, white, blank-walled house with a rabbit-hole door. This is where the merchant bankers from the classier establishments of the City of London gather regularly to talk global money.

Light streams through the old stained-glass windows from the central courtyard. A Bach sonata (courtesy of Aramco's nonstop classical-music station from Dhahran on the Saudi mainland) provides pianissimo background. Numbered lithographs hang on the white, rough-cast walls. These Britishers are having their usual grouch about the difficulty of explaining to newly rich clients that "medium-term" investments don't mean three to six months. They mean three to six years. And as for long-term investments, that will be another education in itself. To boot, Arabs don't trust one basket enough to hold all their golden eggs. They have a distracting habit of spreading investments among banks, sometimes among as many as eight. On top of it all, these bankers are being nudged out of this traditional British territory by the Swiss, as devious and secretive as their Arab clients, and the more highly organized Americans from Wall Street.

The City of London had a good moment last year. The Swiss ruled out any new deposit accounts in Swiss francs in Switzerland. Their resourceful financiers countered by opening branch offices in Luxembourg, which isn't subject to Swiss banking rules. The Arabs can hold their francs there all right. But the Swiss still have only 10 percent of the private Gulf money; the Americans now have 50 percent. These British bankers are trying to hang onto what they've still got of the rest. One of them is celebrating a small coup. He has finally persuaded a particularly good client from Abu Dhabi to grant him a "management agreement." He won't have to waste time tracking down his elusive client in the future to seek his approval for every money move he makes on his behalf.

Lost down another bumpy back street is the one place these merchant bankers in residence go for an evening out. The migrant, minor businessmen stuck in the fluorescent junction of the Gulf Hotel won't find their way there. You have to ring the doorbell to get into Keith's. "In" businessmen, bankers, and a few Bahrainis come to eat and relax over a carafe of wine at rustic tables by the light of guttering candles. It's Chelsea in the late '60s.

Keith, a bronzed delight of indeterminate age, the medallion hanging on his turtleneck jersey catching the light, hovers around one of his regulars, Charlie Colchester. His godfather arranged for him to come to the island to work for Gray, Mackenzie, a prestigious part of the Earl of Inchcape's group. Charlie came to sell liquor.

"After two years here I began to have qualms about selling alcohol in a Muslim country, so I went into business on my own as an agent for foreign companies, things like that. I was absolutely shocked at the attitude of the Westerners who walked into my office. You wouldn't believe their arrogance. Their basic attitude is that Bahrainis are a bunch of darkies. It escapes them that this is a dignified nation of people who have been trading for centuries and who are very shrewd indeed. Firms send such second-rate people if they send anyone at all. Lots of them think a once-yearly whiz-through by a seven-thousand-dollar-a-year sales rep is all it takes. Don't think the Bahrainis don't notice; they're just too nice to let it show."

He downs another glass of *vin ordinaire,* his earnest young face getting longer and longer. "Then you get the British lot that come over here running down industry back home or moaning about the high rate of income tax back home. The Bahrainis rightly reckon they're ripoff merchants out to fleece their joint. The Americans' approach isn't any better. They stroll in as if they're doing the Bahrainis a favor. They come in blind and, what's worse, they go out blind. I get letters from presidents of large American corporations addressed to Manama, Bahrain, Saudi Arabia; to Manama, Bahrain, Oman. More often than not they add insult to injury by ending it off 'The Persian Gulf.' It does so much long-term harm, you can't imagine."

Poor Charlie. But Collingwood's isn't like that. Collingwood, the old established British jeweler, has taken him on with free rein to sell its goods in the tactful way that appeals to him.

Jewelry might not be what the Arabs need most right now. But it's what they want. What they need are solid industries to take over when the oil runs out.

It's not only a question of knowing when to develop, but how to do it so that it works. Bahraini realism acknowledges its limitations but it also knows its strengths. Bahrain works as a service center. Apart from easy communications, there's an educated work force to staff the offices.

This unusual achievement for the Mideast can be traced back to a day in 1919, when a band of local merchants, mostly illiterate, put up money for a private school. The ruler appointed an al Khalifa as Minister of Education to preside over the inevitable boardroom squabbles. Another first in the Gulf.

Today that minister's grandson is in charge of education:

Sheikh Abdul Aziz, graduate of the School of Oriental and African Studies, London University. In his schools boys and girls have only two periods of Koranic instruction a week. "Well, after all," he says, leaning back in his swivel chair sagely, "it's no use teaching religion at the expense of physics." (Tell that to the Saudis.)

An education system that has been going for fifty years has had time to throw up exceptional men, not ones hand-picked by the al Khalifa but brainy boys who got on. The most outstanding is the only man who figures when you're talking about Bahrain's economic future. He's got the feature spot at high-powered international planning conferences; he's the country's showpiece. Yussef Shirawi, Minister of Development and Industry, is respected and heeded by all the merchant bankers and businessmen.

His mother died when he was young, but he was groomed from the start by teachers who pushed him hard. He won a scholarship to the university in Beirut. He followed that with a postgraduate award in chemical engineering at Glasgow University. Back home he eased his way to the top to become Director General of Oil before independence. Now he's Bahrain's Mr. Planning.

Even after this buildup, the physical presence of the man is stunning. It's not just his looks; the grizzled hair, the face of a Levantine shipowner, the second skin of his well-cut suit. It's the performance. It dazzles.

What makes Bahrain different? Quick as a flash Shirawi produces from nowhere a big, old book. He leafs through it with a broad smile. "Look at this. It's a message sent to a merchant on this island in 1996 B.C., complaining about the bad ingots he'd delivered to Mesopotamia. That's what makes Bahrain different from its neighbors. Four thousand years ago we were quarreling about the quality of ingots."

Political trouble ahead? Another broad smile. "There are two groups of people in the Arab world who are really impossible to govern: the Palestinians and the Bahrainis. They're both intelligent, educated, and they won't take no for an answer."

Apart from exploiting Bahrain's tolerance of foreigners to create that service center, he's carefully stoking Bahrain's economy to run on feasible post-oil projects: an aluminum-smelting works, a dry dock—whatever needs the skilled work force that Bahrain can provide. His models are Japan and Switzerland; they too have educated people and no natural resources.

What's on the other side of this success story? May Shirawi, his wife, a Shia. Yussef is Sunni. Shia and Sunni Muslim sects are to Bahrain as Catholic and Protestant were to Ulster before violence. They coexist uneasily. The Shirawi Shia-Sunni marriage, another first, seemed to promise so much. May was brilliant, beautiful.

Today she sits at home, proud but left out of the Bahrain round. "So you've met May?" a drawing room cow. "I don't suppose you know about her first child? It was born without arms. It died at the age of five when it fell out of bed and suffocated on the floor. That's what happens when you mix Shia and Sunni blood."

May's house is simple—an upright piano for the children, the *World Encyclopedia* for her. From childhood she has worshiped Yussef ("My headmistress always used to say, 'If you work as hard as Yussef Shirawi . . .' "). Now she is married to him, and they are very close, when he can manage to get home.

On the wall of her sitting room there hangs an embroidered sampler that reads: "God grant me the serenity to accept those things I cannot change and the wisdom to change those things that should be changed." The Bahrainis are doing their best.

JADED PIECES

AT THE TOP OF THE HEAP IS THE RULER, SHEIKH ISA IBN SALMAN AL Khalifa. (Actually he was promoted to emir on independence in '71, but everyone still calls him the ruler.) Sheikh Isa's salary is nearly $5 million a year; not bad. But he's always in debt; he's such a generous man and he does like to have his old friend from London, Capt. Algernon "Algy" Asprey in to do his place from time to time.

Say Bahrain to anyone (anyone who's heard of the place, that is) and you'll hear about this Don Juan of Arabia who has a telescope in his palace trained on the airport runway. "Be careful, he watches every plane that lands; he watches every pair of legs that comes down the steps. He's on the lookout for new talent . . ." Does he indeed? With planes coming in from all over the place at all hours of the day and night, he'd be a busy man. And incidentally, he can't see the airport from his palace —it's miles away at Rifaa.

"And all those wives . . ." they go on. That makes Sheikha Hasa laugh. Sheikha Hasa is the only wife Sheikh Isa has ever had; he's had her since she was sixteen, and that was nine children ago. She's his first cousin; she puts up with an assortment of visiting European females. But another wife? Oh, goodness me no.

Tuesday morning is Sheikha Hasa's At Home. There's a long walk past dozens of royal stables, through the archway, into the first courtyard. No sign of life. Emptiness. Silence. Down the cloistered walk, and . . . what's this? A heap of slippers outside a door. Inside, a huge space hums with voices. After the sunshine the darkness is blinding. It takes a while before you can make out the long, low room, maybe twenty yards of it. It's flanked by sofas filled with women, women, women.

It's stepping back into the past, into another world. One by one the arriving guests file down the middle of the room, down the gaudy, patterned carpet toward the bale of saffron yellow that is all you can see of your royal hostess at the end. A little closer and her vivacious face takes shape. She doesn't look forty-six until you get very close. And she doesn't let you get very close for long enough to inspect much more than her thick black hair and shining young-girl's eyes. She's having a jolly time. Which is just as well; she's probably the only woman in the room who is. All the others are on their guard. They're aware that Sheikha Hasa, for all her regal welcome, gets uppity if she feels that she's not getting her royal due.

Behind her armchair is a mirrored wall. In it you can see the floor-to-ceiling photograph of Hasa's husband grinning at the other end. No wonder he's grinning. The room embraces an extraordinary collection of women. It seethes with Kanoos, ambassadresses, exhaustingly cheerful American oil wives, old al Khalifas like wrinkled apples, young ones beautifully dressed, and peroxided English hags who have been around so long that they've got black-rimmed empty holes where they should have eyes. Heavens knows what they have seen. The ruler in his boisterous prime?

Among all this coming and going, upping and downing, shaking of hands and sipping of sickly, sticky juice, there's still time for a chat. No jewelers here, no talk of dwarf tomatoes. Everyone's talking about the latest movie. It's not *Jaws* (no one goes to the movies in Bahrain; that's old hat). It's a sensational,

amateur documentary (*cinema vérité*-style) of Bahrain's forty
top ladies tripping around Morocco. It was another Sheikha
Lulua special; it quite eclipsed her bus outing to the Windsor
Safari Park last summer when they were all in London. Sheikha
Lulua is the family organizer. Kanoo Travel, naturally, takes
care of the details.

Sheikha Lulua has had a thorough grounding. She was married at the age of twelve to Salman, a twenty-year-old cousin
she had never seen. That was in the bad old days, but luckily
for her, Salman turned out to be a good thing. "Right from the
beginning I traveled a lot with him," explains the jaunty grandmother. "He made me learn English and then when we were
abroad he would always tell me to go and get the information
and buy the tickets. I was frightened at first and said, 'No, no,
I can't,' but he forced me to. He wanted me to develop. He
always used to say, 'You must be your own person.' " Sheikh
Salman is dead now, but his protégée travels on.

The affair of St. Christopher's is being hotly discussed in the
middle distance on the left. Some remark about the English
school's standards going down since the Arab quota went up. A
cross admirer denies it. Even so, one ultrasensitive woman confesses that she's thinking of taking her children away.

Visiting time is limited to fifteen minutes. You know when
your time is up, when you have to make room for the second
sitting. The cue is the censer of burning sandalwood borne
around by another gauzy bundle. The women lean forward in
turn to fumigate their hair or drapes. A second ample bundle
follows, bringing ounces of Miss Dior to splash over their sugary
fingers. On the way out, there's a last glimpse of the cardboard
ruler with his Cheshire cat grin. But where is the Cheshire cat?

The ruler is all over the place. He likes to be active. I drive
to his palace to see him. From the outside, it's another of those
silent, monastic, white-walled affairs, like Sheikha Hasa's across
the road. It's not difficult to get past the armed guards. I talk
to them in English. They don't understand a word (that's

puzzling for Bahrain), so to be obliging they let me in. Across the courtyard there's a modern plate-glass, sliding door into a plush suite of offices ("Algy" Asprey's been here all right).

I'm not too surprised to hear that Sheikh Isa isn't at his shiny black desk, subtly carved with gilded Arab motifs. I'm just passing by. But on the way back into Manama a white Mercedes is gliding out. A familiar face peers through the window. It's the ruler, bowing and beaming, waving his hand at all he passes. That's Sheikh Isa ibn Salman's way. His friendliness is as legendary as his generosity.

It came as a comfort to everyone when he succeeded his mean, conservative father, Sheikh Salman (let alone his meaner, even more conservative grandfather, Hamad). "Sheikh Salman's death in 1961 was a longed-for relief to the family," says one grateful al Khalifa. "Sheikh Isa allowed us to start traveling more, educating ourselves, living our own lives a bit."

There are other differences. The father and grandfather inclined to boys; no one accuses Isa of that.

Money problems Sheikh Isa may have, but with the National Assembly now "subject to delay," he has come into his own again. He's flanked by one brother as Prime Minister, the family muscle man, and another as Foreign Minister, the family brain trust. Isa's only al Khalifa rival is the island's richest and meanest man, younger brother Mohammed. Mohammed has lost any chance of a government job now through his quarrels with brother Isa. The Bahrainis aren't heartbroken: They won't forget how he shone as chief of police (1965: riots, eight killed).

Sheikh Mohammed broods in his white fortress of a palace and competes with Isa wherever he can. Isa runs a *majlis* for all the island's men to come for a moan and a prattle. Brother Mohammed must have one too. Isa takes delivery of a new Rolls-Royce; Mohammed doesn't waste a moment ordering his.

Mohammed sulks but he doesn't forget the call of business. A merchant, well placed to know, puts Mohammed's income at about $200,000 a month. Add up just a few of his many interests: $25,000 a month rent from the Delmon Hotel, $20,000 from the Jashanmal office block (home of Manama's biggest department store on the lower floors, the garish new dinner-dance spot, the Pearl, on the top, and a crop of bankers' suites between—Kleinwort Benson, Union Bank of Switzerland, British Bank of the Middle East . . .). And don't forget $25,000 a month rent for the National Bank of Bahrain Building. At least Mohammed is a rich sulk.

Sheikh Isa has never been a sulk. But he's happiest on Fridays; his weekend timetable is a fixture. He sits in the *majlis* early in the morning, goes to the mosque and then to the seaside. Not any old seaside. The ruler has his own.

I'm scooting along in a dune buggy, and there's a holiday feeling in the air. Twenty-three miles out of Manama (having got past the depressing view of the Awali American oiltown and the old ruler's palace rotting in the scrub) we come to a crossroads. The Datsuns, Toyotas, and Bahrainis turn left to the BAPCO (Bahrain Oil Company) beach. We turn right, down a mud path to a riot of green trees (at last) and the ruler's beach.

A soldier stops each car at the gate, to check in cameras. He hands out a cloakroom ticket and hangs up the camera on one of the hooks hammered into a nearby tree. It's already jammed with Pentax, Nikon, Leicaflex, and Kodak Instamatics. This unusual cloakroom attendant stops the buggy, glares hard at me, and then gruffly addresses the Englishman at the wheel. "What nationality does it have?" This takes a while to sink in; he means me.

"It is British," I answer indignantly. A long, thoughtful stare. "Hmm. You look like Arab lady. No come in if Arab lady." Only the sight of a British passport satisfies him. Then he's so embarrassed that he breaks gate rules by having a chat. "Me speak English well. Me one of few who can. That why I am gate job." So that's it; the ruler has twenty-five soldier bodyguards brought in from North Yemen (the okay one, not the Communist one). Why North Yemen? Because it's a long way away; they don't speak English, there's less chance of—well, whatever.

The soldier even hands over his treasured rifle for inspection. It's cleaned, in working order—and loaded.

("They don't have bullets in those things," says a regular, watching the soldiers on their beach patrol. "They're only for show." Some show.)

Satisfied now that I'm no "Arab lady," the guard waves us on. Only two Bahrainis (plus their secretaries and servants) are allowed onto the ruler's beach. The ruler is one; his oldest son, Crown Prince Hamad, head of the army, is the other.

The ruler comes because he likes the view. The Crown Prince comes because he likes to see his father. Hamad doesn't come too often because he also likes to see his vivacious wife, Sapiqi. Hamad is trying hard to be his own man; he's even gone as far as revolting against the faithful "Algy" Asprey in favor of looking for his own decorator. Front runner: a blond *woman* from London, a one-time receptionist in a seaside hairdressing salon.

Needless to say, Bahraini society hums with talk of terrible goings-on at this "out of bounds" territory. There are rumors of taxis scouring Manama to take unattached European women to the beach (no fare charged). There's talk of "Mrs. Manchester's" beachhouse. Mrs. Manchester is the locals' nickname for a middle-aged wife of one of those limp-shouldered technicians. She, they say, is a particular favorite. Then there's all that old stuff about the closed-circuit television in the ruler's beach palace with cameras trained on naked bodies sunbathing outside.

This scene of iniquity turns out to resemble nothing so much as Nantucket circa 1948. Small children build sandcastles and paddle. Reg and Bill discuss the price of beer and what it's like back in Liverpool. Elsie and Joan drop their knitting to sort out some intricate dressmaking.

The ruler's beach palace is nothing more than a green-tile-roofed bungalow with candy-striped hammocks and chairs around it, facing the parking lot. Inside is the living room-den with sofas and plastic tables.

It's true there are a mass of girls lying around listening to transistor radios or munching sandwiches. Although they're all wearing bikinis, they have unappetizing, flabby thighs and they're hardly going out of their way to pose like something out of a sexy Bacardi Rum advertisement.

About ten men ask if I'm a stewardess. By now this much used Bahraini term is acquiring the same innuendo as the word *model* in the '60s. But, it seems there are "stewardesses" and stewardesses. The first kind provides a good business for some people in Manama who are sent chick gathering in Europe by various other people. Not the ruler; he's settling down, and there are enough around for him already. The second brand are bona fide cabin staff based here because Bahrain is the headquarters of Gulf Air. At any one time there are four hundred of their girls in Manama, mostly with flight-staff boyfriends.

There is a lawn on one side of the ruler's bungalow. Here Elsie and Joan have gone back to their knitting, Reg and Bill are snoring slightly, and their children are playing on the strip of beach. The beach runs beyond the bungalow, beyond the parking lot to open onto a broader sandy stretch. At the far end is "Mrs. Manchester's" famous house. It's just a house. It's empty and it could belong to anyone.

Only the soldiers and the long new pier looking out to the ruler's white tub (you can hardly call it a yacht, even if it is another of Algy's jobs), suggest that this is anything more than a two-star seashore spot. Of course, the waiters in snowy white uniform aren't the usual ice-cream vendors. At eleven in the morning and four in the afternoon they serve coffee and iced cakes on trays to anyone at a table under an umbrella by the shore. The cups and saucers are something of a jumble; earthenware flowered cup on gold-rimmed white china saucers, that sort of thing. But it's all free, so no one complains.

The white Mercedes sweeps into the parking lot. His Highness plonks himself down on a towel on a bench in a corner by the bungalow. The Mercedes departs, and the ruler recovers from the strain of attending the Friday races. "I'm worried about my horses. I don't think the jockeys are good to them. I won't let them race for a while and see if that helps." His Highness is terribly pleased to see me. He's terribly pleased to see everyone. He enjoys sitting here watching the world go by. He's very, very short and very, very round but he's very, very charming.

He makes room on his towel for me, sends for an orange juice, and offers a Benson and Hedges cigarette ("English, for you"). To my amazement, he's shy. He thinks I'm making a play for him; enough girls do this afternoon.

I find a way in; I mention Sheikha Hasa. Now he relaxes. He's on home ground. I tell him how impressed I am by the way building goes on day and night on the Sheikha Hasa office block in Manama (she's something of a property tycoon). He smiles proudly. He sends a servant to fetch something from the shuttered bungalow. It's a photograph of the Sandhurst- and Mons-trained Crown Prince rising high over a fence on an Arab show-jumper. He shows it to me; now he's bursting with pride.

"My son is a wonderful rider. He's wonderful. I have nine children, you know; they're all wonderful. Two are still at school in Switzerland. They write to me every week." He confesses that he has had to stop telephoning them. Sheikha Hasa put her foot down because he fussed every time one of them complained about some minor school misery.

He also has a mischievous sense of humor. He says that if I want anything more than a good gossip, he'll be only too delighted to discuss how bad British industry is on delivery dates. A big wink, a bigger beam.

He greets everyone going past. "How nice to see you. I do hope you had a pleasant day," this time to an elderly couple shuffling off. Everyone stops to thank him for a lovely day, and he thanks them all for coming. He shakes hands with one blonde, aged four, and admires the older ones, who have now pulled themselves together for a good flaunt past. "I love sitting here," another twinkle, "but I do get a crick in my neck."

After a long, crick-making time he rises, shakes his tummy, and calls for his red car. He's off to the high point of the Bahraini social week. He's looking forward to it enormously; he offers a lift.

Outside the gate where the Yemeni soldier is now awkwardly trying to keep his rifle in place while checking out the cameras, up to the main road. A stream of cars is zooming along. But this isn't the customary Bahraini thirty-five miles an hour. Something is up. Cadillacs, Chevrolets, an odd Lamborghini, and hundreds of tin boxes are rushing into the distance. His Highness joins in the current. A herd of camels looks down on the procession. The cars are crowded with families, squads of girls, makeup flashing through dusty windshields; young men, eyes flashing through even dustier windshields. Every Friday afternoon in summer all Bahrain drives to Thompson's Beach. Every Friday afternoon in winter all Bahrain drives to the old, no longer used, airfield.

At last we arrive at Thompson's Beach. Through a storm of sand kicked up by thousands of wheels the social zenith of Bahrain is realized. There are cars as far as the eye can see. Some are parked, others drive slowly around them. A few people, mostly families, get out and sit on the beach watching the huge red sunset. The teenagers stay put, drinking Pepsis, eating their picnic snacks. This is the nearest "decent" Bahrainis get to dating.

This is it; nothing else happens. The game is to find out who the girls are who are watching the boys who are watching the girls. Every now and again there's a slight nod here, a suspicion of a smile there. The atmosphere is tense with puppy love. Many a marriage has started through two panes of glass, over a strip of tarmac in winter, a haze of sand in summer. The ruler's car joins the parade and then slowly nose-to-tail bumps back through the traffic jam to Sheikha Hasa. An hour later as dusk falls Bahrain, the Philadelphia of the Gulf, goes home after celebrating its day off in its usual style.

His Highness has had his idea of a good weekend. He does try, but he doesn't have a flair for more cultural occupations. His British aide-de-camp, Major Green, recently thought that the time might be right to encourage him. There were empty niches in his newly decorated *majlis*. Just right, said Green, for a few choice pieces of jade. If he hoped to interest his royal master in the Western pastime known as "hunting out something tremendously special," he was wasting his time. "Splendid," said his Highness. "Go out and buy me a jade collection."

That's Bahrain. "We're not rich, but we're comfortable, thank you."

PART

KUWAIT—

"PEERING INSIDE,

AFRAID TO LOOK OUT . . ."

CHAPTER

17

THE MEN WHO CAME IN FROM THE COLD

THE OIL ARABS HAVE A GREAT GAME. IT'S CALLED BITCHING ABOUT the Other Oil Arabs. Westerners mustn't be tempted to join in, but it goes something like this: Bahrain, say the Saudis, is a dump. Kuwait, say the Saudis, is arrogant. (King Faisal summed it up in a withering remark: "There are three superpowers: Russia, America—and Kuwait.")

The Saudis, say the Bahrainis, are fanatics. The Kuwaitis, say the Bahrainis, are punks. ("What do you want to go there for? It's a dead city.")

The Kuwaitis look down on everyone. They reserve a particular spite for Saudi Arabia. ("Who *really* killed King Faisal?" they ask in a loaded way.)

It's part of the contradiction that at the same time there's another standard game. It's called: We're All the Same at Heart. As they're fond of reminding you, the royal families of Saudi Arabia, Bahrain, and Kuwait are connected. This means they were all hoofing around in the same desert a few hundred years ago. The al Khalifa of Bahrain and the al Sabah of Kuwait are even tribal cousins. But they've traveled far, in separate directions, in a mighty short time.

In Bahrain, you're always aware of the al Khalifa. In Kuwait you could almost get by without hearing of the al Sabah.

211

They're the most inscrutable bunch of all. The al Sabah men are the epitome of all that's well bred, well dressed, and thoroughly modern. At least, that's the picture they project. The emir (not ruler) is hardly seen and no one publicizes his idea of a holiday treat: riding around the London subway. Handsome, educated al Sabahs go out to important embassies abroad: Oxford-educated charmer Sheikh Salim (now a government minister) polished his ambassadorial posts in Washington and London until they gleamed. His brother-in-law Sheikh Saud is another in the Omar Sharif mold. He brings to his new ambassadorial office suite in London the sleek showmanship of an attorney (called to Gray's Inn in 1968).

No one talks anymore about how Emir Mubarak "The Great" bumped off two brothers to get to the top job in 1896. The mid-1950s antics of the present emir's older brother, Sheikh Fahd, are all in the past too. Apart from Fahd's minor weakness for chartering planeloads of prostitutes, he had the more distressing habit of rifling the national cash register when he was head of the Development Board. Eventually the family put their heads together in private and threw him out of office. Shortly afterward he died: officially of a heart attack on a pilgrimage to Mecca. Intelligence sources favor the version that he died on his yacht in Bahrain from eating something disagreeable—probably poison.

The al Sabahs have always been good at putting their heads together at the right moment. That's how they got to rule the place. After a shocking drought in the desert in 1710 some of the more aristocratic Bedouins went down to the Gulf for a sight of water. They wandered around until they settled on a convenient spot, Kuwait. Someone had the bright idea of sending one of their clever young men off to see the nearest Turkish governor to get permission to stay put, on condition they kept quiet. His mission was a success; his name was al Sabah. His family has been top dog ever since; everyone else who was around at the time is "heritage."

At first I'm impressed by the mere sight of all those godlike highly educated al Sabahs with their faultless Western dress in

Europe and tightly hugging jeans off-duty in Kuwait. Then I start to admire the family's desert-conditioned sense of timing. There are the little touches: early risers can catch a glimpse of a good-looking, keen-eyed man wandering around the fish and meat markets at five in the morning. It's the conscientious Crown Prince-cum-Prime Minister checking on prices again. The al Sabahs have caught onto the idea of consumer protection for their faithful citizens. There are the bigger flourishes: the lively National Assembly (admittedly packed as far as decent with al Sabah supporters, including a ragged horde of highly vocal Bedouins). The emir himself, reputedly sick, still knows that the al Sabahs have to keep one jump ahead of getting the boot.

But his family has always had trouble with its women. No sooner had they settled down in the 1760s than a grizzly tribe attacked them, dying to carry off a particularly beautiful al Sabah daughter, Maryam. The al Sabahs' band fought well; Maryam's honor was saved.

They still haven't mastered that weak spot. Not that one likes to bring it up, but there was that small bother over Sheikh Saad's daughter a while ago. Sheikh Saad, Hendon Police College-trained in England, is Minister of Defense and Security. His daughter made the mistake of falling for a Muslim Lebanese when she was at the university in Beirut. They eloped to Cyprus. No question of the girl being forced to come home; she was too old to be treated as a minor. Much to the family's horror, Interpol nearly got involved with the errant daughter; someone alleged she had stolen some of her mother's jewelry. It was all a terrible misunderstanding.

The unfortunate Sheikha now works in Australia. No one knows how to undo the bitterness, but certain female cousins secretly send her money. "It's disgraceful. After all she married an Arab; what more did he want?" one Sheikha says after I tactlessly mention that another Sheikha has mentioned it to me. "I feel for the girl, I really do. But that's not what matters. It's that incidents like these ruin everything the rest of us are doing to live down the old days."

The al Sabahs like to keep their dirty linen to themselves. The fact that at the moment there's interfamily strife of a somewhat awkward nature going on is kept strictly behind Kuwaiti palace walls. When they've sorted out the jobs among themselves, Kuwait will get to hear the results. Meanwhile all that most people care about their ruling family is that they keep the state steady and don't hog the jobs. In the sixteen-man Cabinet there are now eleven commoners; that's democracy at work, you'd think. Not exactly: the commoners are all heritage men from families close to the al Sabah.

From behind the scenes the al Sabahs run a very different kind of setup than their cousins do in Bahrain. The city's so large compared to Bahrain's suburban offerings. What's more, it works. The broad roads are lit at night. Decent town planning from way back gave rise to directions as endearing as: "Off the sixth ring road." And then there's the hot water: Kuwait has virtually no fresh water of its own at all, but by spending a fortune it manages to make twice as much as it needs. Whoever's into desalination in Kuwait must be cleaning up. I've just come from places where every tap was an adventure. Sometimes cow-brown water came out. More often nothing. If I was lucky, clear water came out, cold. Occasionally, I had a Klondike water strike—hot, fast-running. Kuwait's reliable running hot water, taken as a matter of course, sums the city up perfectly.

And Kuwait State is a city, give or take six thousand square miles of sand (half the size of Rhode Island, that's all) with more oil under it than anywhere but Saudi Arabia. Paradise? Take a look at a map. Kuwait's too close to too many people who don't like it. Those Socialists in Iraq, over the border; if only they'd stay there. Iraq's invaded before now; it wants to again (What do you think Kuwait's 150 new Chieftain tanks at $400,000 a throw are for? To fight Israel? Forget it). Then those Aryans over in Iran. Friends? The Iranian Embassy in Kuwait counts as a "hardship post."

One way or another Kuwaitis are in a chronic state of paranoia. At least it's not the same paranoia as Saudi Arabia's. It's the result of being a minority group in your own country and refusing to face it.

There *might* be 1,000,000 people in Kuwait (golden rule: never trust official population figures around here. Merely a reminder). There *might* be 300,000 Kuwaitis, plumped up by bought-and-paid-for Bedouins.

Proper Kuwaitis, with a talent for sticking their heads in the sand and ignoring reality, lead a good life. They believe that you're closer to Allah in their country than anywhere else on earth. The most proper Kuwaitis (the al Sabah and the eight or so families who arrived with them in 1766) know better. As they've grown richer and richer, they've become cannier and cannier. They understand the full extent of their insecurities.

One of their greatest is that a quarter of the population is Palestinian. Before I started this journey "Palestinians" meant to me Arafat; guns and refugee camps; bomb outrages and hijackings. Here I am in a city where Palestinians are what makes my life comfortable. They make things work. But *their* life; that's another question.

I'm in a nightclub, watching a young man of twenty-five, a qualified engineer, the only one of his kind in Kuwait (he has some unusual specialty). Even if I didn't know who he was, his slick Western suit would mark him as an outsider. Only proper Kuwaitis wear national dress. As it happens, he's the son of a Palestinian who helped to create a key ministry in Kuwait twenty years ago. I can't name him. As a Palestinian, even though he was born here, he'll never be safe.

He's as taut as a whippet. He's concentrating hard on a pretty, unusual-looking English girl. He's not out to make her; it's not that kind of concentration.

When the crowd moves to the table, he gets to sit next to her. I listen as he zeros in on her; I can hardly believe it. "The minute I set eyes on you I knew I'd be able to talk to you. You look so wise; you're the first girl I've met since I got back from the States four years ago who I feel can respond to me as a person." The girl has a kind face, but she hasn't said much to justify his conviction that a "meaningful relationship" lies ahead over the giant Gulf shrimps. I'm about to switch off when I sense an intense, low-pitched eruption. "Do you think I'm odd? Do you like me? I'm not odd; I'm not drunk. I'm tired, that's all, very tired. I get up at five thirty every morning, I stay in the office until late at night. I only go home to sleep. I'm killing myself with work. Why do you think I do it? Do you think I like work? Do you think I need the money? I've got all the money I need. But I can't stand going home. What else have I got? I've had to wait four years to find one girl I can talk to. Girls in Kuwait are all the same. They only care about money and clothes. Talking to them is like talking to a bit of wood. I will never marry a girl from Kuwait."

Anywhere else this would sound like afternoon soap opera. But he's right; he won't marry a girl from Kuwait. No good Kuwaiti family would have him. No matter how much money they have, how trusted they are on high, Palestinians are second-class citizens.

Every year the Minister of the Interior can, if he chooses, naturalize fifty people as a reward for long service to the country. This engineer's father gave such service. He's still Palestinian; a man of no existing nationality and temporary traveling papers.

The young man in the nightclub's lucky; he's got brains, money, a future. What does the next Palestinian I meet have? He drives for a civil servant, he works for the government. For sixteen years he has had the same job; he can't get another. He makes $320 a month; a Kuwaiti would get $660. The driver pays $100 a month rent for rooms in a squalid street. At least his children can go to school. The government now offers free schooling to non-Kuwaiti children (an important, new civil-liberties advance)—*if* they arrived here under the age of seven. The driver's five children were born in Kuwait, so they go to school—with $1.50 a day in their pockets. "All other children have same money. Kuwait rich country."

There's a note of whining desperation in his voice. It's as distinct as the smell of poverty. His life is made up of dreams.

Dreams of the family orange grove he knew as a child in Palestine. Dreams of renting a small shop (non-Kuwaitis aren't allowed to buy property): "Then I will be my own man." Dreams that his children will escape. When he gets home at night he sits over them as they do their homework, reminding them it's the only way out.

And mostly he dreams of spending more time with his wife. "My wife no learn English like me, she no write. But she so good; she better than me." He will see her in eighteen hours' time, his usual working day. That's his future.

At last I meet a Palestinian I can name. It's a big enough name. Khaled Abu Saud, Director of Investment at the Ministry of Finance. He moves $4 billion a year around the world. It's the Kuwait government's investment abroad.

The Ministry of Finance has a lot of doormen; forty is a usual count. The Bedouins on the door are Kuwaiti and every Kuwaiti is entitled to a government desk or door to sit at. The building reeks of piss. It's a long smell up to Abu Saud on the top floor. His office has two naked light bulbs and a few tattered chairs. Khaled Abu Saud is round and gray with fatigue.

He's had this vital job for eighteen years. He arrived from Palestine only two years after the old mud walls of Kuwait city were torn down. There was nothing much here but the start of an oil boom. The polish and education came later. He caught the eye of an al Sabah who recognized the faithful nature of the man and the fast brilliance of his mind. He's risen to a position of fantastic financial importance. At last he was made Kuwaiti in '74. But he's still not Kuwaiti Kuwaiti. He can't vote; he doesn't wear national dress.

To give you an idea of the complexity of his job, I must tell you a typical Kuwaiti financial arrangement. I've just met an American investment banker who knew that Iceland needed money and knew a Japanese who knew which Kuwaiti had 4 million dinars (local currency; about $13,300,000) he wanted to lend abroad. The Icelandic government has its loan.

Khaled Abu Saud will have heard about this. It's his job to know every money move in Kuwait. Thirty telexes an hour drop on his desk. He holds up bundles of paper: "I have the movement of every share all over the world here in my hand. We have our own offices and representatives everywhere. I've never given business to any banker who has walked through that door on his own initiative. But hundreds of them come every week, and I know they can't go back empty-handed after coming all this way. At least they should go back with a visiting card saying 'Khaled Abu Saud.' "

I'm surprised at his apologetic tone. I've heard the way bankers talk about him in the hotel lobby. They question each other closely like small boys waiting to know who the school principal has chosen for some special honor. "Have you seen Abu Saud? You've *met* him," they say with envy to a peer who has pulled it off. But of course the nuances of the hotel lobby are meaningless to Abu Saud; he's been conditioned by Kuwaitis, and to them he's still known as "brilliant but Palestinian." It was only a while ago that there was a public fuss about having a Palestinian in such a key position.

Other things hurt: he's laying down a pensioned future for a Kuwait without oil. Even so, some of his long-term, feather-bedding designs ricochet. He masterminded the Kiawah Island real-estate deal, buying up the only totally unspoiled resort coast along that stretch of South Carolina. He's calculated, probably correctly, that more and more Americans will be taking vacations at home. Miami? Another big city. If you're not in the Palm Beach bracket, the choice is pretty limited. Really carefully developed (and the Kuwaitis won't have to save the dimes; they can afford to buy the best), Abu Saud figures Kiawah could net a fortune long-term. But "long-term" hasn't yet entered the time scale of any but the most sophisticated Kuwaitis, so he's already being accused of buying a slice of nothing.

He was hurt most when he pushed through the $214 million takeover of the St. Martin's Property Corporation in London (making Kuwait the landlords of the "New Scotland Yard," the police headquarters). The headline in a London newspaper screamed: "THE ARABS ARE COMING." Kuwait winced. Abu

Saud gave up. How could he ever explain to the hostile British public that no less a patriot than the governor of the Bank of England, Sir Gordon Richardson, had made a personal appeal to him over lunch to take some action that might help to stop the bottom from falling out of the quivering London real estate market?

He learned. He's organizing the purchase of 5 percent and 7 percent block shares in big banks all over the world, especially America. He's buying silently, protecting himself and Kuwait from unsavory publicity.

It's late. It's the weekend; we're both tired of talking money. He asks me to lunch to meet his wife. "My wife is an angel. She lives with a man who is diseased. What else am I? I have the disease of buying, selling, and making transactions. My son came home from school the other day and asked whether he was Christian or Muslim. I'm ashamed that I've given so little time to my children that my son doesn't even know what being Muslim means."

Somehow I know it will be all right to mention Israel. (Normally I never mention it at all; if trapped, I call it Palestine—if I didn't, I might be in for a three-hour marathon about being the brainwashed victim of Zionist propaganda.) Abu Saud answers simply. "Israel is a reality. I'm in a position to say that because I know at what price; my family have paid part of it. My father was killed in Jersusalem in the 1948 war. My brother was killed at the same time by Jews in our house. We had the misfortune to live near a mosque, you see. My mother is seventy-eight, she still lives in Jerusalem, but she's too old to travel. She'll never see her grandchildren again."

I leave him knowing that this gentle Palestinian—sorry, I mean Kuwaiti—feels many things. Bitterness against Jews is not one of them.

CHAPTER

18

SHOPPING AROUND THE SNOBS

PROPER KUWAITIS DON'T FEEL GUILTY ABOUT THE WAY THEY treat Palestinians, even top Palestinians. It's not as if they reserve their condescending ways for them alone; they treat everyone that way. At their worst, Kuwaitis are terrible snobs. They go on and on about their ambition to have a theater to house the Bolshoi Ballet (much to Saudi disgust Kuwait has diplomatic relations with Communists). So nothing less will do than having the best man over from London to advise them on building their own National Theater. "Something like the Paris Opera House is what we have in mind," says the minister unpretentiously. Then you find out that the same Kuwaitis oohing and aahing about hosting the Bolshoi never bother with ballet when they're abroad. So what's the point of all the fuss? It's easy: if the Bolshoi dance for New York, they should for Kuwait. Kuwaitis can't stand being left out of anything chic.

Nearly all of them have perfected the art of seeming to be arrogant; most of them are. They're also sarcastic and cutting: "I suppose you could call us the English of the Arab world these days. We have the same kind of reputation for standoffiish- ness; only we're so much better at it." Is that 15-love for a complete putdown, or love-15 for stooping so low?

All this one-upmanship shows itself at its worst with the

married. Kuwaiti women are legally more advanced than any in the area—they even got the vote in 1975—but some of these liberated women are insufferable.

There are the ones who are mad about their appointment books (a latest craze): "I can spare half an hour on Wednesday week," they say to a close friend on the phone after poring over their advanced bookings. And then you find out they've nothing on all day tomorrow; but they couldn't face owning up to the failure of being left with a blank page.

There are those who lie about education. The biggest craze of all among married women is enrolling at Kuwait University—to pass the time; not many get around to passing the exams. Most of these superstar students are delivered to the university each morning by chauffeur (yes, of course they can drive but they don't have to score small points like that anymore). They come home to bookshelves crammed with books (unopened), wear their courses like monogrammed neckchains and spout undigested academic jargon off the top of their heads.

They lie about knowing people. "Don't tell me you haven't met Princess Grace of Monaco!" No, I haven't; but I'd lay money this woman hasn't either. They lie about knowing places. "Acapulco's pleasant enough, but we're trying to persuade our friends to come to Puerto Vallarta." Then try calling a Kuwaiti on one of these oh-so-cool remarks and watch her squirm.

I try it on one society matron when I've finally had enough of her patronizing. I haven't hung around places like Nassau for nothing; I know the meaningless dialogue backward:

She serves: "We used to stay at the Byblos in St. Tropez, but now we take a villa up in the hills instead."

"Don't tell me you still go to St. Tropez. I *am* surprised. Don't you find it's unpleasantly vulgar these days? I gave it up years ago and tried Sardinia instead, the Costa Smeralda, naturally."

"Oh yes, we go there, too. But you do have to choose the right hotel . . ."

"Cala di Volpe?"

"Of course, we were there last summer."

"Mm. I *used* to go there but now they've extended it, they let *anyone* in. I can't bear it now but that's probably because I remember it *before* it was spoiled. But frankly, for a hundred dollars a day by the time you get through, I think there are so many more *interesting* places to go."

Now I have her completely; this kind of Kuwaiti snob longs to know only the best places but she can't stand the thought of being "had." (Kuwaitis see themselves as too sophisticated these days to be flashy with their money.) She collapses; changes the subject and glares at me. She'll get her own back later somehow.

But who wants to spend hours playing verbal Ping-Pong with cookies from Kuwait? I get tired of being crushed by their cold, withering remarks and even more tired of bothering to hit the ball back to them. But, hey, what's this? Underneath all that surface frost the Kuwaiti women don't enjoy it either, would you believe. In fact they hate it. It's hard to get past their face-saving chill, but you know when you have. It happens to me thanks to Countess Clanwilliam.

A bit of background fill-in: In December, 1974, Gainsborough's *Countess* was packed up with a load of other canvases and flown to Kuwait by Roy Miles, thirty-eight-year-old London art dealer. She went on show in the Sheraton Hotel's Blue Room with an $84,000 price tag, a few Stubbs, and a complete set of Pieter pastels (which once graced Lady Sassoon's country-house). This show of old masters was reported back to journalists in London from Miles as the social event of the season. There was no talk of a firm sale but a big deal was hinted at. The British press gave him a good splash.

A year later I'm sitting in a drawing room making small talk. My hostess, her eyes fixed somewhere above my head, is friendly but reserved. My eyes are glued to her expensive, soft leather boots. I cast around for a name to drop and come up with that of Roy Miles. My hostess raises a supercilious eyebrow and produces a clipping from a London newspaper. She hands it to me to read. The punch line is in the last paragraph:

"One thing which really fascinates the Kuwaitis is the way

the eighteenth-century subjects frequently posed adorned with pearls. Kuwait was traditionally a pearl exporter (before the oil, naturally) but, as the Arabs never wore them, they didn't know what they were used for."

I snort. She gives me that know-it-all smile I'm learning to hate. Then suddenly I recognize the article. I should; I wrote it. I break up. It all seemed so plausible a world ago in London. "I know I should apologize," cracking with laughter, "but it's so funny." The women are watching me carefully. I can't stop laughing enough to worry about saving my face: "You must think I'm an idiot. I certainly do."

The thaw sets in, and six snobby Kuwaiti ladies laugh too. I know I've broken through. "Ah, another for the collection of the Blue Room stories, a good one," says my hostess, looking at me at last. "But I can cap it. I was at the airport one day when a European dealer was clearing customs for a Blue Room exhibition. His embassy had sent someone to meet him so the stuff was cleared fast, but someone must have told the dealer in Europe that you can't do a thing out here without a bribe. So out came his wallet with a wad of notes for the customs man. Imagine the confusion of the diplomat. There he was, trying to make the dealer understand that the packages had been cleared long ago, but nothing would satisfy the stupid man until he paid his bribe. The customs man thought he was mad. But he wasn't a fool. He took it."

And yes, the story's true. Incredulous, I checked it with the embassy concerned.

Saving face is what the whole Kuwaiti performance is about. And in order to keep the chorus line of saved faces neat, there are definite rules about how proper Kuwaitis go about matters. It's increasingly "the wrong thing," for instance, to fly in a designer to do over one's house. "Farther down the Gulf they're like the Americans in the early days—new rich and title hungry," sniffs one Kuwaiti. "They go to New York and London and pick up any decorator with a fancy name as if money can buy breeding."

John Sellers is Kuwait's very own Princess Lee Radziwill. He's a protégé of the al Ghanim family, and you don't come higher than that—the al Ghanims aren't mere heritage, they're the best heritage. It's Sellers's task to coat some of the city's richest houses with Kuwait's newly acquired sense of tastefulness.

He's a thin-hipped, streaky-blond cockney from the East End of London who landed on Kuwait in 1966 during his flowerpower days en route to Japan via India. His story involves Beirut, a New York ex-cop, an Italian-Swedish blonde hoping to make a killing (her only offer of employment was as a stripper), and finally a Lebanese architect who took to Sellers. He was impressed enough to rope him into his practice in Kuwait. Four years later Sellers opened on his own. Now he has twenty designers working for him, a large brown-and-red office with leather-buttoned sofas and a parrot in a cage. He's the dearly beloved of the kind of Kuwaiti women whose appointment books *are* full.

Sellers has to find ways of doing their homes in near-furtive conditions. It goes without saying that his clients are lying through their teeth that they did it all themselves. (Face saving, right.) The fact that Kuwait's so small that everyone who's had a Sellers job knows everyone else who's had a Sellers job is beside the point. Sellers is careful never to repeat himself in any two drawing rooms, and the mistresses of each can coo at one another about how clever they both were to scheme it so well.

His discretion and taste don't come too expensive. He's too shrewd to price himself out of the thrifty Kuwaiti market. He charges under $4,000 to design a room and only $13,000 to put everything in it.

"When I arrived here there was decor chaos." Sellers, talking through his shaggy moustache, remembers to signal to the Indian teaboys brewing up on the other side of a glass wall. "No one knew what they wanted and they were scared stiff of choosing. They didn't have the confidence to let me do anything new. One guy gave me carte blanche to do up his den, so I designed a fantastic room in simple colors but with huge cushions covered in beautiful fabrics around the room. It seemed so obvious—every time Kuwaiti men get together, they always end up slouched on the floor. Well, the guy was horrified; he wanted 'proper seats,' and yet I knew he'd be sitting on them just the way he would on a cushion; but he didn't have the self-confidence to do anything new like that.

"It's all different now. Now I can do pretty much the same sort of thing I'd be doing in England. Well, to be honest, a great deal better; they've more money to spend here." The tea arrives in a second. Seller's operation is geared to instant delivery. "When I was working in London I used to go around being Artistic and Temperamental, and I'd have to wait until I was in the right mood to choose colors. But here, wham, you've got to have it all drawn out by tomorrow morning." His clients want it *now;* they don't want to wait. After all, in a short while they'll be on the move again.

That's no joke; one architect who designed and carefully landscaped a house, saw it bulldozed five years later to build something better. Nothing unusual. At one stage they didn't even have to be bulldozed. They simply fell down. Sellers is already drawing up plans for a new house for a family whose last million-dollar-decorated domain acquired his costly finishing touches only a few weeks ago. That's how fast Kuwait moves.

You can see their progress clearly laid out. Start off in the middle of Kuwait city and there're still a few old houses left over from the mud days of not so long ago. Drive out to where the development started when the oil money came in. Here are the early, garish, rainbow-colored houses complete with jutting balcony, copied unthinkingly from foreign magazines—what on earth is the use of a balcony here? In summer no one can sit out on it for the heat. In winter the cold winds drive sand into feet-high heaps on anything as dumb as an exposed balcony. Drive on to the more functional copies a few miles along: neo-Georgian mansions complete with columns. But they look damned silly in a desert capital. Another couple of minutes' drive and you're into the Americana-modern belt that went up a couple of years ago. Nice enough if this were California. It isn't; nor is it Spain—which didn't occur to the next lot of progressives who started getting an Arab nationalist itch in their house plans and put up Spanish-Moorish villas. But right out on the edge of the Kuwaiti suburbs, in the smartest residential district of all, Salamieh, where Sellers has his office, you'll find the avant-garde of today. Sellers's taste-hungry clients are now into designing homes on more purified "classical Arab lines" (whatever they are). Basically that means blank, fortresslike walls with slit windows and huge spaces inside. Don't let on to the Kuwaitis, but it's a mixture of mainly Persian and slightly Arab designs splotched together. Purified? Hardly. But beautiful all the same.

Don't run away with the idea that the whole of rich Kuwait is on the hunt for good taste. Near Sellers's office is Mobilia House, Decor and Furniture. They still do a brisk trade in hideous casts of Venus de Milo and three-foot-high Botticelli's *Birth of Venus,* (complete with shell). There's a ready market for their Lebanese carved, hand-painted, white-gold-and-powder-blue bedroom suites with seven-foot double bed, twelve-foot wardrobe, two matching chests of drawers-cum-dressers with mirrors, twin triangular corner tables also with mirrors (only $5,000 the package, says the salesman. Can he mean it?). And they sell plenty of those "old gold" antiqued or cut-glass Syrian chandeliers ($200 each) to add a soft, romantic haze. This is what Sellers calls "the Louis de Lebanon look." It's what he had to do before his clients could be persuaded that there was an alternative to plush velvets and tasseled brocade. What his clients haven't discovered, it seems, is that there's an alternative to getting a decorator in and claiming to have done it yourself. It's called "having the confidence to get down and do it yourself." No, they haven't gotten that far yet in Kuwait.

Where Kuwait excels is in its shops. The main street of Salamieh might not be the Via Condotti, but it's getting there.

Lanvin and Chloe couture from Paris hangs artistically in a boutique appropriately named "Versailles." "Ruban Bleu" (they are stuck in old-fashioned notions of what's chic; if the name's French, it must be okay) sells only the best from the Paris houses of Dior, Scherrer, Patou, Givenchy, and Nina Ricci. There's Charles Jourdan in "The Red Shoes," and Carita of Paris runs a beauty parlor. And there's not the faintest whiff here of that bargain-basement mess in the shops of Jeddah and Riyadh. No hint of the seedier end of Greenwich Village that Bahrain's boutiques take after. The window displays, accessories —it's all good Madison Avenue stuff in Salamieh.

I overlook one characteristic Kuwaiti dig: "Our Yves St. Laurent is ravishing compared to yours in Bond Street." I don't bother to point out it has the same clothes, the same displays; I'm resigned to the fact that Kuwaiti has to be best. At least I'm not the only target, they dig at each other the same way. One Kuwaiti was caught wearing the same Yves St. Laurent suit as another woman, who's telling me the story: " 'Where did you get yours?' she asked me. I told her Beirut. 'Oh there,' she said. 'Yves St. Laurent made mine especially for me.' It's a lie, it has to be a lie. Because her suit was identical to mine. I'm sure she gave it to her Indian maid that night." (Incidentally, the woman telling me her story didn't get hers in Beirut—she bought it in Salamieh.)

They sure get their roles confused in Kuwait. Do they want to be the smartest, most exclusive things on two legs wearing all the right labels? Or do they want to be sharp chicks who buy cheap? Now they know that old money's more careful than new, they can't make up their minds which role is the more sophisticated. So at one moment an al Sabah sheikha will say she doesn't go shopping with her cousins because she hates the way they spend more than $400 on a dress. (To a rich sheikha spending $399 on a dress is still cheap; it's all relative after all.) The next she'll say that only Charles Jourdan boots will do because only their leather is soft enough for her. They're keen on boots in Kuwait. Leather boots, here? They want to be like Europe or America, you see. That's why none of those smart boutiques would make a cent if they dared to hang out an Arabic name above their shop.

When you come down to it the Kuwaiti women's arrogance isn't solid. It plates and protects a sense of deep insecurity. That's why I can forgive them for all those stabbing remarks. I learn what's on the other side, the private one. Away from the shops and the beauty parlors, life isn't half so grand for these rich women. How could it be? No less here than in Saudi they exist only as daughters, sisters, wives, and mothers. The parameters of their lives are staked out by the men.

It's only in Kuwait, where national dress means more than any amount of gold braid on a soldier's uniform, that I start to focus properly on what superiority this dress gives a man. In Saudi I couldn't tell one *thobe* from another. Here (where the dress is the same, only the name's been changed—it's called a *dishdasha*) I begin to notice small but significant variations.

National dress does have a language that gives something away after all. Is the material rough or fine? Higher collars make an important man keep his head up; the downtrodden sink into their lower-cut collars. If a man doesn't do much, he'll fasten the front with studs—he has the time to fiddle with them. If he does something, he'll probably make do with buttons. If he's very conscious of his position, he'll go to the trouble of having his dress made with hidden fastenings. It's more elegant.

Lowlier mortals have short hems with heavy-duty shoes poking out inches below. Higher ones have long hems (they don't have to bother about dirtying their clothes. What are a few extra laundry bills?) and you don't even notice their shoes.

Above all, there's the headdress, which can say more about a man than his best friend would. Chic variation number one is to throw up the sides of the headdress. This takes a certain style and can only be done by a man with good ears and a firm jawline. The movement can be seductive—especially in

Saudi Arabia, where every square inch of revealed skin is charged with meaning.

There are, therefore, dozens of ways of wearing a headdress without any style at all. Too much left hanging over a man's forehead makes him look like a halfwit. If the rope (originally used for hobbling his camel) is jammed too far down on his head, he looks like a neatly tied parcel.

And national dress betrays an interesting difference between Kuwaiti and Saudi men. In Saudi their attitude to it is an extension of their attitude to their country—a bundle of contradictions and complexities. For them, national dress is a straitjacket. It's another of those insidious ways in which the free play of their individuality is stifled and suppressed. They pine to break out, get abroad, and change into a Western suit. In Kuwait their attitude is that national dress is a mark of rank. Only Kuwaiti Kuwaitis wear it. They'll make noises about how inconvenient it is with the same convincing tone as a much-decorated statesman groaning at having to put on yet more badges, sashes, and medals.

Throughout Arabia you can tell a man who spends most of his time abroad. He's the one who's forever scratching his head. That "tablecloth" over it makes him itch. He's one of the few that probably looks better in Western clothes. Few Arab men bother with a good tailor. They rush into a store and buy ready-made, usually badly fitting suits because they haven't the patience to wait for fittings. And they look dreadful in them.

But national dress? Ah, that's different. It makes the tall and slim look like film stars. The ascetic like saints. Figures paunchy and stooping, gutted by years of outrageous living, become venerable vessels of wisdom. Then you see in London or New York the figures you last met in Kuwait, Jeddah, or Abu Dhabi. It's an appalling shock, better avoided. The film star has turned into a waiter, the saint into a beggar, the wise man into a carpet vendor.

Besides what it does for his figure, national dress confers an advantage on an Arab, especially on a Kuwaiti, over everyone else he talks to who doesn't wear it—and that means women, Westerners, and foreign Arabs. It also enables him to get up to all those tricks that become possible when you're wearing long drapes—it turns the crow into a peacock.

Sitting down becomes a whole performance; the vain man won't crease his apparel. Then there's the question of pockets. A man's role is circumscribed by the fact that he can't carry anything but the odd, minute gold lighter around with him. The thin cotton reveals the contents of his pockets to all the world—he couldn't be disfigured that way. So the oil-rich Arab can't play the role of the Useful Man who's always equipped with string, cigars, spare handkerchiefs, pens, and other white rabbits ready to whip out in an emergency. It renders him "helpless," in need of an entourage.

Worrying about all these problems means that on top of feeling he's running the world, an Arab man has to be all those things women have long been accused of—excessively pre-occupied with details, obsessed with self and therefore doomed to look at other people and his surroundings through a de-licious haze of subjectivity.

Oh yes, their women may spend a fortune dressing up like the rich usually do everywhere else—but that's the whole point. No matter how much they spend, how well they dress, how much they go for chic or exclusivity, rich Arab women now look like any other rich women throughout the world. And the Western world isn't agog to know what's next in the minds of those all-powerful oil sheikhas. They're only interested in the all-powerful oil sheikhs. It's the modern way of setting their women physically apart.

And the men are going to keep it that way. Don't listen to any Kuwaiti man who tells you he wears national dress be-cause it's more practical. It might be in summer, but he won't often be here in summer. He wears it because it stamps him as a superior being. It's written all over him in black (his cloak) and white (his dress) that he's the thing to be right now—Arab, from an oil state, and a man. How could the Kuwaiti women fight that?

CHAPTER

19

NO EXIT

"ALL CHANGE, PLEASE" SEEMS TO BE THE MOTTO OF KUWAITI society. All those new houses; all those independent females. Kuwait even claims to have a world-renowned women's movement. In case you haven't heard of it, it has thirty members. As a status symbol, it's fine. As anything more potent, it's a total failure. Kuwaiti family life is all too often a desolate mockery of freedom and companionship. In its own way it's more segregated and harsher on women than Saudi Arabia's.

Most men in Kuwait spend their time with other men. There's homosexuality, but that's not the main reason. There's a Kuwaiti institution: the *diwania*. It's a large room with a separate entrance, tacked onto or under a house. Every evening most men from the inner circle of Kuwait (some three thousand in all) go to one another's *diwanias*. They play cards, gossip, do business, watch television, and, occasionally, import belly dancers. It's respectable enough; it merely excludes wives. (The latest stand of Sheikha Awatif, the ruler's daughter, and her husband Sheikh Saud has caused some consternation. They have desegregated his *diwania;* husbands and wives are both invited now. Too bad this bold couple have been posted to the embassy in London; no one else has yet had the courage to follow their example.)

Then there's adultery; rather a great deal of it. Among men,

231

that is. I don't know how men are supposed to commit adultery with women without women committing adultery too, but that's the marvelous paradox of the double standard at work again. Kuwaiti men are even less inhibited about their sexual activities than Saudis.

Their attitude to Western women in their country is equally less inhibited. I'll never be able to smell sandalwood again without being reminded of a conversation I have with one young Kuwaiti who's reeking of the stuff. It goes on for an hour or more. The gist: Why am I so prejudiced against Arab men that I think all they're interested in is sex? (I haven't mentioned the subject; he's brought it up.) And why, while we're talking about it, won't I sleep with him? And if I won't sleep with him, why do I go around looking like the kind of girl who can cope with life and therefore with sleeping with him? That's the Western woman's Catch-22 in the Gulf: either you're not tough enough to be able to cope in the country, or you're tough enough to cope and that's synonymous with being tough enough to sleep around. It's like being stuck on a carousel.

You're also tough enough, it seems, to be beyond surprise. This man is from a heritage family. He's in his late thirties (he looks fifty). He's on public boards and corporations and owns his own company. He plops himself down next to me and, without invitation, treats me to the saga of his private life. Since I'm fondling my notebook at the time and he's perfectly sober and knows perfectly well that I'm a journalist, I wish I could name him. He's old enough, and certainly big enough, to know what he's doing. (Alas, I can't.) He launches forth.

"At last I'm going to Cairo to see about my flat. Every week I book a flight, every week I'm so busy I cancel. I bought it some months ago and gave the decorator ten thousand dollars to start work. But he's spent that, and I have to go and arrange matters. Of course I buy it and I do everything. My wife wouldn't know how to make a house. Our house in Beirut, I did everything. Even my house in Kuwait, I made everything and then I called her in and said, 'There you are.'

"My wife is very busy. My mistake was in making five children, one nine or ten months after the other. My wife clings to the children so much. I come home at nights and find our children in our bed. I tell her very often, 'I do not like to sleep with children, I like to sleep with you.' Finally I say, 'All right, you go and sleep with your children. I'll sleep in my bed.'

"Now it's not so bad. I feel sorry for my wife. She loves me too much. I can't help it, but I don't like to be with her so much. Last summer in London I said to her one Sunday, 'Today I will be with you. I will take you for a walk in the park.' She loved it, but me, I didn't like it. If I go with my friends for a walk I say, 'There's a pretty girl.' I can't say that to her and so we have nothing to discuss.

"I'm very hot and strong. I must have a woman every day or I can't sleep. But my wife, she only wants three times a week. So I have four girlfriends in Kuwait, two in London, and one in Cairo. Every morning I leave my house at eight o'clock and I go and take one of my girlfriends to my private flat and we enjoy ourselves for say one and a half hours and then I go to the office.

"Today I make my wife at one thirty, I make one girl at three, and then I go to the *diwania* until twelve and then I make another girl and then I go home to my wife. Today after lunch my wife in bed she made five times and I made one. All my girlfriends are the same. I wait and then I say, 'Is that enough?' and then they sigh and say, 'Oh, yes,' and then I roll on top and that's that. My French girlfriend in London says she has never had man in her life like me.

"I don't know if my wife knows or if she doesn't. I say to her many times, 'If you don't like me, you can go away.' But she loves me. What can she do? My wife wouldn't want another man. What would I do if I found out she had one? I would push her straight out with her children and tell her to go back to her home. Of course it's different for me. I'm very hot man."

I'm too stunned to react. What can you say to such a man?

I ask him if he thinks his wife is happy with her lot and what she does every night when he goes to the *diwania.* "Happy? She has me. She loves me so much that we have four servants but she washes all my clothes herself; she would kiss my feet if I told her to. What does she do? I don't know. She stays inside our home, she talks to her children, watches TV, and is on the telephone very much."

He's incapable of recognizing his wife as a person. No wonder she spends so much time on the telephone. All over Kuwait there's a network of telephone addicts supplying each other with fixes. There are women telephoning women, women telephoning men. It's a most curious fantasy life.

The most sorry story of all was told me by a young girl from a good family. She had a "love affair." It was pure fantasy, until she got hurt. Then it was real enough. She's twenty-five, dark, pretty, thin—too thin. "One day I was so bored that I picked up a telephone and dialed a number. Any number. A man answered the telephone and we ended up having a conversation. He pleaded with me to give him my number and that's how we started having a romance. It was all on the telephone. It went for for six months and we hadn't even seen each other. We were dying to, so I arranged to meet him in a supermarket by such and such a counter. I said I'd wear a pink shirt. I took a girlfriend and he took a boyfriend.

"We were able to see each other and talk for a few moments. He was wonderful-looking. After that we used to arrange to take drives at the same time just to be able to wave and smile. This went on for five years. But then my family found out about it, so he said it was time for him to be formally introduced to me.

"He met my brother and it was obvious that there was going to be a proposal. One friend even gave me a betrothal present. I was happy—you understand?"

I understand. Marriages are still arranged, mostly because they have to be. There's a limited circle from which a girl of a certain family can take a husband. To find one from it for herself would be happiness indeed.

"Then it started. First I got threatening calls from his mother and sister warning me off. His mother said he had been promised to another girl from birth. The man said he didn't care. The summer came and his mother went away, taking him with her. He went for a week. After one and a half months I still hadn't heard a word. Then someone told me he was back; still no word. At last I worked up enough courage to telephone. His mother hung up on me.

"One day he telephoned. He didn't even say hello. He asked me a question: 'Listen, do you hear that noise?' I listened and I could hear a faint swishing. 'That's my wife. Sweeping.' That's all he said."

At least her family stuck by her, even though she had broken every law of their society. Everyone in that limited circle from which she could marry knows about it. Not much hope of a husband now.

Not all Kuwaiti women allow themselves to be drawn into loneliness. They don't all remain passive. There are single girls who work, who lead an independent life of sorts. All too often their mothers push fathers or brothers into cutting down these girls' freedom. They want them back in the family prison. It's a question of jealousy. Older women resent having missed the opportunities. "Imagine, all those hundreds of years of purdah and the veil," said one educated older woman, "and I had to miss real freedom by twenty years."

More forceful girls marry an acceptable man and then bully their way into getting what they want—freedom to go out to work, to public places, restaurants, Europe, and the United States. The more fortunate find a man who doesn't want only the *"diwania* and separate existences," and knows how and when to compromise.

Hind al Naqib had an uncertain, disturbed childhood. She was born in Iraq but the family moved to Kuwait soon after the revolution there—they got instant Kuwaiti citizenship. They were cousins of the Iraqi royal family, and here that counts for something. Her family were received as "proper

Kuwaitis." Unfortunately for Hind later, her father goofed by moving to Beirut—it was easier to make money in Lebanon in those days. *That* the Kuwaitis didn't forgive: "They still say to me sometimes, 'When we were poor you were in Beirut, now we're rich you want to be here,' and they do feel bitter about it."

Hind's an aristocrat and she's married to one, a Kuwaiti from a heritage family. She's nearly thirty; has been a mother for most of her twenties, was a headmistress, and is now a university teacher. She is one of the rare Kuwaiti women who entertains for her husband, Abdul Rachman, a deputy minister. She's one of an even rarer breed of Kuwaiti women; she has a certain insight into herself.

"I was a very spoiled child and very precocious. I behaved like a child when I went to the university in Beirut. I never did a stroke of work. I don't know how I passed the exams. I always tried to live up to my reputation for behaving badly—it gave me a kind of distinct identity.

"But at home we lived like Kuwaitis. I was never allowed out in the evenings, so I used to rage and scream at my father, 'Let me, let me go out like everyone else.' And then right after I graduated I got married. It was arranged for us, but afterward I used to get terribly angry whenever my husband admitted it. I was so embarrassed about it that I used to go around saying that we had fallen in love.

"Those first two years back in Kuwait were awful. It wasn't Kuwait; I was used to a sheltered life in Beirut. Getting used to each other was difficult. The trouble with us Kuwaiti girls is that we're spoiled. We get married young and go on treating our husbands exactly like our fathers: 'want, want, want.'

"I was bored to tears shut up in the house all day and I used to lie in wait for Abdul Rachman and nag him with questions, wanting to know every single little movement he'd made since he left the house. I was mad to have his attention; he was normally so unaffectionate. I got so bored that I spent every moment of my life when he wasn't at home on the telephone.

"That was when Abdul Rachman pulled me up short. He told me that I would be appalling in ten years' time and that I had to do something useful. He sent me out to teach. They all got their knives in then. 'Poor girl,' they said, 'he can't even make enough money to keep his wife.' He was a good deal wiser than his years, Abdul Rachman; he didn't care. It did the trick. All that energy I'd been turning in on myself suddenly had an outlet. I started making friends of my own. It was good for my confidence.

"Abdul Rachman does go out quite a lot in the evening with his friends. But now the women take it in turn to entertain. We can't go to a public restaurant, not our kind of women, so one group invites the men one evening and the other group the women. It works. But the one thing that has made my marriage easier is that I can truly say I never fell in love and I don't believe in it. I'm very grateful for that."

Less grateful women resort to cunning. If they're single, they weave a refined mesh of coverups involving friends, sisters, drivers, maids. All this to go to occasional mixed tea parties or dinners. "Wherever I am, I always say I'm with my best friend and my best friend always knows to back that up when my mother calls her to check." This from an al Sabah. "And it's not as if this is the high life. It's so innocent. What's wrong with a little dinner party once a week and maybe a drink? Fortunately my driver is very loyal. Mother once tried to trip him up, saying she knew I'd been to a house with a mixed party and Europeans. He wouldn't give me away."

Other girls get out of the country altogether. They go to a university abroad and regard Kuwait as an obligation; they come home for a few months, do nothing, grow fat, and can't wait to get away again. But that has its drawbacks when the inevitable time comes for marriage: there's the all-important matter of virginity.

Before the troubles everyone used to go to Beirut for their trousseau. Some girls threw in a quick bit of hymen stitching, too. One Kuwaiti girl asked a gynecologist why he went in for (her words) this barbarous practice. "I was outraged when I came back from the West and was asked to perform such an operation," he replied. "But what can I do? I know these girls haven't done anything wrong. It's their society and the men that are at fault. I can perform a simple formal ritual that will make it possible for them to go on with their lives. Yes, it's disgusting and it's barbarous. I can't change society but I can protect the girls. And after all, I'm an Arab too. I understand."

I'm sitting around with a few Kuwaiti girls. They're having the same old rap I know from Greenwich Village and Hampstead: "consciousness raising," "ecology," "alienation." But it's not Greenwich Village. One of them mentions that she's by no means certain that one of her relations wouldn't kill her if she was found not to be a virgin. "Everyone says, 'I'll kill my wife if . . .' or 'I'll kill my sister if . . .' You never know who means it *literally*. I had a girlfriend whose father took her out to the desert when he found her with a man. We never saw her again. Whenever we went over to tea we'd ask after her. Eventually we stopped asking. How do any of us know that that wouldn't happen to us?" Her friends nod.

"What men want when they get married is blood and pain. Unless they get blood on their wedding night, they might send back the goods. And don't tell us that not all girls bleed, or about horseback riding and sport. Tell it to the men. It's an obsession with some of them. In the old days women who were worried used to go to a 'wise woman' before the wedding and she'd give them a sheep's bladder with blood in it. They'd stuff that inside on the wedding night and that did the trick.

"Some men may not mind if you're not a virgin or if your hymen is already broken. Some would understand. But how do you know when you get married which type you're getting? You've only seen him a few times. I wouldn't take the risk."

Some wives, when they get lonely enough, take an even graver risk for Kuwait. They resort to cunning and boyfriends —their drivers or stray foreigners. This one, who looks unassailable, regularly books into a beauty salon for a day's massage and facial. She turns up all right. Then she tips the receptionist heavily for silence and slips out—to see her German boyfriend. When *he* told me I didn't believe him—another bigmouthed boaster was my assessment (it still is). When *she* told me I thought she was nuts.

Can it be worth it? There's a woman in Kuwait who was caught talking on the telephone to a man. Her husband shot her in the neck and called her brother: "If you want to see your sister again alive, you'd better come around at once." Her brother secretly got her to the hospital. Next morning all Kuwait knew about it.

She now leads a quiet life and everyone agrees that it's forgotten. The end of an ugly scar juts below the scarf around her neck.

Sometimes I long to say to women I meet, "You don't have to be victims, you don't have to be underhanded and afraid. The way out is through the door; take it. If not, wake up and fight back." Then I realize how futile and out of place my Western conditioning is here. And anyway, can I be so sure that I'd be any different had I been born to this life? Not after meeting Najat Sultan, certainly.

Najat Sultan *has* woken up; she's working for change. "In 1972 I tried to get a group of women to work together. I contacted some thirty-five of the two hundred and thirty women graduates there were in Kuwait then to come to a meeting. No one showed up. I tried the same thing in the traditional way—arranging a tea party. No one came. And then I realized it was the wrong approach, that I had to work more gradually, talking to individuals and concentrating on women who were already working or were in important positions to give me a lead." What is she trying to accomplish? Her aims are so modest as to appear prudish. "I just want to make women aware of themselves and of their position." *Just.* In Kuwait that's like asking Palestinian commandos home to tea.

People talk of Najat as articulate, tough, and cold. She

sounds alarming. She works at the government's Planning Board during the day and every evening sits in the art gallery she and her brother Fawaz have started together. Najat Sultan is holding her salon. Here she's at her most slick and buoyant.

She's a beautiful girl, with a cloud of fluffy, dark hair down to her waist. She has a small, neat-featured face—with huge, rather anxious, deep brown eyes, not so certain of themselves after all. She's unusually dressed for Kuwait: dark trousers, loose Peruvian-style jacket over a white shirt, and loads of necklaces—Bedouin jewelry and some she made herself.

This *could* be New York; the prints on the walls of the white, deliberately austere, gallery may be by Kuwaitis and other Arab artists, but they all trained at Western art schools. The sophisticated, slightly Bohemian girls around her talk intensely, and with a certain contempt, about other Kuwaiti women. Some of Najat's phrases are good, if obviously well rehearsed and much aired: "In Kuwait we suffer from double apartheid: class and sex. Kuwaitis and non-Kuwaitis, men and women. They are separate societies within one society." Yes, it's good, and I've heard other patter like it in Kuwait.

But there are other Najats: the simpler, gentler, warmer creature that is Najat at home with her mother and "Baby," her sister. She's more honest. "I've clipped my wings a lot recently and I'm much less sociable. I had to; my brothers and cousins objected to my seeing so many people." The way she talks about other women changes too. She shows more understanding, more compassion. "Husbands complain about their wives' extravagance! But how can you possibly blame the women? Things are all they have to fill the vacuum."

And then there's the unself-confident Najat. European friends invited her to a party; she came, slightly out of control from fear and uncertainty. Her defense was to turn up in an outrageous fancy-dress costume, Edwardian, with a big, floppy hat. ("That was when I first felt affection for Najat," says a friend. "The moment when I could see how much it cost her to come into that room, she suddenly became vulnerable.")

But I know people in London who'd laugh at such a story, say it's hogwash. They remember her when she spent years at a posh art school there, taking a jewelry course. She bowled everyone over: beautiful, cool, very together, and right on top of the social scene. She never talks of those years now; she's buried them completely. The Kuwaiti social scene has defeated her since then. What's ahead for her? She may look twenty-four but she must be in her midthirties. No Kuwaiti man would take her on, and there's no question of her marrying a foreigner; she's from far too good a Kuwaiti family. Those brothers and cousins (guardians of *her* and, therefore, *their* honor) wouldn't complain; they'd behave as though she were dead.

She enjoys her work, but it's not much fun living in a society that sees you as a freak, an oddball. The most daring thing she can ever do is to go out for dinner alone with a man in a restaurant. But she has to care enough to run the risk of being seen. Najat's far too honest to resort to scheming and cover-ups. "If it's important enough to me, yes I'll go and take the consequences. But I won't go just for fun."

If I lived in a society where going out for one lousy dinner would turn me into a social outcast, I guess my self-confidence and independence might cave in too. Najat's certainly have. When she went back to London on vacation recently she was given Germaine Greer's number to call and lots of other trendy introductions. She didn't use a single one. Kuwait has undermined Najat Sultan.

What woke her up? Maybe it was seeing her aunt's life. Her aunt married a good-looking man, who left her after two years. He left her with two children, never divorced her, and she had to stay with his parents. Maybe it was seeing her own parents, who were much happier—during the sixteen years they spent living in India, away from Kuwait. Knowing another life made a difference to Najat, but she never belonged wholly to that other existence either; she went to boarding school in Cairo as a girl and hated being cut off from her family. Once was enough; she wouldn't do it again. She came back to Kuwait in 1959 hardly able to speak the Kuwaiti Arabic. She doesn't fit in and she doesn't want to get out. There's no exit for Najat.

Kuwait talks about Najat Sultan rather a lot. They don't say very much about Sheikha Badria. They mention her frequently enough, all right, but it's in passing. They take her for granted. She's exceptional; what else is there to say?

A lot, frankly. It's something I keep coming across, time and again, in Arabia. There's that handful of women whose personalities soared above their society's limitations at a time when women were literally boxed in, bundled up, and blotted out (as far as the outside world was concerned, anyway). In Saudi Arabia, for instance, there was Princess Hassa, the strong, forceful mother of the Crown Prince and his six full brothers. In Kuwait there's Sheikha Badria.

At the Hilton Hotel the top women of Kuwait are gathering for a luncheon in honor of a British schoolmistress—Audrey Callaghan, doing a grand Arabian tour with her husband James (in his capacity as Foreign Secretary). If you haven't heard of Sheikha Badria and meet her here for the first time, you might not think anything of her at all. You might not even notice her. She's a plump, middle-aged woman who's quiet. Unlike most Kuwaitis, she's listening rather than talking. Perhaps she doesn't understand a lot of the jabbering going on in English around her?

Then slowly you may become uncomfortable under the scrutiny of a pair of extremely active eyes, Sheikha Badria's. Of course, she understands every word. She's renowned for the way she slightly unnerves people with her quietness, making them talk more than they expected to. She's summing them up.

Maybe when you were searching out the state of the dollar in this morning's paper, you noticed the name above an announcement of today's foreign currency prices—the United Trading Company. That's Sheikha Badria's outfit. She owns one of Kuwait's two largest moneychanging and financial in-

stitutions outside the banks. She has real estate valued by conservative locals at $165 million and she not only makes deci-
sions about her company's long-term strategy and day-to-day
dealings—she makes all of the decisions.

Take another look at that face; it gives no clue what's on
her mind, but it's tough and canny. At home she's different.
And then again she's not. She's welcoming and warm, unusually so for Kuwait. But there's still no clue what's on her
mind. You won't get one, either, from chatting with her. You
will if you watch her drawing her Palestinian manager to one
corner after dinner and talking business. In a moment she
changes: leaning forward, she delivers a low, rapid, decisive
burst of words while her eyes continue to scrutinize the room
as if she's looking for a mouse. Then she listens intently to her
manager, nodding briefly.

She rejoins her guests; she's smiling and retiring again. Take
a closer look at that face: the bones show, it alternates between
looking gracious, imperious, and maternal, almost without
moving a muscle. She's great company, but you won't learn
anything about her from Sheikha Badria herself. You will from
looking to her background, her home, and her daughters.

"Ah yes, Sheikha Badria," say Kuwaitis, "of course she's different. She was the creation of her husband." At first I go along
with that view. At seventeen she married Sheikh Fahd, a first
cousin, twenty years older, who was the first al Sabah to be
college-educated abroad (the American University of Beirut).
He went on to run substantial portions of Kuwait's government
before his death in 1959. Yes, Sheikha Badria is the widow of
that Sheikh Fahd—the one who went in for an imaginative life-
style and got pushed out of his jobs by the family. She's also
the granddaughter of one of those two brothers murdered by
a third, Emir Mubarak "The Great." Her family was exiled,
so she grew up in Iraq, away from the al Sabah conforming influence—that made her different for a start.

When Sheikh Fahd asked for her hand Badria's mother
(who had black blood) was opposed to the marriage. He was
poor and he was black, too. "Ethiopian blood, they tell me,"

says Badria's daughter, Lulua, whose long neck, straight features, and tiny bones speak the remark anyway. Badria married her cousin regardless, and in the early years they traveled abroad together a great deal. Another difference.

In the early fifties Fahd started taking over government responsibilities. He asked Badria to work with him. He was serious; he wanted her to do things, not just carry the titles. History has not been kind to Sheikh Fahd, but he had some fine qualities; intelligence was one of them. At first Badria refused: "I lacked the self-confidence and experience." Then came a trip to the States in 1954; she spent a few months looking around hospitals, improving her English, and acquiring enough confidence, when she returned to Kuwait, to go without the veil and to accept the post of Director of Hospitals. It was the start of the country's health service (which, incidentally, is a good one. Kuwaitis don't need to fly to London for everything. They choose to).

Sheikh Fahd hadn't made a mistake; Badria showed her mettle. She hired good people (good Palestinians) and worked hard herself. "People used to ring me up at all times of the day and night and ask me to accompany their mother to the hospital or sit through an operation on their wife because the doctor was a man and that frightened a woman."

She was also busy having several children and earning a reputation that stuck among foreign diplomats as "the Sabah wife who entertains." Now if she was purely Fahd's creation, her career would surely have lost momentum after his death. The reverse has happened; today she's the first al Sabah visiting foreigners approach to open their exhibitions. "They all need sponsors. None of them are frightened to come to me. How can I refuse?"

Of course they're not frightened. She may be guarded with you but she treats you immediately as a friend, an equal. (This need I remind you in Kuwait, not Jeddah.) And the United Trading Company, which she started in the sixties? "My mother was a born businesswoman from way back," says one of her daughters with a huge smile. "While other women were

always given jewels by their husbands, my mother turned them
down. She always asked my father to give her property instead."

So that's Sheikha Badria's background. Now for her house—
correction, palace. Picture a flying saucer, wildly extravagant
and all curves. That's Sheikha Badria's home. Next to it nestles
a very normal old house with straight lines. That's her old
home; the hermit crab's discarded shell. Her daughters live in
that now. Badria's domed living room (really domed: it has
the silhouette of a perfect blancmange) is magnificent, grand,
enormous—any words you can think of to describe a pale fawn
marble floor with every item on it rare and carefully chosen.
Sofas follow the curve of the room; there's an Arab urn in its
center, Chagall lithographs on the walls, a French eighteenth-
century dresser, fine art nouveau glass. On a low table is a
chess set, made of gold and enamel, inset with turquoises.
Plants, tapestries, stained-glass panels; it's a Parthenon for a
princess, with a touch of the Assyrian tarbrush in style. Yes,
it is truly magnificent. It copies nothing; it's restrained and
yet studded with color. Badria never learned this from Fahd.

Then look at her daughters: Amina, stunning. With her
American accent, she could be a wealthy black from the States,
only there's something wilder, freer about her. Maybe it's those
Grecian curls bubbling over her head. Maybe it's her mouth,
soft, sensual, always looking as if it's about to fill with laughter.
Irresponsible in a way no educated American could be today;
black consciousness doesn't mean much to you if you're royalty.
Why the American accent? The Scottish-American Mrs. Stevens
—Sheikha Badria was the first to introduce a foreign nanny to
Kuwait. Later she sent her daughters to school in the U.S.;
it means that English is their first language and their Arabic
is poor. "I can't speak Kuwaiti," says Fatma, "and that's aw-
fully important." (Not quite the problem it was for Najat
Sultan, however; Fatma's an al Sabah, remember.) "I can manage as long as we're talking about nothing in particular, but
as soon as there's an interesting conversation, about politics
or philosophy, I simply can't follow what they're saying."
Okay; they can't speak Kuwaiti Arabic but Fatma's interest

in philosophy and Kuwaiti politics is no pose. That's one bonus. The daughters' sense of humor is another.

Take Amina, for instance. Her cult figures, she says, are the British Prince of Wales and Barbara Cartland. Everybody laughs and jokes about it for a while and then she slips in again with an innocent look on her face. She inquires whether, if she were to marry the Prince of Wales, the British newspapers would carry the headline: OIL QUEEN FLIES IN. Amina, in the nicest possible way, is having a dig at the Western media.

Who teaches them now? Who's grounded them to be so at ease with foreigners? Their mother, of course. When Sheikha Badria's said good-bye to the last of her Lebanese and Palestinian guests ("Mama is always most at home with foreigners . . ."), she draws two of her daughters into a small antechamber. She sits down like an Arab man in national dress, legs apart, hands on her knees, and briefs them—on business, current affairs, and the only politics they need to know about, family politics. It's the one moment in the evening when they stop larking about and become quite quiet. As long as they keep the rules (i.e. in the palace, under their mother's eyes, when they're not abroad studying), Badria's daughters get the protection of this astonishing woman.

But what made Sheikha Badria so different? I still don't know. Why does one superb actress become a star while another equally superb actress merely stays employed? It's an indefinable quality. Every now and again Arabia has always thrown up the odd "star"—Sheikha Badria is one. And even *her* daughters admit that in Kuwait it's better to be a man. It's a far far easier station in life to be called to.

20

RACING AROUND WITH A ROYAL

THE BEST KIND OF THING TO BE OF ALL, OF COURSE, IS AN AL Sabah man—like Sheikh Nasser. He and I are bowling along one Monday in his silver sports car (complete with statutory Japanese LM-IM Mobile carphone with push-button dialing). We're off to the races. Sheikh Nasser's in a cheery mood; news from the track has it that the going's soft. Good for his horses; Nasser keeps forty at his Amneaf Stable outside Kuwait and he's in keen competition with Uncle Khalid who has seventy at his stable, Al Salam.

The horses are already in the paddock for the two o'clock race when he screeches to a halt in the desert parking lot. Nasser goes off for a quick word with his Egyptian jockey Hisham, walking his three-year-old maiden, Hakima. The sheikh has a feeling that his quartered green-and-red racing colors will show to advantage this afternoon.

Sheikh Nasser ibn Sabah al Sabah is the son of Kuwait's Foreign Minister and son-in-law of the ruler. A royal plum, in fact. At twenty-eight he's chairman of United Fisheries and director of Gulf International, the largest Kuwaiti conglomerate. More significantly, he's a director of Lonhro, the British stock exchange-listed company whose front-page boardroom rows a few years ago (involving tax-free payments in the Cay-

man Islands and so on) led British Prime Minister Edward
Heath to coin that bon mot "the unacceptable face of capitalism." The press coverage of Sheikh Nasser's first attendance at
the annual Lonhro shareholders' meeting after several million
shares passed expensively into his hands, wasn't flattering. The
usual Arabs-are-coming Western treatment. Kuwait winced
again.

Nasser takes me up to the members' stand, where a large
party of his relations are already installed. Uncle Khalid, a
correct man, as befits the president of the emir's *dirwan* (court)
sits stiffly in his front-row armchair behind his telephone and
two Venetian vases of plastic yellow flowers.

Here is the result of past generations' greed for wives, from
white to ebony. Half of the al Sabah royal family present are
pitch-black. Khalid's half-brother, Misha'al, the son of a slave,
keeps up a nonstop flow of jokes, shouts, and anecdotes, while
he cracks nuts and scatters shells everywhere. He stamps on the
stand boards to hurry along the servant below who scurries
up and down all afternoon with trays full of teacups. Ahmed,
the Crown Prince's son, a slimmer version of his father, slips
in and hardly opens his mouth. He's the only one to keep
quiet. It's a gang of the lads having a tremendous outing. The
powdery sand track is indeed soft. There's much peering
through binoculars, learned race-talk, and cruel slashing of
whips by eager jockeys.

It takes a while to absorb the sight (and sounds) of all these
royal sheikhs, normally so dignified, rushing around like a
bunch of loonies. But it's not long before I notice that I'm the
only woman; apart from Myra Davies. Myra's a blunt, Welsh
outdoor type who looks after Khalid's horses on an informal
sort of basis. Kuwait is a small city and it didn't take long for
Khalid to hear that there was an excellent horsewoman in
town who'd be only too delighted to help work out his magnificent Arabs. Apart from the dour-faced Khalid, everyone thinks
it's a lark having a woman here. Myra doesn't count. With her
hair tied back from her face, her absent husband off doing a
day's work for the Kuwait Oil Company, she's almost one of

the lads herself. Every racing afternoon involves at least one lengthy discussion between Myra and Khalid about how his beasts are doing on their new Indian barley feed.

She finds time from dietary matters to fill me in on this extraordinary assembly. Don't the sheikhas ever come? Myra laughs. "With rare exceptions, being married to an al Sabah," she explains patiently as if to a child, "isn't like being a wife as we understand it. It's like being a brood mare." Mares at stud in al Sabah palaces don't go to the races.

Sheikh Nasser is one of the exceptions, explains the all-knowing Myra. Not that his wife, Hasa, would be here either. "It's just that they're, well, different in other ways." In any case, Hasa is under a doctor's care in Paris. She's resting in her apartment, trying not to have her third miscarriage in a row.

Nasser is having a smashing time. He strides to and fro in his two-inch platform shoes (he's very short, for an al Sabah, and wishes he weren't). He stuffs his hands into the pockets of his long brown national dress and digs into the betting. Highest stake, after much angry haggling, $35. They're off for the first race: 1,000 meters, entry fee $10, first prize $270. Nasser's Hakima starts well but finishes third. His big face (it's big enough for a man wearing twelve-inch platform shoes) registers thunder. It soon passes.

Jockey Hisham walks by on Hakima. He looks up apologetically at Nasser. But Nasser's already involved with ribbing Khalid and any number of his cousins. They're generous to each other over winners. When Major General Abdul Latif Thuweini, undersecretary at the Ministry of the Interior, leads in his winners in the second race and then the third, they're all pleased for him. Misha'al and Nasser do point out, though, how keen the general is to rush down and be photographed with his horses. At last a winner for Nasser—Mashalla in the fifth race. He almost falls down the steps in his hurry to get in front of the camera.

It's an afternoon of laughter, teasing, sand driven into my eyes. Whenever he remembers, Nasser is the perfect host. When he forgets, the rest of his family do the honors—even Uncle Khalid comes around, offering an occasional nod. It's about as formal as a donkey derby.

Now I understand why Arabs, even royal Arabs, don't like to keep their horseflesh in Europe, where it could gallop around more fashionably in the Arc de Triomphe of St. Leger. Where would the fun be for these exuberant owners stuck with the champagne and shooting-stick crowd?

Nasser's servant comes to give him a nudge. Has he forgotten that he's flying to Cairo in an hour's time? Nasser's expressive face registers panic. Then he looks me straight in the eye: "Would you like to come to Cairo tonight? I'll send you back on my plane tomorrow." The back of Uncle Khalid's head freezes. I don't hesitate. "I'd love to. I've always wanted to see the pyramids."

It's seven o'clock in the VIP lounge at Kuwait airport. Sheikh Nasser is impatient. Officials stand around, edgy to anticipate his every wish. His only wish is to get off the ground. Unfortunately he forgot to tell his air crew about going to Cairo.

At last the English captain arrives to announce that the crew's all present and correct but there's another problem: fuel. The Falcon is carrying too much baggage to fly without refueling. Luxor is out of gas, so is Syria. Would Sheikh Nasser mind cutting across to Jeddah first? Sheikh Nasser doesn't have much option, and all he wants to do is split from the crowd in the VIP lounge, swelling by the minute. He's very royal here, which means too much bowing and scraping for Nasser's taste. At this point the captain learns that he won't be flying back until tomorrow. "Can someone telephone my wife?" he asks with the resignation of a man who left for a day trip to Khartoum last time and came back a fortnight later.

I don't have a visa for Egypt. Nasser waves that aside. I don't have a visa to reenter Kuwait. Another wave. When it's time to board I'm trying to make him understand that mere mortals can't hop into Egypt like a Kuwaiti royal (my passport isn't stamped "member of the ruling family" like his). Okay, we'll play it his way. Sheikh Nasser marches across the tarmac followed by a large troop of well-wishers and a small troop of passengers. We're off. With the plane so full there's no room to watch a video tape; it's Shirley Bassey on the stereo hi-fi instead.

Two hours later the Falcon approaches Jeddah. I'm up in the cockpit with Captain Jim, who's trying to put me at my ease: "Don't feel uncomfortable, we've had plenty of girls aboard before." Jim was enjoying a quiet afternoon with his wife, and copilot Rudi was fishing six miles out to sea when someone was sent to find them. Adrian, the blond, delicate-looking steward was playing with his new dune buggy on the beach ("I borrowed the money for it from Sheikh Nasser; I'm counting on him not to ask for it back").

The generator has failed. The windshield is iced up. "Where's my shammy?" mutters Jim. "I can't see a bloody thing." What a life; he had only just gotten the Kuwait ground staff used to servicing the old HS 125 when Nasser bought this second-hand Falcon from Lonhro. To cap it, he's now talking about ordering a long-range, intercontinental Gulfstream GU2.

Jim moans all the way to landing point but somehow brings the jet down smoothly. It's the last smooth moment for hours. *Of course* Jeddah doesn't have fuel. It's the middle of the pilgrimage season and the place is littered with planes. What a contrast to the crisp cold of Kuwait as the hot, humid air of Jeddah hits me. I never thought to be back, at least not *this* soon.

Nasser wishes he had never agreed to come. Takeoff will be ten thirty, then eleven thirty. Nasser stomps between the VIP lounge (as luxurious as a Greyhound Bus station) and the plane, angry but helpless. Everyone is surprised at the predicament. "I don't understand this country. How can Saudi Arabia of all places run out of oil?" At midnight the Falcon takes off and Nasser creeps into the back with me to dine on

Adrian's sensitively cooked chicken. His exuberance of the afternoon has been crushed. "It makes me feel terrible. All this waiting. I'm so scared at what you must think of me that I don't know how to talk to you."

Nasser is an unusual al Sabah, he's upsettable. He feels responsible for the inconvenience in Jeddah because I'm his honored guest. He looks like a small child, which is an appealing combination—Nasser's another extremely attractive man. He may be short but he has a well-built torso. His face is too big for it; but he has huge brown eyes with long lashes. He's also very rich, which you'd think would give him more confidence. He's not just as rich as all al Sabah are automatically (as the al Saud are in Saudi Arabia, etc.); he's riding a company, Gulf International, that was started by his father with a Sudanese vet and is growing vast.

The Falcon comes in to land at Cairo at 3 A.M. The cockpit window on Jim's side is so iced up that Rudi is bringing her down. This is always a nerve-racking hop. One captain (I'm not surprised to learn that Jim's the third in a year) tried cutting corners over Luxor and the next thing he knew there were five military jets screaming around. The plane was heading directly toward a missile site. The jets didn't shoot it down because a SAM missile was waiting for the honor a few minutes on. There was a rapid change of course in the nick of time. We cut no corners this morning, but not being able to see makes Rudi jumpy.

Wheels are down, flaps are down, when Jim remarks in a tight British voice, "I say, Rudi, you're landing on the road actually. The runway's over there." A quick swerve and we make it.

The embassy official has been dutifully waiting for ages—he expected the plane six hours ago. There's more Sheikh Nasser this and Sheikh Nasser that—until he sees my passport. What? No visa? He's mesmerized by horror. Nasser grabs his briefcase and my arm and drags me out of the VIP lounge into the Cairo night. It's three thirty in the morning and an al Sabah is marching along a deserted road with a strange woman in dirty jeans. The funny side hits us; it's hardly jet set but it's fun.

Eventually we find a taxi to take us to the Meridian Hotel. This glossy tower boasts a view of the Nile, fourteen floors, a swimming pool, a nightclub with reputedly the best belly dancers in Cairo and a receptionist-night manager who has a wonderful way of lifting a surprised eyebrow.

Nasser's long brown dress looks silly in this international marble lobby. The manager has to see his passport before he'll take him seriously. Yes, he's found the suite booking but could he please have, pause, "the lady's" name. Nasser remember's "Linda." He sticks. I don't help him out. There's a long, long silence before I add demurely, "Blandford." The eyebrow's working overtime, and Nasser's glaring fit to kill.

It's four o'clock when we walk into Suite 727. Disaster. It has a sitting room with kidney-shaped sofa but only one bedroom. Nasser refuses to take the bedroom and leave me on the sofa. I refuse the bedroom too; I point out that he's too fat for the sofa. Impasse. We break so that I can take a much needed bath. The only suggestion he never makes is that we share the one bed. (Can you picture a Westerner carrying an obligation to a guest that far?)

We compromise, order a nice cup of tea, and sit on the balcony overlooking the Nile. It's the kind of night they make movies about—only the dialogue is wrong.

By now I understand more than enough of the Arab fear of losing face to be astonished (and impressed) by Nasser. He admits that he flunked his law degree at Kuwait University, some achievement in itself for an al Sabah. "I was twenty-one and I didn't know what to do. So I went to my cousin Hasa and asked her to marry me. I told her that I couldn't think of anything else to do. It was very hard for me because Hasa was the clever one of the family and I'd always hated her for being intelligent.

"Hasa said she'd think about it. She said yes and that gave

me the confidence to finish a two-year course in business studies. We had a small flat in London, knew no one there, so I had the chance to get to know her. We were together all the time. If we had married and stayed in Kuwait, it wouldn't have been possible." So that's what the Welshwoman at the races meant about Nasser's marriage being "well, different."

He's leaning on the balcony, looking across at President Sadat's guesthouse. His father often stays there. The president has invited him, too—Nasser's company has the fishing rights for the Aswan Dam and he's putting up a four-hundred-bed-room, dam-side hotel. He rocks backward and forward on those strange platform shoes. "People say I'm a big international businessman now. It doesn't make sense to me. I'm running a company my father started. I have to prove myself. It will take years before people stop saying I'm only bringing my father's money to Gulf International while others do all the thinking."

He feels he's running a race against his deficiencies. He swivels around and asks a very un-Arab question. "Do you think I have an inferiority complex? Of course I do, why ask? Sometimes I wonder if I should see a psychiatrist. Maybe if I know more about what's wrong with me, I'll be more clever and confident. Hasa says failing my exams was the best thing to happen to me. It's made me work to prove myself. But I feel so stupid. I love to meet new people, but what can I talk to them about? Someone in London promised to organize a dinner party for me and invite some society people, but I'm too scared. I could talk to them about Islamic art, but who wants to hear about Islamic art?"

It's nearly dawn. Nasser remembers that the crew will be turning up after they've cleared the airport's red tape. They're expecting rooms at the Meridian. Needless to say there aren't any. But his father has a house—on a five-acre estate near the pyramids. He concedes that I won't take the bedroom and that I won't even take the suite while he goes to the villa. (Alone in a Cairo hotel with no visa? He's crazy.) "You're being stupid," says Nasser, "but let's go."

The receptionist-manager puts his own interpretation on our reappearance. It isn't easy to walk out of a hotel with wet feet (the cleaners are drowning the lobby) and dignity. We camp on the curb until the crew turns up and then we pile into taxis to head for the villa. Nasser hasn't stayed there for ten years; nor has his father. I hate to think what we're going to find, *if* we get there at all. Somehow Nasser guides the driver through the back alleys of Cairo, shakes open a pair of creaking gates—and we're there.

It's the garden that hits me first in the dawn light. It's beautifully tended, rose bushes and flowers everywhere, screened around the outside by lines of trees. Nasser runs around it shouting at the top of his voice—he's *hoping* that there are still some servants. They come running out, kissing his hand, beaming with delight, looking not an inch put out at his unexpected arrival. The sun is coming up as we get to bed. Jim and Rudi take one room (Jim's moaning at the musty smell). Adrian is on his own downstairs (shuddering at the bathroom's rusty taps). I get the master bedroom (with a hard, lumpy bed that feels like swansdown by now—by this time I couldn't care less exactly how long ago it was made up). Nasser sleeps in the gardenhouse.

At ten o'clock the sheikh and I are having breakfast. The servants have hurriedly unwrapped and polished a fleet of cars. A refrigerated truck has turned up from nowhere: it was sent over by Nasser's younger brother, Sheikh Hamad. He's gotten back unexpectedly from a hunting trip in Libya and couldn't think where else to send his record catch of five hundred birds. ("I bet we get stuck with those disgusting things on the flight back," Adrian flinches.)

In Kuwait I wanted to see the pyramids. "Right," says Nasser, "eat up, time for a Sphinx." He's super to be with. We do the whole tourist trip, riding camels, looking at the pyramids. It's worse than the Acropolis in August; far worse. I've never seen so many tourists with so many cameras; the Sphinx doesn't get a moment's peace. Nasser sees through my disappointment: "It's marvelous," I lie.

"You're pretending; I know they're not what you expected. Please don't put on an act." Touché. Driving to lunch another side of Nasser slips out. The radio is on softly. A lush orchestra changes tune. "It's Beethoven's *Fidelio*," exclaims the "stupid one," turning it up. We park at the restaurant and eat roasted pigeons under the trees while their unknowing relations coo on the branches above us. He talks knowledgeably of music and literature; of paintings he's been buying through agents at auctions; of his and Hasa's new home in Kuwait. He's persuaded a French professor from the Sorbonne, an expert in oriental architecture, to design it for them. His talking of *their* home is significant. He's the first Kuwaiti man I've come across who doesn't call it *mine*. Hasa weaves in and out of the conversation. She's had two miscarriages, and he's terrified of her having a third. Then he takes a photograph out of his wallet and shows it to me. It's a snap of a delightful little girl. "It's our daughter, isn't she lovely?" Now, wait a minute . . . Another shock. They gave it to his mother; it was the firstborn.

At first he pretends that it was only because his mother had lost her youngest child in a car crash when the girl was born. "She was very depressed, you understand, and we felt it would help her." Finally he admits that in the al Sabah family, modern as they are, the paternal grandmother still has the right to the firstborn child. Sheikha Awatif, his sister-in-law, wife of the new Kuwaiti Ambassador to London, gave *her* eldest son to her husband's mother. Ambassador Sheikh Saud was himself brought up by his grandmother. Nasser won't talk about it. (Sheikha Awatif is much more forthright when I ask her how it feels to give away your first child after carrying for nine months. I don't mind asking her; she's a very easy, honest woman. "It's not so hard because you know it will happen. I see my son every day, just as Nasser and Hasa see their daughter. But I know that my son loves his grandmother more than he loves me, just as my husband loves his more than his mother. It's natural that that happens.")

Nasser won't talk about it. Perhaps he can't accept the apparent contradiction between the thoroughly modern image his family's trying to project and the way they stick to this practice that many might find archaic if not a little strange.

No, he's neither simple nor stupid. He directs the talk to international politics, away from treacherous personal ground. I direct it to Israel. He looks hard at me (watch an Arab watching you if he's trying to measure you—he'll stare straight into your eyes). "My lawyer in America is a Jew. Does that answer the question you were really asking?" Right on. Lunch lasts for hours, but it's time to make for the airport. Nasser insists on driving me there. It's not only because I'm his guest. He wants me to see something. He drives the Mercedes into the center of Cairo and makes me look; look hard, the Arab way.

The street stinks; stick-thin children sit in what would be gutters if this was a road. Women, eyes hollowed by poverty, crouch against grubby walls, selling sticks of sugarcane. Egypt has nearly forty million people. This street is rich living compared to the life most of the others know. "Now go back to Kuwait and remember your sight of the pyramids." I get the point; Nasser drives the car on.

The Falcon flies home nonstop. I'm the only passenger— along with brother Hamad's record catch from Libya. Adrian wasn't wrong; those bloodied, dead birds have gotten on board. Nevertheless, Adrian's in a confidential mood: there was that bag of diamonds ("as big as nuts, they were") Nasser took to Paris last time he went to see Hasa. There's that solid silver Rolls-Royce stuck in Bombay that Nasser can't get out of the country. And what happened on Nasser's nine-day trip to Acapulco, well . . .

"Still Sheikh Nasser works hard, I'll say that for him." I'd say a lot more. So too did all of Kuwait next day.

21

WATCHING THE HERITAGE GO BY

THE NEXT BEST THING TO BEING AN AL SABAH MAN IN KUWAIT is being an al Ghanim. It says it all: heritage, glamour, money, power. His Excellency Abdullah al Ghanim is Minister of Water and Electricity and a good job he makes of it. Not that his department has to scrimp to make ends meet. Kuwait isn't going bust.

Until he went into government Abdullah, a small, lively man with a booming, deep voice, was in business—contractors, pharmaceutical chains, importer of engineering equipment, toys and gifts, manufacturer of sanitary napkins. His wife, Lulua, runs all that now.

Lulua is the Lauren Bacall of Kuwait; she has the face of a Dior mannequin, there to show off clothes. But she's a brainy clotheshorse; she was taking a course at the London School of Economics (and you don't walk in there on the strength of being Kuwaiti heritage) before she married Abdullah.

Everyone in Kuwait says that Lulua al Ghanim has two husbands, Abdullah, thirty-seven, and his younger brother, Diraar, thirty-one. She cherishes them both. Every night she sends her chauffeur over to Diraar's place with a full-scale dinner—on the off chance that he'll be in. And in return Diraar adores Lulua just as he adores Abdullah. That's very fortunate because he doesn't fall over himself with enthusiasm for his father, who lives conveniently far away overlooking an English golf course. Diraar is the Jet Set of Kuwait, says one diplomat admiringly. That means that he's the only bachelor around who's old enough and from a good enough family to count.

One Friday I'm invited to join Diraar for a weekend picnic on a nearby island. His high-powered speedboat sets off late; it takes a while for Diraar to stir his stewardess girlfriend, Vicky. She flew in from London late last night. She flies out to Bombay tomorrow. At first she's rather cross and sleepy. Slowly she wakes up as the fresh sea air rushes past the boat. Vicky, Moroccan-born, Egyptian nationality, is a sultry piece with sensuous lips and fluid hips. These show to advantage later when she treats the party to a display of belly dancing. Her act is all hips and tidy footwork—spoiled somewhat when Diraar joins in, wearing a couture beach suit that doesn't conceal his friendly paunch. He waves it around like a sexy schoolboy.

Diraar apologizes profusely for the whisky and gin bottles littering the island's beach. "When will these people learn that there's more to life than spirits," he sighs. He has organized champagne; on ice. He left the food to his houseboy. That's obvious. The picnic hamper contains some fruit and a few sandwiches. It's a hot, relaxing day. Diraar steams about in the boat trying to locate brother Abdullah, out fishing with some friends on the family yacht, *Bibi*. Lulua is at home with her two daughters; she doesn't like the sea, she says. *Bibi* doesn't want to be raised so Diraar goes back to making a fuss over the enticing Vicky.

She has her own flat in Kuwait. "No, of course I didn't get it for her," he says later, crossly. "She wouldn't want me to, and anyway, I'd never respect a woman that let me keep her. Mind you, I didn't feel right dating Vicky at first. She works for Kuwait Airways and I audit their books. It almost seemed unethical."

Diraar runs an accountancy practice. He has three hundred

fifty people working for him today in eighteen offices. It's the only private professional firm to span the Mideast. He's in partnership with Price, Waterhouse (of New York and London, etc.) and a Palestinian, Tallal abu Ghazaleh. He's touchy enough about trading on the al Ghanim name to run the company under his Palestinian partner's. Don't underestimate what that means in Kuwait.

There's no excuse for his not being a success as a playboy. His late brother-in-law was that legendary Badr Mullah, founding member of Annabel's nightclub in London. His closest international playmates are Princes Bandar and Turqui ibn Faisal from Saudi Arabia. Sure enough, he goes in for the right kind of nightlife in the right kind of places.

"The Bahamas, Nice, Rome, New York, London, and all that are fun, but it's artificial and all the same. I go for a few days. The first night I'll be out until the morning looking around every discotheque, every club. Then finished. It's always with a group of Arabs. Not many other men can afford the time or money for our way of life when we play." At home in Kuwait he organizes lively parties that have people who go in for that kind of thing scrambling for an invite.

The evening Diraar and I spend lounging around his sloppy sitting room in his seashore bungalow is nothing like that kind of thing. He sent his driver to collect me. Not for my sake, oh no. "I'm an al Ghanim. I can't be seen in the Sheraton" (he doesn't add "picking up a woman" but that's what he means). If that makes him sound self-important, then picture Diraar sitting on the floor in his national dress, eating Lulua's nightly offering, playing his favorite tape. It was recorded in a workingmen's club in Scotland. It's a totally incomprehensible comic turn. The Glaswegian accent is so broad that it takes me a while to work out that it's the English language I'm listening to. Diraar's roaring his head off. He knows the tape backward.

"If you ask me where I've made the most friends, I'll tell you it was Glasgow. I understand the Scots; they're a tribal people like us, and they accepted me." After private schooling in England, he spent seven years in Glasgow training with a firm of accountants. He somehow crossed the line between his basement flat with evenings in the local pub, and the society clique—balls and debutantes' dances. "I did it on my own," he says proudly. "The name al Ghanim meant nothing there." Too right. "Do you know I returned to Glasgow a while ago and went back to that same pub. An old boy said to me, 'Hello, Diraar, you've come home then. Where've you been?' That's being accepted." In Kuwait what he is counts; in Glasgow it was who he is. Having grown up in the West, this Kuwaiti accepts me as a friend. There's no feeling of strain. He tries his Glaswegian accent on me. I don't understand a word but I can recognize that it's perfect. He breaks into English to tell me that there was a girl in Glasgow. She was the only girl he has ever wanted to marry. Something held him back. It was the same logic that would hold him back from marrying Vicky, or any other foreign Arab. Unlike Jeddah, that's not "done" here. "Lulua and Abdullah would accept her for my sake and they'd force our friends to accept her. But what kind of a life would she have? Being Arab isn't enough; she'd spend her life fighting against being an outsider. Kuwaiti women have their own dialect; that's how tight the circle is."

Kuwait means a lot to him; so does his work. He has a habit of rushing off for a few days without warning. But it's to look for new clients, not girls. "I can have plenty of women; I wouldn't pay but I don't have time to play romantic games either. I was in Morocco recently and an American girl came over to me and started talking, so I took her out to dinner. Afterward we went back to my room, but it was getting late so I told her right out, 'I've a business meeting at seven thirty in the morning. Are you coming to bed or not?' She went through a performance about it being only our first date so I simply said, 'I'm here for three days. If you think it's more correct for us to wait until the last night, fine. But while you're making up your mind, there are three alternatives. I can take you home now because I'm tired; you can sleep on the sofa, or you can get into bed with me.' " He can't remember which she picked. (That's one way the callous-Arab-playboy myth takes shape.)

Diraar has two heroes: brother Abdullah and Abdlatif al Hamad. Al Hamad, thirty-nine, born with a silver spoon in his mouth and Harvard-educated to a golden touch, plays King Arthur in a fair and beautiful castle in Kuwait's Camelot—the Kuwait Fund for Arab Economic Development.

He has at his command $3,325 million to buy the goodwill of the Arab world with selective aid-giving. The fund was set up in 1961, soon after independence and the inconvenience of buying off Iraqi intervention with $100 million. Whatever the motivation behind it, King Arthur himself has become the world's model of how to run an aid agency.

I've seen Abdlatif at work in his ivory tower. He's impressive. Diraar and I are having tea with the al Hamads at home. Abdlatif has a sheaf of papers to put away for tomorrow: progress reports on an irrigation scheme in Yemen (the Communist one, not the other one this time), a thermal power project in Socialist Syria, and an appeal from a Western television producer for another kind of project—a prestigious, historical, drama series. That one will get a firm but polite no.

Fattda and Abdlatif al Hamad puzzle Kuwaitis, who sarcastically nickname them "the lovebirds." Despite her attendance at the inevitable university course, Fattda is less like a Kuwaiti than a Mother Earth: she's soft, flowing with silk, and feminine. There's a drawback, though, to being married to a knight: he spends months off in foreign parts. "I'm no different from my mother. My father was a captain of a ship, like most men were then. He sailed to India and Africa and once he was away for a whole year. My mother spent her life waiting for his ship; I spend mine waiting for Abdlatif's plane." Diraar chips in to remind me of an old Kuwaiti proverb: "Those who go to the sea are lost; those who come back are born." It's his way of saying that even the richest, oldest, heritage families have known loss and hardship.

Kuwait might not understand the al Hamads' ideal of being

together whenever they can, but Diraar admires it, just as he admires Abdlatif's intellectual luster. Their home is serene, expensive (an al Hamad doesn't have to stint), and it has some of the loveliest old pictures, calligraphy, and furniture collected from Islamic lands everywhere. It's a long, long way from the Louis de Lebanon look.

As Diraar and I drive off to another of Lulua's prepacked feasts he talks of Abdlatif and Fattda with a mixture of respect, envy, and pride. He shies away from any mention of his own marriage; there aren't many girls fit for an al Ghanim and, secretly, he's afraid of being tempted outside the circle as he nearly was in Glasgow. "I haven't time for marriage." He puts his foot down hard on the accelerator. "And anyway, as you've heard, Lulua al Ghanim has two husbands, Abdullah and Diraar."

Lulua recently achieved a feminists' landmark (by Kuwaiti standards). She became head of the social committee of an institution unique for this part of Arabia. It's an everyday version of the Royal Enclosure at Ascot. It's equally as overdressed, has twenty founding members (five royals, the rest heritage) and only they can put up new members.

The Hunting and Equestrian Club is miles from anywhere. As you drive up it looks like a military base. It's fenced in, walled at the front, and its gates shut firmly on outsiders. Inside it's the Elysian fields compared to Kuwait's dust bowl of desert and concrete—it's green. Those generous donations mentioned in the club report have built stabling for forty-seven horses, a nine-hole golf course, and a skeet-shooting range.

But Kuwait comes less for the sport than for the pièce de résistance—an American-style country clubhouse. You'll find everyone on the daily-sprinkled lawn, neatly hedged and bordered, sitting at tables in mixed and family groups. This is the Brookline Country Club all over again: Boston brought to Arabia in 1974.

Mustapha Behbehani, another heritage offspring, has just come from work—at the emir's *dirwan*. The blue sky over his head makes a change from the ninety-one English turn-of-the-century pictures of busty women in various stages of undress that decorate the ceiling of his office at the palace. (They're left over from some earlier sheikh.) A couple of ravishing American-educated al Sabah girls compliment him on his new season's stock. Behbehani owns a boutique in Salamieh. The role of storekeeper seems an odd one for this court official from an old family. "Why did I open it? Because it's the only thing my father's never done in business," he explains bashfully. Knowing the size of his father's empire, I can believe it.

There's a roar as one of the emir's grandsons makes his entrance in his steel silver-red-and-black-decorated Trans-Am with Trac Action 60 Big Boss tires. He's come for a ride on a horse. The sheikh is sixteen. There's a flurry of Kuwaiti youth as he opens his car door and puts out a chubby, jodhpured thigh. This is the city's one legitimate flirting ground.

Diraar al Ghanim's greatest pal, Khalid al Rodan, doesn't join the crowd. He's too old for that kind of thing and anyway he has his position to maintain. He's another storekeeper. He opened "Sportsman" a few months ago. It's a chrome-and-carpeted exercise wonderland of rowing machines, saddles, tennis and squash equipment, marred only by a windowful of grotesque silver trophies, made in Japan, for Kuwaiti football clubs.

In the cool of the New England clubhouse lounge the color television is on. No one's watching; there's too much to talk about. "Bassima, darling," one woman spots a friend flicking through some comics, "you're looking marvelous. I can't take my eyes off you." Nasty moment as I wonder, not for the first time, who dresses for whom around here. A young mother in a clinging jersey teagown (whom I see here nearly every day) has one scrap of talk to cover her presence: "I'm determined to learn to ride. I'm taking my first lesson tomorrow."

She shrinks back as Lulua al Ghanim strides in with a file of supporters. She's come to see how her arrangements are going for the al fresco Malaysian social on Saturday night. But there's some rival excitement outside. The careless watchman had forgotten to close the gate after the last sheikh. A grubby family jalopy trundled in. Out spilled delighted children who made a beeline for the swings in Kiddies Korner.

The faded, gray figure of Mrs. Cullinan, wife of the club manager, hovers in horror. She collects herself to go for Mr. Cullinan, who walks over to the newcomers, tugging the club's guard dog behind him to make his point. The dog sits down and falls asleep. The family tumble back into the jalopy obediently and trundle out again. They're Bedouins who took "Kuwait for the Kuwaitis" too seriously.

In between the black-haired, spirited al Sabah and their friends, I spot a few Europeans. It's an honor for them to be invited here. They won't be invited much further into the circle. At one table, waiting for her children to come back from their ride, is a pretty blond Englishwoman. She's Primrose Arnander, wife of Christopher. This merchant-banking whiz kid came out two years ago to a big Kuwaiti job. He's now doing another big Kuwaiti job. They're as far into the inner circle as any resident Westerners. They've been invited to two Kuwaiti homes for dinner in as many years.

At every Kuwaiti table a story does the rounds. My favorite today concerns the farce of the heritage son who decided to martyr himself in the fight against "Kuwaiti hypocrisy over drink." The country is officially dry; the rich all have bootleggers and the poor get stuck with Flash, a local brew mostly made from distilled scent. It blinds and maims.

The would-be martyr packed his suitcase full of whisky bottles, flew into Kuwait, and presented himself at customs. He hoped to be brought to trial, to become a cause célèbre. To his chagrin, the authorities outwitted him. They confiscated the Scotch, sent him home, and ignored the affair. Shrewd, these Kuwaitis.

It's been another lovely afternoon at the club. Some might complain that Lulua's Malaysian tent is blocking the view of the sunset and that the sprinklers are dousing the teacups. Everyone complains about the flies. They're everywhere; a continual headache for Mr. Cullinan. The club's backers have put aside enough money to build a swimming pool with cabanas, another $4 million to knock down the present clubhouse and erect something more fanciful. No one will cough up the money for Mr. Cullinan to do something about the horse manure.

The members hate the flies, but the flies love the shit.

22

THE LONER

EVERY THURSDAY AFTERNOON AND SOMETIMES ON FRIDAY AN unobtrusive car drives into the Hunting and Equestrian Club. A dignified man with a shock of white hair and an impassive, quizzical look gets out. There's something about him. You know he doesn't belong, but all the sheikhs, ministers, excellencies make a point of going up to him.

He acknowledges them, smiles, chats, and then goes off to the stables where Jamida, "the crazy one" as he calls her, is waiting with her Texan saddle. She's one of the rare Bahraini Arab horses to be sent off the island. The ruler of Bahrain chose her himself as a present for Sheikh Khalid, Kuwait's top horse owner. Sheikh Khalid, president of the emir's *dirwan*, presented her to this man. He mounts Jamida; rides off by himself. He's a loner; that much is clear.

Where does he come from? He holds Kuwaiti, Syrian, Algerian, Jordanian, and, most recently, Saudi Arabian passports. It's the last that gives the key. He was the man who had the idea that became OPEC. He was the first Arab to talk of nationalizing oil, the first to say "Arab oil for the Arabs." Abdullah al Tariki was the first Saudi Arabian Minister of Petroleum and Mineral Resources.

The story of oil in the Mideast is the story of his life, except that he would never compromise and he was an honest man. Abdullah al Tariki can't be bothered to tell that story. He looks to the future; the past doesn't matter to him. But eventually he unlocks it for me.

His father had a caravan that went between Riyadh and Kuwait. When Abdullah was born in 1919, in what is now Saudi Arabia, there were no countries, no borders. His father took him to Kuwait slung over the side of his camel in a sack ("I was only six and he expected me to stay on the back of a camel all night. I kept losing my headdress or my stick"). He was to stay with a half-brother and go to school. "In the mornings I'd get up and clean the house and in the evenings I'd collect our goats out in the desert. It's all villas there now."

His apprenticeship started at eleven. He was sent alone on a steamship to Bombay to work for a merchant. The merchant couldn't read or write; Abdullah could do both. He became his secretary and bookkeeper. The next trader he worked for felt this quick-witted urchin should be given a chance. He sent him back from India to Arabia with a letter of introduction to the Saudi Minister of Finance. Abdullah had to ride a camel from Kuwait across to Mecca to present it. On the basis of that letter he was chosen to receive schooling in Cairo.

To this day he boasts of being the school's swimming champion ("breast stroke"); mostly he studied. "I wanted to be an engineer even though I was very dumb in chemistry. An Egyptian officer told me that when God created people, he created their wealth with them, but it was up to them to find it. He told me that when he served in Turkey, he saw geologists running up and down the mountains looking for minerals, looking for wealth. That sounded like a good idea."

Next came a scholarship to Cairo University and after that a master's degree in geology and petroleum engineering in Texas. He was to become the first Saudi oil technocrat. "In Cairo the Americans were something new to us. They meant a lot of gold watches, gold rings, a lot of chewing gum. I just got the idea that I would like America very much."

New York? He hated it. "I had no money but I got a guidebook and walked into the first hotel I saw listed. It was the Waldorf-Astoria—can you believe I was that naïve? I ended up in the best I could afford, a mattress on a floor behind Times Square."

Texas? He loathed it. "They thought I was just a skinny Mexican." He was lonely. "I met an American, a blonde, who wanted to marry me; she liked me." She liked him enough to marry him and go back to Saudi Arabia with him.

When he returned the Saudis placed him with Aramco in Dhahran. He was the only qualified Arab in an American joint, and Aramco didn't like it. They wanted to house him in the Arab workers' barracks. He held out for an American-executive apartment. That solved nothing; his wife was ostracized for marrying a native. "It wasn't a happy time." A typical Abdullah remark.

In 1958 King Saud moved him to Jeddah to be the country's top man in oil. In 1960 he was made minister (Yamani was nothing then). Abdullah was a power. He had a house by the sea, full of people, laughter, gazelles, dogs—King Saud's cast-offs. "King Saud brought five greyhounds from England because he felt like racing them. When he got tired of the idea I took on the dogs. They were males and females, so I ended up with seventeen." He always turns everything into a joke.

The oil-company men hated Abdullah. He found some weak points in their bookkeeping. He forced Aramco to pay back $145 million. "My own aim was to break our fifty–fifty participation agreement with them. I spent a year negotiating with a Japanese company to give us fifty-six–forty-four. Then I found out that Faisal's brother-in-law, Kamal Adham, was their agent. They'd already given him a million dollars' commission, but on top of that they had a secret agreement to pay him two percent of their profit. I got mad," one of his favorite phrases. "I forced the Japanese to cancel the two percent commission to Adham. I think Faisal never forgave me for that."

When the al Saud family forced King Saud to abdicate in Faisal's favor, Abdullah al Tariki went too. "I chose to resign. If I hadn't, I would have been fired. It was obvious: Aramco

wanted my head. I couldn't stay in the country without working and so I went to live somewhere else. I wasn't bitter about
it. I can't hate."

The Algerian and Kuwaiti governments immediately took
him on as their oil adviser, posts he still holds. He lived happily in Beirut with his second wife (the American had left
years ago) until 1970. The Lebanese kicked him out without
warning or explanation. The long arm of Faisal's unrelenting
spite had reached Beirut.

He tried working from Cairo, but who can with a telephone
system that takes two days per call? The Kuwaitis were delighted to have him when he moved here. "He's come home,"
they say. For the last ten years he's been an oil consultant to
many governments (just look at that list of passports). He also
publishes a magazine: *The Oil of Arabs*. When King Faisal
was shot, Abdullah flew to Saudi Arabia to make peace with an
old friend, now King Khaled. He got his passport back but he
can't see why I should find it surprising that soon afterward he
published an article in his magazine headed: "Remove the
Parasites from Around the Crown." It attacked everyone around
King Khaled. "Khaled is my hope, but he's surrounded by
parasites and since I've always said what I believe, why stop
now?"

This Don Quixote and I talk in many places: his office, his
club, his car. One day he invites me to dinner. He wants me
to meet his son. At the club he's a respected figure. In his office
in the ten-story Kuwait Airways "skyscraper," he's a commanding figure. To oilmen everywhere he's an historical one. I walk
into an apartment where the television is almost bigger than
the living room. The food is ample, his hospitality warm, but
the flat is too small for it to be anything but simple. He doesn't
mind. I don't mind. His son, Zakhr does.

Zakhr is tall, slender, and as good-looking as Abdullah must
have been at his age—he's twenty-four. What strikes me is the
contradiction of his outer shyness and inner anger. He doesn't
know whom it's directed at. He hardly knows his father; from
his childhood in Jeddah he remembers a big, powerful bear

living in splendor. He's stuck with an aging man, who (naturally) seems small to him now. He can only talk to him through a servant who's been with his father for years. He doesn't know what to say.

What is he supposed to have in common with Abdullah? Zakhr is the son of the divorced American wife. He grew up hating his absent father; he still won't see his Lebanese stepmother and six-year-old half-sister (fortunately, for the moment they live in Cairo. Abdullah goes there for a week every month).

Why is Zakhr here at all? Because he's not American, although he sounds like one. He was brought up in Beirut and the U.S. He's graduated from Yale University and he needs a job. Every time he goes to the States he has a hassle with the immigration people; he has Saudi traveling papers. He needs his father to help him get work in the only country where he's legally supposed to belong—Saudi Arabia.

"Am I an Arab? I wouldn't be if I'd been allowed to settle in the States easily. So, I don't know what I am. But I've come to live here anyway. The outward things aren't hard. I can put on the headdress [I always see him wearing jeans and a red sweater], and it's like a wall around my eyes, my security blanket if you like. The inner things, those are what I can't work out."

Zakhr went to Jeddah recently. The Juffali merchant family, powerful enough I'd have thought to make their own appointments, promised him a job. He's sitting here at supper; he's heard nothing.

(Later in London, I'm told by a top Saudi that word probably went to the Juffalis that Abdullah al Tariki was all right again, but not all right enough for them to hire his son. Zakhr may be a twenty-four-year-old much needed Yale graduate and what's more a Saudi. But in traditional Arabia he's first the son of his father. No one claims that Abdullah al Tariki was dishonest or subversive. The way it was put to me in London by a man close enough to the throne to know was, "He was ahead of his time. Nationalization wasn't in fashion then; it was a word al Tariki should never have used.")

Abdullah al Tariki is planning on going back to Saudi

Arabia. Mostly for his son's sake, although he'd never admit it; partly for his own. He's going to buy a ranch and speak his mind. "You have to be in a place where you can be effective. Look at them, every one of them is corrupt. It's disgusting. No one is secure in that country. No wonder they just want to make their money fast and get out. I'm fifty-six. I shall go back to Saudi Arabia and I shall go on saying what I believe. And if a truck 'accidentally' runs me over or I suffer a 'premature heart attack,' better that way. I would rather finish it like that than learn to be afraid.

"Once I thought revolution might be an answer. Now I see what the military ones have done in other countries—they change the old bad ways for new bad ways. I feel—I hope, that all it needs is time. Give them enough years and the people, even the royal families, will learn enough to make changes from the inside. It's safer that way."

One day we're driving along the sea road ("the Arabian Gulf Road") and Abdullah falls silent; it's unlike him by now. He thinks for a while and says with deep feeling, "It's useless to be a Kuwaiti or a Saudi. It's a piece of a thing, it's not a thing in itself. This is what oil has done. This change is not normal. Rags to riches can happen to individuals, not to nations. These artificial creations like Kuwait, drawn on a map by other powers, they'll never accomplish anything. They'll always spend, never produce. We open a tap, let out the oil and change it into dollars. They call us the 'oil *producing* countries.' That's a joke.

"What we have is a torrent of rain and no dams. We are so, so stupid. I remember once the Britisher St. John Philby told King Ibn Saud that he shouldn't touch the people, that he shouldn't let the oil touch their lives. At the time we thought he was a colonial, an imperialist stooge. I remember how I laughed at him. Now I wonder if he wasn't right after all."

PART

QATAR—

"A PIECE OF A THING . . ."

NUTTY PRESENT, DOTTY PAST

IN THE CUSHIONED ATMOSPHERE OF KUWAIT, ABDULLAH AL TARIKI is briefing me on the lower Gulf: "When I was oil minister for Saudi Arabia, I went to Qatar for the day to see the emir. He gave me two suitcases jammed with Rolex watches and silk clothes. I thought it was terrible. After I had to leave my country I went to see the same emir. He wouldn't give me five minutes, he was so afraid of offending the Saudis. Now every statesman and leader in the world is flying in to see the head of that tiny place. Isn't it a joke?"

Abdullah is appalled by the news that Leopold Senghor, President of Senegal and international prize-winning poet, has rearranged a whole tour to suit the convenience of Qatar's present emir, his Highness Sheikh Khalifa ibn Hamad al Thani. Uganda's President, Idi Amin, is next to turn up, waving his begging bowl with less finesse. He evidently hopes for more than the $3.5 million that is all the emir apparently considers he deserves. Emir Khalifa aspires to be a leader of global dimensions. An adviser prefers to translate this as, "He's aware of his place in history."

It *is* a joke. Qatar's only been independent since September 1, 1971; before that it had a "Treaty of Protection" with the British. When its first oil was shipped out in 1949 the capital "city," Doha, didn't have one paved road, let alone electricity or water. Not that it could have felt very funny to the people living there then—only there weren't many of them. A few thousand, maybe, mostly desert nomads. There aren't many more now, but its oil revenues bring in billions of dollars.

With that financial security behind him, Emir Khalifa's continuing his relentless pursuit of his rightful historical position. He was a wild success at the Elysée Palace when President Giscard d'Estaing gave a formal banquet in his honor. Now he has his eye on fame in America. He went to all the trouble of flying in a private English tutor, who hung around the palace for a while before flying out again. His Highness kept skipping lessons. He's made progress, though, on his personal set of Linguaphone records.

This Napoleon rules over a sandpit slightly larger than Kuwait, with less than a tenth of its population. Sheikh Khalifa had a miserable, misunderstood adolescence. He has risen above it. In spite of the handicaps of his chronic sinusitis and lack of formal education, he keeps himself busy from six thirty in the morning until late at night, unstimulated by alcohol, cigarettes, or skirt-chasing.

He turns up unexpectedly on building sites to make sure the cement is of the right consistency. He watches carefully the productivity estimates of the Qatar Flour Mills. He doesn't neglect the West Bay Land Reclamation Project where he (and his detachment of security guards) frequently checks out how dredging is getting along. And if programs on the new television station aren't up to scratch, he's on the phone right away. You should have heard him going on about the low standard of entertainment during the long Ramadan evenings. Fortunately, he missed the studio runthrough of a recent documentary on Qatar's history. It took a visiting businessman discreetly to point out that there was something amiss with the soothing background music. It was the theme song from *Exodus*.

It's clear that he means it when he says, with one of those smiles intended to disarm, "My first and last hobby is to devote all my time and power to serve my nation. When I see all these industrial and constructive projects, I feel the happiest man in the world."

Not happy enough though to dispense with the bodyguards, even for a short promenade in Hyde Park on his annual summer holiday in London. This manic, aggressive, chubby-cheeked emir suffers from an insecurity complex. Can you wonder? His grandfather had always promised him the throne, but it accidentally ended up in the hands of his greedy first cousin Ahmed. Khalifa pottered on as Minister of Finance and Petroleum until 1972 when Emir Ahmed's son took to making a "death list," with Khalifa figuring prominently at the top. There was one of those autocratic family councils and Ahmed was packed off to exile. His son lives across the Gulf in Iran.

Sheikh Khalifa nobly took over the throne and gathered a posse of his own al Thani fans around him. These don't necessarily include such notables as his brother, the Foreign Minister —he's competition. No; more dependent, dependable fans. He's taken his first new wife in fifteen years, an educated young cousin. Unfortunately, he's been too busy to let Qatar know whether or not she has "publicly appeared." Society women tactfully carry on, visiting his last wife. He's hauled his oldest son, and Crown Prince, back from Sandhurst Military Academy to head the army. He's plucked younger son Abdul Aziz from his American university and handed him the Ministry of Finance. These sons don't matter much in power terms. The only man who makes a decision in Qatar is Napoleon himself from his office palace in the capital of Doha.

His office is easy to see from the outside; I can't miss it. It's a landmark. I walk in; there are two floors around an open courtyard. Every door opens onto an empty, unfurnished room. There's space for five hunded: forty people work here ("I think it's forty, we've never counted"). His Highness's stylish suite, decorated by David Hicks with his usual flair, is right up in the corner on the second floor. Lots of empty space before I get there.

Then there's the rest of the city. Doha reminds me of a dress store on the last day of the sale. There's just a background

jumble you don't notice for the one purple organdy extrava-
ganza in size eighteen that won't move and a few other outsize
atrocities. Doha is a very pleasant town; clean, gentle, with small
streets and low houses. But it's dominated by a handful of the
city's equivalent of those purple extravaganzas: the al Thani
palace, the Wall Street monolith that's the new Ministry of
Finance, and the dazzling white museum that's the display piece
of Qatar and the personal pride of Sheikh Khalifa. It was all his
own idea.

I learn a lot about the differences between these countries by
the way each wears the past and by getting to know the people
involved with it.

In Saudi Arabia a twenty-six-year-old Chicago-trained archeologist has a budget of $225 million to freeze history while every-
one else is busy destroying it. The Saudi Director of Antiquities,
Abdullah Hassan Masry, Ph.D., was born in Mecca, youngest of
ten children from a poor family. He's black; like many "Arab"
Saudis he has African slave blood somewhere in his not too
distant ancestral past.

While studying in America he lived through what he describes with cool academic interest as "those days of rage," the
height of student rioting. Abdullah had digs in Chicago near the
corner taken over by extreme Black Stone Rangers. He was
there for the Weathermen, the Chicago Seven, the blood-letting
of America.

Today he sits in Riyadh in his unsullied white *thobe,* demo-
lition noises outside deafening us, and remarks after deliberation, "No, I didn't feel involved in any way, why should I have?
No one did *me* any harm, although someone did scratch the
paint of my car. But how could the students and their anger
affect me? I was always too conscious that their T-shirts and
ragged jeans cost as much as a conventional middle-class wardrobe and that the clothing manufacturers were having a field
day."

This superior supergrad has summoned the finest architects,
archeologists, and designers to compete for a museum to glorify

the splendid heritage of his country. By the time $225 million has gone, the heritage may have gone too.

Now how about Bahrain? There's a museum. The government driver has been designated to take me to it. The journey goes from a camera shop (don't ask me why), to Government House, to a slipway by the marina, to the airport customshouse. It isn't that he thinks the museum is hidden in any of these unlikely places. He doesn't know what a museum is, nor do any of the people we ask. I never reach the official museum but I find the country's real treasure trove in the house of Sheikha Haya al Khalifa. Yes, a female member of the royal family wraps a turban round her head, puts on a pair of trousers, and goes out to dig for the past. "Look, he has painted fingers, he must be a woman," I heard a workman say once.

This plump, passionate enthusiast had to leave school at fifteen to marry her first cousin. She acquired a degree by correspondence after having five children, and Bahrain's past is now piled on the tables of her house. "My interest started in 1960 when a bulldozer came into our garden. When it started tearing up the ground everywhere, I rushed in and grabbed everything I could lay my hands on." She points to a Hellenistic bronze sculpture. "But I'm afraid the bulldozer did dent that a bit."

Now I'm in Doha. There's hardly anyone on the streets and the papers are full of some new industrial project that was pulled off. It's nuts. The place is an empty toy town, all it has is oil, and every day they firm up deals that would make sense in a developed city like Detroit, with a decent labor force. How do you like the idea of 300,000 tons of steel a year being spewed out in Qatar? That's the aim of one $318 million-plus project that Sheikh Khalifa has signed up with the Japanese. Who's going to work on the shop floor? Imported Japanese? And if you want to hear about Sheikh Khalifa's pharmaceutical plant or the ten-million-egg-laying-capacity battery farm, I could go on forever . . . .

If the future sounds ludicrous, the past is beyond belief. In the center of this nowhere stands a white fortress sparkling like choppers in a toothpaste advertisement. The Qatar National Museum on "the Corniche" (where is this—Monte Carlo?) is centered around Sheikh Khalifa's old home. It's a shrine to his childhood and to the dead father whose memory he worships.

It was the very first thing he decided to build when he got the throne. On the night it opened he decided to marry his young cousin as a way of celebrating. Who do I find masterminding this place? A sacerdotal, safari-suited public relations man, opera buff and self-taught archeologist from the smarter end of Sloane Street in London, Michael Rice.

Rice is an old friend; he's been around this area for many years, though he doesn't speak Arabic, but I've never seen him ruffled. He's the kind of Englishman Arabs dream about. Sheikh Khalifa patently did. He entrusted him with his favorite jewel in the development crown—the $4 million museum.

Some people may wonder why the emir didn't go for a big archeological name? In this part of the world they don't come bigger than Michael Rice's. He doesn't have any fancy paper qualifications, or any paper qualifications at all for that matter. But he designs superb museums and, what's more, he's a wizard with the Arabs, who can be a trifle irritating. You'd never guess from *him* that Michael Rice's Qatari venture was anything but a smooth, enjoyable experience.

Nor would any of the visiting heads of state suggest that a trip around the museum isn't exactly what they most wanted. They'd be fools if they did; it's obligatory before money flows from the Qatari piggybank. I had the luck, at least, to go around it with Michael Rice. His concept and its realization are magnificent.

No matter that a few rooms are locked because the guards didn't feel like staying around all through opening hours. No matter that they've displaced his lighting system so that I miss the exhilarating view of the room where the young Sheikh Khalifa touched his Koran. No matter that above the stunning first floor showing antiquities and films of Bedouin life, everything you wanted to know about this country and didn't know who to ask—there's a whole floor dedicated to Sheikh Khalifa. It's fitting. Downstairs, movie pictures of life in the tent, and at the top, the show of photographs of the emir of Qatar with an array of world leaders. Shaking hands, having a confidential word over a coffeetable, but always upstaging his costars.

There's only one Qatari that comes into the (well-guarded) open and that's his Highness the emir Sheikh Khalifa ibn Hamad al Thani.

It isn't that there aren't any other Qataris. But anyone who has ever painted pictures by numbers knows that moment when blobs that were eight, thirteen, twenty-one, and forty start to make a pattern. It's sky. Other blobs shape into trees. I've been in Arabia long enough now to begin to recognize patterns. The silences and the spaces in Qatar mean something.

This thumb of sand that is an "independent nation" juts out from Saudi Arabia. Qatar caught Wahhabism from its huge next-door neighbor when the zeal was in the air in the eighteenth century. But because it's tiny and was never locked away like Saudi (the British colonials were here, too, remember) it's not quite as unrealistic. Women drive and work. Itinerant business-men who've been tipped off make their way to Room 501 in the Gulf Hotel. This is a "dry" country but Room 501's the hotel's unofficial bar. The penthouse restaurant has a reasonably good wine list: as long as you know to ask the hotel manager (dis-creetly) for a pass to get in and find the concealed express elevator up there.

But these are nuances. Compared to Kuwait or Bahrain, this country's an Islamic model town. To boot, Sheikh Khalifa has embarked on a moral rearmament program. In the past the al Thanis, and their richer subjects, lived it up with the best of them. Sheikh Khalifa's ideal of the moral straight and narrow isn't something you pay lip service to. The time has come for Qataris to keep a low profile, shut up, and mind their own businesses.

There's literally no social life to be had in Doha for the

Qataris. The sophistication of the Jeddah Group or even the *diwania* male japes of Kuwait are jet sets away. Even the Westerners have to be careful. Those who are caught offering Qataris alcohol can be, and are, thrown out. The government won't stoop to handling liquor permits for residential Christian foreigners, so they've made an unofficial licensing authority of a European embassy (which has to be nameless for the sake of those stranded non-Muslims). Nothing allowed the Qataris but hard work and boredom.

There aren't many people in the country so there aren't many millionaires. Sultan Saif al Isa is one of them. He lives in an anonymous, walled-in, background affair that you wouldn't look at twice.

I'm having coffee with Sharifa, his wife. She has at last solved the mystery of the disappearing furniture. On her annual summer visit to London she bought up a large section of the eighteenth-century-repro department of a department store, Waring and Gillow. It never arrived. Someone's just told her that Waring and Gillow is on the "Israel boycott list." The furniture will never arrive. She'll have to make do with the present, gloomy mahogany dining room. She isn't too bothered; they never eat there anyway.

Sultan, Sharifa, their seven children and two spouses stick to the long trestle table in the family "canteen" upstairs. Sultan looks like Charlie Chaplin and talks like Edward G. Robinson. Sharifa, minute, lumpy, overrides his grumpy silences with a nonstop flow of affectionate gossip. I'm back in a scaled-down model of the all-embracing Saudi household.

Sharifa never wears the famous *burqa*, the leatherlike black mask. Many women here do; some cover nearly the whole face, these are old women. This is the last generation that will see the mask in the lower Gulf. Sharifa's next-door neighbor, a darling little sprite, has finished making her latest creation—the briefest of *burqas* fringed with fat Gulf pearls. She's playing with the idea of giving it up altogether. The unmasked Sharifa does, however, still wear a long black cloak outside the house. Her daughters don't even do that.

Imagine sitting in this old-fashioned house, spotlessly clean but as pretentious as a genteel boardinghouse with sales-room bargains and stuffed chairs inherited from dead aunts. That's Sharifa's home. And through the door walks a Schools Inspector, second daughter Johara, aged twenty-one. Her miniskirt makes my eyes pop. The skirts that follow get better and better. There's Johaina's; she's doing her Ph.D. in Cairo. She's twenty-seven, unmarried, beautiful, sexy with long scarlet nails and high platform shoes. I don't get time to catch breath until fifteen-year-old Harla, another beauty, walks in—at least she's wearing her navy floor-length school uniform. That soon goes. Sharifa finds my surprise (Surprise! Stunned shock) amusing and teases: "It's a new generation. You and I are out of date."

The intriguing Sharifa was born in Bombay, went to the university in Beirut and has family scattered everywhere across Saudi Arabia, Kuwait, and Bahrain. She's generous to a fault, with a habit of stuffing too much food down her children and friends. "Downstairs is for guests and you can eat what you like. Up here we're family and you must eat more."

After dinner we always move onto the second-floor landing—it's the family den. There's a heap of garish shoes discarded at the top of the stairs. One pair protrudes: the Gucci moccasins of twenty-four-year-old Mohammed. He's being groomed to take over Sultan's business (the Rolls-Royce diesel concession, machine shop, construction company and so on), and is taking his part seriously. There's not much talk. What is there to say when the same eleven people meet every night? "Pass another Seven-Up." "Are you washing your hair tonight, Johaina?" "How about a game of backgammon?" A game of whist is played with concentration. Sharifa gossips on in her friendly way throughout. The patriarch slumps in front of the television as usual. He has one laugh at least: some cowboys stroll into a saloon and order whiskies. Sultan translates the Arabic subtitle for me: "May I have an orange juice?"

Johara sits apart, tearing her nails to the quick. She's the only one who hasn't been able to put a thermostat on her emotions. She wants to get married or get out. She wants a release of some kind. So did her older sister, Wafika. She married a penniless Egyptian. Sultan bought them a home but they're always over here. Johara envies Wafika. She envies Mohammed's wife, who has a small baby. She envies Noor, who leaves next week to start at Cairo University. Johara has done Cairo and there isn't much in the way of husbands for an educated girl in Doha.

All over the city it's the same scene. Families gather every day because there's nothing, absolutely nothing else for them to do. I'm not surprised to run across the familiar refrain: "Why do you spend time with the Sultan Saifs? They're not Qatari; they're not typical." Who is? The al Thanis are too busy playing copycat to Emir Khalifa to seem real these days. The Darwish millionaires? They're pushed at me as "real Qataris." Their origins are as Bahraini as Sultan Saif's.

This place was a deserted wilderness until recent years. Now it has schools, hospitals, working women who can drive, an ultra-modern television station, and all those other developments, like the steelworks. And it's as dull as dishwater. This is the country that sends out the Qataris who are known in London for one thing: if you sell a property, if you lease a flat, if you rent a hotel room to them, they'll leave it in squalor.

It's worth spinning forward a couple of months. I'm home and the phone rings. Sharifa and Sultan are in town. I must come over. Number 5 Green Street is about the most exclusive address you can have in London. It's one of those perfect Georgian townhouses that fewer and fewer English can afford these days. The Saifs' duplex apartment has fine plaster work on high ceilings, scalloped niches and an Adam fireplace. It's not pretentiously furnished but it's spotlessly clean.

Sharifa has a full timetable. They've flown in from Bombay (holiday for her, business for him) and she has to make time for her dentist, for the toothache; and her doctor, for the rheumatism. In between she's negotiating with a decorator and with Waring and Gillow again.

The family's on the move to a larger establishment in Portman Square. Fitting eleven beds into a four-bedroom Mayfair apartment is no longer the thing. The new place around the corner is larger and more suitable. Sharifa's slightly horrified at the old tenants. "They did leave the place nice and clean but they didn't have a bidet anywhere." More johns and many bidets are on order. By the time the family swoop down again in May, complete sets of sanitary equipment will have been plumbed in, the new Japanese silk wallpaper will have had time to dry out, and the Waring and Gillow stuff will have been delivered safely. It's only to Portman Square this time.

Sharifa's expensive, tailored outfit is what I expect. It's the change in Sultan that amazes me. This is where Mohammed learned about wearing the right shoes. Sultan's suit is Savile Row's best, his shirt is custom-made, he looks as if he's just come home from an exclusive male club. No trace of grouchiness here. He's relaxed, warm, and alive; he's out of Qatar. Sultan Saif al Isa is too educated, too sharp, not to be worn down by the strains of living in toy town.

Sultan's baffled, too, by the Qatari reputation in London. "I can't think of anyone who comes here who would deserve it and I know practically everyone. Doha's so small." Dead right.

The problem with complaining landlords and other know-it-alls is that they suffer from geographical imprecision. They get everybody mixed up, and somehow the Qataris have been handed the monopoly of being messy. If *anyone* deserves it (and most of the complaints aren't based on truth—they're a way of voicing simple anti-Arab prejudice), it's the spend-happy crew from the United Arab Emirates. And are they spend-happy . . .

PART

ABU DHABI,

DUBAI,

AND SHARJAH—

"MORE PIECES OF THINGS . . ."

CHAPTER

24

ROYAL FLUSH

THE STORY SO FAR: THE UNITED ARAB EMIRATES WAS FOUNDED when Britain formally withdrew in 1971. It's a Federation of seven small sheikhdoms. The President of the UAE is his Highness Sheikh Zayed ibn Sultan al Nahiyan, ruler of Abu Dhabi.

Sheikh Zayed's father, Sultan, came to power by inviting his ruler brother home to dinner and shooting him in the back. Sultan enjoyed his new job—for four years before *he* was chopped down. The next brother lasted two years—he was duly murdered in 1928. It's that kind of family.

Enter handsome, twenty-five-year-old Sheikh Shakhbut, elder brother of Zayed. He took over and became the legendary sheikh who kept his oil revenue in paper notes at home where the rats got at it (untrue) and who didn't want to ruin his people by development (true).

Time for Shakhbut to go, thought the British in 1966. Fortunately, Shakhbut's mother had made all her sons promise not to do one another in. Shakhbut was eased into gentle abdication. Brother Zayed (The Desert Falcon) was reluctantly persuaded to take over. He's been spending money like crazy ever since. Now READ ON:

I'm determined to enjoy Abu Dhabi. After Doha how can I

fail? I've read about the Kentucky Fried Chicken houses, the wall-to-wall-carpeted mosque lit by one hundred chandeliers, the oil income that makes it the richest state in the world per capita (not many capita: perhaps 25,000, more likely 15,000). I figure I'm prepared.

But nothing prepares you for this weird atmosphere. The foreigners don't plan to be around long enough to bother about being nice to one another, let alone the Abu Dhabians. "In business we all behave like people who aren't going to have to live side by side for very long. We're out for what we can get and fast, no matter how. We rent a house and fix it so that we can take everything out at a moment's notice. That's how unstable we feel." This from a bulky sheikh's pet builder.

Nothing prepares you for the sight of Zayed's cost-crazy, lunatic concrete overpass in the middle of a desert, while a simultaneous "cheapest is best" policy in town insures that new buildings are always falling down. Sheikh Zayed is moving into his seventh palace in Abu Dhabi. It's not because he's bored with the old ones. They keep collapsing around him.

Foreigners end up working seven days a week. They may take a day off. A few Britishers go out to examine the desert flora and fauna. Others go down to the sea in boats. The Lebanese, and they're here in swarms, tend to get stoned in the morning and go into the office in the afternoon when the high wears off and there's nothing else to do.

Only the sheikhs have the power to do anything they like. And they LIKE. I'm in a hotel dining room and an elderly sheikh is making up his mind whether or not he's taken a fancy to a girl at another table. She hides in the room of a friend, just in case. If royalty wants something, even a foreign girl, he can bring in the police, if he so pleases, to help him get it.

What else did I expect? All the British cared about in the old days was keeping the lower Gulf quiet. They stopped the local slave trading as unseemly and the piracy as troublesome. They didn't bother to start anything. And once the Indian Empire had gone and East of Suez had been debunked, only a few Foreign Office Arabists minded about what happened in

Abu Dhabi. To everyone else it was a quaint twenty-six thousand square miles with oil coming in where only a few years ago nomads and pearl divers retched with poverty.

The British left Zayed in charge because they saw him as a cooperative chap who wouldn't let the country slip into the wrong hands. They didn't leave behind one school or one decent road. Zayed's been trying—he's built schools and roads all over the Federation. His pride and joy is the highway linking Abu Dhabi town to Al Ain (formerly Buraimi), two hours' drive inland. Sheikh Zayed graduated summa cum laude as governor of this oasis; he still keeps a few wives there, not to mention his deposed brother, Shakhbut.

What the Qatar National Museum is to Sheikh Khalifa, the Hilton Hotel in Al Ain is to Sheikh Zayed—a personally chosen monument to his past. No one much stays in it, but it makes him feel good. As for his present, to hear talk of Zayed in Abu Dhabi is to hear of a character that combines the wisdom of Socrates with the leadership of Lincoln.

That comes as a bit of a surprise to me; in London the man has a different image. Newspapers regularly show photographs of his gangsterlike visage above stories celebrating yet another property coup. There was his August '75 Kensington mansion; everyone caught a whiff of that. But hardly anyone penetrated as far as the Bonsack Bathroom inside. Catch this and you've caught it all. In Abu Dhabi his Highness rubs along with one tumbledown palace after another. ("Sheikh Zayed? He's not living here anymore. He moved last week; the ceiling fell down.") In London nothing less will do Zayed than thousands of dollars' worth of sensuous Bonsack bathing. Godfrey Bonsack ("chandeliers converted into showers are my specialty") of Mayfair is famed for his zoo: frogs, toads, rhinos, turtles, elephants, and any other creature to order if suitable for faucet conversion. (Price per faucet: $500 to $1,600.)

Zayed's country place was another coup—Buxted Park, a former health farm still fully equipped for the resting statesmen and starlets of yore. The locals don't see much of their resident sheikh (he comes and goes by helicopter) but one farmer was astonished to find a rare snow goose scratching around among his barnyard hens and ducks recently. It had strayed off from Zayed's new wildlife park at Buxted. He hopes it won't be the tigers next.

Apart from other British estates, like an interest in a prime cut of beef-rearing Scotland, there's a palace or two in Pakistan where he hunts for two months a year. "It's not fit to repeat the sort of things that are happening around here," reports my pukka Pakistani correspondent, none too pleased to find his estate close to Sheikh Zayed's. But he's got to have somewhere to stay with his $6 million worth of new falcons, and his subjects wouldn't begrudge their hero that. The generous sheikh gives to his people first.

There can be only one thing worse than being in London and opening my morning newspaper to yet another black-and-white photo of Sheikh Zayed. That's being in Abu Dhabi and seeing his Highness moving, and in color, on television, at intolerable length, night after night, on the "world's news." All those outdoor shots with the wind catching his black cloak, enhancing that aura "which appears to combine a breadth of vision and a political acumen." All those closeups that show "the generous and expansive personality of the ruler." That's the way the British press writeups go. He certainly has a breadth of vision, and he is generous, but he's so heroic that he's a pain in the neck.

His Abu Dhabi defenders might do better to let his people see a few shots of Sheikh Zayed when he's off the stage. Why not get some of those tireless photographers into the breakfast room at Keir, the Scottish baronial estate where Sheikh Zayed often goes to stalk deer and shoot grouse?

Across the table from his host, friend, and business acquaintance Col. "Bill" Stirling, Zayed still looks like Sean Connery but when Bond is off screen, minus his toupee. Zayed, balding, in his cozy buttoned cardigan with a woolly scarf around his heroic throat is an altogether more appealing personality. He banters over the long-stemmed glass goblets of orange juice and plates of kippers, kidneys, kedgeree, and other gentry fare. And although he doesn't speak English, he's made himself a regular favorite with the dour, outdoor-minded Scots.

They've got so much in common to grunt about—the nasty nip in the air, the outdoor life, the passion for the hunt. Zayed, always aloof in Abu Dhabi gatherings, is what's called "a jolly good guest"; the kind of man who puts an arm around children and makes them laugh. Hunting in Pakistan may be an even greater delight, but he can't relax in quite the same way. There's the power play of the fellow sheikhs maneuvering around him. To head the al Nahiyan clan is not a rest cure.

No Abu Dhabian thanks you for opening the old sore about Sheikh Zayed's wives. He's on number eleven; intimates say fourteen. But all those wives have created a succession problem. Crown Prince Khalifa may have seen the error of his ways and been working hard to atone, but Sheikha Fatima (Zayed's number one wife) has her own young coming along. She may be his number one now but he'd had four before her, so it doesn't ease the atmosphere that she's steely ambitious for Sheikh Mohammed, her eldest.

Zayed also has to carry around the big bag of family skeletons. There was his favorite Sheikh Said, who was his brother and ruler Shakhbut's son, and married to Zayed's daughter. Sheikh Said shot his sister and her pimp and died of diabetes in exile abroad. He was such a blue-eyed boy that Zayed couldn't risk flying home his body in case it became a political bone.

There was his other nephew who used to bury people up to their necks in sand and leave them there all day—for fun. He died of drink. Then there's Sheikh Shakhbut himself, the brother and ruler whom Zayed deposed. He makes do on $1 million a year, living the peaceful life of a manic depressive in Al Ain. Zayed keeps in touch with him on the phone but still feels responsibility for the past.

Shakhbut's palace courtyard is deathly quiet: a cricket sings. An emaciated figure, apparently anchored to the ground by his heavy black shoes and socks, stands in the doorway. Sheikh Shakhbut likes visitors. Meeting him is a peculiar experience. He asks questions through an interpreter: "How many students are there at Cambridge?" "When was electricity first used in Europe?" "Do bananas grow in Canada?" Once his idiosyncratic test has been passed, he relaxes and talks of his three months in London this summer, staying at the Grosvenor House, going to the Wellington Hospital for treatment: "It was so cooooolllld that I never went out at all. I had to keep warm by walking around the hotel." He's the only Arab I meet who doesn't complain that London boiled all summer. It's hard to put together a jigsaw that includes this old man and the statesmanlike Zayed whom I see in Abu Dhabi.

Then there's Zayed's other brother Sheikh Khalid: the one you never hear about. He's also strange and, incidentally, owns half of Abu Dhabi. Sheikh Shakhbut was reputed to keep his money and jewels in tin boxes. Sheikh Khalid actually did until the day he was burgled in a London hotel. A man walked into the room carrying a bucket telling the servant in her *burqa* that he'd come to clean the windows. He walked out with a bucketful of jewels. She identified every man the police paraded in front of her. "That's him," she kept crying. But of course: all Europeans looked the same to her.

Fancy trying to cope with a family like this and govern a country like this when all your palaces are falling down and your court is, to put it politely, in disarray. Trotting around Zayed's offices is an exhausting business. Everyone you talk to claims to be doing everything and you know perfectly well that only the ruler, and his trusted servant of the moment, the Foreign Minister, do do anything. There's no organization or routine but Sheikh Zayed's personal office is always on the verge of beating the problem: "We're organizing ourselves on the lines of a mini-White House," says his Highness's personal assistant. "It should be ready any month now."

When the White House of the Gulf gets itself together, when Sheikh Zayed has planted enough trees to turn his sheikhdom into the Maine of the United Arab Emirates, one castoff in Al

Ain hopes he'll be remembered. Col. Sir Hugh Boustead has survived British colonial service in the Sudan, Yemen, Oman, and six years as Sheikh Shakhbut's political agent. He retired to England only to be flown out again at the invitation of Sheikh Zayed to run his stables. That was shortly before Zayed developed a green thumb and forgot his other hobby, horses.

Whatever time of day you arrive at the royal ranch, it's bound to be feeding time for the fifty-six horses flown in from all over the world, munching hay flown in from Iran, barley flown in from Karachi, served up by fourteen Pathan stable-boys flown in from Pakistan. And the sun-pickled figure of Sir Hugh, in his two-gallon hat, will be overseeing it all in the absence of Sheikh Zayed, who might, or might not, one day regain his former passion for these beasts.

In the meantime Sir Hugh plays medicine man, dosing the Bedouins ("They come in in heaps") with eyedrops and remedies for dysentery. It's an unusual way for a politico to end his days, but then this is Abu Dhabi. "By the way, if you need a bed for the night," throws out Sir Hugh over the sore Bedouin foot in his face, "you're welcome. Archdeacons and brigadiers have slept right here."

The ruler of Abu Dhabi, President of the UAE, hasn't only given his desert people the promise of green. He's given them something far more substantial. Far more substantial even than the schools and roads he's built—he's given them time.

That surprised the diplomats, who didn't reckon the Federation could survive more than six months. For that alone he deserves the grateful admiration of the oil-thirsty outside world. And he's upped the emir of Qatar to the leading role on the global stage. He runs his embassies abroad on a suitably lavish scale. So lavish that one of them is known locally as the Ph.D. (Prostitution and Hashish Department). Of course Sheikh Zayed can't know that.

Nor can word of it have reached the one commoner whom he really trusts. There is only one at any time and now it's Foreign Minister Ahmed Suweidi. Besides Zayed, only Suweidi has the power to decide anything in Abu Dhabi, so there's a clamor of diplomats, bankers, businessmen all wanting decisions. Every yes is going to mean money for some sheikh or other, so it's a delicate business working out whose bid to accept. No wonder this busy minister has to relax sometimes.

Ahmed Suweidi lives in a modest white family house. It's not where you go when he invites you to dinner. You go past his home along many hard, muddy lanes, around many corners to a truck-infested parking lot. There's a bungalow on one side. Inside, the harsh lights don't flatter the bare room ("cheap but decent," a landlady would say). There are nuts on the low table, a pile of cutlery on a sideboard, a program running on TV, and a well-stocked bar.

This evening there's a vintage crop of bankers, Ahmed's cousin, honored Western visitors, and Ahmed's retinue from the upper crust of his Foreign Office. The door opens and a girl comes in. She's tall, buxom, and beautiful with long black hair, big liquid eyes, and pouting lips. She appears to be the hostess for the evening. "I'm Lilian," she explains. It explains nothing.

Who is she? Not Mrs. Suweidi, that's certain. (Abu Dhabi isn't ready for ministers' wives entertaining men, let alone foreign men.) For the time being no one's quite sure who she is. She entertains the company with talk of Lebanon, the United States, and mutual friends. She's poised, intelligent, and in control.

Suweidi sweeps in straight from work. It's ten o'clock. He's everyone's idea of a lordly Gulf Arab. He's tall, good-looking, and he knows it. Knows it too well. Over the Campari sodas, gin and tonics, Scotches, and a buffet table laden with lamb, fish, and rice, Lilian nourishes the conversation. Who the hell is she? No one's going to explain her, that's clear.

Lilian eventually reveals that she's Lebanese, a doctor's daughter, a college girl, and one of the chosen few who has served as stewardess on Sheikh Zayed's private VC 10. "It's Sheikh Zayed I really admire. I love him like my father. He bothers about little things. He once stopped on his way to the plane and said to me, 'What do you do to your eyes that makes them more beautiful every day?' Why should he have ever bothered to notice us; we were only stewardesses."

When she left the VC 10 she went back whence she came to Middle East Airlines in Beirut. After the troubles started one of her thoughtful friends from the Foreign Office telephoned her and invited her to the haven of Abu Dhabi. "They did everything for me; paid my flight, my hotel, everything. But I'd never abuse their hospitality by boasting that they're paying. Anyone could choose to misunderstand it."

Lilian has a headache. One of Ahmed's retinue tries massaging her temples. He's never done it before but seems rather good at it. "My wife does it to me," he explains. Lilian encourages the masseur with playful scolding. "And why have I neither seen you nor heard from you for two whole weeks? You've no excuse. You know where I'm staying. You're neglecting me."

The masseur is undeterred. "But Lilian dear, I know you're not neglected. I hear news of you from everyone." Even Ahmed's been keeping up with Lilian because she's been giving him French lessons. He's off to visit President Giscard d'Estaing soon.

He's experimenting with his French on a visiting merchant banker. *"Est-ce que tu veux encore du thé?"* he asks. The banker looks pleased and holds out his whisky glass for refilling. But he's got it wrong. Ahmed was choosing his words carefully. He meant tea all right, but he'd better clear up the subtleties of *"tu"* before he gets to Giscard. France's pro-Arab policy hasn't gone that far yet.

Everything's going swimmingly in Ahmed's foreign department at present. Though the Saudis aren't exactly popular around here, at least everything's hunky-dory on the surface. It hasn't always been that way. The "Buraimi Oasis" dispute over their shared border ended up in the international court and involved skirmishes with foreign troops and endless legal wrangling. What neither international arbitration nor brute force could achieve was finally settled last year. Details were not published but afterward Zayed played his part by showing his characteristic generosity and ceding to the Saudis an important oil well.

The United Arab Emirates are in with the Saudis but they're going all out to make friends with Iran. The Shah has made claims to the whole area before now, but he minds most about who rules close to the vital entrance to the Gulf. ("Do you know the value of the oil which flows through the strait every day?" the Shah asked recently. "One hundred and eighty million dollars." Not long ago his mighty army overwhelmed a couple of the Federation's tiny islands, so Ahmed Suweidi is jubilant that Zayed and Company, Incorporated made such a hit in Tehran last week. What are a few islands among friends?

After all this Ahmed feels he deserves an evening off. He stretches into his chair, tipping his headdress provocatively forward. He's one of the few Abu Dhabians who matches those Iranians for style.

Toward one the party breaks up. Caught in the car headlights on the way out of the parking lot is a view of the beautiful Lilian. The Foreign Minister and his top man are playing make-believe tug-of-war with her, each pulling a healthy bronzed arm. The Foreign Minister wins. The headlights move on.

I see Abu Dhabi men; I see Abu Dhabi women. I never see them together. I know which of the two I prefer. The women are the most rewarding part of this place—women like Sheikha Osheh.

Sheikha Osheh may be in her late thirties. It's hard to tell. She never takes off her *burqa*. "But it has shrunk, you see," she says in a muffled voice through her abbreviated helmet.

Sheikha Osheh, daughter of Sheikh Shakhbut, is married to Sheikh Mubarak, perhaps the most powerful royal besides Zayed. She's graceful and gentle, in a high-necked, long-sleeved, full-length dress with strings of pearls lying lightly on her bodice. Above this is the frightening mask. It fades as her personality comes through.

She lives in a protected nest, heavily scented, where time and space intrude only through other people. If only *harem* weren't such an emotive and misleading word, this is what I'd call Sheikha Osheh's brightly colored velveted room. Women drift in and out, servants, daughter, grandchildren, English-language teacher; and all the while Sheikha Osheh entertains her guests.

She's at her most fascinating when she talks about falconing. She takes down a stuffed bird from the wall and starts to explain the way it's downed; how you have to cover the dead bird in sand to hoax the falcon into believing it's lost its prey. Otherwise it won't let go. And how you mustn't let it have more than one peck at the bird's brains or the falcon will lose its appetite and won't hunt anymore. She describes it minutely; she has the zest of a devotee. Sheikha Osheh has never been hunting. Her husband once took her out in a car—to watch. But when he comes home he sits with her for hours bringing alive a world she never sees.

She doesn't know the town of Abu Dhabi at all. She never goes out in it. But she has one extension to this room that few other women like her share. Every morning after dawn prayers her husband drives her out to the desert. They sit and drink coffee together before he brings her home and goes off to his ministry.

Sheikha Osheh is the adored and only wife of Sheikh Mubarak. Polygamy still thrives, but people are becoming sensitive about it. "It's tiring for the man and very hard for the women," admitted one sheikha, herself not an only wife. It'll take time for most men to catch up with their closeted sheikhas and stop equating quantity with quality.

Ever since I first saw a *burqa*-ed woman in the Gulf I've wondered how these masked enigmas manage the simple task of drinking. A little girl brings in a huge Thermos of cardamom coffee. Sheikha Osheh lifts up her *burqa* like a car hood, takes the egg-sized cup, and awkwardly tips in the coffee. Women take off their masks for prayers and husband. Going to the doctor is a trauma. One English female physician still hasn't found a way of coaxing her patients out of their *burqas* in her office. "When they come to see me the first thing they do is throw off their clothes, without my even asking them. They're completely uninhibited about their bodies. But they won't take off their masks. Their face is for them what our private parts are for us. You put on a *burqa* for the first time when you menstruate. The connection's obvious."

An Afghan lady balloonist in a Chanel suit arrives to say hello. She's brought some photographs with her. Sheikha Osheh has never seen a hot-air balloon before. She studies intently the photos of the blue and white contraption and immediately asks the question to which most people have always longed to know the answer. "Hmmm. I understand how it goes up. But how do you get it down again?" Satisfied that this obstacle can be overcome, she earnestly presses the balloonist to come along to next year's National Day Parade. It would add color. Sheikha Osheh knows; she watches the parade on television.

It sounds strange because I don't believe in shutting women away. But even without comparing these women to the men, with their smack of corruption and the stamp of spoiled children, they are entrancing. They're open, preserved from double-think by the thick walls around them, and they understand the essentials of a world they're never allowed to see.

What about London? Can't they kick up their heels there? A sheikha gets into a flying metal tube, transfers to a black limousine, and is shut away in a private apartment. It's Abu Dhabi again. Those black bundles I've seen all summer in Harrods (the Gulf invasion of New York hasn't even gotten started yet; wait another couple of years and then go to Bloomingdale's) aren't these women. They're their Bedouin servants. They're doubtless the ones who earn the reputation for messing up pristine rooms and apartments. It's certainly not the sheikhas.

Sheikha Fatima has often been to Britain. She's stayed at that Kensington mansion with the Bonsack Bathroom, and at Buxted Park with all that keep-fit machinery, but even the First Lady of Abu Dhabi doesn't go out. Sheikha Fatima may have been the fifth, but she's Sheikh Zayed's favorite wife now; the only one he keeps in Abu Dhabi (the rest are in Al Ain); the only one he takes abroad.

You have to work hard to remain the favorite wife of Sheikh Zayed for fifteen years, and Sheikha Fatima is a clever lady. They say she was ravishing as a teenage bride. She's had nine children since then and under the *burqa* who can tell? Compared to tender Sheikha Osheh, Sheikha Fatima's the tough career wife of Abu Dhabi. She's the talk of the town.

She comes in for some criticism from traditionalists who say that she doesn't do her stuff for the Bedouins anymore but that's because she's cultivating the foreign Arabs. She makes it seem as if she's merely fulfilling her First Lady entertaining role. In fact, she's culling everything they have to offer that she wants to learn—current affairs, news of international personalities, a whole picture of the world she wants to master. It's working; she's just returned from her first official visit abroad—to Mrs. Sadat in Cairo.

This week Sheikha Fatima is setting yet another precedent. She's presiding over a special event at the new Women's Club, the only place sheikhas can go. Four avant-garde female Western artists conducted by a "French princess" are having an exhibition. It's opening night: there's the friendly buzz of masked and veiled women, who rarely have the chance to meet. The unveiled young are radiant. Expectancy is in the air. Sheikha Fatima finally arrives and heads the fleet that sails into the exhibition room.

They're the kind of pictures that a self-conscious Western critic might call "a deeply significant comment on our troubled times." Abstracts. Psychedelia. A field day for the Freudians.

There's a nonplussed lull as the ladies sweep around. One black back starts to shake with laughter. "Uterus," she says, pointing to one canvas. "Ovaries," to another. It takes women like these to see the second-rateness of it all. Game, set, and match to the Abu Dhabi ladies.

25

THE DAY DISASTER STRUCK

DUBAI IS THE SECOND LARGEST SHEIKHDOM IN THE FEDERATION (1,500 square miles small). It seems to be a place with a sense of humor; its contribution to the National Day Parade procession this year is a float disguised as a dhow. It features dozens of blacks being foully whipped by an Arab slavemaster. I'm looking forward to a place that has the gall to pull that one off before some gawping African ambassadors on the VIP stand.

My trip starts well. I choose to drive across the desert highway from Abu Dhabi. There's a tourist delight of sand and camels with no road sense, spoiled by the view of Pakistanis road-building in the scorching winter sun. They're always telling you in Abu Dhabi that the Baluchis are the only people who can stand the midday summer heat. A Pakistani millionaire in Dubai hooted at that one: "I suppose the British POW's didn't notice the heat when they were building the Burma railway for the Japanese." At least they're not prisoners of war; they're prisoners of money. The Pakistani road-builders get $220 a month, they point out in Abu Dhabi. That's for working seven days a week; for $75 they can share a hut for four with no facilities. Well, it gives them a chance to save. The middle-class Pakistani businessmen in Dubai make a fortune, live well, but they're mostly scared stiff. They and the Indians own a good slab of Dubai—known as the Venice of the Mideast (more aptly the Shanghai). As foreigners they have no legal right to own real estate—what am I talking about?—they've no legal rights at all. And they haven't forgotten what happened to six hundred fellow countrymen at the docks. They met to discuss the shortage of water taps on site. His Highness Sheikh Rashid ibn Said al Makhtum, ruler of Dubai, locked the gates and shipped them all back home. Bad precedent, he said.

With all these pleasant thoughts going through my mind I miss the vital clue to what makes Dubai tick. It's the sculptured concrete clock tower at the entrance to town. All four faces tell a different time.

I roll up to the Intercontinental Hotel, resplendent with hanging plants and creeping businessmen. "Yes," says the girl at reception, "the Ministry of Information asked for a room for you. But the problem with the ministry is that they think they only have to ask for something and they get it. Well, there isn't one. Come back later."

I'm feeling a trifle queasy—sunstroke probably. Two hours across the desert even in winter is a long, hot haul, and I'm not Baluchi. The telephone seems a good idea. I cling in hope to the name of Mohammed Zayed Bejaseem, director of information in Dubai. The office recognizes the name immediately and sounds very welcoming. "Come and see me. Come right away." Promising start. But I have another number to call: it's the ruler's office. There, I've been told, Oscar Mandody is a great power in the land.

Oscar Mandody sounds very welcoming too. "Come and see me. Come right away." Going there first makes sense; the director of information should be relieved at my initiative. I call him back and explain the dilemma of the room (which he says he'll sort out) and that I'm on my way to the ruler's office. He gives me his home telephone number, wishes me luck, and urges me to call in case of trouble.

This is how it all begins. Bear with me, this tale is Dubai in miniature.

Oscar Mandody is Indian. That doesn't surprise me. Dubai

has long enjoyed a special relationship with India and Pakistan: spice trading, the pearl trade, gold smuggling, that sort of thing. Oscar Mandody is very sleek indeed. He sits behind his desk manipulating a roomful of people through half-closed eyes in a carefully measured voice. He's a snappy dresser; glistening pink silk tie, almost shiny blue mohair suit; long oiled locks. He's quite a sight among all the Bedouin elders, who burst in wielding sticks and promises they've just extracted from Sheikh Rashid in his *majlis* along the corridor.

I can't help liking Mandody. In all this chaos I think he's one sharp operator whom I'll be able to talk to. He's the trusted top man of Mehdi al Tajir, businessman, fixer, UAE Ambassador to Britain and France, described by an admiring banker as "a cross between the devil and the grand vizier."

Oscar supervises the Department of Petroleum in Dubai in al Tajir's absence, keeps watch on the ambassador's businesses, has day-and-night access to Sheikh Rashid. Oh, yes, he's the man to get things done.

He's toying with some Australian city planners who've flown in with model underpasses. While I watch him beguile and confuse I make a tally of what I know of his boss's wealth. Let's say al Tajir doesn't sue when people call him "the richest man in the world." But it was only nineteen years ago that al Tajir descended on Dubai from Bahrain as a lowly customs officer. Somewhere along the line he and wily Sheikh Rashid got together. Al Tajir's a fast earner.

I cast my mind back to September: the UN in New York. I met al Tajir's nephew, a diplomat with the UAE mission. I was having trouble in London over a visa. "My uncle is the only man who can help," said Mohammed, bushy-eyebrowed, the image of his uncle. He wrote down his address on a piece of paper and shoved it across the table. He downed another drink and added: "In Dubai we're all businessmen. Come to my apartment at six thirty and afterward you'll meet my uncle." It's all coming back to me now. After I threw a frosty British fit he caused such a scene that an Egyptian First Secretary came up the next day to apologize. "Those Gulf Arabs. We can't do a thing with them, and they're all too big for their breeches."

I have a nasty fit of shivering. If it's not sunstroke, perhaps it's an omen. Oscar keeps me there until two thirty. "Trouble with a room, my dear Linda; we must see to that." One telephone call to the general manager of the Intercontinental and the room is fixed. "Come to my house this afternoon for tea. You can meet my girlfriend and we will talk."

At the Intercontinental the room is indeed fixed. The general manager sends fruit and champagne. Oscar's at work. I telephone the director of information at home to tell him the good news. An Englishwoman, his wife I think, answers, and I leave a message that I have a room and I'm very grateful.

Oscar practically lives in a zoo. There are goats, birds, dogs, and people. I'm parked on the porch while he finishes a business meeting. At last I'm allowed in to meet Monica. Monica is Swedish, blond, given to throwing herself around. She bristles at me at the first instant and hands Oscar his newest kitten. "Go to Daddy, darling." She makes tea and accidentally forgets to give me some. Oscar strokes the kitten as he goes through the liquor bill. It seems Monica is extravagant on his behalf, but they do have to entertain so much.

"Poor Oscar," confides Monica in a meaningful woman-to-woman way when he's out of the room, "his wife gave him such a dreadful time, and he was so unhappy until he met me. Now we're very much in love, but there are people who talk about us behind our backs." I believe the last line. "I met Oscar when I came out from London and he fell for me at first sight and begged me to stay here and live with him. It's worth it. I don't care what they say."

Oscar returns and announces that Asprey of Bond Street (and Oman, Dubai, and Abu Dhabi, with Kuwait coming soon) has opened a temporary Christmas shop in the Intercontinental. We'll all go together. Monica and I have tacitly agreed that we're not going to be bosom chums. Asprey has everything laid out to tempt Dubai; John Asprey, the young, sandy-looking export director, and his wife greet Oscar warmly. Monica ends up somewhere near the diamond watch case. "I'll lay you two dollars that she'll get one out of him," says Oscar's friendly brother. It's a bet I don't take. Monica gets a watch and buys him a little something, too, a very little something. "Call me, Linda, will you?" purrs Oscar as I take my leave.

By now I'm feeling dizzy. I go up to the room and work out that it's not sunstroke, it's not the atmosphere—I am ill. The housekeeper obliges with a thermometer. It registers way, way over normal. I have Gulf flu. My voice is going, my body's aching, I feel very sorry for myself. At nine o'clock the phone rings.

"Linda, this is Zayed. Why did you do that to me? You have no right to telephone people's wives and tell them what you did."

It's not only flu. I'm evidently going mad. Zayed? It takes ten minutes to work out that the by-now-screaming maniac on the end of the phone is Mohammed Zayed Bejaseem, Director of the UAE's Ministry of Information in Dubai.

I've almost got a grip on myself and manage to explain that I telephoned to say that the hotel problem was sorted out and that I was grateful. That does it.

"Why didn't you come and see me this morning? I waited in the office for you until three o'clock?" Liar.

"I was with Oscar Mandody in the ruler's office," I explain patiently. Another explosion.

"How dare you go to see a filthy foreigner before you come to see me, an Arab? I am from Dubai. How dare you insult me like this?"

"But Mr. Mohammed—"

"Zayed; my name is Zayed, Zayed . . ."

"But Mr. Mohammed Zayed, Mr. Mandody is an adviser to the ruler, Sheikh Rashid; I didn't think that I could be doing anything wrong by seeing him."

"I know. You hate Arabs. You think we're scum who don't work. Well I've been to Cambridge," at a language school as it later turns out, not the university, "and I'm a man you should respect. And if you don't show respect, I'll have you thrown out of the country as soon as I feel like it."

At nine twenty-five I interrupt the threats and histrionics, hang up the phone, lie on the bed, and burst into tears of frustration and misery.

Day two dawns in wonderful downtown Dubai. The sun is rising and so is my temperature. I call reception. There's a hotel doctor; he'll be up to see me. The telephone rings. It's that bad dream from the Ministry of Information. But what's this? A sweet, gentle voice on the other end of the line.

"Linda, why don't you come to my office to see me. I know we have had a small misunderstanding, but my wife is not an understanding woman." Oh, no; it wasn't a dream.

"I have flu and I can't get out of bed."

"I'll send you a doctor."

"Thank you, Mr. Mohammed Zayed—"

"Just Zayed—"

"—but the hotel has arranged one already. I'll call you as soon as I'm better and we'll pretend nothing happened."

"You're in bed ill! That's terrible. I'll come around to see you myself this afternoon."

"Thank you, but that isn't necessary—"

"I'll be there at four thirty." Click.

I quickly ring Aftab, a Pakistani businessman whom I know through a reputable contact in London. I explain that the last thing I want is to be alone with an apparent maniac in my room. Will he please come over for the afternoon? Of course.

The hotel doctor comes, diagnoses bad flu, and leaves me dosed with promises of recovery and antibiotics. I trust neither. The Pakistani arrives in the afternoon, settles down to a stack of newspapers. We wait.

At five o'clock there's a knock on the door. Aftab opens it to admit Mohammed Zayed in national dress bearing one red rose. He has innocent big black eyes; he looks as if butter would melt in his mouth. He mistakes Aftab for the doctor at first so he treats him with a certain caution.

Zayed (it's as catching as the flu) climbs on my bed to stroke my face. Aftab tactfully brings forward a chair. "My neck aches," I whisper hoarsely. "Perhaps you'd be kind enough to sit over there where I can see you." All is peaceful enough in the sickroom until he asks where the doctor came from. I know what he's getting at but I play for time.

"From the hotel."

"What's his name?"

"Dr. Nimr."

"Didn't you know he's a Palestinian?"

"I didn't ask him."

"Dr. Nimr, a Palestinian. What do you want with foreigners? Why is it always foreigners? What's wrong with Arabs?"

I squirm for Aftab. Aftab, a big noise in soap powder from Lahore, is too worldly to be annoyed. He eventually dusts Zayed out of the room, still muttering with anger. Aftab gives me two aspirin for a Zayed-induced headache, orders hot chocolate, and leaves.

Day three is no better. Behold, yet another side of the director of information.

"Linda; it's Zayed."

"Zayed, it's eleven thirty at night."

"Yes, but you're staying in a room booked by the Ministry of Information. I am its director in Dubai; you're staying in my room. I want to come over."

"Zayed, that's not a good idea. I will come to see you in your office when I am better to sort things out. And please remember that I'm the guest of Ali Shammo, the ministry's Undersecretary." Mistake.

"Him, he's a Sudanese, he can do nothing. I'm an Arab. I'm the one who counts. You'll want a car, won't you? Well, you won't have one. You won't go anywhere or see anyone in Dubai unless I drive you there." He sticks to his word. I stick to taxis.

Once I totter out of bed, Zayed's telephone calls become a part of everyday life. "Linda, it's Zayed. I won't pay for your room unless you let me come over to see you. I've spoken to Sheikh Rashid, and he won't see you."

Relief. I've seen that Highness already and the way I feel,

the last thing I want to do is see anyone else in Dubai. Enough is enough. I'm heading for Sharjah, a few miles up the coast.

"I've spoken to Sheikh Sultan, the ruler of Sharjah, and he's too busy to receive you. But if you let me come over, I'll find a way to make Sheikh Sultan see you." I slam down the phone.

One day the telephone rings and it's not Zayed. It's none other than that power in the land, Oscar Mandody.

"I hear you've been having a spot of bother. Why didn't you call me?" Word travels fast. "Never mind, pack your suitcase and come over and stay here with us." I notice that he doesn't say he'll do anything about the director. Nobody does; it would take the combined might of the UAE Cabinet to censure or remove him. He's a local Arab.

I phone Monica to tell her what time I'll arrive. Her tone suggests that I'm the last thing she wants in the house. I can't face more hassles; not on top of Zayed and *après*-flu. I decide to stay put.

At seven thirty on the morning I'm leaving to go home, Oscar phones again and invites himself over for coffee. He walks into the room and makes it clear that he's hurt.

"I've just come from the airport. I've been seeing the ambassador off. We were talking about you, Linda." Am I supposed to be grateful? "You knew I liked you the moment you walked into my office. You should have called me. I admire you, Linda, you have something pure about you." Oh no, not that.

Mandody starts on another tack. "I don't believe in people anymore. Everyone is rotten, everyone is selfish, everyone is cruel. You may be wondering why I've worked so hard." The last thing on my mind.

"I wanted to prove that I could do something on my own without the magical name of Mandody." What? Oh yes, his father is a local doctor.

"I had nothing when I came here and you may not believe this, but for the first ten years I worked for Sheikh Rashid and the ambassador, I never took advantage of my position.

"Now Dubai is too small for me. I'd like to retire and lead a simpler life." He laps his coffee and elucidates.

"I'll buy a place in India, a place in the country in England, perhaps a flat in London and a place in Europe, the South of France, maybe, and I'll need a house in the States. I've seen what money does to people. I admire the ambassador more than any other man on earth. But I'm thirty-four now and I'm bitter."

The confessional at this time of the morning is too much. "And I feel I can be cruel to people I love but I can't help it. I'm sorry about Monica; she can be such a nuisance. But I'm an extremely sensitive person and I wanted you to know how much I admire you."

He leaves me bewildered. I have no clue whether he's trying to pump, compromise, flatter, or even threaten me. I can't wait to hit the runway back to London.

Suddenly it strikes me. I think I know what he came for. While recuperating from flu, I've spent time in the neighboring sheikhdom of Sharjah. Dubai and Sharjah aren't the greatest of friends.

What gave Oscar away was a line that I almost missed. "By the way, Linda," he asked casually, "how *did* you get to see the ruler of Sharjah?"

All that Dubai and Sharjah have in common is membership in the UAE—and oil.

26

GOOD-BYE TO ALL THAT

THERE'S NO AURA ABOUT HIS HIGHNESS SHEIKH RASHID, RULER of Dubai. He's declared himself to be a businessman. I see him sitting in his *majlis,* lean, sparkling still, in his seventies and a character. He wouldn't be in the least offended if it got around that one of his favorite tricks is to pull up his long dress. He then waits to see which of his stiff courtiers will be the first to whisper tactfully that his Highness's balls are showing. Oh no, Sheikh Rashid would be the first to laugh. He doesn't stand on his dignity; he doesn't need to.

He's chomping at the bit, eager to be off to Pakistan for his month-long hunting trip. He packs his private Boeing 707 with his retinue and any spare Bedouins around at the time. One of his officials is preoccupied at present trying to hire a private train for him in Karachi. It's going to be a whale of an outing.

The women are not all delicate hothouse plants either. There was one energetic sheikha who, according to the British man on the spot at the time, had an endearing habit of "pointing a pistol at the breast of the biggest and strongest servant and asking him to oblige."

Nor is Sheikha Hasana anything too unusual. At nine she loaded cannon and rifles as her family fought off their bitter desert rival (none other than Sheikh Rashid in his youth). The family lost; Sheikha Hasana saw her father slaughtered, her relations' eyes gouged by swords. And then at thirteen she was forced to marry Sheikh Rashid's brother. She came from a tough school, so who would be surprised that Hasana took umbrage and a gun and shot her husband's charming fourth wife? Now she lives in the desert, alone in her tent encampment, wearing her *burqa* and her independence as the badges of another age.

Sheikh Rashid doesn't go in for polygamy himself. Apart from anything else he's far too artful. He has stuck to one strong, influential wife so as not to have a brood of half-brothers squabbling for power. Crown Prince Makhtum is a nice, fat, lean-living guy, popular in Dubai, especially among some of the younger set who figure there won't be room for the al Tajir individual style of operating once he's in charge.

Ambassador Medhi al Tajir is affectionately called Mr. Five Percent in Dubai, or Mr. Twenty Percent (according to how large the contractor you're talking to). He's full of bright ideas for Dubai's expansion: the dry dock, the aluminum works, etc. His collection of priceless Persian rugs, pearls, and attractive women acquaintances are much publicized too. He can be very kind and cooperative to journalists. But, says Oscar Mandody, he never stays in Dubai unless Sheikh Rashid is there. It's such a small country that it doesn't surprise me to learn that the ambassador is going global. He won't be leaving anything behind in Dubai—that fabled villa doesn't add up to much when you finally see it. Not compared with Mereworth, his Palladian ideal in the English countryside, with its eighty-foot-long gallery-cum-drawing room "with magnificent frescos and a painted ceiling of utmost splendor by Francesco Sleter" (as featured in *House and Garden*). Al Tajir's worked hard and he's done well for himself.

But his isn't the only success story in Dubai. It's the place that got rich on gold smuggling to India; it's something people are almost proud of. There's so much less savory "reexportation" going on, "pharmaceuticals," for instance, that they're glad to divert attention to anything as harmless as gold. It's an oil state bursting with the character that Abu Dhabi lacks. It's the place to be if it's buccaneers you're after.

There's a funny thing though: even Mehdi al Tajir has never set foot in the sheikhdom of Sharjah. Oscar Mandody hasn't been there either: "I've been too busy." Sharjah is five minutes' drive from Dubai—seven, depending on which border you accept. The UAE borders are a mess, even the ones that aren't under dispute like Dubai-Sharjah's (which is just a main road with no "border" marking to be seen anywhere, unless you count any of the advertisement billboards).

You're never going to believe this, but Sharjah state is divided into four bits stuck all over the UAE. It shares half a patch of desert with the sheikhdom of Fujirah, half a village with another country (Oman), and half an island with yet another country (Iran). When you're driving along the coast from Sharjah town to the fishing village of Hamriyah, there's a bend in the highway. It straightens out after a few miles. You've just missed the sheikhdom of Ajman.

Until recently, Sharjah's main claim to fame (among a handful of cognoscenti) was that it produced the red asphalt for the road outside Buckingham Palace in London. It's newest claim is that it's the youngest oil-producing sheikhdom. Half an oil-producing sheikhdom, to be accurate. Its oil income is a secret; its only production so far is on that island it shares with Iran. They made a gentlemanly deal over it; unlike the sheikhdom of Ras al Khaimah, which lost a couple of islands altogether to the Iranian army when its six valiant policemen had to capitulate. One even died heroically in combat.

So Sharjah's an oil state, and development is raging all over it. It's even building a new multimillion-dollar international airport a few miles away from Dubai's new multimillion-dollar international airport. Joining the oil stakes (in 1974) is one thing. It's far more interesting to me that his Highness Sheikh Sultan ibn Mohammed al Qasimi is the first university graduate to rule anywhere in the peninsula. It was another of those accidents, another of those families.

Ruler Saqr of Sharjah was deposed in 1965 by the British for being as stingy as Ruler Shakhbut. A duly cooperative chap, Sheikh Khalid, was put in his place and all went well —until '72. Sheikh Saqr wanted his state back and shot Khalid dead in the attempt to seize it. Tricky business all around. The UAE President, Sheikh Zayed, decided a fair trial was called for. It was meant to be an open trial. It got tangled up in some unwelcome local publicity and Sheikh Saqr now lives under "house arrest" in Al Ain, around the corner from Sheikh Shakhbut.

Another new ruler was needed for Sharjah, but it would have been embarrassing to choose one of the assassin's powerful sheikhly brothers. In those days, Sheikh Sultan, Khalid's younger brother, was spending his time on his farm, trying out air conditioning on his summer vegetable plants. Sheikh Sultan, a former technical-college teacher, had recently come back from Cairo University where he went to take a degree in agriculture.

Today, at thirty-eight, he's ruler of Sharjah and a delightful man. He's resting outside in the dark, in his palace garden when I arrive. He knows about my flu and sympathizes. He's getting it too. We move inside but one of his tame gazelles tags along, spilling a vase of flowers and trampling the armchairs. Sheikh Sultan smiles and smiles. Eventually the gazelle is shooed outside and the ruler explains that he wants his country to be different from certain others he's too tactful to name.

Bart Paff, an American economics master, sits in, hands folded over his briefcase. He came here to do a short feasibility study and is now the ruler's permanent adviser. (How do they plan? "We play it by the seat of our pants.") Paff has a touch of Steve McQueen about him, especially when I ask if he's Sharjah's answer to Mehdi al Tajir.

Sheikh Sultan, raised in the desert, and Bart Paff, raised

in comfort, know what they want: no middlemen, no percentage cuts, no ban on foreign Arabs owning property, no obligatory local partners, no everything that makes buildings fall down in Abu Dhabi and doing business complicated in Dubai.

Sheikh Sultan is bright. It's not only his university education or his fluent English, Urdu, Farsi. "He has his head screwed on right," as Paff puts it. They're much more alike than they look, this Arab and this American. Except for his national dress, Sultan is light-years away from the old-fashioned Bedouin-style sheikhs down the road. He doesn't take months off from running his state to go hunting; he takes two weeks' vacation each summer. He's the way they'll all be in a few years' time. The rulers I've seen are already moving into history.

He doesn't drink and he's careful not to offend conservatives by being seen publicly with his delectable young wife, Mosa. But that doesn't stop him inviting an English ballet dancer home to give Mosa conversation classes and private tutors from Cairo to coach her for a degree.

They live together in this house with their new daughter, the gazelles, and soldiers at the gate. Without the soldiers I wouldn't know it was a palace. And Sultan isn't adorned by cufflinks to make the right impression. He's past the stage of gewgaws. He's not going to set Bond Street by the ears by walking out of Asprey with a hundred pairs of gold cufflinks and five Piaget eighteen-karat white-gold, diamond-set watches, as Sheikh Rashid has done. Sultan's almost embarrassed at the white yacht he inherited from his dead brother Khalid. He could moor it anywhere; the Sharjah coastline is his. He chooses to leave it on the quay opposite the camel slaughterhouse.

I must tell you about the slaughterhouse; there's a queue of patient camels waiting their turn, and the stench is hellish. It's almost as if Sheikh Sultan wants to remind himself of the inevitable human condition.

His flu is getting worse. His almond-shaped eyes are turning pink. "I want you to see Sharjah and I want you to be happy here. My cousin, Sheikh Ahmed, brought you to me, and he will look after you."

How I met Sheikh Ahmed is another of those tales.

I'm in the lobby of the Intercontinental dodging those phone calls from Dubai's attentive director of information. I've never felt so blue. Which of us is delirious—me or Dubai? A young American and an even younger, owlish Arab peer at me anxiously. "Are you all right?"

Since I'm obviously far from all right, they gingerly escort me to the coffee shop. Barry Qulick is a movie producer (*Sitting Target,* etc.). Sheikh Ahmed ibn Mohammed al Qasimi is from Sharjah.

Sheikh Ahmed quickly grasps the Dubai disaster. Five minutes later he's arranged a visit to his cousin the ruler. Over the next three days Barry Qulick will wish he had ignored my plight. He doesn't get much done while Ahmed takes seriously the ruler's injunction that I'm in his care. He and Barry are going into partnership in an eight-lane bowling alley, movie, snack bar, and restaurant complex. That must wait.

Ahmed decides that a day in the country for me comes before a visit to the bank with Barry. He commandeers his Lebanese office manager (whom he met and hired in a furniture shop) with his Irish girlfriend. I discover on the ride out that Leena, bouncy, rosy-cheeked, sells encyclopedia sets to Arab businessmen around the Gulf.

"Of course they always ask me for dinner, but I say, 'I'll call you tomorrow.' They sign, I never call, and someone else goes to deliver the sets and collect the money. They never go back on a deal once they've given their word. That's what's so nice about them." It's still crazy, but I feel better already.

We drive to the famous Dhaid oasis. So this is an oasis; a shriveled collection of shops, donkeys, a few wilting trees, and a farm belonging to Ahmed's father. Nothing much grows. I suppose it's all comparative. We drag a couple of armchairs out of the living room (Ahmed's father has installed air conditioning, much to the son's disgust) and sit on the verandah. The others fiddle with the barbecue and swill beer.

Ahmed's twenty-one. Father Mohammed didn't get on with his brother, ruler Saqr, so he took the family to Saudi Arabia, where he worked as a clerk for Aramco. Later he came back to Dubai, went into business, and packed Ahmed off to college in London. "I lived in a raincoat in one room; I was cold, wet, and lonely."

His father swiftly became the richest, most powerful sheikh in Sharjah, apart from the ruler. The ruler is grooming Ahmed as a symbol of al Qasimi reconciliation. "My father will never get over the fact that his brother murdered the ruler's brother. Sheikh Sultan wants it all to be forgotten. He's given me land and told me what to build on it, apprenticed me to Bart Paff so I can learn. It's a strain, frankly. I've no money of my own, only land. I have to borrow capital from the bank like everyone else and I don't think I'm that clever."

Ahmed is engaged to cousin Aisha, daughter of the man his uncle killed. That's another reason he's so important. This marriage will help to darn the past. We don't talk about that; we just watch the sunset in Dhaid and drive back to Dubai.

Next day Ahmed comes to take me to the beach. I don't recognize him. He's wearing jeans. Al Qasimis don't walk into the Intercontinental in jeans; there's got to be a reason.

We're sitting cross-legged on the sand about an hour later throwing pebbles into the sea at Hamriyah. Where better could Prince Alfonso Hohenlohe be building a new Marbella Club but in Sharjah? It's better than beaten-up Spain any day, and there's oil money on tap.

In jeans and a short-sleeved shirt, Ahmed still looks owlish behind those thin-rimmed spectacles. But he looks more vulnerable without his headdress; he's also handsome, which hadn't occurred to me before.

"Wouldn't it be marvelous if Aisha could be with us? I talked to her on the phone for hours this morning. I do every day. Although we're engaged I can't see her alone or take her out like this. My family say, 'What are you waiting for? Get married now.' But I don't want to be married their way, living in a huge house with soldiers at the gate.

"I want the ruler to give us a small house, somewhere quiet, but Aisha's mother insists that the daughter of a former ruler must live in a certain way. I don't mind taking a house from the ruler; he gives one to every al Qasimi, but I want to earn the money to furnish it myself and to furnish it our way. No one understands that."

He'd like Aisha to go abroad to study for a while. "Her mother won't hear of it. But I want Aisha to be the kind of wife who comes out, goes to dinner parties, does things with me. As long as she's only known her mother's old-fashioned ways, she'll always think it's wrong for a wife to do anything like that.

"The jeans have made a difference, haven't they?" I click. "I couldn't have talked to you like this in national dress. It doesn't matter to me but it puts up a barrier for you." He's right; even now those white robes still make me think of the men wearing them as set apart from my world. Some are; some of the younger generation, like Ahmed, aren't.

On the road back to Dubai a "Cadirolls" speeds past with a young tiger at the wheel. Ahmed looks sad. It's his sixteen-year-old brother, Salim. "He goes to London in the summer and stays in the Britannia Hotel alone and my family encourage him; they say he's sixteen and a man. He drinks whisky, chases girls, and he's still at school.

"When I was his age, no one had even heard of Sharjah; we didn't have the money to live like that. Now I'm an oil sheikh and wherever I go it's 'Sheikh Ahmed this' and 'Sheikh Ahmed that.' I can't stand it."

We walk into the hotel. Barry Qulick is waiting, a picture of triumph. "Ahmed, I've got it. We're going to have a special section in our snack bar serving 'Sheikh Ahmed's Milk-shakes.'" The new oil sheikh from Sharjah goes dead quiet.

ANNETTE LeBOX

Circle of Cranes

DIAL BOOKS FOR YOUNG READERS
· *an imprint of Penguin Group (USA) Inc.* ·

For my sworn sister, Leah Lindsay
Friendship, love, loyalty

DIAL BOOKS FOR YOUNG READERS
A division of Penguin Young Readers Group
Published by The Penguin Group

Penguin Group (USA) Inc., 375 Hudson Street, New York, NY 10014, U.S.A. * Penguin Group (Canada), 90 Eglinton Avenue East, Suite 700, Toronto, Ontario, Canada M4P 2Y3 (a division of Pearson Penguin Canada Inc.) * Penguin Books Ltd, 80 Strand, London WC2R 0RL, England * Penguin Ireland, 25 St. Stephen's Green, Dublin 2, Ireland (a division of Penguin Books Ltd) * Penguin Group (Australia), 250 Camberwell Road, Camberwell, Victoria 3124, Australia (a division of Pearson Australia Group Pty Ltd) * Penguin Books India Pvt Ltd, 11 Community Centre, Panchsheel Park, New Delhi—110 017, India * Penguin Group (NZ), 67 Apollo Drive, Rosedale, Auckland 0632, New Zealand (a division of Pearson New Zealand Ltd) * Penguin Books (South Africa) (Pty) Ltd, 24 Sturdee Avenue, Rosebank, Johannesburg 2196, South Africa * Penguin Books Ltd, Registered Offices: 80 Strand, London WC2R 0RL, England

Library of Congress Cataloging-in-Publication Data
LeBox, Annette.
Circle of cranes/Annette LeBox.
p. cm.
Summary: Taken from her small, impoverished Chinese village and forced to sew in a New York City sweatshop, thirteen-year-old Suyin is visited by the cranes with which she has a strange connection and learns she is the daughter of the Crane Queen, who needs her help.
ISBN 978-0-8037-3443-2 (hardcover)
[1. Identity—Fiction. 2. Supernatural—Fiction. 3. Cranes (Birds)—Fiction. 4. Human-animal communication—Fiction. 5. Sweatshops—Fiction. 6. Kings, queens, rulers, etc.—Fiction. 7. Chinese—United States—Fiction. 8. New York (N.Y.)—Fiction.] I. Title.
PZ7.L46975Cir 2012 [Fic]—dc23 2011017583

Designed by Jason Henry * Text set in Agfa Wile
Printed in the U.S.A.

1 3 5 7 9 10 8 6 4 2

"For sister, the attic.
For brother, the great hall and study.
We embroider a thousand patterns,
Younger brother reads a thousand books."

—Nu Shu scripture

Contents

Prologue   3

PART ONE: *Cao Hai, Guizhou, China*

1   Home   6
2   A Circle of Cranes   16
3   Snakehead Lao   31
4   The Sisterhood   42
5   Duped!   53
6   Desperate Times   70

PART TWO: *New York City*

7   Gold Mountain   84
8   A Stitch in Time   102
9   Crane Meadow   111
10 Mrs. Tang   126
11 Sister Fang-chou   135
12 A Secret Revealed   148
13 Joy and Misery   159
14 Happy New Year!   173
15 Disturbing Revelations   186
16 Betrayal   202
17 Bird   214
18 The Gray World   241

19	Return to Earth	252
20	A Clarion Call	262
21	Two Birds. One Stone	274
22	Hope	289
23	An Uneasy Alliance	297
24	Missing the Root	305

PART THREE: *Cao Hai, Guizhou, China*

| 25 | Home | 320 |

	Glossary	334
	Author's Note	338
	Acknowledgments	340

CIRCLE
of
CRANES

Prologue

On a high plateau in the mountains, in Guizhou Province, China, there was a far-off village called Cao Hai. The village was known for its poverty and a flock of black-necked cranes that wintered on the nearby lake. Normally the shyest of birds, the cranes approached the villagers as if they were greeting their long-lost relatives. The villagers believed the cranes to be supernatural beings that carried the souls of their ancestors. The birds were particularly gentle with children and were known to bend their long slender necks to allow a child to stroke their feathers. If a villager killed a crane, even if that person was starving, the village would suffer a run of bad luck.

Cao Hai Village was also the home of the Miao minority people. The Miao women defined themselves by the skill of their embroidery. Miao girls learned to stitch at an early age, embroidering their history on their festival dresses. By the time a young girl reached the age of thirteen, she could stitch needlework of unparalleled beauty.

The villagers would gather around a fire and spin tales that lasted long into the night. These stories were as familiar to the villagers as sticky rice, but they never tired of hearing them. Once, a visiting shaman told a story of a man who saw a beautiful woman dancing with a flock of cranes beside a lake. The man fell in love with the woman and begged her to marry him. The woman agreed to become his wife on two conditions—that he promised never to follow her when she went dancing with the cranes and never to open the door to her sewing room as she did her weaving or embroidery. But eventually the man became curious and one day he followed his wife to the lake to spy on her. To his shock and horror, he watched his wife transform into a crane. When the crane wife realized that her husband had witnessed her transformation, she disappeared, never to be seen again. When the tale was finished, the men and women of the village began to argue. The men proclaimed that the man was a fool to have married a woman who'd forced him to make such promises. The women argued that the man was a scoundrel for betraying his wife. The shaman ended the story with these words:

"Never make a promise you can't keep, for the consequences of a broken promise could change the course of history."

Part One

CAO HAI,
GUIZHOU, CHINA

1

Home

Teacher Zhang was in the middle of her English lesson when Zhu Suyin heard the high-pitched rattle.

"It's a crane," cried Suyin. Her classmates stared at her in surprise. To interrupt Teacher Zhang's lesson was foolhardy.

"The cranes have already migrated." Teacher Zhang frowned. Still, she opened the door and listened. A blast of chilly mountain air entered the building. Sixteen students began to shiver as they sat elbow to elbow in the study room of the crumbling Ancestral Hall that served as a makeshift school. Three pails were set on the floor to catch the rain as it dripped from the leaking roof.

"It's only the wind," said Teacher Zhang, looking annoyed.

"No, it's a crane," insisted Suyin. "A young one."

"It's *May,*" said her teacher, pointing to the calendar. "The cranes migrated in March or April."

"Maybe it lost its way or it's injured?"

Her teacher hesitated. To ignore a crane in distress would mean that one had refused to help a dead relative. This would bring the village a run of bad luck. But if a villager helped a crane, the village would be rewarded.

"Did anyone else hear it?" asked the teacher, folding her arms.

"No!" answered a chorus of male voices, stifling laughs.

If only Shan-Shan were here to defend her, but her best friend hadn't come to school that day. She wondered if her friend had fallen ill. She and Shan-Shan were the only girls in a class of sixteen boys. The school fees were too expensive for most families in the village. And if a family managed to scrape enough money together to send a child to school, a son would be chosen, not a daughter. Daughters were expected to work in the fields or care for a younger sibling. But as Shan-Shan was the only child of a successful merchant, a woman who baked the best turnip cakes in the county, her family could afford to send their daughter to school.

When Suyin had asked Auntie Cho-Ye why she, a poor orphan girl, had been given this wonderful gift, her auntie had replied curtly, "Accept your good luck with a humble heart and don't ask questions."

"Don't ask questions" was Auntie's favorite response.

"Suyin's been talking to the birds again," whispered the oldest boy in the class.

She reddened at his taunt. She had always talked to the birds. They told her when they were hungry or cold. They warned her when a storm was brewing. They led her to the best fishing spots on the lake. The fishermen called her Lucky, for whenever she accompanied them, the fish swam into their nets.

If Shan-Shan were here, she would have put that boy in his place with a few well-chosen words. Shan-Shan was fourteen, a year older than Suyin. Suyin admired her friend's daring. She was known for speaking her mind and had even challenged the village council on occasion. But Shan-Shan spoke with such eloquence that even the elders listened.

"We will continue with our lessons, then," said the teacher firmly, "with no more interruptions.

"What is the weather like today?" asked Teacher Zhang in practiced English.

Suyin raised her hand. "Suyin, you have answered the last three questions. Let someone else try, please."

Reluctantly, she lowered her hand. Sometimes she felt sorry for Teacher Zhang. Her teacher struggled over her English lessons. Sometimes she imagined that her teacher was learning from her.

When the crane called again, Suyin stared at the blank faces of her classmates. They were repeating Teacher

Zhang's phrases from lesson three of the English textbook. *"What is your name? Do you speak English? Where are you from?"*

Suyin winced. Teacher Zhang was pronouncing the English words wrong again. Her English sounded like scratches on a chalkboard, but to correct her would cause the young woman to lose face. It would also be an insult to the villagers who had pooled their money to send her to school.

At dismissal time that afternoon, Suyin grabbed her jacket with its embarrassing lack of embroidery and hurried down the muddy road. She knew Auntie would be angry, but she didn't care. As she passed the ancient stone houses, she came upon a group of Miao girls. Each carried an embroidered *hebao* over one shoulder and a baby brother or sister strapped to their back. If only she had a pretty *hebao,* she thought, rushing past the girls.

She remembered a time after her parents had died, when her grandfather had caught her holding a pretty spool of yellow thread. The old man had cuffed her hard, sending the thread across the room.

"Don't touch!"

"Why not?" she'd asked stubbornly.

"Your mother was possessed," spat her grandfather. "Her embroidery was stitched by a malevolent spirit. She forbade her own husband to watch her work! How do you explain that? Everyone knew she used magic in her stitchery. At what cost? My son's life! If he had married his own kind, a noble Han woman, not a cursed minority woman, my son would be alive today."

And so that crazy old man forbade Suyin to touch her mother's needles, her embroidery floss, and her small wooden sewing table. And when her grandfather suffered a stroke less than a year after her father's death, he summoned the village chief to his deathbed. His dying wish was that the women of the village refuse to teach Suyin to stitch.

"If the girl can't sew," declared her grandfather, "she can't lead an innocent man to his death." Her heart ached remembering her grandfather's words.

Suyin's aunties protested her grandfather's edict. "A Miao girl is judged by her skill in needlework." But in a moment of weakness the village chief made a promise to ensure the old man's wishes were carried out. If the women disobeyed him, it would have been insulting to the chief. Her grandfather's revenge was complete when he willed his stone house and a half a *li* of land to a neighbor boy who drank with him. He would have given his property to a passing beggar or a mouse rather than to a granddaughter who carried the bloodline of the Miao minority woman he despised.

When she was a little older, the village gossip told her that her mother had mysteriously disappeared and her father had died on Wushan Mountains searching for her. The villagers found him frozen in the snow, his head resting on a pillow of frost. She had pleaded with her three aunties to tell her about that fateful day, but they refused to discuss it.

She glanced at the sun, slowly slipping behind the Wushan Mountains. She had two hours before nightfall.

A long wheezing rattle cut through the air. The sound came from the fen, a favorite roosting spot for the cranes. Auntie Cho-Ye had forbidden her to go to the fen because three local fishermen had drowned there. But she pushed her auntie's warnings aside and followed the crane's cries.

She raced past Old Auntie Dou, the oldest person in the village. No one knew her exact age, not even Auntie Dou herself. Yet the old woman seldom seemed tired, working day and night dyeing batik cloth and embroidering finery fit for an empress.

As Suyin passed Fisherman Pei-Pei's house, his four-year-old daughter and her two friends were sitting on the steps embroidering dolls' clothes. Suyin flushed with shame. She was probably the only minority girl in China who couldn't embroider, who'd never held a needle and thread, who'd never sat in a ladies' sewing circle—and all because her nasty grandfather had forbidden it.

In Cao Hai Village, everyone knew that a girl's embroidery skills were more important than her looks, for it was through her needlework that a person could glimpse a girl's true nature. Even if a boy showed interest in marrying Suyin, she knew that his parents would reject a prospective daughter-in-law who couldn't sew. They would think such a girl soft in the head.

Rounding the bend in the dirt road, Suyin recognized Shan-Shan's mother, Auntie Huishan. Shan-Shan wasn't with her. Suyin hoped her friend wasn't sick. Auntie Huishan was carrying a bag of rice flour on her back. Auntie was as round and sweet as the turnip cakes she baked; she couldn't bear waste. If a cake didn't sell in Weining Town, Auntie Huishan felt obliged to eat it herself.

Suyin had lived with Auntie Huishan and Shan-Shan for two years before Old Auntie Dou, and then Auntie Cho-Ye, had offered to take her in. But it hurt that since the time her parents had died when she was three, she had lived with three different aunties. Whenever she grew attached to one family, another stepped in to care for her. Although each of her aunties had been wise and kind and they'd told everyone she'd brought them good luck (she'd cured Old Auntie Dou's aching joints, doubled Auntie Huishan's profits in the bakery, and brought a smile to Auntie Cho-Ye's face for the first time in years), not one of them had loved her enough to adopt her. She felt like a stray dog that people took in out of pity.

But today, as she raced toward the fen, she felt hopeful. If she saved a crane, the spirits of her ancestors might grant the village good fortune. Her aunties could buy more rice and corn, some books for her and Shan-Shan, and perhaps some silver jewelry to wear on festival days.

As she followed a narrow winding path, a bright yellow butterfly landed on her arm. She stopped, amazed.

"Hello, Butterfly Mother," she whispered. Butterfly

was the ancestor of everything on earth, the Miao people, flowers and trees and birds. Surely seeing her ancestor was a good sign.

The path led past stands of willow and thornbushes, punctuated with grasses, sedges, and wild onion. Slowly the ground gave way to tiny islands surrounded by murky water. When she reached the heart of the fen, the crane's cries grew more insistent. She had been right all along, she thought. She *had* heard the crane's cries, even if no one else had. And then she saw the small dark shape sitting in a thornbush. She knew at once that the bird was young because its yellowish gray and pale brownish feathers had yet to turn black. The crane was shaking with fright, but when it saw her, it gave a loud, joyful trumpet.

She leaped to the island, but the ground gave way and she sank to her knees in the icy muck. Suyin struggled to pull her feet free, only to sink to her waist. Fisherman Pei-Pei's warnings came back to her. "If you ever fall in a sinkhole, don't struggle. Lie on your back and float."

To her relief, the mud held her up, though the cold water felt like a thousand needles pricking her skin.

The crane peered at her with large doleful eyes. Paddling with her hands, Suyin inched her way toward the young crane, speaking softly to calm it. She reached into the thornsbush and freed the bird's wing, but her sudden movement sent her sinking deeper. She spat out a mouthful of sludge.

The crane gave a loud squawk, flapped its wings, and

hopped onto high ground. The sun was slowly sinking behind the mountains.

"Fly away," said Suyin, but the crane fixed its gaze on her, cocking its head from side to side.

She could feel the quicksand ringing her neck like a noose. She stiffened, too terrified to move. As the darkness settled in, the temperature dropped, and her teeth began to chatter uncontrollably.

Suyin's mind raced with thoughts of death. Her grandfather's stroke, so soon after her father's death, her grandfather's dying wish, like a curse, wrenching the promise from the village chief that the women not teach Suyin embroidery. If she died like her father, cold and alone, she imagined her grandfather would be laughing from his grave. He would consider her death a just revenge. Since the old man blamed Suyin's mother, An-Lan, for his son's death, then her offspring deserved a similar fate.

The cold mud pressed against her chest. I'm going to die here, she thought, and no one will know where I am. I will disappear off the face of the earth like my mother.

And there it was again, the sadness that accompanied thoughts of her mother. Even when her mother was alive, she would leave the village every year to visit her relatives in the high country. Every spring, her mother would say good-bye to her husband and daughter and she wouldn't return until the first snowfall. Suyin never understood how a mother could leave her family for so long.

A freezing rain began to fall. Suyin shivered in waves,

each one stronger than the last. The little crane kept its vigil, its eyes two beacons of hope.

As time passed, her muscles stiffened. She lay on her back, floating, her arms outstretched. She imagined herself sprouting wings and flying across the marsh as she closed her eyes and gave in to the cold.

2
A Circle of Cranes

Suyin woke to the sound of reeds rustling. Night had fallen. She was still floating in the mud, though she'd lost all feeling in her body. Above her, a full moon shone on the surface of the lake. The ripples on the water were bathed in liquid gold. Four dark shapes moved out of the shadows, three black-necked cranes and a smaller exotic-looking bird.

"We're going to get you out of the muck, little one," said the tallest of the black-necked cranes. "Hang on to my neck."

As she clung to the black-necked crane, her companions clamped their beaks on to her jacket and tugged. The mud made a loud *thwack* as it released her. The birds dragged her to a reedy island, where she lay shivering.

"Thank you," said Suyin.

The tallest black-neck bowed to Suyin.

"I am Li-Wen," she said. "And that's Grandmother Crane."

Suyin bowed her head in respect, for Grandmother Crane looked ancient. Her pearl-gray feathers were tattered and her eyes were rheumy. Yet despite her bedraggled appearance, the old crane carried an air of authority.

The third black-necked crane was plump with an ungainly walk. "That's Hazrat the Wise," said Li-Wen. We often look to her for advice. And that's Mulaba."

Mulaba had a pale gray neck, a red throat wattle, and colorful plumage of black, white, and gold. But her crowning glory was a gorgeous head plume of stiff spun gold feathers.

"What kind of bird are you?" asked Suyin shyly.

"I'm a gray crowned crane," replied Mulaba imperiously. "From Africa."

"That's a long way from here," said Suyin, surprised.

"Thank you for rescuing Little Sister," broke in Grandmother. "A selfless act deserves a reward."

Li-Wen nodded. "We're flying to He Shan. Crane Mountain. Please join us."

The world above the earth. Auntie Cho-Ye had often told Suyin stories about He Shan, but Suyin never knew what was made up and what was real.

"Is Little Sister going too?"

"Not this trip," said Li-Wen firmly.

"You'll have to climb on Li-Wen's back," said Little Sister.

Suyin felt her courage falter. *Were the four cranes taking her to heaven?*

"Will you bring me back home?" Suyin asked.

"Of course," Li-Wen assured her.

Wrapping her arms around the crane's neck, Suyin felt the crane's wing bones move beneath her, then a rush of cool air. She laughed as the crane ascended. Li-Wen uttered a series of loud bugles and the other three birds joined in.

Li-Wen took the lead.

Suyin could see the lake and the roofs of the stone houses of the village below. Along the eastern shore of the lake, she saw a long line of bobbing lanterns. Her people were searching for her.

"I'm up here!" she called down to them. But the wind off the lake stole her voice.

As the four cranes soared higher, the flickering of the lanterns grew smaller, until finally, they disappeared. Soon the flock was flying over the mountain. The clouds smelled of seawater and sulfur, the cranes of damp feathers and roses.

The air grew cold and thin. She began to shiver.

Suyin burrowed beneath the crane's primary feathers and found the downies. In a few moments, she felt dry and cozy. With only her head exposed, she found the winds rushing past her refreshing. And she loved her panoramic view of the stars.

The flock flew across wide plateaus and rocky steppes.

They passed small lakes and villages tucked into mountain valleys. Along the way, more cranes joined them. Some had strange-looking wattles and pale blue feathers. Others were small and delicate with pretty white plumes on their crowns. Soon there were hundreds of cranes flying in a wide V.

As time passed, the flock grew to thousands. It was a migration of such magnitude, the cranes blotted out the sun. Then suddenly she saw a bright blue stretch of water below her. The air smelled salty.

"We've reached the sea," said Li-Wen excitedly.

As the flock flew across the great expanse of water, the cranes grew quiet. Li-Wen's wings whirred beneath her like the gentle strains of a lullaby.

Below Suyin lay a wild and lovely marsh. The landscape thrummed with color. The greens sang. The blues danced. The yellows shimmered. Beyond the marsh lay a meadow. In the distance rose mountains covered with dense evergreen forests. Everywhere she looked, she saw abundance. The air was thick with birds and butterflies, the fields alive with animals, the rivers with fish.

Suddenly Grandmother Crane took the lead. In a burst of energy, the old crane announced her descent with an ear-splitting bugle. The flock folded their calls into hers. When the old crane's knobby legs touched the ground, a cry of joy burst from her bill. "He Shan!"

"He Shan," echoed the flock.

Suyin climbed off Li-Wen's back. The crane shook her feather bustle. Suyin looked around uncertainly. Hazrat the Wise had wandered off.

"Where's she going?" Suyin asked.

Li-Wen chortled. "To the wild turnip patch. She heads there to feed after a long journey."

Suddenly Suyin heard a series of low booming honks. It was Mulaba. The crane had inflated her wattle like a balloon. She was forcing the air out in sudden bursts.

Mulaba sounded more like a goose than a crane, thought Suyin.

As the rest of the flock landed, the cranes greeted Suyin with a bow.

"What kind of cranes are those small ones?" Suyin whispered.

"The demoiselles," answered Li-Wen. "We call them the lovely birds. The tall cranes are the sarus. And that's a brolga from Australia. Brolgas love to dance."

Suyin couldn't take her eyes off the birds. Li-Wen told her there were fifteen different species in the world family, and she promised to introduce her to them all.

The whooping cranes were pure white, except for their black wingtips and their crimson crowns. Their javelin beaks made them look fierce and proud.

"Come and dance, Suyin," called the whoopers as they kicked up their legs and did pirouettes. It was hard not to laugh at their antics. They whooped and snorted like pigs.

They purred like cats and growled like dogs. Soon the brolgas joined them in the dance.

At first Suyin was shy, but soon she was flapping her arms and leaping into the air until she almost forgot she was a girl, not a bird.

Later that day, a flock of sandhill cranes led her to a mud flat. She watched the cranes use their beaks to paint their feathercoats with marsh mud. Soon their pale gray feathers were a rusty brown.

"Camouflage," explained Li-Wen.

"Try it," urged a sandhill.

Suyin laughed. Why not? She was already covered in muck from the fen. Scooping up a handful of red mud, she smoothed it over her skin. Using her fingers, she painted circles on her hands, wavy lines on her arms, and jagged lines on her legs.

"Now you are one of us," said the sandhills.

Suyin felt her eyes well up. Everywhere she looked, she saw beauty, in the cranes' dances, in the grace of their flight and the warmth of their friendship.

The moon rose. The snowy peak of He Shan glistened in the moonlight.

Li-Wen uttered an ear-splitting bugle. The cranes responded with low rattling calls that rose from deep within their tracheas. The calls sounded like a drum roll. And then suddenly the flock grew quiet.

Suyin looked up to see thousands of cranes staring

expectantly at her. She gave Li-Wen a puzzled look.

"She has no idea what's going on," sputtered Mulaba, shaking her golden head-fan. "How could she? She's never sat in a ladies' sewing circle. She's never even sewn on a button."

Suyin flushed with embarrassment.

"This is the feather ceremony, Suyin," explained Hazrat. "A girl must choose a feather before she is initiated into the Crane Women Clan. It's an honor."

Suyin's eyes lit up with anticipation.

"Long ago," began Li-Wen, "there was a magical era before living memory when a girl could become a wolf, a deer, or a bird, and every being could move between worlds. We call it the Dreamtime, but there are many different names for it. As time went on, men spent their time building cities and waging war. Gradually they lost their connection to nature and with it, their transformative power—though women retained it. Eventually, women also lost this gift. Now only *a few* women can become cranes—those who are the direct descendents of crane women. For a girl to become an initiate in our sisterhood, she must have inherited the gift from a relative, she must have reached the age of thirteen, and she must have demonstrated courage and selflessness." Li-Wen met Suyin's eyes. "You rescued Little Sister at the risk of your own life. That is why you are here today."

Suyin opened her mouth to speak, but she felt too shy.

If a crane sister's power was inherited, had her mother belonged to the clan?

"Under normal circumstances," continued Li-Wen, "a girl must be proficient in needlework, since an initiate can't transform until she is able to communicate through the most ancient of the female arts, the grand tradition of embroidery."

Suyin was confused. How could a girl who couldn't stitch become an initiate?

As if reading her thoughts, Li-Wen said, "You are an exception to the rule because your apprenticeship in the needle arts was delayed through no fault of your own. But it is never too late to learn."

"Don't you understand?" blurted Suyin. "I've been *forbidden* to stitch."

"In your village perhaps," said Grandmother Crane. "Not on He Shan."

Were the cranes offering to teach her to sew, she wondered.

"The feather ceremony is the first step on a girl's path to her transformation," said Li-Wen.

Suyin blinked. "Transformation?"

"To a crane," said Li-Wen.

"You mean . . . I could become a crane?"

"After your initiation . . . in theory," replied Li-Wen. "But heed my warning. You must not transform until you prove yourself worthy of a place in the clan. If you do, you may not have enough transformative power to return to your human form. Much of our power comes from the collective energy of the sisterhood."

Suyin swallowed hard. "You mean I could be stuck as a bird?"

Li-Wen nodded. "Yes . . . and your absence from the human world would affect others. And another warning— you must also take great care that no human outside the clan witnesses your transformation. Our safety depends on secrecy. If this should occur, you may never return to your human form."

"Never?"

"Never," answered Li-Wen firmly. "The Law of the Clan is immutable."

Suyin shuddered. It was hard to imagine never returning to her human body. She would miss Shan-Shan and her aunties. She would miss Auntie Huishan's turnip cakes and fishing with Uncle Pei-Pei and writing Nu Shu poems.

"But how will I know if I've proven myself worthy?"

"A feather will sprout on your wrist," said Grandmother. "A natal feather."

"The initiation," prodded Mulaba, anxious to begin.

"Wait," said Suyin. "I need to know. Was my mother a crane sister? Or Shan-Shan? Or the cranes I danced with by the lake?"

"Initiates aren't privy to all of the clan secrets," said Mulaba sternly.

"But some secrets can be shared," countered Hazrat.

"The cranes you danced with by the lake, Suyin, are called grus. Grus are cranes with no ability to transform. They are beloved to us, but they are not clanswomen."

"Oh," said Suyin, disappointed at the crumb Hazrat had thrown her.

Li-Wen stepped forward and opened her wings with a flourish.

"Pluck a feather from my feathercoat," said Li-Wen. "The feather you choose will inform the path you must follow to earn your wings."

The crane made a slow turn, lowering her head and fanning her tail.

Suyin felt her hands begin to shake. "I can't decide."

"Take your time," said Li-Wen. "Your choice will decide your future . . ."

"And ours," said Hazrat under her breath.

Suyin shot Hazrat a questioning look, but the crane refused to meet her eyes. Perhaps she was unaware of what had slipped from her tongue like a drop of oil on water, a tiny glistening globule of truth.

Suyin was suddenly struck by the weight and solemnity of the ceremony. The cranes watched her, motionless, wary. It seemed as if the entire flock was holding its collective breath.

She gazed at the sea of feathers: the short stiff feathers of the under-wing lining, the long elegant feathers of the primaries, the tiny down feathers blanketing the crane's breast. Each was exquisite in its own way. She closed her eyes, touched the crane's breast feathers, felt the steady thumping of the crane's heartbeat, cushioned in down. And then a small white feather, soft as silk, curled around her finger.

This is my feather, she thought. She tugged gently, then harder.

At the feather's release, Li-Wen let out a cry and crumpled to the ground. The others stood over the fallen crane, fanning her with their wings.

"I'm so sorry," said Suyin. She held a tiny white feather between her fingers. It was so small and delicate, she feared it might blow away.

"Do not be sorry," said Li-Wen. "You chose the heart feather. It was a courageous choice and worth the pain."

The flock gazed at Suyin awe-struck, their beaks open, their eyes wide. She could tell by the excitement in the birds' eyes that *something* had occurred.

"What does my feather mean?" she asked, frightened.

"It depends on the girl and circumstance," said Li-Wen cautiously. "A girl who chooses the heart feather must forge her own path."

That told her nothing.

"Maybe one of you could take a guess?" pleaded Suyin. "Grandmother?"

The old crane cocked her head to one side. "Perhaps it means opening your heart."

"But how?"

"There are as many ways as the feathers on a duck's rump," said Grandmother.

Suyin smiled sadly. "I wish I'd chosen an easier feather."

"The path to worthiness is never easy," said Hazrat. "You must be prepared to sacrifice your own desires for the good of the clan."

Suyin peered at her feather. "What do I have to do to transform, Hazrat?"

"Besides proving yourself?"

"Yes."

"Close your eyes, tug on your heart feather, and concentrate hard."

"That's it?" asked Suyin.

"No, but that's all you need to know for now," said Hazrat secretively.

Suyin felt her anxiety growing, but before she could say another word, Grandmother had pulled out a needle and cord from under her wing. Then the old crane stitched the heart feather to the cord and tied the ends around Suyin's neck.

As soon as the feather lay against her skin, Suyin felt a sweetness enter her body, as if all this time she had lost part of herself and suddenly found it. Looking around her, she felt surrounded by mothers, by the mother she longed for, by the mother she couldn't remember. It was as if her mother had returned to her in the guise of the feather.

When Suyin looked up, she saw hope and expectation in the cranes' eyes. The birds gazed at her in silence.

"Where are your feathers, sisters?" Suyin asked the flock.

The cranes poked their beaks into the ruffs of their neck feathers and pulled out their feather necklaces. Suyin was fascinated. The cranes' feathers were of different sizes, shapes, and colors. Some were black or gray. Others were shades of white or gold, though none looked quite like hers.

"What's your feather, Li-Wen?" Suyin asked, hoping to discover a clue to the meaning of her own.

"Mine's a tail feather," replied Li-Wen, holding up a large, elegant black feather. "A tail feather is used as a rudder. I used to be a follower. I learned to steer my own course."

"I too chose a tail feather," said Hazrat. "For a different reason. A tail feather is used to brake as well as steer. I was once impetuous, but I learned to think before I acted. That is how I earned my name and my wings."

"Hazrat the Wise," said Suyin.

"Do you recognize my feather, Suyin?" asked Grandmother. Grandmother's feather looked so old and tattered that Suyin feared it might disintegrate.

"It's a wing feather," said Suyin proudly.

"Yes," said Grandmother. "A wing feather gives a bird lift. For much of my life, I carried the weight of the world on my shoulders. Only when I learned to find joy in the moment did I earn my wings."

"What does it feel like to transform?" Suyin asked.

"It's a joy and a burden," said Hazrat. "Yin and yang. To glide effortlessly through the air, to feel the sunlight on your feathers, to feel completely at one with all things green and growing is enthralling. But you will always be torn between earth and sky. Yin and yang." The cranes nodded in agreement.

Auntie Huishan often talked about yin and yang, thought Suyin. They were opposites that were interconnected. *Dark and light. Warm and cold.*

"Transformation depends on harmony," said Grandmother Crane, "though the sisterhood's been lacking that since we lost our queen."

"Your queen?" asked Suyin.

"There will be time to discuss that later, Grandmother," said Mulaba gently.

"Now, what I was talking about?" said the old crane, flustered.

"You were telling Suyin about harmony," said Mulaba, jogging the crane's memory.

"Harmony is essential when you transform," said Grandmother Crane. "If your mind is on one path and your heart's on another, you could end up being neither human nor bird, but something in between."

A picture of a girl with wings came to Suyin's mind, a fairy creature or an angel, but she could tell by the look of horror in the cranes' eyes that what Grandmother was referring to was something monstrous.

"Transformation is a state of grace," added Li-Wen. "But it's not for the faint of heart."

"Or the foolish," added Mulaba.

As Suyin reached for her heart feather, a sudden calm swept over her. If her feather could speak, it would have said, "Take heart. This is a new beginning."

Standing among her feathered friends, she felt part of something bigger than herself—a sisterhood that stretched back thousands of years.

Then it was time to leave.

As Li-Wen took flight, Suyin turned her thoughts to her people. They would be worried about her. They might think that she had disappeared as mysteriously as her mother—that she had used up her store of good luck as Auntie Cho-Ye had used up her store of pickling spices before winter.

3

Snakehead Lao

The blast of a cow horn pulled Suyin from her dream. Two stretcher-bearers lowered her to the ground near the entrance of the village. The villagers swarmed around her like bees.

She heard Uncle Pei-Pei's shout above the murmurings of the crowd.

"Suyin's alive! We found her in the fen."

Old Auntie Dou, Auntie Huishan, and her daughter, Shan-Shan, came running toward her. They were red-faced and breathing hard.

Shan-Shan reached Suyin first.

"Dear friend," she whispered, throwing her arms around her. Suddenly Shan-Shan pulled away from her, laughing. "You're covered in mud!"

Suyin looked down at herself and smiled, remembering what fun she'd had.

"Our little daughter," cried her aunties as they knelt to hug her.

"Where have you ladies been?" asked the chief sternly.

"At home," said Auntie Huishan. "Waiting for word that our daughter had been found."

Suyin felt a sharp stab of hurt. If Shan-Shan had disappeared, nothing would have kept Auntie Huishan from joining the search. And Auntie Cho-Ye was nowhere in sight.

"You'll come fishing with me soon, Suyin?" asked Fisherman Pei-Pei. "My nets have been empty since you disappeared."

Suyin tried to smile. "Yes, Uncle Pei-Pei."

"What happened!" urged Uncle Pei-Pei. "You've been gone two days. We had almost given up hope that you were alive."

It was hard to concentrate. She was still reeling from the excitement of the feather ceremony. She reached for the heart feather circling her neck. No, she hadn't dreamed it. The feather was proof.

When she'd finished telling her adventures, Uncle Pei-Pei laughed uproariously.

"She flew on the back of a crane!" said Uncle, slapping his knee.

"The poor girl's in shock," said Teacher Zhang.

"She needs rest," said the village chief.

"And something to eat," added Auntie Huishan, pulling a turnip cake from her pocket.

"Make way for the shaman!" said Butcher Yong.

Auntie Cho-Ye looked like a brightly colored bird. She wore her festival dress every day of the year. The sleeves of her dark blue blouse were intricately embroidered in red, yellow, and green linen. Her headdress was bright red and pink, and her skirt of a thousand pleats was creamy white. Draped loosely around her neck were five large silver neck rings. Hanging from her neck rings were silver coins and beads of amber and turquoise. Around her left wrist, her bracelets tinkled like tiny bells. The shaman lived by magic and secret spells. The villagers respected and feared her, for on many occasions she had foretold the village's misfortunes: a flood that took dozens of lives, three drownings, and many downturns in business. But she had also predicted joyful events like weddings or unexpected good fortune.

Cho-Ye took a pinch of dried herbs from her medicine pouch and placed them under Suyin's nose. Suyin recognized the familiar fragrance of thorn-apples, the trumpet-shaped flowers that grew in abundance outside Cho-Ye's window. The plant was poisonous, but a shaman's gifts could harness its healing properties.

"Ah!" said Suyin, feeling the calming effect of the herb. Everyone began talking at once.

"Hush," said Cho-Ye. "How can I see into the child's future with so much chatter?"

Chastened, the villagers waited in silence.

"I see you've painted yourself with mud," said Cho-Ye.

"Yes, Auntie."

"Mud painting was an early practice of your ancestors," said Cho-Ye. "The circular marks on your hands are auspicious signs. You will go on a long journey, but you will never forget your roots. The wavy lines mean that you will cross water; the jagged lines mean that you will face danger. You must be cautious in all you do."

Suyin shivered at her auntie's words.

"The cranes took me to He Shan, Auntie. They gave me this feather."

Auntie's eyes narrowed but she made no reply. The villagers exchanged nervous glances.

"Suyin's always had an overactive imagination," chuckled Butcher Yong. "She talks to the birds and the fish."

"I'm not imagining it," said Suyin.

Shan-Shan took Suyin's hand. "I believe you," she said quietly.

Cho-Ye scowled at Butcher Yong. "Do not doubt the child's word. In the Book of the Ancients there are many references to He Shan. The daughter of our village has been blessed and cursed by fate. We should show the spirits gratitude for her return."

Butcher Yong shrank under the shaman's gaze.

"We should celebrate our good fortune!" croaked Old Auntie Dou, fluttering her wrinkled hands.

"I will bake a fresh batch of turnip cakes," said Auntie Huishan. In her bright green eyes was a mysterious glint.

"And I will slaughter my finest pig," announced Butcher Yong. "We will have a feast tomorrow."

The villagers cheered. A feast after a winter of hunger! Suyin's mouth watered at the thought. A roast of pork was reserved for weddings and funerals. Butcher Yong's family would have to go hungry for many weeks afterward. She couldn't believe such sacrifices! She was so happy to be home.

As the villagers walked back to the village, their songs rang out over the water, where their voices flushed a flock of ruddy shelducks into the farthest reaches of the fen.

After Suyin bathed and changed into clean clothes, she made her way to the Ancestral Hall. The hall was a hive of activity. Preparations had already begun for the feast the following day. A tall thin man with a wide forehead, tiny jagged teeth, and oily skin leaned against the door of the hall. His eyes darted nervously from person to person as if he were sizing everyone up for a meal.

"What happy occasion are you celebrating?" asked the stranger.

"A lost daughter has been found," said Butcher Yong. "I am on my way to roast a fine pig. Tomorrow we will hold a banquet. You are welcome to be our guest."

"I would be honored," said the stranger, extending his hand in greeting. "I am Lao from Fuzhou."

"What brings you to our village?" asked Chief Wu.

"I'm looking for Cho-Ye, the shaman," said the stranger. "I've come to seek her advice."

"I am the person you seek," said Cho-Ye. "Wait here, Suyin, until the two of us return."

When Auntie Cho-Ye and the man reappeared a short while later, the man was wearing a smile, though Auntie looked upset. Why had the stranger come to see Auntie, Suyin wondered.

"What business are you in, Mr. Lao?" asked Chief Wu.

"The travel business," said Lao. "I take people to Gold Mountain—America."

"How I would like to go there!" said Butcher Yong.

"Me too," added Uncle Pei-Pei.

Lao's eyes brightened. "That could easily be arranged, for a price."

"How much?" Butcher Yong asked.

Lao took an abacus from his coat pocket. He moved the beads rapidly back and forth as he calculated. "Train transportation to the coast, cost of the passage on a ship, plus meals and a recruitment fee for myself as a snake-head."

"You catch snakes?" asked Uncle Pei-Pei.

"No, you fool," he muttered. "I'm a travel agent, Snake-head Lao."

Auntie Cho-Ye raised an eyebrow. "No one in our village has travel documents."

Lao sniggered. "I make arrangements for people *without documents*."

"That's illegal," said Uncle Pei-Pei.

"And risky," added Old Auntie Dou.

Lao rolled his eyes. "If you want to become rich, you have to take risks. In China, people are like snakes confined to cages, poor and powerless. But once they are set free in the Beautiful Country, the snakes become rich and powerful dragons!"

"How much does it cost to become a dragon?" asked the village chief.

Lao sucked his teeth. "Fifty thousand American dollars."

A gasp rang out through the crowd.

The chief's jaw dropped. "We are poor farmers and fishermen." He pointed to a rusty pail filled with rainwater. "The roof of our Ancestral Hall leaks, but we have no money to fix it. Even if we worked for an entire lifetime, we could not earn that much money."

"Hear me out," said Lao. "If everyone put a few yuan in a pot, you could raise enough for a down payment on a single passage. My boss, Sister Fang-chou, will guarantee a migrant's loan until the debt is paid off."

"What's a migrant?" interjected Uncle Pei-Pei.

Snakehead Lao sighed with exasperation. "A person who moves from one country to another, usually without documents. A person in need of a trusty people smuggler."

"How would that benefit our village?" asked Butcher Yong.

"Your village would become prosperous," said Lao. "The overseas relative would work for Sister Fang-chou. They would give a portion of their earnings to her and a portion back to the village council. American dollars go a long way in China."

Chief Wu's eyes filled with interest. "We need electricity in the village, drainage tiles for the fields, and a new roof for the Ancestral Hall."

Cho-Ye fixed her stare on Chief Wu.

"We need a proper school," she said firmly. "Not just for sons, but for daughters too."

"You could build ten schools with overseas money," said Lao.

Auntie Huishan looked worried. "Is the ship safe?"

"Of course," said Lao. "It's a cruise ship! It offers first-class accommodations, twelve-course banquets, an orchestra, dancing, movies, swimming pool, the works!"

"How do we know you're telling us the truth?" asked Auntie Cho-Ye.

"You have my word," said Lao, placing his hand on his heart.

Auntie Cho-Ye's brow darkened.

"This sounds like a wonderful opportunity," said Farmer

Chan. "But choosing *one* person would be impossible. Everyone would want to go."

I wouldn't, thought Suyin, though it would be nice to visit the beautiful parks and tall buildings she'd seen in the photographs in her English textbook.

"Pshaw," said Lao. "Set the qualifications, then choose accordingly."

"What qualifications would you suggest, Mr. Lao?" asked Chief Wu.

"Someone young, healthy, brave, hardworking, and lucky. If they speak English, all the better."

Suyin pondered Lao's words. His criteria would eliminate the old, the sick, and the fearful. After considering all the people of the village, she could think of only one suitable candidate: Teacher Zhang. Still, it was hard to imagine the village council placing their fate in the hands of a woman.

Lao picked up his bag and slung it over his shoulder. "If you need time to raise funds, I'd be willing to stay a little longer than I'd planned."

"Thank you, Snakehead Lao," said Chief Wu.

"Is it true that the streets of Gold Mountain are paved with gold?" asked Uncle Pei-Pei.

"The streets, the buildings, the statues," snapped Lao. "Everyone's rich in Gold Mountain, except lazy people, and they deserve to be poor."

"If I were younger," said Butcher Yong, "I would go in a moment."

Yong's wife frowned.

A little boy carrying his baby sister on his back tugged on Lao's jacket. "I'd like to go to Gold Mountain, sir."

"You will have to wait a few years," said Butcher Yong, patting the boy on the head.

"I will go," said Teacher Zhang, stepping forward.

"No," said Chief Wu sternly. "You are needed to teach the children."

"While you decide, could I interest anyone in a game of mahjong?" asked Lao slyly. "Or perhaps a small wager or two?"

"We are too poor to waste money on gambling, Mr. Lao," said the chief. "Now, if you will excuse us, my people have much to discuss."

Lao shot the chief a sour look. "As you wish."

When Lao was out of earshot, Auntie Huishan pursed her lips. "How can we trust a smuggler?"

"Smugglers are smart businessmen," said Butcher Yong. "They're good for China's economy."

"But if the person we send gets sick or dies," said Teacher Zhang, "the village will be mired in debt."

"How would we recover?" asked Uncle Pei-Pei.

"If we want to get ahead, we have to take a chance," said Chief Wu.

"I could never leave my family," said Shan-Shan.

Suyin breathed a sigh of relief. She wouldn't want Shan-Shan to be sent away.

"Suyin, you're exhausted," said Auntie Cho-Ye. "Yong's

roast pig won't be ready until tomorrow." Cho-Ye gently took her arm. "Go home and rest. All the children are leaving. We grown-ups have business to discuss."

"I'll see you tomorrow," said Shan-Shan, hugging her. She and Shan-Shan had been best friends all their lives. Even when Suyin had been shuffled from one household to another, Shan-Shan had been her playmate. She was loyal and true, a perfect friend and ally.

4
The Sisterhood

W hen Suyin woke the next morning, she read the note Cho-Ye had left on the table. The village council had spent most of the night in meetings and more were scheduled that day. She was to remain at home until Auntie returned for her.

She opened her Nu Shu notebook and began to write the graceful characters of the women's script.

Since my initiation the world seems a place of mystery and enchantment. I feel as if I've suddenly been reborn.

As she paused in her writing, her mind spooled back to that special day two years ago when her aunties had told her and Shan-Shan about Nu Shu.

"In the distant past," Cho-Ye had explained, "women in China were forbidden to read and write. So a small group of women invented their own women's script. They called it Nu Shu. It was a closely guarded secret. With Nu Shu, women could communicate with one another without fearing reprisal. They could write missives in poetry and song and express their anger toward the men who oppressed them."

"They could call their husbands donkeys' asses or pea brains," cackled Old Auntie Dou.

Suyin's apprenticeship in Nu Shu script had begun that day when she and Shan-Shan and the aunties had sworn lifelong friendship, love, and loyalty to one another. That was the day they became sworn sisters.

Like all languages, written or spoken, Nu Shu had come easily to her. It was an accomplishment she could take pride in, a substitute for the needle arts.

"Sisterhood is eternal," the aunties had told her. And when she and her sworn sisters shared what lay deepest in their hearts in Nu Shu, Suyin felt as if she truly belonged.

She spent the day trying to keep busy. She scrubbed Cho-Ye's pots and pans and cleaned the coal stove. These were small things, but she hoped that every task might add up in the ledger of her worth.

When Cho-Ye returned that evening, her auntie seemed even more upset than the day before.

"It's time to go," said Auntie Cho-Ye. "We must hurry."

"Did the village choose someone?" asked Suyin.

Cho-Ye's face darkened. "The men are convinced an

overseas relative will bring prosperity to the village. Their opinions carry more weight than the women's. It has always been so."

She followed her auntie in silence through the streets of the village.

Entering the hall, Suyin saw her father's portrait sitting on the altar alongside others who had passed away, yet her mother's portrait was absent. This was a slight that never failed to upset her.

The hall was crowded. Everyone was there, from the smallest child to the village elders. Suddenly she felt the villagers' eyes on her.

Chief Wu welcomed her with a smile.

"After much deliberation," he said, "we have chosen you, Zhu Suyin, granddaughter of Grandfather Chen, daughter of Zhu An-Lan and Chen Yan, to become the benefactress of Cao Hai."

She stared at him in disbelief.

"Our decision was unanimous," continued Chief Wu. "You are young and in good health, and you are a hard worker. And we all know of your gift with languages."

Uncle Pei-Pei jumped in. "Remember that Korean merchant, Suyin? He said you spoke his language like a fellow countryman, and you've never left the village."

"You could speak to that foreigner from Germany too," said Butcher Yong. "You helped him choose a pork roast, remember?"

"But—" Suyin began.

"You must let us finish," said Chief Wu in a gentle voice. "You showed bravery when you risked your life to rescue the crane chick. And everyone agreed that you have been blessed with luck."

Suyin's heart sank. Would a girl blessed with luck be sent away? She didn't want to leave her village—it was the only home she'd ever known. Especially not now! She had just been initiated. Would the cranes know where to find her in a foreign land?

"I am honored," she said, trying to remain calm, "but I am an unsuitable candidate. Ask my aunties. I am impatient and disobedient. I ignore their warnings by sneaking off to the fen. I've caused the whole village to worry and I often daydream in school. Ask Teacher Zhang."

"It is true that you daydream and your impatience leads you to act without thinking," replied Teacher Zhang, "but you learn quickly and you speak English as if you were born to it."

She turned to Cho-Ye in desperation.

"Auntie Cho-Ye needs my help with the rice harvest."

Cho-Ye smiled gently. "I don't need your help, Suyin, though I will miss you terribly. We all will."

Even Cho-Ye had not tried to keep her. She was dispensable, not a blood daughter.

"I don't want to go," she said. "I'm too young."

Chief Wu frowned. "We will not force you to go, child. Your aunties will explain things, then you can decide."

The neighbor boy who had claimed Grandfather's

house gave her a sheepish look. He would be glad when she was gone. He would no longer have to face her.

As her aunties led her through the crowd, she knew the sisterly talk was just a formality. The die was cast.

When her aunties reached the lake, Shan-Shan came running toward them. Seeing her best friend, she felt a pang of jealousy. Auntie Huishan would never send her own daughter to a foreign land. But when Shan-Shan threw her arms around her, her resentment dissolved into sadness and she began to cry. As her aunties comforted her, she felt the finality of their parting. They were the only family she'd ever known.

"I don't want you to go," whispered Shan-Shan. She wondered if her sworn sisters would keep their vow of eternal friendship. Or would their promises fade like the green of summer?

The moon shone over the lake, leaving a bright coin of gold on its surface. The call of a night bird echoed in the stillness. She gazed at the snow-capped mountains and the swaying reeds and the stars reflected on the lake. She drank in the scene, knowing she might never see it again.

"The lake was your mother's favorite place," said Old Auntie Dou. "In the winter months, she would dance with the cranes. Just like you! She would spend hours talking to them. She too had the gift of languages."

Suyin looked at Old Auntie Dou in surprise. She hadn't known that until now. Her aunties seldom talked about her mother, even though Suyin had plagued them with questions over the years. The thought of her leaving must have loosened their tongues.

"What was she like, Auntie Dou?"

"She was beautiful inside and out," said the tiny woman. "And her embroidery was exquisite."

"How could you let my grandfather sell it?" accused Suyin.

"An art dealer from the capital offered your grandfather a tidy sum, then he promptly left the village. By the time we discovered her embroidery gone, it was too late. Her works are on display in the museum in Guiyang City," said Old Auntie Dou. "But her greatest gift was an open heart."

Suyin started. *An open heart.* Grandmother's words at the initiation ceremony. Was this the key to her proving her worth?

"What's the matter, Suyin?" asked Auntie Cho-Ye.

"Nothing, Auntie."

"Your mother loved you and your father very much," said Auntie Cho-Ye.

"If she loved us so much," said Suyin defiantly, "how could she leave my father and me for half the year?"

"She had responsibilities," said Auntie Cho-Ye.

It was the excuse she had expected, as old and worn as her shoes.

"That explains nothing," Suyin snapped. The mere mention of her mother's name was enough to plunge Auntie Cho-Ye and Auntie Huishan into a black mood.

Only Old Auntie Dou remained cheerful, though she too was stubbornly tight-lipped about the subject.

Cho-Ye brushed a lock of hair off Suyin's face. When she spoke, her voice was tender.

"Sometimes our own wishes must be put aside for the good of the collective. Even the poorest family in the village contributed to your passage. Some gave money passed down from their ancestors. Others dug up their trove of silver, treasures they were saving to pay for a daughter's dowry. Each gave what they could, but it was not enough. You'll have to work off your debt when you reach Gold Mountain."

"I will go," sighed Suyin.

Cho-Ye hugged her. "It is an honor to become a benefactress."

Then why did the honor feel like a betrayal? Her people seemed more interested in riches than her leaving. She wanted to lash out at them, but she knew that words spoken in bitterness were better left unsaid.

"Be wary of Mr. Lao, Suyin," said the shaman. "He has a black heart. He sought my help to reclaim one of his lost souls."

Suyin suddenly felt frightened.

"I tied a white string around his wrist to keep it inside. But unless that man changes his ways, it will escape again."

"How could you send me away with a man like that?"

demanded Suyin, no longer able to hide her resentment.

"The men in the village trusted him," said Cho-Ye. "And I have faith in you."

"What work will I do?" she asked sullenly.

"You will become a seamstress in a garment factory."

"But I'm not allowed to sew!"

"Pah!" said Cho-Ye. "In Gold Mountain, you can sew! Who's going to stop you? Not the chief. Not when the future of the village is at stake."

She was furious. The village elders seemed more than willing to overlook a promise when it was convenient to them.

"I've never sewn a stitch in my life!" she said, crossing her arms.

"You'll learn," said Cho-Ye. "Stitchery is in your blood."

My sworn sisters have betrayed me, she thought, but she held her tongue.

Her three aunties gave her farewell gifts: a notebook of Nu Shu missives and a pair of slippers embroidered with butterflies. And Shan-Shan presented her with her mother's silver embroidery scissors. The scissors were shaped like a crane, the blades forming the crane's moveable beak.

"How did you get these?" she asked, shocked.

"I stole them from your grandfather's house," said Shan-Shan softly.

Suyin hesitated. A gift of scissors meant a severed relationship.

"They're not a gift," explained Shan-Shan, reading Su-yin's thoughts. "They're your inheritance."

"Your mother would have wanted you to have them," added Cho-Ye.

"Oh, Shan-Shan," said Suyin sadly. "Thank you." The thought that she might never see her friend again seemed almost too much to bear.

"Your feather, your scissors, and your Nu Shu notebook are your secret trinity," said Cho-Ye. "They will remind you who you are, a girl of Miao heritage, daughter of Zhu An-Lan, the finest embroideress that ever lived."

"One more word of advice," said Auntie Huishan, frowning. "And this is for your ears too, Shan-Shan. Watch out for bad apples. Red on the outside, rotten on the inside."

"Better an ugly boy of upstanding character than a good-looking crook," added Old Auntie Dou.

"Long on looks, short on character," chimed the three aunties.

Shan-Shan giggled. "Suyin's only thirteen."

"I married your father at fourteen," said Auntie Huishan.

Shan-Shan frowned. Suyin tried to smile. Her aunties had told her that in Gold Mountain, she would learn to stitch factory clothes, but there would be no time to embroider. She would probably never marry. A Miao girl who couldn't embroider would never be accepted by a boy's family. The only person who would marry her would be an old man, someone soft in the head or mean.

*　　*　　*

After packing a small bag, Suyin returned to the Ancestral Hall. The succulent aroma of roast pork welcomed her. She fixed a smile on her face.

"Come sit beside me, Suyin," said Uncle Pei-Pei. "What a send-off—the finest pork you have ever tasted."

She caught the snakehead eyeing her as he stuffed meat into his mouth. He was a big talker, rough in looks and manner, with eyes that reminded her of mouse droppings. She stared at the white string circling his wrist and thought *lost soul* and *black heart*. What if he wasn't who he claimed to be at all? What if he kept the villagers' money and murdered her?

But her people seemed oblivious to her fears. They lost themselves in merriment, for they knew it would be years before they could afford another celebration like this. As soon as Lao had eaten, he was impatient to leave. One by one, the villagers hugged Suyin and said their good-byes.

"Promise me you will never forget us," said Cho-Ye. "You carry the hopes and dreams of a village."

And those of He Shan, thought Suyin desperately.

Since Snakehead Lao had already made his way up the road, Chief Wu kept his farewell speech short.

"Zhu Suyin, good luck in Gold Mountain. Our village has sacrificed much to send you. If you succeed, we will prosper. Work hard, for we are your people." Then he gave her a toothless smile and a final hug.

"Go quickly," said Old Auntie Dou, "or Mr. Lao will leave you behind."

When she finally caught up to him, he threw his bags at her.

She hoisted the bags onto her back, swaying under the weight. Lao pushed her for the sport of it, laughing when she lost her balance and fell, skinning her knee.

"I don't know why your people chose *you* to save them," he sneered.

Glancing over her shoulder, she took a last look at her village. Then she wiped the blood from her knee, straightened her skirt, and hauled the bags up on her back, determined to prove him wrong.

5

Duped!

Sworn sisters, it took five days to reach Fuzhou City by train. From there a second snakehead took us to a warehouse where we met three girls and thirty-five boys. We were herded into vans and driven to a remote bay along the coast, where we are waiting for two sampans to ferry us to the cruise ship. I'm scared and excited about the journey before me. A few minutes ago, Lao spotted my Nu Shu script. He said I was writing nonsense. He's mean and stupid. I'll be glad when I see the last of him.

When Suyin boarded the small boat, she sat beside two frightened-looking girls named Jade and Wing. The girls were from Fuzhou City, though the two had just met.

"The three of us should stick together," whispered Jade, pointing to the boys behind them. "Safety in numbers."

Jade was fourteen, a year older than Suyin. She had

a moon-shaped face and flashing eyes. She had straight black hair, cut to her ears, and a fringe covering her forehead. At first glance, Suyin thought her plain, but when Jade smiled, her face radiated warmth and friendliness.

Wing was the youngest of the three at twelve. She was small and delicate, with wispy hair, doll-like features, and a shy smile. She wore tiny gold teardrop earrings and a gold ring with a jade stone. Her dress was of pale yellow silk with a deeper gold trim. She must be rich, thought Suyin.

A tall, strikingly handsome boy in his teens called Pang sat beside her. When he shook her hand, she saw that his fingers were long and graceful. When he smiled, he displayed a perfect set of pure white teeth.

"This is my friend Kwan-Sook," said the boy, running his fingers through a mop of thick black hair. The girl was pretty, despite a sharp face, scowling mouth, and wary eyes. She reminded Suyin of the beaten and hungry stray dogs that sometimes wandered into her village.

"My father, Han-Bo, adopted me," continued Pang, "and I adopted Kwan-Sook."

Kwan-Sook's eyes lit up at Pang's words. The girl leaned toward him, smiling. Her face was so openly affectionate that Suyin thought that perhaps her first impression had been wrong.

Suyin offered her hand, but Kwan-Sook ignored her. Suyin noticed a thick ugly scar circling the girl's neck. Had someone tried to slit her throat? She felt a rush of pity.

The sampans hugged the coast, sailing past twinkling lights of cities and towns. After several hours, Pang nudged her, grinning. He put on a fur cap with earflaps that fluttered in the wind.

"Like my hat?"

"It looks warm," she said, flustered.

"It's made of rat," said Pang boldly. "Ten pelts. In Fuzhou I was called Rat Catcher Pang. The restaurant owners hired me. They paid me one yuan per rat." He removed his hat and handed it to her. "Would you like to wear it? It's warm."

"No thank you," she said. The boy laughed nervously. *He is trying to cheer me up,* she thought, *by pretending he is brave.*

Gazing up at the Milky Way, she remembered her magical flight to He Shan. Instinctively, she touched the heart feather. Since then, she had relived the experience countless times: dancing with the cranes, painting herself with mud, and choosing her feather. But where were the cranes now?

After several hours at sea, Pang whispered, "There's the boat."

The boat emerged from the inky dark like a silent ghost. The hull was rusted. Paint was peeling from its bow. The rickety rust bucket was no more than a few hundred feet long, too small to carry thirty-nine passengers plus Lao and the crew. Too small to cross an ocean!

Suyin could hardly believe her eyes. "That can't be it," she said, glancing over at Lao, who was snoring. "Lao told my people it was a cruise ship."

"Smugglers always lie," said Kwan-Sook in a haughty voice. "Especially to unsophisticated country people."

Suyin's fear dissolved into anger. "There's no excuse for lying."

"Country bumpkins," muttered Kwan-Sook. "So naive.

"Mr. Lao!" shouted Kwan-Sook. "Our boat is here."

Suddenly the captain, a gaunt, swarthy-looking fellow with a weather-beaten face, appeared on the bridge. He was carrying a lantern. Tucked into his belt was a revolver.

"How many migrants?" he asked.

"Thirty-nine," answered Lao.

The captain cursed. "There's barely room for half that number."

"Sister Fang-chou's orders," snapped Lao.

Suyin touched Pang's arm. "What's Sister Fang-chou like?" she whispered.

"Aiiya! She hasn't heard about Fang-chou?" said Kwan-Sook in a mock innocent tone.

"Kwan-Sook," said Pang sharply.

Pang explained that in Fuzhou City, Sister Fang-chou's reputation was well-known.

"She's the biggest snakehead in Gold Mountain. You girls will be working in one of her garment factories. I'll be working as a dishwasher in her restaurant the Golden Palace." Lowering his voice, he said, "Fang-chou's friends call her Sister, her enemies Sharktooth. Lao's her lackey."

"Why do they call her Sharktooth?" asked Suyin in a low voice.

"If you cross her, she's vicious."

Suyin shivered with fear.

The captain threw down a rope ladder and everyone climbed on board. When Suyin stepped onto the upper deck, two rats scuttled by her.

"I've changed my mind," whispered Wing.

"It's too late," said Jade. "The boats have already set sail."

Our fate is sealed, thought Suyin.

"I'm not staying in the hold," Lao shouted to the captain.

"We need an enforcer down there to keep order!" barked the captain.

"I don't care if they kill each other," muttered Lao.

Suyin leaned toward Pang. "Why would we need an enforcer?" she asked quietly.

"There have been problems on the smuggling ships. Beatings, rapes, murder."

She glared at Lao. If it weren't for that fast-talking snakehead with his sugar-coated lies, she'd be safe at home in her village.

The captain opened an iron hatch and led them down a short flight of stairs into the hold. The hold was small and dark like an underground cave. The air was thick with mold. Curtains of cobwebs hung from the low ceiling. The beam of light from the captain's lantern shuddered with each pitch and roll of the boat. When the captain reached the midsection of the boat, he switched on a ceiling lamp wired to a car battery.

With growing horror, Suyin took in the dismal surroundings. There were ten bunks on either side of a central passageway, five upper bunks and five lower ones. Water dripped from the ceiling bolts and pooled onto the aisle between the bunks. A thick black mold edged its way along the walls. At the far end of the exit hatch was the latrine. The sleeping quarters were no more than sixty feet long, about the size of the kitchen and pigpen in Cho-Ye's stone house. It was hard to imagine forty people living in such a cramped space.

Her people had thought her lucky. If she had ever been lucky, her luck had run out as soon as she'd left with Lao.

"We should reach open water in less than an hour," growled the captain, turning to go. His keys jingled as he climbed the stairs and closed the hatch with a thud.

"He's locking us in the hold like cargo," whimpered Wing.

"Shut up, *yazi*," said Lao. "Stupid little duck. You *are* cargo. I get paid whether you reach Gold Mountain or not. So stop your quacking."

Wing paled. She grabbed Jade's arm and held on tightly.

"Two to a bunk!" said Lao, placing his belongings on the first bunk nearest the hatch. "You three girls will have to share." He patted the bunk directly across from his and turned to Jade with a smirk. "Unless one of you wants to bunk with me."

Jade bristled. "No thank you, Mr. Lao."

Kwan-Sook clasped Pang's hand and led him to a lower bunk halfway between the hatch and the latrine.

"We'll have to be careful what we say," said Jade quietly, watching Kwan-Sook. "Miss-Know-It-All is close enough to eavesdrop."

"Her friend is sweet, though," whispered Wing, glancing over her shoulder at Pang.

The three girls lay on their sides like pickled river fish. The bunk was too narrow for three. If the boat lurched, the girl lying near the aisle would find herself dumped onto the floor.

Suyin had a sinking feeling. For the next two months, they would be sleeping on top of one another like the caged birds of Weining Town market. *Had her people had any idea what lay ahead of her?*

"Switch off the light," ordered Lao.

"Mr. Lao," said Kwan-Sook sweetly. Everyone turned to the girl with interest. "I would like to express my gratitude to you for providing us with this opportunity to go to Gold Mountain. Please be assured that we will bear the hardships ahead without complaint."

Pang grimaced, but Kwan-Sook's fawning hit its target, because Lao flushed with pleasure.

"It is good to hear young people willing to sacrifice themselves for the next generation," said Lao. "Your name is . . . ?"

"Kwan-Sook."

"The name means 'gold,' does it not?" asked Lao.

"Yes, Mr. Lao," said Kwan-Sook coyly.

"I'm sure such an auspicious name will bring you good fortune," said Lao.

Kwan-Sook bowed her head in feigned humility.

"Thank you for your kind words, Snakehead Lao."

The girl has a mouth as soft as tofu and a heart as hard as nails, thought Suyin.

Moments later, the hold was plunged into darkness. The boat creaked and groaned as it pushed into the open water.

"We're on our way!" said Pang. Someone began to clap softly until gradually everyone joined in, even Suyin. And in that moment, she forgot her homesickness. She forgot everything but the happiness and good fortune that awaited her in Gold Mountain, where snakes became dragons and the streets were paved with gold.

Sworn sisters, today is our seventh day at sea, though it feels like a lifetime. Lao told us the voyage might take from forty to sixty days, depending on the weather. I am always cold and my bones ache from the damp. Our daily ration is a half a cup of rice porridge, a few pickled vegetables, and a cup of weak tea. Everyone is hungry and scared, though the boys pretend to be tough. The boat is overrun with rats. There was a rat in our bunk yesterday. I feel angry at my misfortune. Why must I sacrifice everything dear to me—my home, my education, my best friend?

*   *   *

As she and her new friends lay in the darkness, unable to sleep, they talked about their families. Wing removed her photographs from a plastic bag. She shone her flashlight on each image: a beautiful woman in an evening gown, a stern-looking father in a business suit, and Wing posing under a willow tree with a flower in her hair.

"My mother was a singer," said Wing. "She sang at the Min Opera in Fuzhou City. She taught me many lovely songs."

"Sing for us, Wing," called a voice. It was the rat catcher named Pang. Suyin stiffened. There was no privacy, unless they whispered, and sometimes, even then the others could hear them.

When Wing began to sing, the hold went quiet and Suyin glimpsed the happy girl Wing used to be.

"You have a voice like a nightingale," said Jade.

"My singing is terrible," said Wing, trying to be polite. "Worse than fingernails on a chalkboard. My mother's voice was a marvel, though. On stage she looked like a tiny porcelain doll." She sighed. "So beautiful."

"Like you," said Suyin.

"Not so much," replied Wing. "Not anymore. Used to be, though. Lots of fine clothes. Servants and parties. Very glamorous."

To Suyin, it seemed a life of shimmering moments.

Jade began dabbing her eyes.

"What's wrong?" Suyin asked.

"I miss my little brother. Min-Jun is only seven, but he has no one."

"He has your mother," said Suyin.

"Not really," said Jade, staring at her brother's photograph. "She's too care-worn to look after him. He was mine more than hers. When my mother returned to work, I looked after him. I treated him like a doll at first, but then I grew to love him like a mother. When I was old enough to get work in the garment factory, Min-Jun played at my feet as I stitched. In the last year, my brother has become a thief. It's not his fault. He steals to feed himself. If I fail in Gold Mountain, my brother will be lost."

"What about your family, Suyin?" asked Wing.

"My parents died when I was small," said Suyin. "My mother was an embroideress, but my grandfather refused to let my aunties teach me to sew. Maybe you could teach me?"

"I'm sorry," said Jade. "I didn't bring a needle and thread. Did you, Wing?"

Wing gave a bitter laugh. "Why would I? I thought I'd be enjoying myself on a cruise ship!"

Wing reached for Suyin's hand. "Who cared for you when you lost your parents?"

"Three aunties."

"It must have been hard for them to let you go," said Wing. "My mother cried for days before I left."

Suyin pushed down the hurt flooding her chest.

Her aunties hadn't shed a tear. What a fool she'd been to think they'd loved her.

*   *   *

"All my suffering will be worth it if only I can send Little Brother to school," said Jade, swatting away a rat as it scampered across their bunk.

"We'll be old ladies by that time," said Wing bitterly.

"Nonsense," said Jade. "If we work hard, we'll send American dollars home to our families. We'll wear fine clothes and speak English like big shots."

"I studied English in school," said Wing. "But I still can't string two sentences together."

"My parents couldn't afford the school tuition," said Jade.

"I could teach you English," said Suyin shyly. English would help her friends in their new life. It might also help Suyin earn her wings and escape from the boat.

Wing raised an eyebrow. "You?"

"English comes easily to me," said Suyin, trying not to brag.

Wing looked unconvinced. "Say something in English."

"My name is Zhu Suyin. I am from Cao Hai Village."

"You are a wonder, Suyin," said Wing.

"Will you teach me too?" asked Pang, whose ears had pricked up at the word *English*.

"I'll teach anyone who wants to learn," said Suyin.

"Kwan-Sook," called Pang. "Suyin's going to give us English lessons!"

"English lessons? From that silly little child?" Kwan-Sook glared at Suyin from her bunk. "Not on your life!"

Pang shrugged. "Maybe you'll change your mind later."

Before Suyin finished teaching her first lesson, everyone had joined her class, except Kwan-Sook, who sat in her bunk sulking.

At first her students listened quietly, too shy to pronounce such strange-sounding words. Only Pang was brave enough to try. The boys laughed at him, but he persevered until he was able to say his first sentence in English. Seeing his success, the others began to try too. Learning English made the days pass more quickly. And for the first time, there was laughter in the hold.

"When we are rich in Gold Mountain, we will repay you in gold," the boys told her.

"Stop fawning over that fake," hissed Kwan-Sook. "She's a peasant pretending to be an intellectual. How can you be sure she's not teaching you nonsense? Lao says she's writing chicken scratches in her notebook."

No one came to her defense. They feared Kwan-Sook because she was Lao's favorite.

Despite Kwan-Sook's taunts, Suyin discovered that she loved teaching. And for the first time since she left her village, she saw some value in her journey.

Sworn sisters, we have endured three weeks in the hold of the boat. How you would weep for me if you knew my suffering. The hold is dark and crawling with rats. There is no water to wash or brush our teeth, and the boat stinks. The latrine is a subject no one talks about—the slop pails caked with nightsoil, the large iron scoop, the stack of garbage bags, and no privacy. My only comfort are my friends Jade and Wing, whom I have grown to love. Hardship has drawn us closer. We have promised to stick together no matter what our future holds.

Wing spent the night throwing up and crying. Unused to hardship, she was like an orchid in a windstorm. She was falling apart. The boys thought her spoiled. She wasn't the only one suffering.

Jade was more patient. She understood that Wing had never been hungry, thirsty, or dirty. She talked to her like a mother.

"We've been down here a month," said Jade. "And we're still alive."

"Barely," sobbed Wing.

"Quiet, Wing," whispered Suyin. "Lao's in a foul mood."

"Shut that stupid girl up," Lao roared.

Wing turned on Lao, furious. "How dare you speak to me like that! You're a nobody! I am from a good family. My father gave you his life savings. He would never have sent me away if he'd known I would have to suffer like this."

Lao spoke between clenched teeth. "Poor little rich girl," he taunted. "Are you going to miss your precious house on the hill? Your singing lessons and servants?"

"My father will have you beaten when I tell him what I've had to suffer," shrieked Wing.

Jade squeezed Wing's arm in warning. "Quiet, Wing, please."

Suyin broke into a cold sweat. Wing had called Lao a nobody. She had insulted him in the worst possible way.

"Your daddy was greedy," hissed Lao. "He didn't think twice about sending you away. He was more interested in overseas money than a spoiled daughter."

"Liar!" screamed Wing between sobs.

Lao pulled Wing from her bunk. He smacked her face.

"We're going for a walk up on deck," he said, pushing her toward the exit hatch.

Wing swallowed her tears, shocked into silence. She gave Jade a helpless look as Lao grasped his keys.

Suyin froze. He was going to throw Wing overboard.

Jade tugged bravely on Lao's coat. "Please, Mr. Lao. Give her another chance. If she makes another sound, I'll stuff a rag in her mouth myself."

Lao hesitated. He pursed his lips. "I guess the sharks will go hungry today." He poked his finger in Wing's face. "I won't forget this."

Wing had made an enemy.

"Kwan-Sook!" barked Lao. "The captain needs an extra deckhand. Do you want the work?"

Kwan-Sook leaped to her feet. "Thank you, Mr. Lao," she gushed. "You won't be sorry."

Jade grimaced. "Did you see the look she gave us when she passed?"

"Yes," said Suyin. "She was gloating."

"Lao threatened to kill me," said Wing, her voice quaking.

"You must be careful from now on," said Jade.

"I was foolish," said Wing, hanging her head.

Suyin winced. Shame washed over her like scalding oil. She'd felt no compassion for Wing's suffering, and when her friend's life had hung in the balance, she'd done nothing.

Jade had been brave. She had saved Wing's life.

When Kwan-Sook returned to the hold, she wore a triumphant smile. She had swabbed the deck, but she'd felt the sun on her face and breathed in the salt air. She couldn't stop talking about how lovely it was.

"What a braggart," muttered Suyin.

"I feel sorry for her," said Wing.

"Why?" Suyin asked. "She doesn't care about anyone but Pang."

"She doesn't have a family," said Wing.

"Neither do I," said Suyin bitterly.

"You had aunties," said Wing.

"They sent me away."

"So did my father," said Wing softly.

Suyin's feelings about her aunties were as changeable as the weather. Sometimes she loved them with every inch of her being. At other times, she hated them for sending her away. Seeking comfort, she read the missives that her sworn sisters had written in her Nu Shu notebook.

Even on the Third Day after my wedding,

When I leave my village,
You will remain in my heart. Shan-Shan

Reading Shan-Shan's words, she felt the reality of her plight. Shan-Shan wasn't even betrothed yet. Her best friend was talking about the distant future, a future in which she would have no place.

Wing was terrified of the rats. She pleaded with Pang to do something, anything, to rid the boat of the vile creatures. She was too scared to fall asleep.

"You're a rat catcher, Pang," begged Wing. "Surely you can help."

"I didn't bring traps," said Pang, scratching his head. "But I'll see what I can do, little Wing."

Turning to Suyin, Pang smiled, and when their eyes met, Suyin felt her cheeks grow hot.

When Suyin looked up, Kwan-Sook was standing beside Pang, scowling.

"Xiaoli's bothering me, Pang," she said angrily.

"I'll be right there," said Pang. "Don't worry, Kwan-Sook. I'll talk to him."

He shot Suyin an apologetic look before he hurried after her. Now Suyin understood what Kwan-Sook saw in Pang. It wasn't just his good looks but his kindness. But a boy like Pang could break a girl's heart without even knowing it.

Jade rolled her eyes. "That girl has him wrapped around her baby finger."

"He wants to take care of her," said Wing wistfully. "She's his only family."

The next morning, Pang had a surprise for Wing. He held up a snap trap he'd fashioned from a small piece of wood and some wire he'd found wrapped around the hanging lamp. A rat was caught in the trap.

"This should help you sleep," said Pang proudly. "I used a few grains of rice for bait." He released the rodent from the trap and dropped it into a plastic bag. "Lao can throw it overboard."

"You're my hero, Pang," said Wing, her eyes shining. But Suyin's distress showed in her face.

Pang reached over and touched her arm.

"Don't worry, Suyin. All our trials will be forgotten when we reach Gold Mountain."

6
Desperate Times

The weeks passed slowly, each day a test of the migrants' spirit. Tempers flared like a match to kindling. Lao had coaxed some of the boys into playing mahjong for cigarettes and coins. Xiaoli, their ringleader, was full of swagger. He belched and broke wind and whispered behind the girls' backs whenever they passed his bunk on the way to the latrine. When a fight broke out between Xiaoli and his friend Wen-Ching, Suyin expressed her worry to Pang.

"Someone's going to get hurt," she said.

"I'll be back in a moment, girls," said Pang. When he returned, he pulled a fistful of mahjong tiles from his sleeve. As he fluttered his fingers, the tiles disappeared, then magically reappeared in Wing's pocket.

"How did you do that?" Wing asked, returning the game pieces to Pang.

"Sleight of hand," said Pang. "I'm the best pickpocket in China. Actually, my adoptive father is the best. I'm the second-best."

"I thought you were a rat catcher," said Jade.

"That was my first career, then I became a pickpocket."

"You mean a thief," corrected Suyin.

"Not a thief, a pickpocket," said Pang firmly. "There's a world of difference."

"What's the difference?"

"Anyone can be a thief," said Pang, "but a good pickpocket demands intelligence, patience, speed, coordination, and a willingness to take risks. The best pickpockets are masters of disguise and keen observers. They must take note of a victim's face, the way they walk and talk, their style of clothing, and their shoes—most particularly their shoes."

"Why their shoes?"

"You can tell a lot about a person by their shoes," said Pang, meeting her eyes. "Yours, for instance."

She flushed, embarrassed. Her shoes were hand-stitched and made of cloth. They were village shoes, unlike Pang's and Kwan-Sook's store-bought sneakers and Wing's dainty cream-colored leather shoes.

"If my shoes could talk, they would say I am poor."

"Perhaps," said Pang quietly. "But whoever embroidered those shoes did it with love."

She felt her heart soften, but only a fool would trust a pickpocket.

"If those boys find out you stole their game pieces," she warned, "you'll be in big trouble."

"You scold like an auntie," laughed Pang.

"Leave him alone, Suyin," said Wing. "He did it for us."

That was true, but Auntie Huishan's warning rang in her ear. *Watch out for bad apples. Red on the outside, rotten on the inside.*

"Don't you feel sorry for your victims?" she pressed.

"Of course not. I only steal from the rich. I'm the Chinese Robin Hood."

"Here come the gamblers," whispered Suyin. Suddenly she was afraid for Pang.

"What's happening, brothers?" chirped Pang.

"We're missing some game pieces," said Xiaoli angrily.

"And we think you're the culprit," added Wen-Ching.

"You're wrong, boys," said Pang smoothly, "but you're welcome to search me."

After Xiaoli pulled out Pang's pockets and patted his clothing, he gave him a sheepish look. "Sorry. Perhaps I was mistaken."

Pang patted Xiaoli's shoulder. "Everyone makes mistakes, brother."

No sooner had those scoundrels left than Pang pulled the mahjong tiles from his sleeve the way a magician pulls a rabbit from a hat.

Hoping to distract the gamblers, Suyin announced that her English class was about to begin. Wing was her best student, as she'd studied English in school, though her pronunciation needed work. Pang's diligence made him an excellent student, but poor Xiaoli struggled. Suyin offered the boy extra help, but eventually he left her class in a fit of pique. Kwan-Sook soon became Xiaoli's ally, filling his head with lies.

Several days later, Kwan-Sook interrupted Suyin's lesson, speaking in a voice loud enough for everyone to hear.

"Lao told me how Suyin had followed a silly crane and nearly drowned."

The hold went silent.

"When her people finally found her she said she'd flown on the back of a crane to a world above the earth!" Kwan-Sook laughed uproariously. "Pshaw! She's either a liar or soft in the head. Maybe that's why her village pooled their money to send her away. They wanted to be rid of her."

Suyin felt her blood boil. Kwan-Sook had it out for her. Until now, she'd tried not to rise to the girl's bait, but her last insult was too much.

"I'm not lying and I'm not crazy," Suyin said, her voice rising. "You're just trying to make trouble for me."

Her students stared at her, their eyes widening.

"Am I?" smirked Kwan-Sook. "Then explain why you write gibberish in your precious notebook. Explain why you sleep holding that stupid feather and those silly crane scissors."

Suyin folded her arms. "I'll explain nothing to a mean and conniving busybody!"

Pang covered his ears with his hands. "Girls! Stop fighting. I'm tired of everyone fighting."

Suyin gave Pang a black look. "The lesson is over for today," she said, and stormed back to her bunk.

When Wing returned to the bunk, she tugged at Suyin's sleeve.

"Is your feather really magic? Or your notebook and crane scissors?"

"I don't want to talk about it," Suyin said angrily. Her heart feather, her embroidery scissors, and her Nu Shu notebook were all she had of her old life. She didn't want to share them with anyone, not even her friends.

She lay down and wrapped her arms around herself. She was angry with Kwan-Sook for humiliating her and with Wing for being so nosy. She was angry with her aunties and the crane sisters for abandoning her.

"I'm glad you stood up to that bully, Suyin," said Jade softly.

"I hate her," Suyin said fiercely.

And then a terrifying thought came to her. What if Kwan-Sook had spoken the truth? What if her village really *had* wanted to be rid of her?

Later that evening, as she lay in the darkness, she was sorry she'd lost her temper. If the key to transformation was an open heart, she knew she had to do better. She vowed to compose herself from now on and be nicer to Kwan-Sook even though the girl despised her.

*　　*　　*

On the fortieth day at sea, when Lao announced that the ship's cupboards were almost bare, the boys banged their tin cups against their bunks in protest. Lao showered them with curses, then quickly scrambled to the hatch to escape their anger. But Xiaoli lay in wait for him. He leaped on the snakehead's back and began choking him. Pang pulled Xiaoli off Lao with the help of another boy. Pale and shaken, Lao staggered to the hatch.

"You'll regret that," he rasped, glaring at Xiaoli.

After Lao left, Pang set up a portable camp stove on the floor. He filled a stew pot with water, loosened the drawstring of his rat bag, and slowly emptied its contents onto the floor. The dead rats had large staring eyes, tiny whiskers, and little pink ears.

Pang gave Suyin a pleading look. "I was hoping you'd help me skin and filet the meat." He shrugged his shoulders apologetically. "Kwan-Sook has a weak stomach."

Rat is considered a delicacy to Miao people with the family name Long or Dragon. The rat was their ancestor. The Longs were Suyin's aunties' neighbors, and every year around New Year's, they invited her and her aunties to celebrate the Rat-Eating Festival. The Longs baked the rats in hot ovens and afterward the meat was dipped in delicious sauces and served with rice in the shape of rats.

Suyin hesitated. She had always enjoyed a feast of rat, but she'd never had to prepare the meat.

"I will help," she said.

She and Pang worked for hours to filet enough meat

for the stew pot. A rat has tiny bones and more gristle than fat. She felt squeamish as she dropped the carcasses, glistening with blood, into the pot. When the meat was cooked, Pang scooped up a piece with his chopsticks.

"Delicious!" he said, smacking his lips, but she could never tell if he was joking or serious.

Suyin broke off a sliver and brought it to her mouth. The meat was tough and stringy and less tasty than the baked rat she'd eaten at the Longs'. It lacked dipping sauces and sticky rice. It lacked the reverence of ritual and prayer.

Wing shook her head stubbornly.

Jade's eyes grew hard. "If you want to live, Wing, you have to eat."

"Would you keep an eye on the stew pot, Jade?" asked Suyin.

When she approached the latrine, Xiaoli blocked her way.

"There's our little English teacher, Suyin!" he said bitterly. As she tried to slip past him, he grabbed her.

"Let her go, brother," yelled Pang. He wrenched Xiaoli's hands away and pushed him to the floor. Xiaoli scrambled to his feet. Suyin saw the flash of the knife blade. Kwan-Sook screamed. Pang's hand flew up, knocking the knife to the floor. Without thinking, Suyin kicked the knife under the bunk. Kwan-Sook glared at her, her eyes burning with hate. Xiaoli slunk away, cursing.

Squeezing her eyes shut to contain her tears, Suyin left

Pang and returned to the stew. After she composed herself, she gripped the pot handles, rose, and offered each migrant a bite-sized portion of meat swimming in greasy broth. Her hands shook as she approached Kwan-Sook.

Kwan-Sook took a bite, grimacing.

"This is pig's swill," she said, and dumped all the remaining stew onto Suyin's shoes.

Suyin stared at her ruined shoes. Kwan-Sook sniggered.

Suyin wanted to slap the girl, but to retaliate in such a way would be unthinkable back home. She waited for Pang to defend her. Surely this time, he could see the girl was clearly in the wrong. He gave her a helpless look.

Surprisingly, Wen-Ching stood up for her. He picked up the stew pot and glared at Kwan-Sook. "It's not Suyin's fault the food's bad."

Suyin felt like crying, but a teacher who cries in front of her students loses their respect.

Later, as the hold prepared for sleep, Pang stood beside her bunk with bowed head. "I apologize on behalf of my friend. She's led a bitter life."

"Leave me alone, Pang," Suyin snapped, knowing Pang's presence would only cause her more pain. His guard dog, Kwan-Sook, made too much trouble. Pang waited for her to relent, but she turned her back to him.

That night she dreamed she was a crane with lovely white wings and a long black neck. The dream seemed so real that when she woke, she ran her fingers over her limbs to see if she'd grown feathers, but she felt only rib bones, loose skin, and disappointment.

They had been at sea for forty-four days when Pang failed to show up for Suyin's English class. She had only a handful of students left. Most were too sick or weak to learn. Suyin was surprised at how disappointed she felt. Pang always cheered her up with his jokes and quick wit.

Moments later, she spotted Kwan-Sook storming up the passageway.

Jade muttered, "Here comes trouble."

"Listen, pea-brain," said Kwan-Sook, sticking her finger in Suyin's face. "Pang's too sick to be playing school with you. You're so selfish, you haven't even noticed."

Suyin paled. How could she have been so blind?

Kwan-Sook's eyes suddenly welled up. "English lessons won't save us, you fools."

When the class was over, Wing said, "Kwan-Sook is right. What good will English do us, if we die down here?"

"We're not going to die," insisted Jade, though how could anyone know if they would survive.

"No one can live on air!" cried Wing, tearing up. "Not even Kwan-Sook. She has been giving her share of food to Pang. She lied to him, told him that Lao had given her double portions. Pang is too sick to know better."

Suyin's cheeks burned with shame. Kwan-Sook had sacrificed for Pang. Suyin didn't know her at all.

In a strange way, she felt a kinship with Kwan-Sook,

her angry twin, even though she envied the girl's freedom. Kwan-Sook was responsible for no one, except Pang. She did not carry the burden of a village on her shoulders or the future of a crane kingdom. The crane women had deserted her when she needed them most.

Sworn sisters, our situation is desperate. Pang rid the ship of the rats, so we can no longer depend on those poor creatures for our survival. If we don't reach Gold Mountain soon, the hold will be our coffin.

She lay in the darkness, waiting. She waited to see Jade's face each morning, her eyes familiar comforts. She waited for her next meal, a few sips of watery gruel. She waited for her daily ration of water, a few tablespoons, as she dreamed of rivers and creeks flowing down mountains and rain falling into lakes. She waited for Wing to sing away the hardships of their voyage, her voice the summer marsh and birdsong. She waited for a woolen blanket to warm her, for a mother to hold her, for the cranes to save her. She waited to reach Gold Mountain, to take her first step toward a dream. She waited, most of all, to prove her worthiness. She didn't know what to do. She reached for her heart feather hoping and waiting as a bird waits for spring.

On the forty-eighth day of their voyage, the smugglers' boat entered the rough seas of the west coast of Canada.

Lao warned the migrants to expect rogue waves the size of a house, winds so strong they could toss a ship into the air like a child's ball. He warned them that the authorities patrolled these coastlines, so the migrants had better not talk if they were caught. Then he abandoned them to join the crew, leaving them with only two jugs of drinking water. If they didn't reach dry land soon, they would die of thirst. Everyone was too worried to sleep. And no one felt like lessons.

So when gale force winds hit the boat and shook it like a leaf in a whirlwind, Suyin was certain they were about to die.

Stepping over a skeletal body in the passageway, she entered the latrine. She shone the flashlight over a mountain of garbage bags filled with human waste and gagged with revulsion. An army of cockroaches spilled from the overflowing buckets. She slipped, soiling her clothes. Cockroaches fell onto her hair and neck. She swatted at the insects and stumbled outside, retching.

Teetering on the crest of a wave, the boat crashed with a thud, flinging shoes, bags, and the migrants out of their bunks and onto the floor. The panic that had been simmering in the hold for weeks erupted. She heard screams of terror, the scrape of metal against rock. The engines sputtered and then died. Then the ship groaned loudly, and slowly slid onto its side.

Someone shouted, "The ship's run aground!"

Within seconds, the passageway was crowded with

frightened migrants rushing toward the exit hatch. Suyin pulled Jade and Wing from their bunks and joined the stampede.

Suyin and her bunkmates held hands, trying to stay together.

"I can't swim," screamed Wing.

"Water's coming through the hatch!" Xiaoli yelled. "We're trapped!"

A high-pitched wail of grief and terror rang through the hold.

Xiaoli pounded on the hatch with his fist, cursing at Lao.

Pang placed a hand on Xiaoli's shoulder. "It's no use, brother. It's locked and the crew can't hear you."

Xiaoli's toughness melted. He placed his head in his hands and began to sob. But it was not a disgrace to cry when you were staring death in the face.

The three girls froze. They found one another's hands and held on tightly.

Everyone was crying now. The boys cried for their mothers. Even Kwan-Sook spared no tears.

Suyin tried to remain calm for Wing's sake, but as she stared at the water rising steadily in the hold, she began to panic.

I am too young to die. My life has just begun. She thought of all the people she might never see again, the foods she might never taste, the seasons that might come and go without her, if she didn't survive.

She clutched her heart feather, her embroidery scissors, and her Nu Shu notebook. Her secret trinity. She laid her head on Jade's chest and squeezed Wing's trembling hand. She closed her eyes, trying to be brave.

Above the roar and crash of the waves, she heard the clarion cry of the cranes.

Part Two

NEW YORK CITY

7
Gold Mountain

She woke in a dark basement filled with cots and stained mattresses. The basement stank of mildew and backed-up sewer. Every so often, the room seemed to tilt on its axis. She felt nauseous. Someone touched her arm. She bolted up, terrified.

"Shh," said Pang. "Everyone's asleep."

Pang sat on her cot. He leaned over and whispered in her ear.

"I've been worried about you. I couldn't sleep until I knew you were all right."

"Where am I?" she asked. Her head was pounding.

Through the dim light, she could see Jade, Wing, and Kwan-Sook curled up on cots across the room.

"Gold Mountain. New York City," he said in a whisper. "In a safe house. That goose egg on your forehead has gone down a bit." Reaching up, she felt a small raised bump.

"What day is it?" she asked.

"The first of July," said Pang. "The snakeheads dropped us off here late last night. Remember?"

Suyin looked uncertain. She rubbed her forehead, trying to separate her dreams from reality. She remembered the cries of the migrants as they realized they were locked in the hold of a sinking boat, then her relief when she'd heard the cranes calling and discovered that the birds had opened the hatch. She'd caught a glimpse of Grandmother's spindly black legs and her pale gray feather bustle as the old crane had hurried up the stairs leading to the upper deck.

Suyin had shouted to her friends, "The hatch is open now!"

The panic to escape was ugly. Xiaoli and Wen-Ching clawed their way past them, knocking Wing down. She remembered her terror as she leaped into the sea with Wing in tow.

After that her memory turned murky.

"Is everyone safe?" she asked.

Pang nodded.

"How did we get from the water to the city?"

"You don't remember?"

She shook her head.

"The boat was wrecked off the west coast of Canada," said Pang. "A snakehead in a white truck picked us up. We spent three days in the container."

She closed her eyes and the memories came rushing back. Lao herding them into the truck like animals, the snakehead's warning that if anyone made a sound when they crossed the Canadian-American border, he would chop off their arms and legs and feed their body parts to a pack of dogs.

"Where are the others?"

"Lao dropped them off at different safe houses throughout the city. Kwan-Sook coaxed Lao into letting me stay here with her."

She heard Kwan-Sook stir in her cot. Suyin stiffened.

"Don't worry," said Pang. "When Kwan-Sook falls asleep, not even a herd of goats could wake her."

Still, Pang kept an eye on Kwan-Sook as he spoke. He drew closer to Suyin, his lips almost touching her ear, his voice so low that she had to strain to hear him. It would be easy to lean toward him, to let him comfort her. She was so lonely and scared and they'd both gone through so much. If she turned her face toward him, his lips might brush hers. She had never been kissed before. She had never liked a boy enough.

Wanting to be held was natural, she told herself, though it was unwise. If Kwan-Sook found out, she would find a thousand ways to make her life miserable.

"Why does she hate me?" asked Suyin.

"She's had a tough life," said Pang quietly. "I found her on the street. I was eleven years old. Han-Bo had adopted me two years before. Kwan-Sook was eight, a dirty little girl in rags. She was sitting on the sidewalk with a begging bowl. The poor kid was starving. Her father had sold her to a nasty old man who used her as a servant and beat her. That's how she got that scar on her neck. The old man slit her throat because she burned his dinner. A neighbor took her to the hospital. When she had healed, she ran away from the old man. I gave her a few yuan for food and she followed me home. She would have gone with anyone who was kind to her. My adopted father took her in. He gave her food and a roof over her head, but he refused to adopt her. He wanted a son, not a daughter. That was hard on her. It was another rejection. Kwan-Sook lived with Father and me for three years until we left Fuzhou."

"What happened to your parents?"

"They died of the flu when I was seven years old. I was taken to the Linchuan orphanage in Fuzhou City, but I ran away. I survived by catching rats for the restaurant owners until Han-Bo took me in. Han-Bo saved me and I saved Kwan-Sook. She can be difficult, but I'm the only family she has."

Now she understood Kwan-Sook's bitterness and her fear of losing Pang.

Pang leaned closer. "I need to talk to you about something before the others wake up. The night of the boat wreck, Wing saw a wave pull you under. We were afraid you had drowned. We started combing the beach, searching for you. Then I heard birds calling and I followed the sound to a rocky point. As I got closer, I saw three tall birds with long necks and sharp beaks. The birds were pulling you from the sea. At first I thought I was dreaming, until I saw your feather. It was glowing in the moonlight. The birds were bent over you, fanning their wings. I raced to the point in a panic. I didn't know if you were dead or alive. When I reached you, the birds took flight. Everyone thinks I saved your life, Suyin, but I didn't. I think those birds did."

Pang shook his head. "I haven't told anyone else what really happened. Who would believe me?"

"Those birds were my friends," said Suyin. "They were cranes."

Hearing Pang's story, she felt that same sweetness she'd experienced the day of the feather ceremony. The cranes *hadn't* forgotten her. They had saved her life and the lives of her friends.

"The bird on those scissors you used to carry . . . was it a crane?" asked Pang.

She nodded sadly. "Yes, but I lost my scissors in the sea."

"And the feather?"

"A crane feather." Her key to transformation.

Pang looked relieved. "So I'm not crazy. Those birds actually rescued you."

"Yes, Pang, but you *did* save my life. I could have died if you hadn't found me."

"Those birds *led* me to you."

Why hadn't the cranes carried her away?

She leaned closer. "Please don't tell anyone."

"I won't—but you owe me an explanation."

She hesitated. It was pointless to deny what he'd seen with his own eyes.

"The cranes saved my life," said Suyin. "They have extraordinary powers. They belong to a secret society as old as the earth itself. I'm trying to prove myself worthy of a place among them, but I'm not sure how."

Pang drew back in confusion. "I don't understand. A secret society of cranes?"

"I can't tell you any more, Pang. Promise you'll keep my secret."

"I promise," said Pang solemnly. "I'd never believe it if I hadn't seen it myself. Is there anything I can do to help?"

"No, there is nothing anyone can do."

After Pang returned to his cot, she tried to sort out her feelings for him. He was a boy of contradictions. He was kind, but he was a thief. He was brave—he had fought off Xiaoli, and he had saved her life—but around Kwan-Sook he seemed lost, as if his adopted sister were his map and compass.

She admired him, but his presence unsettled her. When he looked at her, she felt as if he could read her heart. And in that moment, she had revealed secrets to him about the sisterhood. Now her indiscretion haunted her. What if it ruined her chances of earning her wings?

The next morning Jade and Wing helped her stand, propelling her toward the door of the safe house. She weaved a little as she walked, her legs unsteady.

"Lao's here, to take us to work," whispered Jade. "He's in a terrible mood."

Lao stood by the door, tapping his foot impatiently. He glared at Suyin, sucking his teeth.

"You'd better be ready for work, missy, or you'll feel the wrath of Sister Fang-chou."

"She'd rather sleep than work," muttered Kwan-Sook.

"She's been sick," said Jade between clenched teeth.

"I'm ready, Mr. Lao," Suyin said, trying to keep her voice steady.

As she climbed the stairs leading to the street, she felt like a mole emerging from its tunnel after a long winter. The sun was blindingly bright.

Wing curled her arm around Suyin's. "You saved my life. I'll never forget that, friend. And Pang saved yours."

"I owe him a lot," said Suyin.

Pang turned, grinning at the sound of his name, while Kwan-Sook bobbed up and down with excitement.

"I can't believe we made it, Pang-Pang," said Kwan-Sook, her eyes shining. "We're here! In Gold Mountain!" Then she stood on tiptoe and kissed him on the cheek.

"You and Pang are heroes," said Wing under her breath.

"Not like Lao and the crew," said Jade. "Those cowards were halfway to shore in a lifeboat while we had to swim or be rescued by our friends. One of the crew must have opened the hatch, but I'm sure it wasn't Lao. If it had been him, we would have never heard the end of his bragging."

"Shh," said Pang, pointing to Lao.

"Sister Fang-chou blames Lao and the captain for the boat wreck," explained Wing. "Lao beat Xiaoli for mentioning it."

As Suyin and her friends walked the city streets, they kept their eyes peeled for gold. Finally Jade gathered enough courage to ask, "Where's the gold, Lao?"

Lao sniggered. "Such gullible country people! The only gold you'll see around here is Fang-chou's eyetooth!"

Suyin wondered what other disappointments lay in store for them.

Sister Fang-chou's restaurant and her garment factory were located a block apart on East Broadway in the heart of Chinatown. The other boys were to work at her string of laundries and small takeouts scattered throughout Manhattan and Brooklyn.

Suyin had hoped to see the end of those snapping yellow teeth and those small darting eyes when she'd reached Gold Mountain, but Snakehead Lao had become Manager Lao.

"If you want to climb Gold Mountain," said Lao, poking his finger in their faces, "you must work hard, save your earnings, and don't complain. If you're slow or lazy, you'll be fired. And you'd better not leave Chinatown or you'll be in big trouble with Sister."

Suyin felt a knot form in her stomach. She wanted to do well at work, but she had no experience like the other girls. What if she got fired? When Lao had finished his lecture, Pang begged Suyin to help him brush up on his English. He was anxious to make a good impression on his first day on the job. He began rehearsing the phrases Suyin had taught him on board ship.

"Hello. My name is Pang and I work as a dishwasher at the Golden Palace. How do I sound?"

"Very good," she said.

"How do I say *I've come to catch rats at the Golden Palace!*"

Suyin's eyes widened.

Pang grinned. "I'm joking."

She smiled, amazed he could be so cheerful after their suffering on the boat.

The Golden Palace had a pagoda roof and an elaborate gold and red archway with a wondrous fire-breathing dragon curling its tail around the entrance.

A meaty-looking doorman in a red uniform and black leather gloves stood guard at the door.

"Good morning," said Pang slowly. "My name is Pang and I work . . . as a dishwasher at Sister's restaurant the Golden Palace."

"Back door," growled the doorman.

Pang looked baffled until Suyin translated *back door* for him.

"Aiiya!" he cried, happy to learn a new English word. "Back door. Back door." He was still repeating it when he disappeared down the alleyway.

Walking down East Broadway, she imagined herself in

the center of a whirlwind: cars whizzing by, horns blasting, people rushing to work, merchants unrolling brightly colored awnings.

Kwan-Sook pointed to a stumpy woman with a humped back and a crippled hip a block ahead of them. The woman was motioning to Lao. Three young girls accompanied her.

"Where's Manager Lam, Mr. Lao?" rasped the stumpy woman, leaning on her cane.

Lao gave her a sour look. "Fang-chou sent him to the Pearl River Factory. I've got my old job back."

The gray-haired woman peered up at him through spectacles perched at the end of her nose. She was taller than Old Auntie Dou, but not by much.

"Humpf," she said. "I see you've brought a new flock of little ducks with you. I'm Mrs. Chin, girls, one of Sister's long-time employees. We'll be working together. I came on a smuggler's ship thirty years ago when I was twenty."

Suyin was taken aback. If what Mrs. Chin said was true, she was fifty, but she looked as old as Auntie Dou.

"And this is Mei-li and Mei-Xia," continued Mrs. Chin. "They're sisters, and that's their cousin, Jin. The girls were born here, but their mothers and I came across on the same ship. I call the girls the Triplets because they look so much alike. Same pointy heads, button noses, and tiny feet." The three girls giggled, taking no offense.

"Stop your idle chattering, old woman," said Lao, checking his watch. "We've got to get to work."

As they walked through Chinatown, the Triplets chattered. They told the girls that they had learned to cut threads at their mothers' feet. At nine years old, they had graduated to stitching hems. By twelve, they were skilled seamstresses, but they had never gone to school. Suyin felt sorry for them. They didn't know the thrill of reading a book or a poem or writing their thoughts.

She thought of her Nu Shu notebook floating somewhere in a distant sea, the ink blurred, the embroidered cover faded by the sun and salt. A dull ache swelled in her chest. Maybe books and poetry would be lost to her as well.

"I never went to school either," offered Jade.

"Can you girls speak English?" asked Wing.

"No," said Mei-li wistfully. "We don't know anyone who speaks English."

"Sometimes Manager Lam cursed in English," said Jin.

"Suyin taught us English on the boat," said Jade proudly. "She's going to continue with her lessons on the way to work."

"Why don't you join our class?" said Suyin. "I'd be happy to teach you."

Clasping their arms around one another, the three girls jumped up and down on the spot.

"English! We're going to learn English!" they cried excitedly.

"We'll meet you at Columbus Park every morning,"

said Mrs. Chin. "English lessons will be good for the girls."

Suyin smiled to herself. Surely this would improve her chances of earning her wings.

"You don't need English to get ahead," said Kwan-Sook. "You need hard work!"

Jin raised an eyebrow. She gave Suyin a knowing smile. She seemed the quieter and more thoughtful of the three. There was a dark bruise under one eye. Suyin wondered if she'd been beaten.

"Mrs. Chin! Do you want to learn English with us?" asked Mei-Xia.

"I'm too old," said Mrs. Chin. "You can't teach an old dog new tricks."

Wing and Jade showed the Triplets their photographs. But the features of their loved ones were blurred and watermarked—ghostly images of what remained of the girls' old lives.

Suddenly the Triplets lowered their voices.

"That's the Lotus Flower Beauty Parlor," said Mei-li. "Mr. Leung, the proprietor, tells people the girls give customers haircuts and sometimes massages, but he's lying. The girls sell their bodies."

"The girls were desperate," said Mrs. Chin. "They lost their jobs. They were penniless."

"They were probably slackers," muttered Kwan-Sook.

Suyin shuddered. If she got fired, would she be forced to work for the awful Mr. Leung? As if her thoughts had been read, the curtain of the window moved. A man looked out, watching them the way a fox watches a flock of chickens behind a barbed wire fence.

"Where's our workplace, Mr. Lao?" broke in Kwan-Sook. Her voice was syrupy. She was always trying to curry favor with Lao.

Lao pointed to a red brick tenement sandwiched between the Waloy Bakery and the Tak Shing Hong Groceteria. Across the street was a restaurant called the So Good Noodle House. Suyin noticed a pair of eyes watching them from the restaurant window. Moments later, a girl about her age appeared at the doorway. The girl looked up at her and smiled.

Suyin was so relieved to see a friendly face, she smiled in return.

Lao's face stiffened. He jerked her up by the ear and pushed her inside an unmarked door with red peeling paint.

"What are you doing?" rasped Lao. "That girl could be a spy for the INS, the Immigration and Naturalization Service! Those devils are always trying to send illegals back home. You don't smile or wave or speak to anyone down here. Make yourself invisible."

She felt a sudden jolt of fear. Was Gold Mountain so dangerous a place that even a young girl could be a spy eager to deport them?

When Lao led them to the stairs, Suyin suggested that Mrs. Chin take the elevator.

"I would if it worked," said Mrs. Chin dryly.

The stairs were littered with garbage, yellowing piles of newspapers, and empty foam packing cases.

Suyin felt her hopes fading with every step. She had expected to find gold in the streets, skyscrapers made of glass, everything bright and new and shining. Instead, she saw chipped concrete floors, fading paint, and writing scrawled on dingy walls.

"Mrs. Chin," said Jade. "Do you and the Triplets live in a safe house?"

Mrs. Chin raised her eyebrows. "Safe house?" she said under her breath. "You mean a prison. Fang-chou only keeps you in a safe house until you've paid off your debt. The girls' mothers and I had to borrow money from a loan shark to pay off that old battleaxe. Now we rent a *gong si fong*—an apartment the size of a closet. Twelve of us share three small rooms and a bathroom."

"Stop complaining, old lady," said Kwan-Sook loud enough so Lao could hear. "If you work hard, you'll pay off your debt quickly."

"I've paid off my debt, Miss Fresh-Off-the-Boat," snapped Mrs. Chin, "but it took me fifteen years. The girls' mothers and I were out of work for a year. We had no income, but the interest kept piling up. The loan shark bled us dry."

"Are you rich now?" asked Suyin hopefully, though the old woman's housedress looked worn.

Mrs. Chin gave a snort. "If I were rich I wouldn't be

working for old Sharktooth! I send half my earnings to my relatives in China and the rest goes for rent and food. American dollars go a long way back home. Not here."

Suyin was speechless. Would she end up like Mrs. Chin, slaving for years with so little to show for it?

On each floor of the tenement was a small landing that led to three cast-iron doors—entrances to small factories.

"Fly-by-night businesses," explained Mrs. Chin, breathing hard. "If the bosses find out there's going to be a raid, they'll strip the factory in a few hours."

On the sixth floor, Lao removed a ring of keys from his belt and began opening a series of locks: a sliding steel bar buttressing the door, a dead bolt, a key lock, and an iron hatch. Once inside, Lao locked the door behind him.

The garment factory consisted of three rooms: a sewing room, a tiny office, and a closet-sized bathroom. Inside the workroom, tubes of fluorescent lighting were suspended from the ceiling with a series of rusty chains and convoluted wiring. Above the lights hung a labyrinth of pipes and plastic bags, spools of thread, scissors, bobbins, buttons, and bags of fabric scraps. Rows of giant spools of thread held by textile machines were attached to a line of sewing machines on long tables. The machines seemed alien to her. No one in her village owned a sewing machine. What use would it be without electricity? The city girls took sewing machines for granted. She wondered if Lao knew how inexperienced she was.

She stepped over paper patterns strewn on the floor.

There were canvas carts on casters beside the sewing tables. Rows of finished garments, waiting to be pressed, hung from hooks on a metal line with wheels. Plastic garbage bags stuffed with fabric scraps were stacked into corners.

"Find a seat in front of a machine," ordered Lao.

Kwan-Sook scrambled for a seat by the bathroom. Suyin sat between Wing and Jade.

"I'm scared," said Wing. "I've never had a job before."

"Me neither," said Suyin. "Do you know how to use a sewing machine?"

Wing nodded. "My mother taught me, but I'm slow."

"You'll start as Merrow workers," said Lao, stacking a pile of dresses beside each machine. "Stitching hems."

"Hems!" muttered Kwan-Sook indignantly. "We're experienced seamstresses."

Not all of us, thought Suyin, biting her lip.

"The starting salary for a seamstress is three dollars an hour," barked Lao. "If you work fast and show initiative, Sister might give you a raise. Your quota for today is five hundred pieces. No one leaves the shop until the order's finished. Start stitching."

Mrs. Chin pulled a strip of fabric over her nose. It was held up by a piece of elastic that fit over her ears.

"What's *that* for?" snickered Kwan-Sook.

"It's a mask for workers," said Mrs. Chin. "There's a pile of them in the corner. You'd better wear one unless you want a hacking cough or a rash."

Suddenly the shop was filled with a deafening sound, like a thousand jackhammers.

Suyin watched the others, uncertain where to begin.

"What's your problem?" asked Lao, his eyes narrowing.

Suyin took a deep breath. "I've never used a sewing machine."

"Pah!" he said, rolling his eyes. "I should have known better than to hire a country bumpkin."

He stomped off and returned with a gown of pale gold taffeta. He laid the dress down carefully on the table and handed her a needle and a spool of gold thread.

"This gown needs hemming," said Lao. "Make your stitches small and neat. The gown is worth a fortune." She was so nervous she tried to thread the needle, missed and then missed again.

"Let me do it, Fumble Fingers," said Lao impatiently. He quickly threaded the needle and pressed it into her hands. "I'll be back shortly to inspect your work."

Suyin stared at the gown with dismay.

"What's wrong?" asked Mrs. Chin. "You're as pale as a ghost."

"I don't know how to sew."

Mrs. Chin raised an eyebrow. "Not even hand-stitching?" She shook her head. "No."

Mrs. Chin grabbed the gown and gave her a quick demonstration, keeping her eye out for Lao. The old lady made hand-stitching look easy, but Suyin's stitches were crooked and the hem uneven. She snipped the thread and began again, but her second effort was no better than the first.

"Here comes Lao," warned Jin. Mrs. Chin hurried back to her seat.

When Lao examined her work, he slapped her across the head. "You've ruined the dress!" he screamed. "A dog could stitch better than you. You must have tricked your own people."

She heard Kwan-Sook stifling a laugh.

My people tricked us both, Suyin wanted to say. They'd sent a girl who couldn't sew to work in a garment factory! And now she had to bear the brunt of Lao's insults. Her only tenderness toward her people back home was reserved for Shan-Shan, who wasn't in on the plot to send her away.

Lao grabbed a pile of shirts and dumped them into her lap. "If you can't stitch, you can cut threads."

So that's how she lost her first chance for success in Gold Mountain. She was given the lowest-paid job in the shop, the job given to small children who accompanied their mothers to work or to half-blind grandmothers who were lonely and had nowhere else to go: a lowly thread cutter.

8

A Stitch in Time

On the seamstresses' second day in Gold Mountain, they met Mrs. Chin and the Triplets at Columbus Park. It was a good place to teach the English words Suyin loved: *sparrow, tree, grass, flower—sun* and *sky*. As usual, Manager Lao walked ahead of the seamstresses with his cell phone glued to his ear. He was busy making bets.

"What's the English word for *takeout,* Suyin?" asked Pang.

Before Suyin could answer, Kwan-Sook interrupted, "English sounds like sandpaper rubbed together."

Suyin inhaled sharply. "Walk with Kwan-Sook, Pang. I don't want any more trouble."

"You've got to teach me too," begged Pang. "How can I climb Gold Mountain without English? A big-shot owner of a Chinese takeout *has* to know English."

"Kwan-Sook is angry with me already," she said,

keeping her voice low. "It will only make matters worse."

"She's not angry with you, she's angry at the world," said Pang. "She's sweet when you get to know her."

Suyin gave him a look of incomprehension. The girl was as sweet as pickle juice!

"I'll think about it," said Suyin, knowing in her heart that she wouldn't be able to refuse him.

Pang grinned at her before racing toward Kwan-Sook. When Kwan-Sook took Pang's arm, Suyin felt a twinge of jealousy. Her feelings toward Pang had changed the night she had confided in him, but since then she tried to keep her distance. His heart was taken.

When they reached the Golden Palace, Pang waved good-bye to everyone. Before he turned to go, his eyes lingered on hers. Suyin's cheeks grew hot. Sharp-eyed Kwan-Sook noticed.

"What are you gawking at, Suyin?" she spat.

Suyin let out a deep sigh. She'd given up on trying to mend things between them. Nothing but Suyin's disappearance would be enough for Kwan-Sook to leave her in peace.

"Trouble ahead," warned Jin.

The door of the Lucky Eight Tea Parlor flew open and three tough-looking teens stepped onto the street. They were dressed alike: tight jeans, black nylon bomber jackets, and white sneakers. Two of the men had spiked hair with streaks of fluorescent orange; the third man was as bald as an egg.

"Look at the stupid fresh-off-the-boats!" cackled the bald man. He whacked a steel bat against the palm of his hand.

"Who are they?" whispered Suyin.

"The fat boy shaped like a steam bun is Fat Wu, Sister Fang-chou's nephew," said Mrs. Chin under her breath. "The tall one is White Tiger—a nasty piece of work. His sidekick is Baldy Chun, baldhead, big muscles, and lychee nuts for brains. They're enforcers for the factory bosses."

"Aiiya," said Mei-li, clinging to her sister's arm. "Here they come."

"What's he doing with the bat?" Wing asked, terrified.

"Threatening us," said Mei-Xia. "They use bats to crush people's kneecaps."

"If you don't pay your debt," said Cousin Jin.

"Or if you're caught stealing," added Mei-Xia.

Baldy Chun stepped in front of them. Fat Wu and White Tiger came up behind them.

"Mr. Lao!" screamed Kwan-Sook.

"Leave the girls alone, boys!" said Lao. "They work for Sister Fang-chou."

When they were out of hearing range, Kwan-Sook huffed. "Don't those lowlifes know Sister pays protection money?"

"They know," said Lao. "They're just looking for trouble."

The balding man took a small stone from his pocket, threw it into the air, and hit it with the bat. The stone landed behind them.

"That's why you stay in a safe house," said Lao, "and why I escort you to work. A garment worker was found in an alley with her throat cut just last week. She tried to run away without paying off her debt."

A week later, Pickpocket Pang stole Lao's calculator. The seamstresses were anxious to find out how long it would take them to pay off their smuggling debts.

After work, the four girls sat on Pang's cot in the safe house and waited to catch a glimpse of their futures.

Before Suyin had left home, Auntie Cho-Ye had given her a quick lesson in the difference between the Chinese yuan and the American dollar. Her auntie had assured her that she'd be making good money in Gold Mountain.

"American dollars have big buying power in China," Auntie Cho-Ye had told her. "Twenty American dollars can pay for a girl's tuition, books, and uniforms for a year. A Cao Hai farmer earns on average the equivalent of one hundred American dollars per year. Whatever you do, don't let the *lao fan* cheat you."

Wing was the luckiest of the four girls because her father had paid half of her smuggling fee up front. If Wing worked hard she might be able to pay off her debt in three years. Kwan-Sook was the fastest seamstress and she was Lao's favorite, so she would probably pay off her debt before Jade. Suyin was worst off because a thread cutter earned so little. At a dollar an hour, it would take her ten or fifteen years to pay off her debt. The weight of this knowledge pressed down on her like a thick black cloud.

Back home, the villagers had thought her lucky. But how could an orphan be lucky? Or a girl who'd been sentenced to a life of drudgery?

As she lay in the darkness of the safe house that night, Wing sang to them. The music swept Suyin away to earlier times, when she and Shan-Shan would dance with the cranes on the shore of the lake. How the two would laugh as they'd mimicked the cranes' dance steps—the whirls and bows and ecstatic leaps. As her eyelids grew heavy with sleep, Suyin realized only now in the starkness of her loneliness, that the fullness in her chest she'd felt as she and Shan-Shan danced, was happiness.

When August came, a heat wave held the city in its grip. At noon, the temperature in the Good Fortune Shop was like an oven. Mrs. Chin joked that she could fry an egg on her sewing machine. Earning so little and performing a job that a trained monkey could do, Suyin felt like a failure. The cranes had saved her life but then they'd disappeared. Would they wait until she was nearly dead to help her?

Jade and Wing tried to teach her to sew, but she found the lessons frustrating.

Stitching was the sum of all her inadequacies, a mirror held up to her in a harsh unyielding light. She also had to put up with Kwan-Sook's mocking smiles as she struggled. This brought back painful memories.

"Where's your *hebao*?" some boys from a neighboring village had once asked her. When she ignored them, one boy taunted, "A Miao girl who can't stitch is as useless as a chicken that can't lay eggs!"

The boy's words had stung her, for they reflected her own feelings. She was useless, a girl without family, an extra mouth to feed. But the men from her village had gotten their just deserts when they'd placed their future in the hands of a bumbler with no talent for stitching.

She would often plead exhaustion, but Jade and Wing were insistent. They were hoping Lao would promote her to seamstress. And Mrs. Chin prodded her as relentlessly as a mother hen.

"You can't make a living as a thread cutter," she'd cluck.

Sometimes Suyin wondered about the boys from the boat. She never saw them, though once she'd caught a glimpse of Xiaoli from a distance. According to Pang, he was working at one of Sister's laundries about six blocks from the Golden Palace.

Lao's roar pulled her from her thoughts. "Sister Fang-chou's here!"

Suyin heard the thump of footsteps in the hallway. She felt her heart ratcheting in her chest. The newcomers would meet the big boss for the first time. She had heard rumors about Sister's ruthlessness, but she also had her admirers.

"Sister Fang-chou started out with nothing," whispered Kwan-Sook. Her voice was filled with awe. "Now she's the richest woman in Chinatown. She's a goddess to me."

When Sister made her entrance, Suyin was disappointed. Her big boss didn't look like a goddess. She was short and stout with a square face, waxen skin, and jowls that flapped when she talked. A hair protruded from a mole on her chin. Despite her swarthy appearance, however, the factory boss was wearing fine clothes. She wore a black silk dress and a red pillbox hat perched upon a nest of freshly permed hair. Two stumpy legs protruded below her dress, spilling over fat ankles that were stuffed like pork hocks into a pair of dainty high-heeled shoes. At first glance, she looked like a chicken masquerading as a swan, but her eyes were cold and unyielding.

"Welcome to Gold Mountain, *yazi*." Sister grinned, revealing a razor-sharp eyetooth on the left side of her mouth. The tooth was sheaved in gold. Pang's words returned to her. "Her friends call her Sister. Her enemies Sharktooth."

A shark baring its teeth, thought Suyin. Vicious, grinning, trolling for minnows.

"We've got a rush order due tomorrow morning," said Sister. "Mr. Lao, make sure that nobody leaves the shop tonight until the order's finished."

"Don't worry, Sister, the order will be ready."

"It's on your head if it isn't," growled Sister.

"More overtime," grumbled Jade.

"More money," smirked Kwan-Sook, rubbing her thumb and index finger together.

Later that day, Suyin turned to see Lao grab Wing by the hair and shake her.

"Useless girl!" screamed Lao. "You stitched the zipper in backward. No wonder your daddy sent you away!"

Wing fought back tears. She was terrified of Lao since he'd threatened to toss her off the boat.

"Your stupid mistake will cost you a day's pay," snarled Lao.

Suyin took a deep breath, trying to calm herself. Her eyes wandered to Lao's wrist. The white string was still in place, but it was frayed and dirty after their time on the boat. How much worse would he treat them if he lost that soul?

As the day wore on, sweat poured down the seamstresses' faces. It was two o'clock in the morning before the seamstresses had finished their work.

"Quitting time," hollered Lao. "Except for you, Fumble Fingers."

Lao pointed to the carts filled with newly stitched garments. "Every loose thread has to be clipped by morning."

Wing clasped Suyin's hand. "Will you be scared here all alone?"

"No," murmured Suyin. "I'll be glad to work without Lao breathing down my neck."

Hearing Lao's keys in the lock, she felt a sense of relief. It was the first opportunity she'd had to practice machine-stitching. She'd watched the seamstresses often enough, so she knew what to do.

After practicing for several hours, she heard the call of a bird outside the shop window. When she opened the sash, her eye caught a shiny object pinned to the sill. It was a needle and a length of thread. At first glance, the silver needle looked like an ordinary shop needle, but on closer look she noticed tiny flecks of gold. An inscription, perhaps, too small for the naked eye? She remembered the peddler who had showed the villagers a landscape engraved on a grain of rice, so she knew that such miniature engravings were possible. Holding a magnifying glass over the needle, Suyin saw the Nu Shu characters. *All women are sisters.*

Her heart pounded with excitement. She grabbed a fabric scrap and pushed the needle through the fabric. With the first stitch, she felt something loosen inside her. The room began to spin. The floor shifted and the sky came crashing down.

9
Crane Meadow

S he found herself in a sun-baked meadow filled with flowers: daisies and thorn-apples and poppies. She was still holding the needle, her knuckles white. The thread scrolled above her, buoyed by a breeze, then it slackened, falling over her shoulders like a shawl.

She stared at the needle in utter amazement. It had catapulted her to He Shan in the blink of an eye.

A short distance away, she spied a circle of cranes stitching in the meadow. The birds clasped their needles firmly between their primary feathers, using their beaks to pull the thread through the fabric. Their movements were precise and delicate.

As she drew closer, she recognized Little Sister and the three black-necked cranes who had rescued her—Grandmother, Li-Wen, and Hazrat. Mulaba the prickly African crane with the golden head fan was there too.

"Come," said Li-Wen, looking up. "We've been expecting you."

Suyin felt relief that the crane sisters had finally summoned her, but resentment that they'd waited so long. All those days on the migrant ship when she'd faced possible death they'd left her to struggle on her own, saving her only at the last possible moment.

"I thought you'd abandoned me," said Suyin. "It's been three months since my first trip to He Shan."

Little Sister piped up, "They saved your life on the boat!"

"That's true," she conceded.

"And your friends' lives too," added Little Sister.

"Hush," said Grandmother, waving the young crane away.

"Please don't think I'm ungrateful," said Suyin. "I know you saved our lives and I thank you from the bottom of my heart. It's just that . . . I wish you had come sooner. My life has been bitter since the day I left my village."

"We know how hard your life is," said Li-Wen sympathetically. "But you have endured. To endure is a girl's greatest lesson. You have shown your mettle . . . despite a few missteps. So today we are going to ask more of you. But first I'm going to tell you a story. It is a story of the Past, Present, and Future."

Suyin drew closer, listening intently.

"After the Dreamtime," said Li-Wen, "the world slowly

changed. It was no longer safe for clanswomen to share our ways. Secrecy weakened the bonds between us, but our queen was the force that connected us to one another and to the natural world. We are part of nature and nature is part of us.

"Since ancient times, a succession of queens has flown near and far to perform sacred ceremonies with each clan. During these ceremonies, we sang the songs of the Old Ones, danced and chanted and prayed until we felt the blood rise in our veins and we were entranced by all we saw and felt—a butterfly's wing, a leaf, a pebble, wondrous and infused with life. We call these ceremonies the Mysteries because we remember little afterward except our joy and deep sense of peace and harmony with the world."

Suyin hugged her knees, completely enchanted. She couldn't wait to have a place among the sisters so she could meet the wonderful queen and feel the joy the sisters felt.

"As the earth renews itself each spring," continued Li-Wen, "so we too must renew our transformative power. The source of this power lies in nature itself. It also springs from the collective energy of the sisterhood. Our task has always been to bring peace and harmony to the world. Sometimes our challenges have seemed insurmountable—war, famine, and insatiable greed have taken a terrible toll, but we have carried on, undaunted . . . until several years ago when we lost our beloved queen. Without the queen to perform the Mysteries each year, human beings have become more and more disconnected from the earth. In their quest for riches, people are destroying the water, the forests, and the air that sustains them. The earth has grown warmer—drought, fire, flooding, and a melting icecap plays havoc with the land. Lacking the queen's steadying guidance, the sisterhood itself has begun to fall apart. We are beset with conflict and petty rivalries."

"Where is the queen?" asked Suyin.

"She is in the Gray World," replied Li-Wen. "It is a terrible place between earth and the Lower World. There is nothing there but the dark and cold, and time stretches on forever. Without our queen, our transformative power grows weaker with each passing year. Soon our kind may be no more."

Suyin felt the hair on her neck stand up. "What do you mean?"

Li-Wen's voice dropped to a whisper. "Extinction. We'll no longer be able to change our shape. He Shan will be a distant memory of a dream. And our hope that one day the earth will be a peaceful and harmonious place will be forever dashed."

Suyin felt her blood run cold. Extinction was forever.

"Maybe you or Hazrat could perform the Mysteries," suggested Suyin.

Li-Wen shook her head. "Only the queen has this knowledge, and she passes it on to her successor through a long and intense apprenticeship. We have tried to remember the words to the chants, the dance steps, and the prayers, to no avail. According to the scripture of the ancient queens, we are *meant* to forget. This was to protect our secrets, but in the end, it may destroy us. That is the story of the Past. The Present involves you."

"Me?"

"Yes. You are the only one who can save the queen."

Suyin blanched. "But I'm just a girl."

"We have always known you were special," said Li-Wen. "Your connection to nature runs deep. You love birds. You have the gift of languages. And your mother was a brilliant embroideress. But we had to wait until you came of age. When you risked your life to save Little Sister, and then chose the heart feather, we were certain."

"You are An-Lan's daughter," added Grandmother. "Stitchery is in your blood."

Suyin's confusion returned. "What does stitchery have to do with saving the queen?"

"Everything!" croaked Grandmother. "You can't fly to the Gray World until you transform. And you can't transform until you are able to communicate through your skill and knowledge of embroidery!"

"But embroidery is not enough," warned Li-Wen. "You still have to follow the call of your feather." The crane's eyes darkened. "And if you transform before you've proven yourself, there will be grave repercussions on earth as well as He Shan. Humans are communal beings. The loss of one life affects all of us."

Suyin felt the weight of the cranes' need and with it a strange dread.

"You've told me of the Past and the Present," said Suyin. "What of the Future?"

"The Future is in your hands," said Li-Wen solemnly. "But our time is running out."

"Has anyone tried to save the queen?" asked Suyin.

"Several sisters tried and failed," said Hazrat sadly.

"They sacrificed their lives," said Mulaba bitterly, "to attempt the impossible."

Suyin froze with fear. The cranes were asking her to risk her life.

"Some of us believe it's possible, Mulaba," said Hazrat gently.

"And some of us don't," snapped Mulaba.

Reeling from the cranes' revelations, Suyin trembled. The needle fell from her fingers, but she quickly caught it.

"Whose needle is this?" she asked.

"It was your mother's," said Li-Wen quietly.

"I thought my mother's needles were in Grandfather's house," said Suyin, puzzled.

"Your mother's *ordinary* needles are there," said Li-Wen. "That needle is special. It is yours to keep."

For a moment she imagined her mother's long delicate fingers moving the needle in and out of the fabric. She imagined herself stitching beside her mother, the most famous embroideress in all of China.

"The inscription on the needle is in Nu Shu."

"All women are sisters," said Li-Wen. "It's a lovely idea, isn't it—that all women across time and distance are connected."

"So my mother must have belonged to the clan."

"Yes," said Li-Wen.

"And she must have known Nu Shu."

The cranes nodded.

"Do you all know Nu Shu?"

"Only the Chinese cranes," replied Mulaba. "Over centuries each clan developed its own secret communication through the needle arts. Each has its own symbols, though the same symbols might mean different things to different clans."

"How did my mother die?" said Suyin.

Little Sister looked alarmed. She pressed her beak against Suyin's ear.

"Hush, sister. The clan looks down on such questions. A girl who breaks that unwritten law is considered weak or . . . immature."

Suyin ignored the crane. "Why can't I ask about my mother? I'm her daughter."

"Birds live in the present," explained Hazrat. "To speak of our lives on earth is to speak of the Past and Future. Bird life is beautiful because we are at one with all living things—a blade of grass, a daisy, a brook." Hazrat's eyes grew sad. "At least we used to be . . . before we lost our queen. You won't understand this, Suyin, until you become a fully fledged member of the clan."

Suyin felt the gulf between her and the cranes slowly widening.

"At least tell me who put the needle on the windowsill," she pleaded.

"I did," answered Little Sister boldly. "I thought you needed some help to get started."

"Thank you," said Suyin, grateful for an ally. If Mulaba was the most guarded of the flock, Little Sister was the least. Maybe Little Sister was trying to repay her for saving her life in the fen. Or maybe it was simply the crane's nature to speak her mind.

"You seem reluctant to learn," said Mulaba.

"I've been trying," said Suyin defensively.

"Halfheartedly," said Mulaba.

It was true she'd been reluctant, but every time Jade or Wing tried to teach her, she became overwhelmed at the task that lay ahead. A Miao girl started stitching at four or five years old. At thirteen, how could she ever catch up? How could she ever hope to become anything but a mediocre embroideress like that slow-witted girl who lived in the village next to hers. People complimented the poor girl's embroidery out of pity.

The mere sight of a needle brought back painful memories: the dread of festival days when she'd had to watch her friends show off their elaborately embroidered dresses. Among the women, patterns and stitches seemed the only subjects of the day. The cranes had no idea how inadequate she felt.

"Wake up, Grandmother," prodded Mulaba.

Grandmother's eyes flew open. "Nothing like a short nap to refresh an old bird. Come closer, Suyin." The old crane pointed to a tapestry she'd been stitching. "See these motifs?"

Suyin recognized the familiarity of the shapes: squares, circles, whirlpools, diamonds, and ellipses outlined by straight and wavy lines.

"Each symbol has more than one meaning," explained Grandmother. "A centipede means happiness for a grand-child, but it could also mean working on a farm or setting up house. If one symbol is combined with another, the meaning changes. A spiral pattern means good fortune, but three spirals could mean three cranes, the triple god-desses, or Mother Nature."

"That's confusing," said Suyin.

"It was *meant* to be," said Grandmother. "Each clan has its own tricks and ruses. It's our way of hiding the sacred."

Suyin pictured a ball of tangled yarn, one that could only be unraveled by unwinding and tugging at it a little at a time.

"So let us begin your apprenticeship," said Grand-mother. "The magic needle will make it easier."

"Teach her the seed stitch first, Grandmother," said Mulaba, hovering over the old crane's wing. The gray crowned crane was stitching a tapestry that was bold in design and color. She used a large blunt needle and brightly colored yarns.

"What are you stitching, Mulaba?" Suyin asked.

"Africa," said Mulaba, pulling the yarn through with her beak. "Yellow for the desert, ochre for the earth, black for the night sky."

"It's beautiful," said Suyin. She wondered why Mulaba stitched alongside the black-necked cranes. Africa was so far from China and though Mulaba's needlework was gorgeous, it bore little resemblance to the delicacy of the Chinese embroidery. She wondered if the crane was acting as a gatekeeper, to ensure the secrets of the clan were guarded from new initiates like her.

As if answering Suyin's thoughts, Hazrat whispered in Suyin's ear.

"Mulaba's taken a special interest in you. She's trying to discourage you from going to the Gray World."

Under Grandmother's guidance, Suyin learned how to loop skeins of gold filigree between her hands, separating the threads into strands as fine as hair. Using a fabric scrap to practice, she learned how to wrap a single strand of fine silk around her magic needle, then stitch it down. She was fascinated by the way the cranes grasped their needles between their pinions or the claws on their toes, how they pushed their needles through the fabric with their beaks or the shafts of their feathers.

Her mother's needle seemed to move of its own accord. And her fingers felt more nimble.

"Some people call the seed stitch the forbidden stitch," said Li-Wen, "because young girls could go blind with eyestrain. But the Chinese knot and Peking knot can be equally fine and do similar harm. Yet each of these stitches can be used to create works of great beauty."

When Suyin mastered the seed stitch, the cranes took turns demonstrating the cross-stitch, the rice stitch, and the chain stitch.

Hazrat's pale green eyes were warm and strangely familiar. From the first time they'd met, Suyin felt the crane was a friend, a bird who might trust her enough to share a secret.

"Who decides when a girl is worthy?" Suyin asked.

"Who tells a fish when to swim to the sea?" mused Hazrat. "Or a star when to fall? Something unfathomable in nature. Beyond our understanding. Destiny, perhaps, or Fate." Suddenly Hazrat's eyes lit up. "I know what you need! An embroidery sampler. It's a record of each stitch, something for you to copy. It's perfect for a beginner."

The black-necked crane chose a square of fine white linen and a variety of colored embroidery thread. She used a different colored thread to stitch each row.

"Yellow for the fly stitches, blue for the chain, red for the seed, and green for the cross-stitches," said Hazrat. When she had finished stitching the fourth row, Grandmother snatched the sampler.

"I think you need more of a challenge," said the old crane. Tiny feathers floated in the air as the crane stitched. Her rheumy eyes sparkled with an inner light so the crane suddenly seemed young.

"I stitched a missive in the last row," said Grandmother triumphantly.

Suyin looked. "Where?"

"It's hidden in plain sight."

Suyin furrowed her brow. "I don't understand."

Grandmother chortled. "You'll find the answer in the sampler."

But Suyin couldn't see it. She saw elegant stitching and a lovely pattern, but no message.

"Study it long and hard and it will come to you," said Grandmother.

When Suyin's eyelids felt heavy, Li-Wen tapped her on the shoulder.

"It's time to leave."

"Could I use the magic needle to transport me to He Shan?" asked Suyin. "I need more embroidery lessons."

Li-Wen hesitated before answering. "Only if you're alone."

"But I'm hardly ever left alone," protested Suyin.

"Then you must wait. No one outside the clan must see you."

Suyin clutched the needle and the sampler and squeezed her eyes shut.

"Take a deep breath," said Hazrat.

And suddenly she felt as light as the heart feather circling her neck.

*   *   *

A dull throb moved along her temple. Her mind was racing. Her mother had belonged to the sisterhood. The clan had lost their queen. But even more disturbing was the cranes' expectations and their sense of urgency. She had so much to accomplish and so little time.

She began to pace. She had hoped that the cranes might reveal the circumstances of her mother's death, but they had been guarded. Perhaps when she earned her wings, she would be privy to their secrets. Her father still remained a shadowy figure.

She glanced at the clock, suddenly aware of her fatigue. It was five thirty. Dawn would be breaking soon. She had four carts of garments to clip. If she took a very short nap, she could still be finished with her work before seven o'clock when Lao opened the shop. She made a nest of scraps on the floor and sank into it. Within moments, she slipped into an exhausted sleep.

Mrs. Chin pulled at her sleeve. "Wake up! Lao's here."

Suyin leaped to her feet, blinking into the light streaming through the window. Panic gripped her.

"These threads are not clipped!" roared Lao. "The order is due this morning."

He grabbed her arm and dragged her into the hallway, where a girl's screams wouldn't disrupt production.

"Don't resist," Cousin Jin had warned her, "or you'll be beaten worse."

"You are a useless worker!" he screamed, digging a knee into her stomach. "Lazy! A bad element!"

"I'm sorry, Mr. Lao," she blubbered, praying he would have mercy on her. "I fell asleep."

He kicked her. She crumpled to the floor.

"Stand up, you lazy lump of coal! You need to be taught a lesson." He smacked her across the mouth. His jade ring broke open her skin. Blood trickled into her throat.

She tried to be brave, but when Lao loosened his belt, she ran from him. He caught her in a corner and began whipping her legs and bottom with his belt, places where her bruises would be hidden by her clothes. When the blows finally stopped, sweat poured off Lao's brow.

"Wipe the blood off your face," he snapped, and pulled her back to the sewing room by the ear.

"Stop the machines, workers!" he screamed. "The Good Fortune Shop has missed a production deadline, thanks to Miss Country Bumpkin. You will all suffer for her laziness. Every worker will be docked a full day's pay." He grabbed her ear and gave it a sharp twist. "And this bad apple will lose two!"

"Mr. Lao, please don't punish the others," begged Suyin.

"She's right," snapped Kwan-Sook. "Why should we be punished for her laziness?" A triumphant smile crossed her face. "*This* is why she didn't get her work done." Snatching Suyin's embroidery sample, she waved it in the air like a flag. "She's been playing instead of clipping threads."

Lao's eyes glittered with malice. "Is this true?"

"Yes," admitted Suyin, staring at her shoes.

Lao snatched the sampler and tossed it across the room. It landed at the feet of the most elegant woman Suyin had ever seen in her life.

10
Mrs. Tang

The scent of ylang ylang blossoms filled the air of the shop.

"I hope I didn't startle you, Mr. Lao," said the woman in Cantonese. "I found the door unlocked. I'm Helen Tang. Sister wanted to talk to me about the Chinese Benevolent Association. Is she in?"

Lao looked flustered. His face turned red. "No. She's at one of her other shops."

Suyin stared at the woman, mesmerized. The woman's perfume reminded Suyin of the flowering tree growing by Auntie Dou's house. The woman was tall and slender, with large eyes lined with kohl. She had a long neck and broad mouth. Her blue-black hair was pulled back from her face into a shiny knot at her nape. She was wearing a black silk *cheongsam*, a traditional Chinese dress with a high collar and a swirl of embroidered pink flowers scattered along the midline.

"Please give her my card and thank her for her interest in our charity," said Mrs. Tang.

Bending down, Mrs. Tang picked up the embroidery sampler.

"This is very interesting. Whose work is it?"

"Fumble Fingers," sneered Lao, pointing to Suyin. Her cheeks were hot with embarrassment.

"I'm sure that's not her real name, Mr. Lao," said Mrs. Tang.

When Suyin looked at Mrs. Tang, she thought of beautiful things—pink peonies in porcelain vases and pale yellow butterflies lighting on the leaves of a mulberry tree and swaying grasses on Cao Hai Lake.

"What *is* your name?" asked Mrs. Tang.

"Suyin."

"Hello, Suyin," said Mrs. Tang, offering her hand. "I'm Helen Tang. Where did you learn to embroider like this?"

Suyin tried to think fast. The work wasn't hers. But she couldn't say that two cranes had stitched it!

"My relatives taught me."

Not exactly a lie.

"I thought this kind of needlework a lost art," said Mrs. Tang. "Where are your people from?"

"From Cao Hai Village in Guizhou province," replied Suyin. "My mother was Miao. My father Han."

Mrs. Tang smiled broadly. "Ah! That explains it. Miao

minority women are famous for their embroidery." She opened her handbag, removed a brochure, and placed it on the sewing table. "That's my store."

"Tang's House of Fashion," read Suyin in English. "Helen Tang, proprietor."

Mrs. Tang looked surprised. She switched from Cantonese to English. "So you can read. And speak English too?"

Suyin nodded. "Yes." Mrs. Tang contemplated Suyin for a long moment, and then went on.

"There's a market for high-quality embroidered items," Mrs. Tang told her. "These are hand-sewn one-of-a-kind orders. Would you be interested in doing some embroidery for me? I'll pay you for each piece you stitch."

An embroideress! A step up in the world! Suyin nodded hard. She couldn't believe how her luck had changed. From a beating to a promotion!

"She'll have to go through me," interjected Lao. "I'm the girl's agent."

Suyin's smile faded.

"Well, then, Mr. Lao," said Mrs. Tang, raising an eyebrow. "I'll need your assurance that all of her work will be sold to me on an exclusive basis."

"I'm sure we can negotiate a financial arrangement mutually pleasing to both of us," said Lao.

"And to Suyin too," added Mrs. Tang.

"Why don't we talk in my office, Mrs. Tang," said Lao smoothly. "I can draw up a contract before you leave."

"Excellent, Mr. Lao," said Mrs. Tang. "I'll be out of the country for a month, Suyin, but I'll stop by the shop at the end of September. I'll bring some fabric and embroidery thread." She gave Suyin a questioning look. "You speak English without an accent."

"I pick up languages easily, Mrs. Tang."

"She can speak lots of languages," piped up Jade.

"Mandarin too?"

"Yes, Mrs. Tang," replied Suyin.

"You studied languages in school?"

"No, Mrs. Tang. The words just come to me."

Mrs. Tang met Suyin's eyes. "How do you explain that?"

"It's a gift I was born with."

"You're a clever girl, aren't you," said Mrs. Tang in perfect Mandarin.

Suyin felt her cheeks grow hot. "Thank you, Mrs. Tang," she said miserably. Slowly it dawned on her that she wasn't clever at all. Unwittingly, she had backed herself into a corner. She had lied to the lady and in a month's time she would have to face her. In the meantime, she couldn't ask Jade or Wing for help because Kwan-Sook would see through her lie and tell Lao, and if Lao found out, he might fire her. What had she done?

"Mrs. Tang knows nothing about piecework," said Mrs. Chin. "She's not a buyer. She's a big-shot owner. That old swindler will bleed her dry. You too, if you're not careful."

"Kwan-Sook!" barked Lao. "Help Suyin cut threads for that order."

When Lao had left the sewing room, Kwan-Sook rose from her chair, grasped an armful of garments, and threw them into Suyin's lap.

"I'm not a thread cutter!" said Kwan-Sook with disgust. "I work my fingers to the bone to get ahead while you waste your time with silliness. I'm . . . not . . . helping . . . you!" Kwan-Sook wagged her finger. "You pulled the wool over that rich lady's eyes, but you don't fool me. Yesterday you could barely stitch a hem and today you're an expert? But you won't get away with your trickery. Mark my words. Your fortune will turn as bitter as yellow root."

Despite her guilt about lying, Suyin was enchanted with Mrs. Tang. She admired her beauty and sophistication. She admired her stylish clothes and her graceful walk. She admired the way she wore her hair, swept back in a knot at her neck like the pictures she'd seen of ancient Chinese empresses. Suyin wanted to be just like her.

Later that afternoon, Lao bellowed, "Bathroom break! Two minutes each. A second more and you'll be docked a half day's pay."

Suyin sighed with relief. It had been six hours since their break. A line formed outside the bathroom. Kwan-Sook got there first, as usual, tapping her foot impatiently while Lao fumbled with the padlock.

Wing was bent over, crossing her legs.

"Take my spot," offered Suyin. She tapped Kwan-Sook on the shoulder. "Do you mind if Wing goes first? She can't wait."

"First come, first served," snarled Kwan-Sook, slamming the bathroom door.

Jade was furious. "That's not fair! Why should you always go first?"

"Shut up, ugly," yelled Kwan-Sook from inside.

Jade gave the door a kick.

At exactly one minute and fifty-nine seconds, Kwan-Sook flung open the bathroom door and elbowed Jade as she passed.

"Excuse me," she cackled.

"Everyone hates you," spat Jade.

"Your eyes are red with envy," sneered Kwan-Sook. "I'm the fastest seamstress in the shop and you know it."

That was true. Kwan-Sook never stopped to daydream. She never stopped to gossip when Lao went out to eat dim sum. She never told a silly joke or laughed. And though Suyin didn't like her, she held a grudging admiration for how hard she worked.

As she stitched in the dim light of the safe house, a deep cloud of melancholy fell over her. She longed to escape her life of drudgery. If she had wings, she would fly to He Shan and leave her life on earth, maybe forever. Sometimes she wished she'd chosen a different kind of feather, a tail feather like Hazrat or a wing feather like Grandmother. Then all she'd have to do would be to think before she acted or search for a rainbow in the rain.

Her only comfort was her mother's special needle. The

needle was as fine a teacher as the cranes themselves. If she made a mistake (perhaps she twisted the thread the wrong way or dropped a stitch) the needle seemed to sense it and an almost imperceptible vibration flowed through the needle into her fingers. It was as if her mother were sitting beside her, saying *wrong turn* or *loose thread* or *that is a fine row of stitches, daughter.*

Across the room Jade, Wing, and Kwan-Sook were stitching baby bibs for a friend of Lao's, a merchant who had a children's-wear store on Broadway. It was a way of earning extra pocket money.

Suyin had slipped the sampler under a fold of her blanket so Kwan-Sook's sharp eyes couldn't see that she was copying. She quickly studied the final row. What on earth did Grandmother mean by "hidden in plain sight"? She hoped the old crane hadn't played a joke on her.

Later, Wing and Jade curled up on Suyin's cot.

"Your embroidery is beautiful," said Wing.

"You've made amazing progress," added Jade. "Let me have a look."

Reluctantly, Suyin handed her practice piece to her friends.

"Suyin," gushed Jade. "This is almost . . . miraculous!" Leaning over, Jade planted a kiss on Suyin's cheek. "I'm so happy for you."

"That's not a shop needle, is it?" Wing asked. "It's got tiny gold flecks on it."

Kwan-Sook's head shot up. Suyin could feel the girl's eyes boring into her from across the room.

Suyin lowered her voice. "No, it belonged to my mother."

"You never mentioned it before," said Wing, her curiosity piqued. "May I hold it?"

Reluctantly she placed it in Wing's palm. Suyin felt possessive about the needle. She didn't want to share it.

"It feels strange and mysterious," said Wing, lowering her voice. "Does it help you stitch better?"

Suyin nodded. She placed her forefinger over her mouth. "Don't tell anyone."

From the corner of her eye, Suyin saw Kwan-Sook creep softly across the room. A weasel after a rabbit. Suyin hid the sampler.

Kwan-Sook pointed to Suyin's practice piece. "That's not your work."

"Stop bothering me, Kwan-Sook," growled Suyin irritably, waving the girl off with her hand.

"It's hers," said Jade, defending her. "I saw her stitch it."

"So did I," said Wing.

"You're both fools if you believe her tricks," said Kwan-Sook.

"If Suyin didn't do it, who did?" demanded Jade.

"Don't argue with her, Jade," Suyin said under her breath. Jade always spoke her mind, even if the person she was speaking to refused to listen. Jade and Shan-Shan were alike that way.

Kwan-Sook drummed her fingers over her lips. "Maybe . . ." A sly look crossed her face. "Maybe . . . those crane birds she's always going on about did the stitching? Or the sparrows in the park?" Kwan-Sook began to laugh. "Her people called her the crane wife's daughter."

Suyin rose from her cot, her eyes blazing. "That's a lie."

"Ask Lao if you don't believe me," said Kwan-Sook.

From across the room, Kwan-Sook yelled, "It's only a matter of time until Mrs. Tang finds out you're a fraud!"

11

Sister Fang-chou

By mid-September, the air had turned damp and chilly. The songbirds flew south and the leaves on the maple trees turned color. The maple tree was sacred to the Miao people because Butterfly Mother emerged from the maple to lay her twelve eggs. When the leaves on the maple faded, Suyin saw her hopes for a bright future in Gold Mountain fade too. Lao had lied to them. They were drowning in debt.

Sometimes Suyin checked her wrist to see if her natal feather had sprouted. She was trying to open her heart to people, even to Kwan-Sook. She complimented the girl on her work and shared a bag of sugar-glazed ginger with her. Kwan-Sook grudgingly accepted the sweets. But when she tried to persuade Kwan-Sook to join her English class, her efforts backfired. Kwan-Sook gave Pang an ultimatum.

"Choose," she said, folding her arms. "English class with *her*—or me."

"Kwan-Sook, be reasonable," said Pang. "I need English to climb Gold Mountain."

Kwan-Sook stormed ahead and Pang trailed after her.

Jade frowned, shaking her head.

"I've tried to be nice to her," Suyin said.

"She's jealous," said Jade. "It drives her crazy that Pang likes you."

"We're just friends," said Suyin.

Jade smiled. "You're blushing."

Suyin shrugged. "He's taken, Jade. Kwan-Sook will never release her grip on him."

Over the next few weeks, Pang continued to take English lessons and Kwan-Sook continued to sulk. Pang bought Kwan-Sook a bag of lychee nuts from Mr. Ng's groceteria to placate her. She dropped his offering on his toes. When Pang shared the lychees with the seamstresses, Kwan-Sook burst into tears. Suyin watched Pang put his arm around her and the two made up. In the battle of wills, Kwan-Sook had lost, but she blamed everyone but Pang.

Suyin had mixed feelings about Pang's devotion to the girl. He was either foolish or pure of heart. Or maybe both. When Pang bought Kwan-Sook the pretty jade necklace she'd been admiring in the shop window, Kwan-Sook threw her arms around him.

"You have my heart, Pang-Pang," she said. Kwan-

Sook's eyes shone with happiness as Pang placed the necklace against the scar circling her neck. Under Pang's gaze Kwan-Sook seemed tenderhearted, like a hurt child seeking refuge in the only person in the world she trusted.

Suyin's heart softened toward the girl. Kwan-Sook's life had been harder than hers. Suyin's aunties had cared for her. They had fed her turnip cakes and mango pudding. Her village had paid for her schooling. She had Shan-Shan too. The two girls were like blood sisters. They would often lie awake all night talking, sharing their secret hopes and dreams. But Kwan-Sook had no one, until Pang.

Later when Suyin asked Pang if Kwan-Sook was his girlfriend, he looked surprised.

"No. She's my adopted sister. We're family. She thinks I'm going to abandon her because everyone else in her life has, but I never will. I promised I would never leave her. If I broke my word, she would have nothing left to believe in."

Now she understood the depth of the bond between them. Pang was imprisoned by Kwan-Sook's need. Only a hard-hearted girl would argue with a boy's loyalty to family.

One morning as Suyin talked to a little sparrow, Mrs. Chin's eyebrows shot up.

"You remind me of the queen of the birds, Suyin. I've forgotten how the story goes, but the queen could speak to birds like you. She could change her shape too. From a woman to a bird."

Suyin sat riveted to her chair. Did Mrs. Chin belong to the sisterhood? But that made no sense; the sisterhood was a *secret* society. Their members didn't go around blabbing their history to seamstresses in garment factories.

Just to be sure, however, Suyin asked Mrs. Chin if she wore a feather. The old lady looked at her blankly.

"Why on earth would I wear a feather?"

As the day wore on, Suyin pondered Mrs. Chin's words. The queen in Mrs. Chin's story could speak Bird like Suyin and her mother; she could also change her shape. Suddenly a crazy thought struck her. The villagers had found her father's body, but her mother's had never been recovered. What if her mother hadn't died, but she was stuck in the Gray World? What if her very own mother were the queen? Wishful thinking, she told herself; her mother was dead. And yet, a tiny grain of hope began to grow inside her.

The following morning, when Lao ushered a frightened-looking Wing into his office, the seamstresses were on tenterhooks. Was Lao going to fire her? But when Wing returned to work, she was smiling. Suyin felt relieved to see Wing's spirits lift. Wing hadn't smiled in weeks.

"I got a letter from my father today," she said, pressing the letter against her chest. "Lao read it first, but that doesn't matter."

"What did your father write?" asked Suyin.

"He said my mother missed me. He asked me if I enjoyed my voyage on the cruise ship."

"Are you going to tell him what happened?" asked Jade.

"No," said Wing. "I can't tell him the truth. He asked if I'd started working yet and if I'd gotten paid."

"One more week," said Suyin.

"I don't know why we have to wait three months for our first pay," grumbled Jade. "That doesn't seem right."

"The sooner I can pay off my debt, the sooner I can start saving to go home," said Wing fiercely.

"You're lucky to hear from home, Wing," said Jade wistfully. "I don't expect any letters. My parents don't know how to read or write."

Suyin was glad for Wing, but watching her friend hugging the letter from home made her aware of her own lack. Shan-Shan or Teacher Zhang could have written to her in English. Her aunties could have written in Nu Shu. Shan-Shan could have addressed her aunties' envelopes. They could have found a way. Didn't they realize how lonely she was? She felt angry toward her people and then guilty. She felt worried too. Mrs. Tang would soon be bringing embroidery supplies to the shop. Suyin was desperate for more lessons, but Lao had refused to leave her alone in the shop. On two occasions, she'd offered to stay behind to complete an order, but Lao became suspicious. If he thought you wanted something, he would refuse to give it to you on principle.

＊　　＊　　＊

As September came to an end, the seamstresses were beside themselves with excitement. After three months of living off tea money, three dollars a day, Sister was coming to the shop to pay their wages. When Mrs. Tang appeared that morning, Lao seemed surprised.

"I thought you were coming next week," he told her rudely.

"I just got back from my trip," replied Mrs. Tang. She smiled at Lao politely, despite his lack of manners. "I came to talk to that little girl about her embroidery. Suyin's her name, I think. Ah, there she is!"

Suyin felt butterflies in her stomach.

As Mrs. Tang crossed the floor of the shop, trailing the scent of ylang ylang, the staff stopped their work to stare. She looked like a film star in her jade-green silk pantsuit with the delicately embroidered scarf.

"Back to work," said Lao peevishly, giving Wing a quick slap on the head. Mrs. Tang's unexpected visit seemed to unnerve him. He paced up and down the shop, glancing anxiously at the door.

"Lao's acting strange," said Jade in a half whisper.

Mrs. Tang smiled at Suyin, opened her handbag, and took out two squares of black silk, two silk scarves, embroidery thread, and a large spool of gold filament.

Suyin's eyes widened. The silk alone would have cost a fortune back home, not to mention the embroidery thread and gold filament. Her Cao Hai aunties would have been overjoyed to work with such fine materials. Staring at the richness before her, Suyin felt a mixture of nervousness and pleasure.

"I'd like you to embroider two Mandarin squares to adorn a silk jacket."

Suyin looked puzzled. "Mandarin squares?"

"Rank badges," said Mrs. Tang.

Suyin had no idea what Mrs. Tang meant. She felt Lao's gaze on her. She longed to confess to Mrs. Tang, plead for her forgiveness, but she lacked the courage.

"The badges are an ancient tradition, dating back to the Ming Dynasty," explained Mrs. Tang. "Miao women embroidered the badges for the court. The badges were usually couched in gold filament. Cranes represent the highest rank, so I'd like you to stitch a crane on each square. When the squares are completed, they'll be stitched on either side of a lovely silk jacket."

Mrs. Tang's eyes met hers. "Are you up to such a task?"

"Yes, Mrs. Tang," said Suyin in a small voice, though she doubted this to be true, not even with the help of her special needle.

"A plain silk scarf or a shawl won't sell for much on its own," said Mrs. Tang. "They are mass-produced factory items. These are special orders. It will be the artistry of your embroidery that will make the items valuable. Feel free to create your own designs." Mrs. Tang smiled warmly. "I'll pick up your piecework the first week in November, so you'll have five weeks to complete them. My standards are high, but after seeing your sampler I'm certain you'll do an excellent job."

When Mrs. Tang left, Suyin felt overwhelmed. Five weeks? It was impossible. She was a beginner. If only she could fly to He Shan for more embroidery lessons, but she'd had no opportunity to be alone. She threaded her special needle and began to embroider a line of seed stitches. She had barely finished the first row when Lao came flying across the shop, waving his arms. He grabbed a pile of shirts from a nearby cart and without warning, dumped them on Suyin's stitching.

"Sister just arrived!" he growled, thrusting a pair of shop scissors into her hand. "Start clipping. Now."

Lao is acting like a scared chicken around Sister, thought Suyin.

In the hallway, she could hear Sister greeting Mrs. Tang, inviting her to stay for tea and Mrs. Tang begging off.

"Mr. Tang is waiting for me downstairs," said Mrs. Tang.

"It's payday, staff," boomed Sister, stumping across the floor. Her sharp gold tooth glittered in the light. "I'll call each of you into my office to settle up. You'll go first," she said, pointing a sausage finger at Suyin. "The rest of you return to work."

Suyin's knees felt weak as she followed Sister to Lao's office. Sister slid a thick pile of forms across the desk.

"First things first," said Sister. A single hair on her chin swayed as she spoke. "Sign each sheet at the bottom, please. I'll fill in the rest."

At the top of each form were the words *The Department of Labor*. There were columns for dates and numbers of hours worked and a separate column for overtime. The forms were blank. When Suyin had finished signing them, Sister opened her ledger.

"I've been having some cash flow problems lately," said Sister Fang-chou, tapping her nails on her desk. "Nothing to worry about. I owe you three months' pay. July, August, and September, but I'm only paying you for July and August. Not to worry. You'll receive two months' pay at the end of October."

Suyin nodded.

Sister made several quick calculations, then reached into her briefcase and laid out a line of bills on her desk. Three twenty-dollar bills and two tens. Eighty dollars.

"But Sister—"

Sister's eyes narrowed. "Yes?"

"By my calculations, I earned five hundred and sixty dollars in the last two months," said Suyin in a small voice.

Sister laughed uproariously. "You stupid girl. Do you think I'm running a charity? You owe me money for rent, food, heat, and electricity. Half your wages go toward your debt, plus interest. Minus the days you lost for missing a rush order and the cost of a ruined gown. That leaves you eighty dollars."

Sister pushed the bills toward her with her stubby fingers.

"As you can see, *yazi,* New York is a very expensive city."

Suyin's eyes welled up. *What a fool she'd been.* Her situation was far worse than she thought. Her village had paid Lao one thousand American dollars for her passage to Gold Mountain, a fortune for a village so poor, but a drop in the bucket when she owed fifty thousand. Now she owed forty-eight thousand, nine hundred and twenty dollars.

"I'm going to send the money home," said Suyin. *Eighty dollars would buy rice and corn and a load of coal. It was less than she'd expected, but it was something.*

Sister gave her a sly look. "I'll ask Lao to arrange it for you."

"I thought I would send the money in the mail," she said.

"Not on your life!" boomed Sister, rising on her shanks. "There'll be no international money trails for the INS to sniff out! One of my men there will hand-deliver the money to your village chief. Lao will make the arrangements. Didn't he explain that to you?"

"Maybe," she said. Lao hadn't, but she'd rather take the blame herself than face Lao's fury.

She turned to go.

"There's a charge for home delivery and Lao has to be paid for his trouble. Eighty dollars minus twenty for the shipping fee." Sister Fang-chou stuck out her hand.

"But—"

Sister's eyes hardened. "You don't think the service is free, do you?"

Suyin slowly shook her head. She could feel tiny droplets of sweat clinging to her neck, but she pressed on.

"If you don't mind, Sister," she said. "I'd like . . . I'd like to save my money, then send it home later in a larger amount."

"Why?" Sister demanded.

Suyin felt the last of her confidence drain away. "So I can save money on the shipping fee."

Sister Fang-chou's eyebrows shot up. "You won't save a penny! The shipping fee's a *percentage* of your earnings." As Sister spoke, Suyin could see her boss's gold tooth glittering in the black maw of her mouth. She imagined the sharp jaws of a shark biting into her flesh as Sister opened her palm.

Suyin stared at her, her hopes dashed. She placed a twenty in Sister's hand and turned on her heels, unwilling to let that loathsome woman see her cry. Maybe Sister wouldn't send her earnings to her people at all. Neither Lao nor Sister seemed trustworthy. But what choice did she have?

How could her people have gotten her into such a terrible mess? Gold Mountain was a lie, a trap to catch foolish girls and turn them into slaves. Her debt was the mountain and it wasn't gold. It was her grave.

When Sister left the shop, Lao lectured the staff for wasting valuable time gawking at Mrs. Tang.

"As for you," he sneered, fixing his stare on Suyin, "*I'm* your manager, not *Big Shot Tang*, and until you've clipped every loose thread in this shop, you won't be embroidering birds on badges."

"Yes, sir," she said. "I was wondering if you would you give me a chance to machine-stitch. I know I can do it."

Lao gave a low snort. "You're a thread cutter, not a seamstress. You and Mrs. High-and-Mighty Tang have cost this shop enough time and money. Now get back to work."

Somewhere above the fractured din of the city, Suyin heard the ecstatic honks of the geese on their way to sunnier climes. The cranes would be migrating too—fifteen species winging their way from one part of the world to another. Suyin stared out the window, hiding her disappointment in flying dreams.

Mrs. Chin gave Suyin a poke with her cane. "Forget about the past."

Suyin started. "What do you mean?"

"Stop moping. You're spending too much time daydreaming about home," scolded Mrs. Chin. "Face the truth. You'll never set foot in your village again."

"That's cruel, Mrs. Chin."

"It's not cruel, it's reality," said Mrs. Chin, her voice softening. "You're illegal. The only way you'll return home is in the hold of a smuggler's boat."

Suyin closed her eyes against the truth. Mrs. Chin was right. She had no papers and she was too poor to buy them. And she would rather die in Gold Mountain than return home in a smuggler's boat.

Kwan-Sook's ears pricked up. "If your people cared about you, you would have heard from them by now."

"Mind your own business," spat Suyin.

"The mail is slow," said Jade sympathetically. "Sometimes letters get lost."

But the truth stared her in the face. Her people *hadn't* written. Even her best friend hadn't written.

That night she dreamed that Auntie Huishan had brought a matchmaker to the village. Shan-Shan didn't want to be married so young, but her father had insisted. Shan-Shan was leaving the village to stay with her in-laws. The dream was sad. Shan-Shan and she were both crying because they knew they would never see each other again.

12
A Secret Revealed

My needle's missing!" Suyin cried, searching through the pile of unclipped shirts. Panic-stricken, she grabbed each shirt and tossed it into a separate pile, her heart thumping crazily in her chest.

Jade and Wing helped her search. They checked her scissor box, her sewing table, and the floor. They crawled on their knees among the scraps and dust balls.

"It's got to be here somewhere," muttered Jade. "It can't just disappear."

"When did you have it last?" Wing asked.

"Earlier today . . . just before Mrs. Tang left," said Suyin. "I stitched a single row of seed stitches . . . Lao dumped some shirts on my needlework and ordered me to start clipping threads. Then Sister Fang-chou called me in to her office."

"Where do you usually keep it?" asked Wing.

"In my sewing box."

Jade widened her eyes. "Do you think somebody stole it?"

Wing whispered, "I saw Kwan-Sook poking around your table when you were in Sister's office."

"Why would Kwan-Sook steal my needle?" Suyin asked. "She thinks embroidery is a waste of time."

"Because she hates you?" replied Wing.

Suyin studied Kwan-Sook's sharp rat-eyed face and felt her own hatred stirring. She imagined the girl's stealth as her nimble fingers plucked the needle from Suyin's sewing box as she'd walked past. But she couldn't accuse the girl without proof.

As the day dragged on, Suyin could think of nothing else but the lost needle, Mrs. Tang's next visit, and the expectations of the crane women.

When Lao ordered Suyin to stay behind the others to clip threads, she searched every corner of the shop to no avail. If Kwan-Sook was the thief, she must have taken the needle with her.

How could Suyin have been so careless?

Brooding, she ran her fingers lightly over Grandmother's sampler. She fixed her eyes on the row of cross-stitching surrounded by tiny decorative dots. Suddenly, like the click of a key turning in a lock, she saw the Nu Shu—hidden in plain sight. Grandmother had stitched the women's script within the embroidery patterns so cleverly she hadn't seen it. It was the same phrase inscribed on her mother's needle. *All women are sisters.*

She heard a soft whoosh by the shop window. She turned to see Grandmother, Li-Wen, Hazrat, and Mulaba perched on the sewing table.

"Well done," chirped Grandmother. "You solved the riddle."

"I must have been blind, not to see it before," said Suyin.

"It's an open secret," said Li-Wen. "But it requires a special seeing and a trained eye. Your mother was one of the finest practitioners of the art."

"Is my mother the queen?" blurted Suyin.

"The secret is revealed when the seeker is ready," said Li-Wen. "Yes, Suyin. Your mother is the queen."

"And you are the princess," added Grandmother.

A rush of emotions filled Suyin's heart. Joy, sadness, loss. She took a deep breath to calm herself. She was thrilled to be a princess, but even though she had suspected that her mother was the queen, actually knowing it was shocking.

"What happened to my mother?" she asked, her voice cracking.

"I'm not sure where to begin," said Hazrat.

"Begin before Suyin was born," said Grandmother gently, "when An-Lan first arrived in the village."

Hazrat nodded. "Your mother was dancing with the cranes by the lake when your father saw her. Yan fell in love with her at first sight and courted her against his father's wishes. The sisterhood also disapproved of the match. But your parents were blinded by love. An-Lan's greatest strength was an open heart, but it also led to her downfall. She was determined to marry Yan despite our advice. And she reminded us, quite rightly, that a queen must make her own choices."

"But she must choose wisely," Mulaba quickly added.

"She agreed to marry your father on two conditions," said Hazrat. "He had to promise that every spring, she could leave to visit her relatives in the high country. And secondly, that he must never follow her when she left. Yan promised and they were married. When you were born, your parents were overjoyed. We felt blessed as well, for you were our princess, the first and only daughter of the queen. Every spring your mother would kiss you and your father good-bye, leaving you in the care of your aunties. She promised to return at the first snowfall."

"Why did she have to leave?" Suyin asked, though she already knew the answer.

"She had to perform the Mysteries."

"But she left us for months," said Suyin.

"We're a *world* sisterhood," said Hazrat the Wise. "Your mother had to perform the sacred ceremonies. War and destruction can't thrive when humans have a deep connection to nature. Your mother was doing her duty."

Suyin bristled. "What about her duty to my father and me?"

"Suyin," said Hazrat gently, "if she had neglected her duty to the clan, it would have led to—"

"The situation we're facing now," said Li-Wen darkly.

"The threat of extinction," said Grandmother.

"As your mother's reputation as an embroideress grew," continued Hazrat, "so did her earning power. Your father dreamed of buying a new fishing boat and begged her to stay home and stitch. His pride was suffering too. Some of the men in the village called your mother 'the crane wife.' They said she loved the cranes more than she loved her husband. That was untrue, but it stung Yan. That spring, when your mother left the village, Yan's curiosity overtook him. He followed her to the fen where the flock had gathered to migrate.

"He spied on her from behind a bush," whispered Hazrat, a pained expression in her eyes.

"Like a coward," muttered Grandmother, pacing around the shop. "He broke his promise."

"And when An-Lan began her transformation . . ." Hazrat's voice suddenly faltered and her wings drooped. ". . . Yan saw neither woman nor bird but something . . . in between. Unable to contain his horror, he cried out and in that instant, your mother knew her fate. We tried to carry her broken body, but somewhere between earth and He Shan, she slipped from our grasp. We searched for her to no avail."

Suyin held her hand over her mouth to keep from crying out. Her mother would remain a bird forever. Suyin would never look upon her mother's human face or feel her mother's arms around her.

"Why is she still in the Gray World?" asked Suyin. "Couldn't she fly?"

Hazrat shook her head. "Not with one wing. The other was a mass of muscle and bone, a half-human, half-birdlike appendage, useless for flight."

Suyin felt the hairs on the back of her neck stand up.

"How did it happen?"

"Your mother's soul was conflicted," said Hazrat. "She was torn between her duty as a wife and mother and her duty as queen. If you are not at peace when you undergo transmutation, a disruption can occur. Maybe it was the shock of knowing all she'd lost— her husband, her daughter, her place on earth. Maybe it was Yan's betrayal." Hazrat's voice trailed off. "We'll never know for sure."

Suyin listened, stunned. "Why did you wait so long to tell me?" she said. "I'm her daughter. I had a right to know."

"Until the moment you chose the heart feather, we were uncertain as to whether you had inherited your mother's transformative power."

"The heart feather is the imperial feather," explained Mulaba. "We knew then you were the one who could save us."

"You said I was the *first* girl to choose the heart feather," said Suyin sullenly.

"You were the first—after the queen."

Suyin flared. "All my life I thought my mother was dead. You've been heartless. I want to go to her right now!"

"You have no wings," Hazrat gently reminded her.

Disheartened, Suyin lashed out. "What did my mother accomplish to prove herself?"

"It wasn't what she *did*," said Hazrat, "it was what she *was*. She had a loving heart. She put others before herself. She was generous and forgiving."

Suyin felt a lump form in her throat. Her mother was good and she was not.

"She gave of herself in the most generous way possible," said Li-Wen. "She plucked her feathers and wove them into her stitching."

Suyin winced, remembering Li-Wen's tortured cry when she'd plucked the feather from her breast.

"It was painful and exhausting," continued Li-Wen. "When she had completed each piece, she was nothing but a shell, but her sacrifice reflected a beautiful heart. She wove the secrets of the sisterhood so artfully in her embroidered patterns that only through a long apprenticeship could a sister unlock the knowledge." The crane stretched her long legs and strode to the window. She looked up at the moon. "Anyone who gazed upon An-Lan's creations felt the weight of the world fall away."

When Suyin thought of how her grandfather had sold her mother's embroidery, she felt a renewed hatred for him. But she also blamed her aunties and the crane sisters for allowing it to happen. It was as if her mother's existence had been erased on that fateful day, leaving only gossip and a fireside story.

"Now we believe you are ready to receive a special gift," said Mulaba. Lifting her wing, the gray crowned crane carefully unrolled a tapestry and gently laid it on Suyin's lap.

Suyin felt a lump in her throat. It was the loveliest embroidery she'd ever seen. The harmony of the design, the delicacy of the colors, and the perfection of the stitching took her breath away.

The tapestry was covered with a fine white dust. Some of the threads were crumbling and yellow with age.

"The tapestry has old magic," said Grandmother.

"Is it my mother's?"

"It belongs to the sisterhood," said Mulaba.

"I will carry it with me always," promised Suyin.

"The tapestry was embroidered by one of our earliest queens and passed down to each successive queen. Each queen, in turn, studied the tapestry and added her own stitching. The cross pattern near the border at the bottom was stitched by your mother. The secret of the Mysteries is hidden within these embroidered patterns," said Mulaba. "If you could decipher the meanings, then perhaps you could save the clan without risking your life in the Lower World."

"And then?" asked Suyin bitterly.

Mulaba opened her wings and bowed. "Then, Princess Suyin, you would become queen."

"I don't want to become the queen," said Suyin fiercely. "I want to *save* the queen."

"We all want to save dear An-Lan," said Mulaba, "but I fear such a quest is futile."

"Your sisters don't agree," said Suyin, eyeing Li-Wen, Hazrat, and Grandmother, who were shaking their heads in unison.

"No, but they can't deny the risk," countered Mulaba. "If we lose you, there is no hope for our survival."

"There is little hope anyway," said Suyin grimly. "I lost my mother's needle."

"That's why we've come," said Grandmother, pulling a needle from under her wing.

"It will take me years to learn," protested Suyin.

"Patience is a bitter plant, but it has sweet fruit," said Grandmother.

Without the needle to guide her, Suyin dropped stitches. She forgot how to execute an embroidery stitch that had seemed easy before. Grandmother was patient. She would simply point to the mistake with her wing or demonstrate the stitch to jog Suyin's memory.

Suyin didn't mention Mrs. Tang or the fact that she'd lied to the lady to get the job. She was too embarrassed.

"I'm going to stitch another sampler for you," whispered Grandmother, picking up a scrap from the shop floor. The old crane thrummed as she worked.

"Does Mrs. Chin belong to the clan?" Suyin asked suddenly.

Li-Wen was guarded when she answered. "There

are women whose *ancestors* belonged to the clan. These women have little memory of their past, but they share our sensibilities. Now only the stories remain to them, passed down from one generation to the next like heirlooms."

Suyin thought for a moment. "If their ancestors were bird women, why aren't they?"

"Throughout time, women with extraordinary powers have been persecuted," said Li-Wen. "Mothers kept their heritage from their daughters to protect them. The knowledge was lost and eventually their power."

Grandmother cackled. "Use it or lose it!"

"There are others who are born with bird hearts," said Hazrat, fixing her eye on Suyin. "Those are the boys."

Suyin's mouth fell open. "Boys?"

Hazrat nodded. "Their ancestors were among the last males to lose their transformative powers."

"Then there are the fallen ones," said Li-Wen. "Women who once belonged to the clan, but lacked the courage or the will to transform. They were seduced by the pleasures of the human world—ambition, riches, power."

What about love? wondered Suyin. Her mother had sacrificed everything for love. And in doing so, she had unwittingly risked her humanity. Yet Suyin owed her existence to the power of love. Her father had made a fatal mistake, but he'd loved her mother. Maybe he had loved her too.

After hours of practicing her own stitching, Suyin

stopped to examine the ancient tapestry. Gazing on it, she felt humbled. She picked up her needle and practiced a row of cross-stitches on a fabric scrap until she fell asleep. When she woke, the cranes were gone. But they had left a new sampler beside the tapestry.

13
Joy and Misery

On a cool October night, five and a half months from the day he left Fuzhou City to seek his fortune, Pickpocket Pang took his first step up Gold Mountain. His change in circumstance had happened so quickly that no one knew until he burst out the door of the restaurant pushing a rusty old bicycle. It was eleven o'clock and the seamstresses stood gawking at him with tired eyes and open mouths, wondering if he'd stolen it.

"Whose bike?" asked Kwan-Sook, her eyes fixed on the peeling paint.

"Mine!" Pang beamed, grabbing Kwan-Sook's hand. "I got a promotion!"

Kwan-Sook smiled uncertainly. "Congratulations!"

"What happened, Pang?" asked Wing.

"Get a move on," grumbled Lao. "I'm in a hurry." As

Pang pushed the bike along the sidewalk, the wheels made a creaking sound.

"Manager Ren asked me if I spoke English," said Pang, speaking excitedly. "I told him yes, I learned English from my good friend Suyin."

Kwan-Sook bristled.

"Ren said, 'Can you deliver Chinese takeout as fast as you wash dishes?' I told him, 'Faster than any boy in Chinatown.' 'A delivery boy needs a bicycle,' he said. 'Can you get a bicycle?' So I went to Loan Shark Li, borrowed the money, bought this bicycle, and got the job. It's old, but it's in good working order. Look at this basket! It has a kickstand too. What do you think, Suyin?" asked Pang shyly.

"It's a beauty, isn't it, Kwan-Sook," said Suyin, renewing her efforts to be nice.

Pang reached for Kwan-Sook's hand. "There's something else. I'm moving, little sister."

Kwan-Sook's face fell. "Moving? Where?"

"Mulberry Street. Don't worry; it's not far away. We'll still see each other."

"Why do you have to move?" whined Kwan-Sook.

"I'm on call day and night. A delivery boy can't be locked up."

Kwan-Sook's lip began to quiver. For a moment, Suyin thought she was going to cry. Suyin had mixed feelings too. She was happy for Pang's promotion, but sad she wouldn't see him so often.

"What's that?" asked Kwan-Sook sullenly, poking her finger at the paper bag in Pang's basket.

"Dinner! We're celebrating tonight. I got a raise too. I'm now earning three American dollars an hour."

When they reached the safe house, Lao pushed them inside and scurried away. She couldn't blame him. The air of the safe house was heavy with worry and decay.

"You're lucky you're moving, Pang," said Jade, plugging her nose. "Is it a nice place?"

Pang shrugged. "It has windows and the toilet works, but it's cramped. It's a small apartment divided into compartments, plywood partitions, a *gong si fong*. I share it with sixteen other bachelors."

"Sixteen?"

Pang nodded. "I rent a bed from midnight until six in the morning. A cleaner who works the midnight shift rents the bed in the daytime. I don't mind. It's cheap, so I can save more money." He nudged Suyin's arm, teasing. "If the delivery business is slow, I'll be able to make some money on the side."

"If you're caught stealing . . ." said Suyin.

"I don't steal," joked Pang. "I redistribute wealth. I take from the rich and give to poor seamstresses."

"If you enter the lion's den too often, you'll get eaten," scolded Suyin.

Pang grinned. "Don't tell Lao, but Rat Catcher Pang is back in business," he said. "I'm catching rats for Mrs.

Wong, the lady that owns the So Good Noodle House!"

"How did you get the job?" asked Kwan-Sook.

"One day I saw Mrs. Wong chasing a rat out the door of her restaurant with a broom. She told me she'd been trying to trap the little rascal for months. Traps didn't seem to work and she was worried about the health inspector. So I offered her my services. I told her that for every rat I caught, she could pay me a dollar. If I failed, there would be no charge. But then she said, 'Do you think I'm a cheapskate? This is America, not China! Everything here costs more.' So she offered me ten American dollars! For a rat! I couldn't believe my ears. She must be rich."

Pang began humming. He spread containers of takeout food on an empty cot, opening the lids with a flourish.

"What are those dishes?" asked Kwan-Sook.

"Sweet and sour chicken balls. Pork fried rice. Chop suey. Garlic spare ribs and rice. It's American Chinese food. Scrapings from the customers' plates and some leftovers from the kitchen."

"What a feast," said Jade, smacking her lips.

Suyin's mouth watered. It was hard to wait, but no one moved. They were trying to disguise their hunger. Hunger was embarrassing, like wearing a patched skirt or a badly stained jacket.

"Go ahead. Eat," urged Pang.

Suyin chose a garlic spare rib. She took small bites, anticipation sharpening her pleasure. In Cao Hai, hunger arrived in winter and stayed until the first harvest, but she never imagined that this unwelcome guest would follow her to Gold Mountain.

"Any gossip, Pang?" asked Wing, munching on a chicken ball.

Pang nodded. "First Class Fashion and Pearl River Garment walked off the job today. They made a complaint to the Department of Labor."

"Stupid girls," muttered Kwan-Sook.

"Sister hadn't paid their wages for eight months," said Pang.

The girls exchanged worried glances.

"It's about time someone stood up to old Sharktooth," said Jade.

"No bad-luck talk allowed tonight," declared Kwan-Sook. She smiled at Pang. "This is Pang's celebration."

After everyone had eaten, Suyin began practicing Dazi embroidery on fabric scraps before she attempted the complicated pattern on the Mandarin squares. Each tiny knot had to be exactly the same size or the embroidered surface would appear uneven.

Studying Grandmother's sampler, she hoped that the Nu Shu missive would leap out at her, but Grandmother was wily. She had set a new challenge for her.

If the sampler frustrated her, the tapestry inspired her. It spoke to her of that magical era before living memory when the first queen embroidered a missive on a strip of cloth. It spoke to her of her royal ancestry. It spoke to her of the Past, Present, and Future.

Gazing upon it, she felt an absurd kind of hopefulness. She imagined herself as a warrior princess, armed with her feather, flying to the Gray World to rescue the queen. She imagined mother and daughter, queen and princess, returning to He Shan in triumph.

But at other times, she wished her mother *weren't* queen. She wished for a mother who would tuck her into bed and sing cradle songs to her—only her—not to the whole world.

When Kwan-Sook had spotted the tapestry, she sneered. "What's that ugly old thing?"

Suyin was glad that the girl thought it worthless. She'd been worried she might try and steal it.

When everyone had finished eating, Pang suddenly plunked himself down at the end of her cot. Suyin jumped, startled.

"Did you find your mother's needle?" he asked.

"No."

"I hope it shows up," said Pang. "I know how much it meant to you." He met her eyes and held her gaze. Her heart raced foolishly. Could he see how he affected her, she wondered? She turned back to her stitching, ignoring him. He belongs to Kwan-Sook, she told herself. And they both steal.

"Is that the stitching you're doing for Helen Tang?" he asked, trying to make conversation.

She felt Kwan-Sook's broody eyes sending poison darts across the room.

"Yes," she said glumly.

Pang smiled. "You've gotten really good, Suyin."

She stared at him, suddenly furious. He must have suspected that his stupid hanger-on had stolen her needle. He was trying to make her feel better, she supposed, but his compliments weren't genuine. Any fool could see how poorly she was stitching. Kwan-Sook was probably laughing behind her sleeve at her meager efforts.

"Thank you for the compliment," she said coldly.

Finally he crept back to Kwan-Sook to lick his wounds. But once he was gone, she felt sorry for the way she'd treated him. And then she wasn't tired, because she was too upset.

After everyone went to sleep, she continued stitching, even though it was late and she had to get up at six o'clock for work.

It was two in the morning when she deciphered the Nu Shu missive in the sampler.

Defeat isn't bitter, if you don't swallow it.

Suyin smiled sadly. The saying was a favorite of Old Auntie Dou's, as familiar as Auntie's rice porridge and the old woman's wrinkled hands. For a moment, she thought, could it be? Then she laughed at herself. It was hard to imagine Old Auntie Dou as a crane.

Later, as she lay in the dark, she glanced at the three sleeping girls. Wing held a photograph of her family. Jade held a fist of the pink and blue hair ribbons, the piecework she'd been stitching for a local merchant. And Kwan-Sook was curled up like a baby, knees to her chest, holding herself. In sleep, Kwan-Sook's bitterness left the girl's face. And her heart was laid bare.

"All women are sisters," whispered Suyin into the lonely dark. "Even Kwan-Sook."

As she closed her eyes, Suyin felt something soft brush against her shoulder. Blinking into the darkness, she saw two splendid wings. It was Hazrat, her golden eyes full of approval. As the bird bent over her, Suyin felt the crane's blessing.

"Sleep, Princess Suyin," murmured the crane, touching her forehead. Suyin smiled before she sunk into a dream.

November brought the first snowfall to the city. Large flakes of snow cloaked the trees and streets in white. Suyin watched Jade and Wing slide along the sidewalks in the prelight dawn. The two pushed each other into the snow, laughing.

The first snowfall in Cao Hai usually heralded the return of the cranes, a joy to all the villagers. The elders would bow in reverence to the birds to honor their departed ancestors. Younger villagers like Suyin and Shan-Shan would race to the fen to dance with the flock. It was the time of her mother's return, though Suyin was too young to remember. Still, she could imagine her father's joy and her small arms reaching for her.

Last week she had turned fourteen, though she'd kept it to herself. Mentioning it would have only made her feel worse, for there would have been no celebration. She wondered if Shan-Shan had been betrothed yet or if the village had celebrated her wedding.

She felt a sharp pang of homesickness, but she was too worried to dwell on it. Mrs. Tang would soon arrive at the shop to find that Suyin had accomplished little. She was afraid of ruining the expensive silk, so she practiced on fabric scraps. But her stitching was never good enough. It was the work of a beginner and it showed. Countless times over the last few weeks, she'd thrown up her hands in despair.

"Suyin!" shouted Pang, tossing a snowball at her jacket. He laughed, taunting her until she threw a snowball back. Soon she and her friends were chasing each other with snowballs and laughing like children. It felt good to laugh.

Their playfulness was enough to throw Kwan-Sook into a sulk. She crossed her arms and stomped angrily away. Pang, as usual, ran ahead to placate her. Why did she always have to spoil things?

When they entered the shop that morning, the air inside was frigid. Ice had formed on the inside of the windows. The seamstresses bent over their machines in their hats and coats. Suyin's hands were stiff from the cold.

"Sister phoned in three rush orders today," said Lao angrily. "No one goes home until they're finished."

Jade's eyes burned with resentment. "We're behind as it is."

"Sister's too cheap to hire more staff," muttered Mrs. Chin.

"Mr. Lao," asked Jade. "When's Sister coming to pay us?"

"Next month," grunted Lao.

The machines stopped. "She was supposed to pay us last month," cried the seamstresses.

"You can't draw blood from a stone," said Lao, closing his office door.

"Little Brother's tuition is due this month," said Jade. "If I don't get paid, Little Brother will be living on the street." She gave Suyin a pleading look. "You speak perfect English, Suyin. Maybe you could lay a complaint for us? To the Department of Labor?"

Suyin paled. "I couldn't. I could be deported . . . or fired . . . or beaten. I'm sorry."

"Only a fool would complain." Kwan-Sook sniffed.

"That's how the bosses get away with it," said Jade. "Everyone's afraid to complain."

When Mrs. Tang arrived at the shop, Suyin began to shake.

"Do you have some piecework for me, Suyin?" asked Mrs. Tang with a smile.

Words froze in Suyin's throat.

"She's had no time," broke in Jade. "Our boss keeps her busy clipping threads."

Mrs. Tang looked disappointed. "When *could* you have the work ready, Suyin?"

Suyin hesitated. Would Mrs. Tang have enough patience to wait?

"January the first?" she asked weakly. "I have to do

most of my embroidery after working hours, Mrs. Tang." Lately this was true. The shop had been inundated with rush orders for Christmas, the *lao fan* holiday.

Mrs. Tang pursed her lips. "Well, I'll be away on business again. And I won't be back until after January twenty-third, New Year's. Hopefully that will give you enough time."

"Thank you, Mrs. Tang," said Suyin gratefully.

Mrs. Tang shook her head. "Clipping threads is a waste of your talent."

When Mrs. Tang had left, Suyin buried her head in her hands. "What if Mrs. Tang gives up on me?"

"She won't," reassured Jade. "She was impressed with your stitching."

Not my stitching. The cranes'.

Jade's brow furrowed. "You'll make your next deadline, won't you?"

Suyin shrugged. "If I had my special needle . . . I might have a chance."

"Maybe we should confront Kwan-Sook," whispered Jade.

Suyin shook her head. "She'd never admit it."

"Stop the chitchat, you lazy lumps," said Lao. "You'll be working all night at this rate."

Suddenly he fixed his stare on Wing. He stopped at her worktable, picked up a shirt, and inspected it.

"These seams are crooked!" He picked up one shirt after another, tossing them onto the floor. "No good. No good.

169

No good, you useless girl." Grabbing Wing by the hair, he yanked her to her feet. "I'll teach you to do shoddy work."

Suyin's eyes fell upon Lao's wrist. The white string that Auntie had tied around it was gone. The lost soul that Auntie Cho-Ye had retrieved had escaped again.

"Please, Mr. Lao," pleaded Wing, stumbling as he dragged her down the hallway. "I'll try and do better."

For a moment, Wing's eyes met hers. Her friend looked so small and vulnerable that Suyin felt a sympathy pain in her chest.

Why did Lao pick on Wing so much more than the others? Was he still smarting from her insult on the boat? Or did her fragility, as fine and lovely as a priceless porcelain vase, make him want to smash it?

Suyin covered her ears to muffle Wing's screams. Jade was hunched over her machine, stitching hard and fast as helpless tears ran down her face. The others sat frozen in their chairs, resting their heads on their machines.

Suyin's heart urged her to act. Perhaps defending a friend might be enough to prove her worth. Yet fear kept her rooted to her chair.

"I hate that man," said Suyin, angry at her own weakness.

"We all hate him, except her," said Mrs. Chin, tipping her chin in Kwan-Sook's direction. "She's hoping he'll give her a promotion. She thinks the fool's got power, but he's a shrimp in a sea of sharks."

Maybe, thought Suyin, but he had enough power to make their lives miserable.

December came and went with no sign of Sister Fang-chou or the back wages she owed them. Suyin studied the tapestry, but the secrets within the threads remained hidden. Her only success was the pale yellow embroidered scarf she'd completed for Mrs. Tang. In her heart, she knew her embroidery failed to reach the high standards of the sisterhood, but it was the best she could do.

Hazrat had once told her she would be tested on the road to worthiness. Was watching her suffer the crane sisters' idea of a test? Why wouldn't they help her?

Her people had forgotten about her too. Not a letter! Not even a note of thanks after Lao had sent her hard-earned money—if he had sent it.

A cold snap in early January froze the pipes in the shop. The city trees were coated in ice and their branches bent and snapped under the weight. Inside the frosty air of the shop, the seamstresses were sick with worry.

"When's Sister's coming to pay us?" they asked Lao.

"You'll get your money on New Year's," bellowed Lao.

"More empty promises," said Jade. She was desperate because the deadline for the payment of Little Brother's school fees had passed. The boy would be on the street, hungry.

"I think we should join the strike," said Jade. "If Sister hasn't paid her other shops, why would she pay us?"

Kwan-Sook's mouth fell open. "Are you crazy?"

"No," said Jade wearily. "I'm tired of working for nothing."

"Maybe Mr. Lee could help us," whispered Mei-Xia.

"Who's he?" asked Jade.

"A friend of Mrs. Wong's . . . from a worker's help center," said Mei-Xia.

"Mother told us he's looking for seamstresses willing to speak out against bosses who treat them unfairly."

"But Mother warned us not contact him," said Mei-li "She said Sister might fire us."

Suyin hated Jade's strike talk. She couldn't afford to lose her embroidery job. Her work as a thread cutter paid so little; she'd need several lifetimes to pay off her debt.

14
Happy New Year!

Alone in the shop after midnight, Suyin heard a knock on the door. She pressed her eye to the peephole.

"Happy New Year, Suyin! It's me, Pang!"

"Quiet, Pang! You're going to get me in trouble," said Suyin. "That door has a million locks. You'll never get them all open."

"These are baby locks," hollered Pang. "Easy to pick!"

"What if Lao catches you?"

"Pshaw! He's out of town. He won't be back until to-morrow morning."

She heard clicks and snaps and clunks. The door flew open and a triumphant Pang strolled in, carrying bags of takeout and a wrapped gift. She grabbed his arm and pulled him inside.

"Aren't you supposed to be working now?"

"One of the other delivery boys is covering for me. I saw your coworkers leaving the shop earlier this evening."

Blushing, he pressed the gift into her hands. "Happy New Year!"

Pang's gift was a notebook with two cranes on the cover. She pressed it to her heart and then without thinking she lifted her arms to hug him. She stopped in midair, flustered, but he pretended he hadn't seen and pulled her close.

"Thank you for the gift, Pang," said Suyin shyly. Her heart was beating fast. "It's perfect. I lost my notebook in the sea."

She hadn't realized how much she'd missed writing Nu Shu. It was the thread that bound her to the sisterhood. Somehow Pang had understood.

Her face fell. "But I have nothing for you, Pang."

"I made you smile," said Pang. "That's enough."

She tried not to think about Kwan-Sook and the fuss she'd make if she knew Pang had come to see her. But tonight she was lonely and he'd brought her a gift.

"I didn't want to eat alone on New Year's," said Pang. He began opening cartons of noodles in chilies, ginger beef, and sticky rice.

"How can I ever repay you, Pang?" asked Suyin. He was so sweet it was hard to close her heart to him.

"Friends help one another." His face was open in its affection for her.

"I'm glad you came, Pang," she murmured.

"Me too," said Pang. Their eyes met and the world seemed to spin. He leaned closer to her. She reached for his hand. She wondered if he was going to kiss her. For a moment, nothing else existed but the two of them.

When the phone rang in Lao's office, she pulled away, the spell broken.

As they shared the meal, Pang showed her a letter from his father.

"Father asked the neighbor lady to write it for him."

Unlike my aunties.

"He thanked me for sending the overseas money. He said I am a good son and he is very proud of me. Have you heard from your people yet?"

"Not yet."

"I'm sure they'll write soon."

Brushing away her hurt, she quickly changed the subject.

"Do you still like your new job?"

Pang's face lit up. "It's the finest job in the world. Better pay than a dishwasher. More freedom. I can do my rat catching on the side too. I caught three rats for Mrs. Wong. Easy money! I've got a cell phone for my deliveries, and some of my customers speak English, so I get to practice. Between deliveries, I study English using *The Daily News*. I circle all the English words I know, then I study the newspaper photographs to figure out what the news story is about. I miss your morning English lessons, Suyin, but I don't miss being locked up in the safe house." He smiled. "Life is treating me well."

"I'm happy for you," said Suyin.

"How are Wing and Jade progressing in their English?"

"Jade's doing well," said Suyin, "and Mrs. Chin too. The old lady has a knack for languages. I'm worried about Wing, though. She's homesick and the long hours at work are wearing her down. Lao is still picking on her."

Pang frowned. "Lao treats you like slaves."

"He says Sister's going to pay us our back wages tomorrow, after the dragon dance."

"Speaking of money," said Pang, "I have something to show you."

With a flick of his fingers, he pulled dollar bills from his sleeve. The bills fell to the floor around him.

Her eyes grew wide. "I've never seen so much money."

"Five hundred American dollars!"

"Did you *steal* it?"

He nodded proudly. "From that gangster Mr. Chu, the owner of the Lucky Eight Tea Parlor. He has a gambling den in the back room."

"Pang! I'm afraid for you."

"Pah! It took me two seconds to pick his pocket. Mr. Chu had no idea."

"Don't you feel *guilty*?"

"Stealing from that crook? No. Mr. Chu collects protection money from every business owner in Chinatown. If anyone refuses to pay, he has them beaten by hired thugs."

"Have you told anyone else what you did?"

"Only Kwan-Sook."

"Can you trust her?"

"I'd trust her with my life," said Pang solemnly. "Don't worry, Suyin. I'm going to stop stealing when I've saved enough money to buy my papers."

"You're risking deportation to buy false documents?"

"Don't you understand? My naturalization papers will make me a citizen of this country. Once I have my papers, I'll become respectable."

She sighed. There was little use arguing with him.

"I miss Father," he said, suddenly downcast. "When I said good-bye I knew I would never see him again. He's too old to come to Gold Mountain."

Pang reached for Suyin's embroidery, examining it. "That's a beautiful silk scarf. The cranes look so real."

Suyin stared at her work with a critical eye. "The satin stitches on the cranes' wings aren't fine enough."

"You're too hard on yourself."

Suyin shrugged. "Mrs. Tang will be coming to the shop in a few days. The scarf is the only piece I've finished. If I lose that contract, Lao will be furious."

"I thought he disliked Mrs. Tang."

"He does, but he wants the commission."

"How much is Mrs. Tang going to pay you?"

She shrugged. "Lao won't say. He says it's up to Mrs. Tang—how much she can sell it for."

Pang frowned. "I hope she's not taking advantage of you."

Suyin shook her head. "Mrs. Tang has given me a chance. She's the only person in Gold Mountain who has."

The next morning the streets of East Broadway were crowded. People were shouting, "Happy New Year, *Gung Hay Fat Choy!*"

Lao led the staff of the Good Fortune Garment Shop outside to watch the parade. Mrs. Chin had warned them that they'd have to work, but the seamstresses were filled with excitement.

"The dragons are coming!" shouted the crowd. At the sight of the parade, the crowd surged forward. Kwan-Sook elbowed her way to the front. Two large dragons undulated down the center of the street.

Suyin held her breath, clasping her hands, willing the magic to last. As the blue, green, and black dragons drew closer, she could see the legs of the acrobats beneath the dancing dragons. One boy was perched on the shoulders of another.

Suddenly the largest dragon reared up on its haunches and shook its giant mane. The crowd gasped in admiration. The Chinese dragons stopped at each business where the owners gave the dancers good luck oranges and red envelopes of money.

As they pushed their way through the crowds, Jade nudged Suyin's arm. "There's Xiaoli." The boy was slapping his forehead and yelling "No! No! No!" His eyes were full of pain and anger.

The crowd parted, leaving him a wide berth.

"What's *wrong* with him?" asked Wing, clutching Suyin's arm.

"It's that crazy kid," whispered Mei-li. "We see him wandering the streets talking to himself."

"He ran away," said Mei-Xia, "but Sister's thugs caught him. They beat him up, nearly killed him. A few days later, two thugs broke into his parents' home in Fuzhou and murdered his little sister in front of his parents. They told the parents that they were being punished because their son tried to escape without paying his debt."

Suyin almost stopped breathing.

"Kill the monkey to scare the chickens," said Cousin Jin, lowering her voice. "They do it to scare us. I'm afraid it works. You're shaking."

She felt a chill. It was as if someone had lifted another veil from her eyes and she had glimpsed something monstrous.

As the dragons danced down the street, the business owners lit strings of firecrackers, throwing them at the dragon's feet. And then the parade was over. The crowds scattered, leaving the air full of smoke and the streets littered with red, yellow, and pink firecracker papers.

"Back to work, *yazis!*" said Lao irritably.

Wing's face fell. "Already?"

Mrs. Chin placed her arm around Wing's shoulder. She frowned at Lao.

"I'm going to buy some *jiaozi* for the girls," said Mrs.

Chin. "Mrs. Wong makes the best dumplings in the city. We'll only be a few minutes."

As they crossed the street, Suyin recognized the bright-faced girl who had smiled at her the first day she'd arrived. The girl and her mother were selling hot snacks from a pushcart. The two looked so happy together, Suyin felt the loss of her mother as a sharp pain in her chest. Since she'd discovered her mother was alive, she thought of little else. Her embroidery work for Mrs. Tang was important, but compared to saving her mother, her job was a drop of water in a sea of discontent.

Lao called after the staff, tapping his watch with his fingernail. "Five minutes. No more."

"An order of pork-filled dumplings, Mrs. Wong," said Mrs. Chin in Cantonese. The bright-faced girl smiled at her. Suyin smiled back, then she nudged Jade and pointed.

"*Jiaozi. Dumplings* in English."

"You must be Suyin, Pang's friend," said the girl, speaking in Cantonese. "I'm Nancy Wong. Pang told me you're teaching him English. He's working for Mom, catching you-know-what." She laughed. "Mom doesn't want her customers to know. He's caught three so far." Nancy lowered her voice. "Your friend looks upset."

"It's hard on New Year's. Wing misses her family."

"My parents do too," said Nancy. "They were immigrants like you. Sister brought them here before I was born. They came with nothing, but they've done well. It's a prosperous business."

Mrs. Wong looked up. "It's bad luck to boast, Nancy."

"Sorry, Mother," said the girl sheepishly.

"Suyin!" hissed Cousin Jin. "Lao's coming."

"Your break is over, *yazi*," said Lao, tapping his watch. He slapped the keys to the shop in Mrs. Chin's hand. "I'll be back soon."

When Mrs. Chin offered Wing a dumpling, she shook her head.

"Keep your broken arm inside your sleeve, Wing," said Mrs. Chin. "That's how you survive."

Suyin tried to comfort her. "Did you hear what Nancy Wong said? Her parents came here with nothing and now they own their own restaurant." But Wing seemed lost in her own world.

As the seamstresses climbed the stairs to the shop, Wing burst into tears.

"That's it? We're given one hour to celebrate New Year's? Our lives are bitter. Our bosses see us as oxen—good for nothing but work. I want to go home, where people love me. No one loves me here," she sobbed.

"We love you," said Suyin and Jade, hugging her.

"Stop feeling sorry for yourself, Wing," snapped Kwan-Sook. "The harder you work, the quicker you'll pay off your debt."

"Mind your own business, thief!" said Jade.

Kwan-Sook raised her fist. "Who are you calling a thief?"

"You! We all know you stole Suyin's needle!"

Kwan-Sook pushed Jade in the chest. "Take that back or I'll tell Lao."

"Jade," cautioned Suyin, pulling her away.

"Thief!" screamed Jade.

Kwan-Sook stomped up the stairs to wait for Mrs. Chin to unlock the door of the shop.

Wing began to cry. "I hate this place."

"Hush, Wing," said Mrs. Chin gently. "If Lao hears you crying, he'll beat you again. He doesn't want to work on a holiday either."

"I don't care anymore," sobbed Wing. "New Year's is about *family*. I begged Lao to let me telephone my parents, but he refused. He said I'm not allowed to speak to my family until my debt is paid off. I am only a machine worker, without embroidery skills that grow from the mist. I don't have a special feather or bird friends to watch over me."

Suyin was too shocked to speak.

"We know the cranes saved your life the day of the boat wreck," said Jade. "The birds were circling above Pang's head as he carried you."

Suyin swallowed hard. "Did Pang tell you that?"

"No, Suyin," said Jade firmly. "We saw it with our own eyes."

"Don't you trust us?" asked Wing.

"Of course I do," Suyin said, but she felt the lie on her tongue. She wasn't sure if she trusted anyone.

As Wing trudged up the stairs, Suyin and Jade exchanged worried looks. In the last few months, Wing forgot to eat unless they reminded her. She was shrinking away before their eyes. Sometimes Suyin woke to see her friend pressing her face against her pillow to muffle her sobs.

"I'm all alone," Wing had whispered to her one night in the darkness as Suyin hugged her. "Mother used to bring me tea every morning in a lovely porcelain bowl. She called me her little flower." Wing smiled through her tears. "She spoiled me. I never appreciated all the little things she did for me. Now I would give my life to have my mother bring me a little bowl of tea."

Suyin thought about her own mother trapped in the cold and dark. She thought about her three aunties. Old Auntie Dou bringing her rice porridge. Auntie Huishan offering her a freshly baked turnip cake. Auntie Cho-Ye bringing a thorn-apple petal to her nose, saying in her shamanic voice, "Breathe in, Suyin. This is the fragrance of heaven."

Her mind wandered back to the New Year's celebrations back home. During the Spring Festival, Shan-Shan and her aunties would wear their silver crowns with the tiny silver coins hanging down and their heavy silver neck rings and brightly colored embroidered festival dresses. Her own dress was a hand-me-down, worn, but still beautiful. In the evening, she and Shan-Shan would watch the young men and women climb up stony mountain paths leading to the next village. The two girls would sit in the darkness, watching the stars and listening to the young girls and men sing love songs to one another and exchange love tokens. She and Shan-Shan liked to guess who would marry whom.

Shan-Shan would be old enough this year to sing to a young man. Perhaps her best friend would become betrothed. The thought that she would miss that important time in her best friend's life brought a lump to her throat.

The Spring Festival was also a time when bosses would bestow gifts and special favors on their employees. It was the most auspicious time for a worker to ask for a promotion.

That afternoon, after hours of fretting, Suyin gathered enough courage to knock on Lao's door. When she asked Lao for a promotion, his reply was swift and cruel. "I'd rather trust a cat with a mouse than Fumble Fingers with a machine!"

"But you don't understand. Mr. Lao," she pleaded. "I can machine-stitch quickly and accurately, and my hems are straight. I can prove it to you."

"You've got enough to do for Big Shot Tang, young lady," sneered Lao. "Get back to work."

"Why won't Lao give me a chance?" she'd asked Mrs. Chin. "What did I do *wrong*?"

"Nothing," said Mrs. Chin. "Lao is punishing you for being an upstart. Helen Tang thinks that rose petals fall from the sky at your feet. He's showing you who is boss."

A click of sharp heels and a gravelly voice sent a shiver up Suyin's spine.

"Happy New Year, staff," said Sister, sucking air through her teeth. "I'm afraid I have some bad news. You'll have to wait a few more months for your wages. My business partners haven't paid me yet." A murmur of dismay ran through the shop. "Don't worry, *yazi*. My cash flow problems are temporary. Be grateful, workers. You have a roof over your head and tea money."

Suyin's blood ran cold. How much longer did she expect them to wait?

When Sister left, Mei-Xia shook her head. "Only the likes of Sister could deliver bad news on New Year's."

"Pah!" muttered Mrs. Chin. "That crusty old bird spends half her life thinking up ways to cheat people."

"Why would someone as rich as Sister cheat us?" asked Kwan-Sook indignantly.

"That's *how* she got rich, foolish girl."

"I heard two shops on Mulberry Street walked off the job yesterday," said Mei-Xia. "Sister hasn't paid them either."

"I'm ready to walk off the job," said Jade.

"Count me out," said Kwan-Sook. "I'm a loyal worker."

"Wing? Suyin?" asked Jade.

"If my father found out, he'd disown me," said Wing.

"I think we should wait," said Suyin.

15
Disturbing Revelations

As January was drawing to a close, Suyin's mind was pulled between two poles—saving her mother and worrying about Mrs. Tang's impending visit.

"Stop hemming and hawing, Suyin," nagged Mrs. Chin. "If your embroidery isn't perfect, so what! Even the best needles are not sharp at both ends! At the rate you're going, you'll be stitching those Mandarin squares a year from now."

"Mrs. Chin is right," said Jade. "You're never satisfied."

Suyin ignored them and unpicked another row.

When Mrs. Tang walked into the shop, Suyin was so nervous, she felt like throwing up. She quickly stuffed the tapestry into a cloth bag at her feet.

"Good morning, Suyin," said Mrs. Tang. "Let's have a look at your work."

Suyin's hands shook as she laid out the embroidered scarf.

Mrs. Tang removed a pair of tortoiseshell glasses from her purse. She held Suyin's needlework under a table lamp. She turned the scarf front and back, checking it for dropped stitches and other imperfections.

"The dancing cranes are wonderful," said Mrs. Tang. "And I like the floral border. Suyin, the scarf is exquisite. I'm impressed."

Relief flooded through Suyin like a shower after a drought. Her hard work had finally paid off!

"And the Mandarin squares?" inquired Mrs. Tang.

Suyin's voice faltered. "I'm sorry, Mrs. Tang. I haven't finished them yet."

Mrs. Tang knit her brows. "Is Mr. Lao giving you enough time to embroider?" Suyin bit her lip.

"No, he isn't," murmured a voice. It was Jade, speaking for her again.

"I'll talk to your boss before I leave," said Mrs. Tang. Opening a large satchel, Mrs. Tang placed remnants of silk and satin and embroidery floss on the table.

Suyin's eyes lit up. If only her aunties could see such riches.

"When you finish the Mandarin squares, I'd like you to stitch something special for my mother. An embroidered perfume bag."

Back home, a *hebao* would be a record of a girl's growing up, her journey from the child she was at four or five to the young woman she'd become. It was difficult knowing that her first *hebao* would be given to a stranger, but she was determined to make the best of it.

Mrs. Tang placed a small feather on the sewing table.

Suyin recognized it at once. "It's a crane feather!"

"A very old one," said Mrs. Tang. "My grandmother gave it to my mother when she came to America. The feather brought my mother and me good luck. Guess what I'd like you to do with it?"

"You'd like me to weave the feather into the perfume bag?"

"You are well-versed in the ancient ways," said Mrs. Tang. "Not to mention your uncanny gift of languages."

Suyin beamed.

"I'll pick up your piecework sometime in March," said Mrs. Tang. "You could stitch perfume bags, shawls, or scarves. I'll leave it up to your artistry."

As Mrs. Tang turned to go, her eyes fell on the tapestry. "May I have a peek?"

"It's not my work," Suyin said quickly. "It was given to me by my relatives."

Mrs. Tang's expression shifted from astonishment to awe.

"It's a masterpiece," she said softly. "It's been stitched in a variety of styles over a long period of time. The embroidery at the top of the tapestry was probably stitched in the style of the Lakai or Kungrat women in preparation for marriage. Those decorative marks in the pattern represent the double-tailed scorpion."

Mrs. Tang held the tapestry to the light.

"This is a communal piece," said Mrs. Tang in amazement. "Each embroidered strip was stitched separately and then sewn together. The needlewomen who stitched these pieces were almost certainly high-ranking.

"Look, Suyin," she said, her voice growing in excitement. "The second strip is white thread embroidery from India. The third is sixteenth-century Florentine. Every stitch, shade, and pattern reveals the history, culture, and geographic location of the needlewoman who stitched it."

Mrs. Tang stroked her chin. "I'm not sure about the fourth strip, though. The series of three circles puzzles me."

"How do you know so much about embroidery?" asked Suyin.

"I studied textiles at university. My particular interest is in embroidery. This tapestry is marvelous. Each embroidered strip is distinctive, but there's unity in the design as a whole. The cross-stitch pattern at the end of the tapestry is the most recent addition. It is typical of your people, the Miao."

Suyin nodded. "It was stitched by my mother."

Mrs. Tang's eyes grew wide. She pulled up a chair and sat down.

"Your mother?"

"Yes."

Mrs. Tang reached across the table and squeezed Suyin's hand. Then she gave her a final piece of advice.

"These patterns look complex until you separate the background stitching from the foreground. Take away those squares and whirlpool patterns and concentrate on the rest."

Suyin watched with trepidation as Mrs. Tang crossed the shop floor and bravely entered Lao's office. How she admired Mrs. Tang's spirit, her knowledge and beauty. Her friend was a crane among a flock of chickens!

As Suyin waited for Mrs. Tang to finish her talk with Lao, she examined the tapestry. As she studied it, the dots, horizontals, verticals, and arcs of the Nu Shu script seemed to rise above the tapestry like a desert mirage. Suddenly, the missive read as easily as a page in a book. *A queen must place her subjects first.* Whether Mrs. Tang had intended to or not, she had helped Suyin unlock her mother's message.

Suyin reached for her Nu Shu notebook, Pang's wonderful gift, and recorded the missive in women's script. And in the execution of those graceful strokes, she found herself transported back to her village, to those memorable nights when she and her sworn sisters had recited poems and songs in Nu Shu, bound by secrecy and a promise that they would be sisters eternally.

A short time later, Suyin heard Mrs. Tang's angry voice

and Lao's low grumbling above the roar of the machines. Alarmed, Suyin quickly hid her notebook and began furiously clipping threads.

When Mrs. Tang left, Lao rushed across the room and smacked Suyin across the face.

"Your precious Mrs. Tang is an unreliable penny pincher," he spat. "She hasn't even paid me yet." His breath was sour, his voice a hoarse whisper. "Any more complaints, and you'll be out on the street."

Was Mrs. Tang trying to cheat her too? She refused to believe it. Lao was as rotten as the wooden Wind and Rain Bridge near her village.

Sitting on her cot in the safe house in the middle of February, Suyin pondered her situation. She had completed the Mandarin squares and woven the crane feather in the *hebao*. But she had still not grown a feather on her wrist or deciphered another missive in the tapestry. If Mrs. Tang's theory was correct, a high-ranking needlewoman, probably a queen, had stitched each strip. Yet judging from the different styles of the embroidery, the needlewomen were from different parts of the world. But if the ascension to the crown was passed down from mother to daughter, why was the embroidery in the tapestry not typically Miao?

Thoughts of her mother's plight were never far from her mind. The night before she dreamed she was lost in the Gray World. In the distance, she could hear her mother's cries but she couldn't reach her. She was afraid the nightmare was a warning.

A rattle of the safe house lock pulled Suyin from her musings. She glanced at the clock. It was late, almost midnight.

Kwan-Sook's face lit up. "Pang!" she said, rising to greet him.

Water dripped from Pang's raincoat as he pushed his bicycle through the door. Despite the foul weather, Suyin envied the time he spent outside. He could feel the rain, the sun, and the wind on his skin while they were locked indoors like caged birds.

"Why don't you come visit me more often?" whined Kwan-Sook. She threw her arms around him. "What have you been *doing*?"

"Working and sleeping," said Pang. "I don't have time for much else."

Kwan-Sook stuck out her lower lip. "You live only a few blocks away. That's no excuse."

Pang looked at her with ragged eyes. "You're right, friends are important."

Suyin felt Pang's eyes on her, but she was too shy to meet his gaze.

"What's new, brother?" asked Jade.

"White Peony seamstresses walked off the job today," said Pang.

Jade held up her hand. "Don't tell me. Sister owed them back wages."

"Pah! Those girls are bad apples—lazy," snapped Kwan-Sook.

"They're not lazy, Kwan-Sook," said Pang wearily. "They've been treated badly. They haven't been paid in seven months."

Suyin wondered if Mrs. Tang would help, then she had second thoughts. Maybe Mrs. Tang was afraid of Sister too. Everyone else seemed to be.

"I keep telling them we should strike, Pang," said Jade.

"We're one of the smallest shops in Chinatown," said Kwan-Sook. "Sister is rich. If we went on strike, it wouldn't affect her much."

"We may be small, but we turn out two thousand garments per week," said Jade.

"Sister could throw us out and spread the word that we're troublemakers," said Kwan-Sook.

"So?" asked Jade. "How much worse off would we be?"

"Don't you fools know what *blacklisting* means?" shrieked Kwan-Sook. "It means no one else will hire us. Without work, we can't pay our debt. If we can't pay our debt, Sister's thugs will come after us—or our families. Remember Xiaoli's sister?"

"Everyone *knows* about Xiaoli's sister," said Jade angrily. "Her murder was *meant* to scare us. The snakeheads control us by fear." Jade gave Suyin a pleading look.

"If I don't get paid, I can't help Little Brother. Why else would I give up my life?"

"If we strike, we'll have no place to stay," said Suyin in a worried voice.

"At least we'd be free!" said Jade. "This isn't a safe house. It's a prison."

"For once Fumble Fingers and I agree," said Kwan-Sook snidely.

Pang tried to change the subject. "That's a pretty scarf, Suyin."

"It may be pretty," sneered Kwan-Sook, "but it is pig's bones work. I'll take soy sauce chicken any day of the week! Quick, easy, and pays better. Suyin's spent months embroidering for Mrs. Tang and she hasn't seen a cent yet. Big Shot Tang's taking advantage of you."

"I agree," said Jade. "I think she's cheating you, Suyin. You'll make more money stitching baby bibs."

Jade's words hurt her to the quick. Was her friend trying to take away what she'd just gained?

"I trust Mrs. Tang," Suyin said quietly. It was Lao she didn't trust.

"I saw Mrs. Tang yesterday at the Golden Palace," said Pang. "She was having lunch with Sister."

"What do you know about Mrs. Tang?" asked Suyin. Pang had sharp ears. He asked questions and he eavesdropped.

"She's a big shot in the Fuzhounese community, but she mixes with the *lao fan*. People call her Dr. Helen Tang."

"She's a doctor?" asked Kwan-Sook.

"Not a doctor for sick people," said Pang. "She's an intellectual."

"She went to university to study textiles," added Suyin. "That's why she loves embroidery."

Kwan-Sook rolled her eyes.

"Her husband, Edward Tang, is a second-generation American Chinese," said Pang. "He's a rich and successful bigwig. Manager Ren says he's a banker. He says Mr. Tang's wife makes the factory bosses nervous because she's spoken against human smugglers. She says they take advantage of illegals."

"But most of the girls who stitch the clothes she sells are illegals," said Jade.

"She's a phony," said Kwan-Sook with relish. "If she was really against smuggling, she would have helped us."

Pang nodded. "Something's not right. If Mrs. Tang is who she pretends to be, how could she deal with crooks like Sister and Lao?"

That night, Suyin couldn't sleep. Her friends were ganging up on her, trying to spoil what she'd worked so hard for. She'd expected Kwan-Sook to belittle her accomplishment, but not her friends. Her embroidery defined who she was—a girl with a history of needlework that ran in her bloodlines. Finally she knew what it felt like to be a true Miao girl. Somehow Mrs. Tang had understood and for that alone, Suyin loved her.

*   *   *

In March the weather turned warmer. Crocuses and snow-drops pushed their way through the moist grass along the thoroughfares. The magnolia trees and the lilac bushes began to bud. Since Mrs. Tang's last visit, Lao had grudg-ingly set aside three hours every afternoon so Suyin could work on her embroidery. Her needlework had improved in leaps and bounds, but compared to the crane sisters, she was still a beginner. Although she missed her wondrous needle, she no longer needed it. Yet despite her accom-plishments in the needle arts, she had yet to prove herself worthy. Giving English lessons hadn't worked, nor being nice to Kwan-Sook, who had rebuffed her efforts. Deep inside, she knew that her heart was wanting. She hated Lao and Sister for their cheating, but she lacked the cour-age to stand up to them. She loved Wing, but she'd done nothing to defend her.

It was only through her embroidery, in her quest to create beauty, could she find solace. The pattern she was stitching on a silk scarf was based on an ancient Miao tale told to her as a child. A girl was climbing the Wushan Mountains. The girl was alone, exhausted, and hungry. But when she saw a meadow covered with pear flow-ers, the sight was so beautiful that the girl was filled with hope. She was able to keep walking and eventually she found her way back home to her village. From that day on, pear flowers symbolized hope for her people.

Using the seed stitch, a series of tiny knots left open to form loops, Suyin embroidered a finely textured surface of pear flowers. Then she added mountains and clouds to her design. As she stitched, the world of the present slowly faded away. She could forget her loneliness. She could forget her hunger. She could forget her failure to save her mother. When she stitched, she walked through meadows of pear flowers.

When Mrs. Tang arrived at the shop in March, Suyin laid her piecework on her worktable. She was anxious until she saw the pleasure on Mrs. Tang's face.

"They're beautifully stitched," said Mrs. Tang. "I'm going to make a special display of your work in my store window."

Suyin's heart almost burst with pride. The seamstresses were staring at her with envy. The lovely Mrs. Tang wasn't only her boss; she was her friend.

Mrs. Tang handed Suyin a bag of fabric and embroidery thread. "These are for your next projects, Suyin. My husband and I will be going abroad for a while, but I'll stop in as soon as I get back."

Then she carefully wrapped the Mandarin squares, the perfume bags, and the shawl, placed them in her satchel, and bent down to hug Suyin good-bye.

When Mrs. Tang reached the hallway, Lao called her back.

"Don't go, Mrs. Tang! Sister wants to see you!"

Mrs. Tang frowned and tapped her watch. "Mr. Lao, I have another appointment in fifteen minutes."

"Sister asked me to phone her when you stopped by the shop. She's on her way. Sit, Mrs. Tang," said Lao, pulling up a chair. "She won't be long."

Mrs. Chin's ears pricked up. "Sister's coming!" she croaked.

"Maybe she's going to pay us our back wages," said Wing.

"I hope so," grumbled Mrs. Chin. "I had to borrow money from my neighbor to pay this month's rent."

Ten minutes later, Sister stumped in. "Dear Mrs. Tang," called Sister in her best nice-old-auntie voice. "Thank you for waiting. Come inside my office, please. I have a nice surprise for you. And Lao, Mr. Lin needs his dress order delivered to his shop on Worth Street. Now!"

"Sister's here," said Lao nervously. He grabbed Mrs. Tang's materials and placed them in the storage cupboard. "You'd better get those shirts clipped, Fumble Fingers."

As soon as Sister's office door closed, Mrs. Chin rose from her chair. She had a nose for trouble.

"I smell a rat," she said. "Sister's got something up her sleeve."

The tiny woman pressed her ear against the door. When she returned, she was furious.

"Sister just made a twenty-five-thousand-dollar donation to the Chinese Benevolent Association!"

"Impossible," said Kwan-Sook. "She's broke."

"In a pig's eye!" hissed Mrs. Chin. "She's up to her old tricks."

Kwan-Sook crossed her arms. "Why would she give money to charity?"

"She's buying *influence*," fumed Mrs. Chin. "*Guanxi.* Mrs. Tang's the chairwoman for the Chinese Benevolent Association. She's influential with the Chinese community and the wealthy *lao fan.* Sister Fang-chou wants a makeover! Big-Time Crook becomes Sucky Do-Gooder! She's looking for a high-society lady to open doors for her, invite her to fancy-pancy parties! Who better than Helen Tang?" Mrs. Chin shook her head in disgust.

"I thought Sister already had *guanxi*," said Wing.

"She's got her admirers," rasped Mrs. Chin, "but not the *uppity-ups*. They look down their noses at her. To them, she's a criminal. But if Sister makes a sizeable donation to Mrs. Tang's charity, Mrs. Tang is obliged to accept it. And once she accepts the favor, that favor becomes a *ren-qing* debt."

"And must be repaid," said Jade, suddenly understanding.

Mrs. Chin nodded. "Mrs. Tang will be obligated to Sister because she's helping the unfortunates. Sister withheld my pay for eight months while she lived high off the hog. I finally quit. For the next five years I worked for lychee nuts—low-paying piecework. Finally, I swallowed my pride and asked for my job back. That was ten years ago. I'm still waiting for the money she owes me."

Was everyone in Gold Mountain trying to cheat people? thought Suyin bitterly. Sister and Lao more than likely, but surely not Mrs. Tang. Even if Mrs. Tang *did* accept Sister's money, it didn't mean that her friend was a cheat. The money was for charity. Her friends thought that Mrs. Tang had duped her, but it wasn't true. She was determined to prove them wrong.

Suyin spent the next two days finishing the shawl. When she'd tied off the last stitch, she gathered her courage and pushed open the door to Lao's office. Lao was reading the newspaper. A cigarette hung from his lips.

"Mr. Lao, sir, I finished embroidering the shawl for Mrs. Tang."

"Leave it on my desk," he said without looking up.

"About the money I've earned from the embroidery work—"

"I've sent it to your people," grunted Lao.

"Mrs. Tang paid you?"

Lao placed his newspaper down and took a long drag of his cigarette. He blew a smoke ring into the air.

"Yes, she paid me. The flat rate per piece was sixty American dollars, forty dollars for the house and twenty for you. You stitched six pieces—that shawl makes seven, at twenty dollars per piece. I owed you one hundred and forty dollars."

She blinked. "You're lying, Mr. Lao! One hundred and forty dollars for weeks of work? I don't believe you. Mrs. Tang knows my work is worth more than that."

Lao's eyes burned with rage. "Look at the contract!"

he said, slamming it on his desk. "There's your so-called friend's signature. There are the terms!"

Then he grabbed her ear and twisted it until she cried out in pain.

"You cursed troublemaker! No one's interested in bloody embroidery except Big Shot Tang. I'm warning you for the last time. If you breathe a *single* word of complaint to that woman or anyone else, I'll break every bone in your body—your fingers, your wrists, your legs—and when I'm finished with you, you'll . . . never . . . work . . . again." His rage shocked her. Even when he'd beaten her, she'd never see him so angry.

"Now get back to work," he said between clenched teeth. "Two more rush orders just came in. The staff will be working late and you'll be sleeping in the shop tonight."

16

Betrayal

The shop was dark when she woke from the dream. She rubbed sleep from her eyes and stared up at the clock. It was four o'clock in the morning. She had finished snipping threads from the rush order several hours earlier. She had been dreaming of her mother again. Her mother was calling her from the Gray World. The sense of urgency in her voice was palpable. The sisterhood needed help. Time was running out.

As Suyin shook herself awake, the memory of Mrs. Tang's betrayal stung her with fresh hurt. How could she have been such a fool? She had trusted Mrs. Tang. She was a living, breathing dream. But the dream was as much an illusion as Lao's stories of gold.

Was Lao lying? Maybe he and Mrs. Tang had both

tried to cheat her. She kicked the cart full of clipped shirts and sent it flying across the floor.

She rested her head in her hands. Her life was one of pain and loneliness.

She walked to the open window and gazed at the star-flung night. Somewhere beyond those tiny pinpricks of light, her mother was caught, unable to fly. What had she felt as she watched her arms become wings, her skin sprout feathers, her face grow a beak?

As Suyin clasped her feather, she felt her mother's presence flood her being. Her feather was her only chance to mend what was broken. Staring into the night, she made a promise to the stars. *I will find you, Mother. I will find you.*

"Do not ask rashly," cried a reedy voice.

Startled, Suyin leaped back. A tiny crane flew into the shop and landed at Suyin's feet. It was Demi, the demoiselle. Her long snow-white head plume fluttered in the evening breeze. The crane took small graceful steps like a miniature ballerina wearing a feather tutu.

"The clan sent me to remind you," said the crane. "If you transform too early, it is dangerous. Losing your bird self is a risk, not only to you but also to us. And the loss of your human self will affect the lives of your friends on earth."

Had she really intended to transform a moment ago? Suyin asked herself. She wasn't sure.

"You mustn't give up," said Demi. "The fate of the clan is riding on your shoulders."

"I'm tired of being a slave," said Suyin. "I've wasted months embroidering for that cheat Mrs. Tang. All for nothing."

"Not for nothing!" said Demi, her voice rising. "You gained knowledge and wisdom as you stitched. A girl may earn her wings with skill, diligence, and purity of heart, but a girl of imperial heritage must forge her own path. Your destiny is to lead, not follow. The heart feather requires the most of a sister. Skill in embroidery is not enough."

"Then what is?" asked Suyin.

The delicate little crane rested her wing on Suyin's shoulder.

"I can't tell your heart what to feel."

For a moment neither spoke.

"Where are the others?" asked Suyin.

"They're stitching a Miao hundred-bird coat."

Suyin looked surprised. "What's the occasion?" A hundred-bird coat was reserved for dignitaries of the highest rank and was worn only on very auspicious occasions. Suyin had never seen such a wonderful coat, but she'd heard her aunties speak of it with reverence.

Demi wrapped her wing over her beak. "I'm not supposed to tell. I'm here to take your mind off . . ."

"That cheat Mrs. Tang," railed Suyin, her temper flaring again. "I hate her worse than Sister. She's a phony, and I despise phonies."

"Hate is for children," said Demi. "Did you only stitch for the money?"

"No . . . but I owe money. Lots of it."

"If you were as rich as Sister, would you stop stitching?"

She hesitated. Stitchery now ran deep in her. It was the source of her struggle and her joy.

"No."

"A bird does not sing because it has an answer," said the crane. "It sings because it has a song."

"Embroidery is my song," said Suyin, more to herself than to the small being standing beside her.

Demi nodded. "It is an expression of what lies most deeply in your heart. For some, it is gardening or poetry. For others it is dancing or cooking—whatever stirs us. Search your heart for the answer."

She could tell something fishy was going on by the smirk on Kwan-Sook's face as she whispered in Sister Fang-chou's ear.

"Stop the machines," shrieked Sister angrily. Wearing a faded cotton housedress with nylon stockings rolled up just below her knees, their boss looked as if she'd just gotten up after a sleepless night.

"Which ones?" Sister snarled.

Kwan-Sook pointed at Jade. "That one's the biggest troublemaker. Talking strike, strike, strike! But her friends

Suyin and Wing are no better. Always complaining. Stirring up trouble. Even that stupid old lady, saying you cheated her ten years ago and you're cheating her again. I begged them to have patience, but they wouldn't listen."

Suyin stared at Kwan-Sook with disbelief. She was trying to get them all fired!

"You're the troublemaker, Kwan-Sook!" said Jade. "Not us."

Kwan-Sook fixed her eyes on Jade. "You were threatening to strike, you can't deny it."

Jade blanched. Kwan-Sook gave Sister an *I told you so* grin.

Sister scowled, her dark eyes burning with rage. "Bloodsuckers!" she screeched. "Dock the staff three days' pay for insubordination. And lock the three fresh-off-the-boats out of the safe house. We'll see how long the ingrates survive on the street."

"We didn't do anything," said Wing.

Kwan-Sook smiled smugly.

Suyin's heart was pounding. They still had their jobs, but they had no place to live. Without protection, they would be at the mercy of the thugs. Mrs. Chin's horror stories returned to her with a sickening clarity. The seamstress who'd had her throat cut, the woman who had been cornered in an alley by four men who took turns with her. The young girl who was beaten so badly she was blind in one eye. They couldn't complain to the police. They were illegal.

"My photographs . . ." said Wing, her voice trailing off.

My Nu Shu notebook, thought Suyin. Luckily she always carried the tapestry on her person. After her needle was stolen, she was careful never to let it out of her sight.

When Sister left the shop, Suyin stared out the window. It was still raining. Where would they sleep? She heard Kwan-Sook humming as she worked. The girl's betrayal didn't surprise her, but her delight in it did. It was hard to imagine anyone finding so much pleasure in another's misfortune.

After work that night, Suyin and her friends shivered in the doorway of the building. The rain made pinging sounds as it hit the sidewalk. Still in shock, the three girls watched Lao and Kwan-Sook walk down the street laughing.

"You poor little ducks," said Mrs. Chin. "I wish we could take you home with us. But there are twelve of us living in three rooms."

Suyin nodded glumly. She understood.

"It's my fault," said Jade. "I was talking strike." Tears welled up in her eyes. "If something happens to me, Little Brother will have no future."

"Kwan-Sook betrayed us, not you," said Suyin, placing her arm around Jade's shoulder.

"You had a right to complain," said Mei-li. "We haven't been paid in six and a half months."

Wing was silent. She hugged herself to keep warm.

"I hope Lao swindles Sister out of every cent she has," muttered Mei-Xia. "See how *she* likes it."

"He's swindling Sister?" asked Suyin.

"He was bragging about it to one of his gambling buddies," replied Mei-Xia. "My uncle told us."

"Lao would cheat his own grandmother," spat Mrs. Chin. "Come along, my little ducklings. Let's go to the So Good Noodle House. Maybe Mrs. Wong's friend Mr. Lee will help you."

"Are we having tea?" asked Mei-li. "I'm freezing."

"Aiiya," said Jin. "Here comes Mr. Leung."

"Wait, girls," said Mr. Leung, his saggy brown suit flapping in the wind. He had a long thin face and patchy hair slicked down with grease. His fingernails were dirty yellow. A cigarette hung from his bottom lip.

"I heard you girls need a place to stay,"

"I suppose Sister sent you," said Mrs. Chin angrily. The Triplets shrunk back, clutching one another.

"No," said Mr. Leung, picking small flecks of tobacco from his lips. "News travels fast in Chinatown."

"Leave the girls alone," said Mrs. Chin.

Mr. Leung ignored her. "I operate the Lotus Flower Beauty Parlor. I'm offering you girls work. It's good pay."

"We've got work," growled Jade.

"You've got work, but no pay!" cackled Mr. Leung.

"Go away!" said Jade.

"We're not prostitutes," said Suyin in English.

Mr. Leung's eyes lit up. "English! Aiiya! You girls speak English! Me too!" he said, switching from Cantonese to English. "Not prostitution," said Mr. Leung, shaking his head. "No. No. Just touchy-feely. Massage in the back room. Talk heart. Good money. Better than stitching."

"Not interested," said Jade, turning her back on him.

Mr. Leung approached Wing. Wing froze. His claw-like fingers lifted her chin, scrutinizing her face. He had a ring on every finger of his right hand.

"What about you, pretty girl? You look young. Customer like young girl."

Wing drew back. "No thank you, sir."

Jade lunged toward him. "Dirty old man," she hissed.

But Mr. Leung kept on, using soft murmurings to try and convince them. When he made no headway, he got angry. "Lots of girl say 'not interested' but they change mind after few week on street. When you're hungry or cold enough, you come to me beg for work."

"Let's go," said Jade. "We're getting soaked."

As they entered the So Good Noodle House a mixture of delicious smells—lemongrass, chicken stock, and pork dumplings—drifted from the kitchen.

Suyin looked for Nancy until she remembered that it was too late for a schoolgirl to be up. She felt envious of the girl's good fortune. Nancy was second-generation Chinese. She could sit on the shoulders of her parents' hard work and sacrifice. Nancy's future was as bright as a silver coin. Suyin's was as black as a chunk of coal.

Mrs. Wong greeted them with menus.

"How do we get in touch with Mr. Lee?" asked Mrs. Chin as they crowded into a booth.

Mrs. Wong raised an eyebrow. "Labor troubles?"

"We haven't been paid in months."

Mrs. Wong put the menus aside. "First I'll bring you some tea and noodles, and then we'll talk."

Mrs. Chin looked embarrassed.

"My treat," said Mrs. Wong.

The girls smiled in relief. Everyone was hungry.

"Suyin, could you ask Mrs. Tang to help us?" Wing asked timidly.

"No," said Suyin, swallowing her pride. "She took advantage of me. She's just a prettier version of Sister."

After they'd eaten noodles with vegetables and tiny slices of chicken, they told Mrs. Wong their troubles. The frown lines in Mrs. Wong's forehead deepened.

"You can't live on the street," she said. "It's too dangerous. I can offer you girls a temporary place to stay, on Mulberry Street, if you don't mind sleeping in a basement. It's unfinished, but it's beside the furnace, so it's warm and dry."

"We're grateful," said Jade. "It's a roof over our head."

Mrs. Chin looked worried. "Will the renters kick up a fuss?"

Mrs. Wong laughed. "We own the building."

"We'll try not to be a bother," said Suyin.

"Mr. Lee should be able to give you some advice," said Mrs. Wong. "Let me make some phone calls."

Before long, a short, wiry-looking man wearing a baseball cap and chewing a big wad of gum entered the restaurant. He was carrying a pile of signs, printed in English and Chinese. He pulled up a chair and introduced himself in Cantonese.

"I'm Johnny Lee from the CSWA, the Chinese Staff Workers Association."

Mrs. Wong brought over a fresh pot of tea.

"How many workers in your shop?" asked Mr. Lee.

"Eight," replied Mrs. Chin. "But one worker has sided with the boss."

"Your shop is small," said Mr. Lee, "but every workplace is important."

Mei-li picked up one of Mr. Lee's signs. *"Say no to sweatshops.* What's a sweatshop, Mr. Lee?"

"It's a workplace where labor laws are violated, where workers endure long hours for low pay, where wages are withheld by greedy bosses, where bathroom visits are timed and fire-doors are locked and workers are cursed and beaten like slaves."

"That's our shop," said Cousin Jin grimly.

Mr. Lee slurped his tea. "Yours and hundreds of others in the city, I'm afraid."

"Sister hasn't paid us in six months," said Jade.

"A familiar story," said Mr. Lee. "'Next month. Next month.' A broken record. We're expecting more shops to strike tomorrow," said Mr. Lee. "Not Sister's. Another factory boss. Discontent is contagious." Mr. Lee pulled out a pocket-sized Chinese lunar calendar. "Tomorrow is March the fifteenth, a lucky day. If you ladies walk out,

Sister Fang-chou will have to take notice. She's been playing this same dirty little trick for decades."

"How does she get away with it?" asked Jade.

"She hires illegals," said Mr. Lee. "They're afraid to complain. But if enough shops strike, the U.S. Labor Department or the city will be pressured to investigate these workplaces for labor infractions. Sister may figure it's less trouble to pay you than deal with the investigators."

"I'm ready to walk off the job," said Jade.

"What about Little Brother?" Suyin asked. The strike seemed a distraction. The only thing that mattered to her now was finding her mother.

"I'm doing it for him," said Jade. "Give me a picket sign, Mr. Lee."

Jade gave Wing a pleading look. "It's our only chance, Wing."

Wing took a sign. Then Cousin Jin stuck out her hand.

Mrs. Chin's eyes popped out. "Are you crazy, Jin?"

Jin lifted her chin. "No, I'm sick of being Lao's whipping girl."

"Us too," said the sisters.

Jade reached for Suyin's hand. "Remember our pact, Suyin?"

Suyin nodded and reluctantly reached for a sign.

"Join us, Auntie, please," begged Mei-li.

"Not on your life!" replied Mrs. Chin. "I've been blacklisted once. Never again."

Only when Mrs. Chin realized that she couldn't change their minds did she agree to walk off the job.

"I'll probably live to regret it," sighed the tiny woman. "But if you young ones are going to be foolhardy, I can't let you do it alone. Just don't ask me to carry a picket sign."

17

Bird

The following morning, after spending the night in the basement of Mrs. Wong's apartment building, the three girls walked to work.

As they rounded the corner near the Lucky Eight Tea Parlor, Baldy Chun and Fat Wu grabbed Wing from behind. She screamed, hitting the men with her hands. Suyin and Jade dropped their signs and rushed to her aid. They kicked and punched the men as White Tiger watched, taking quick nervous drags on his cigarette. Suddenly out of nowhere, Pang raced past them on his bike. He tossed a bag of Chinese takeout through the air. The bag landed at Baldy Chun's feet.

"For your breakfast, Baldy!" yelled Pang. "It's on the house!"

Baldy blinked. He loosened his grip. Wing stumbled

onto the pavement. Suyin and Jade pulled Wing to her feet and they ran.

"Thanks, brother," shouted Baldy stupidly.

When the girls reached the shop, they collapsed on the curb, heaving. A thin trickle of blood ran down Wing's leg. Pang skidded his bicycle to a stop. He threw their picket signs on the sidewalk.

"How did you know we needed help?" asked Suyin, trying to catch her breath.

"Mrs. Wong called me," said Pang. "She was worried that Sister's monkeys might harass you. Your boss is well-known for hiring thugs to punish workers who stand up to her. Mrs. Wong asked me to keep an eye out for you."

"You're our hero," said Jade.

"Don't be silly," said Pang, kneeling beside Wing. He cleaned the blood from her scraped knee with a wrinkled napkin.

Suyin watched his slender fingers gently ministering to her friend. He has a soft heart, she thought.

"Kwan-Sook told me what happened," said Pang.

"That whiny little weasel stabbed us in the back," said Jade.

"I know," said Pang, shaking his head. "I told her I was disappointed in her." He handed Jade a bag. "I thought you girls might want these." Inside were Wing's and Jade's photographs, Suyin's Nu Shu notebook, and her bag of fabric and embroidery silk that Mrs. Tang had given her for her next project.

Wing and Jade showed their gratitude with hugs and pecks on Pang's cheek. Suyin hugged him but she was too shy to give him a kiss.

"Does Kwan-Sook know you brought us our stuff?" asked Jade slyly.

"Yes," he said, staring at his shoes. "She's angry with me for helping you."

"Weren't you afraid of the toughs, Pang?" asked Wing.

Pang grinned. "No, I have my own system of protection," he said, hopping on his bike. "Chinese takeout!"

Halfway down the street, Pang turned and waved. "Good-bye, Suyin!"

"Good-bye, Pang," said Suyin quietly. Jade was watching her.

"Do you like him?" asked Jade.

"He's a good friend," said Suyin.

Jade looked her straight in the eye. "That's not what I meant. Do you like him as a boyfriend?"

"It doesn't matter how I feel, Jade. Circumstances are against us."

When Jade agreed with her, Suyin was crushed. Even though she knew that falling for Pang was like trying to reach for the moon.

When Lao saw the seamstresses picketing, he snickered.

"Do you think Sister cares if you strike? For every one of you, there are a hundred girls desperate for work. Old

Sharktooth runs the garment district. No one will hire you now."

"Except for Mr. Leung," snorted Kwan-Sook.

By mid-morning, the sky had clouded over. By noon, it was raining hard. Lightning flashes lit up the sky. The seamstresses huddled together in the doorway of the tenement until Mr. Lee brought them thin plastic capes to wear over their clothes and plastic wrap to cover their signs, but the dampness seeped into their bones.

On Mr. Lee's advice, they set out a tin can to collect donations for a strike fund, but people crossed the street to avoid them.

"They're afraid of the factory bosses," said Mrs. Chin.

Suyin felt her spirit sinking with every hour.

Only kind Mrs. Wong and Pang donated money.

"For your supper," said Pang, stuffing bills into their can.

"Did you steal it?" asked Suyin, frowning. But the Triplets got angry with her.

"We're hungry," growled Mei-Xia. "Let him help us."

The rain continued the next day. Puddles formed on the roads. A thick fog blanketed the city. The sky was black. As the seamstresses marched past the Good Fortune Garment Factory holding their signs, Suyin taught them the English words for *strike*, *sweatshop*, and *picket*. They were cold, wet, and miserable.

*   *   *

On the third day of the strike, Mrs. Chin pushed her spectacles back with her knuckles and checked her watch.

"Lao and Kwan-Sook are late for work. Something's fishy."

No sooner had Mrs. Chin uttered those words than Kwan-Sook led six sleepy-looking little girls past their picket line. The replacement workers were young, ten or eleven years old. They wore bewildered looks and filthy clothes. Their bodies were skeletal.

"Fresh-off-the-boats," said Mrs. Chin under her breath.

Wing gripped Suyin's hand. "They're taking our jobs!"

What fools they were, thought Suyin bitterly. They had hoped their strike would disrupt Sister's business and force their boss to pay them their back wages. Now Sister would continue to get rich while they were cold, hungry, and jobless.

Kwan-Sook was dressed in a navy suit and a crisp white blouse. She wore a brass name tag that said *Manager* on her lapel.

When Mrs. Chin spotted Kwan-Sook's name tag, she poked her cane in Kwan-Sook's face and sneered, "Scab!"

"What's that mean?" asked Suyin.

"It's a not-very-nice word for replacement workers," said Mrs. Chin.

"I'd like to wipe that smug look off Kwan-Sook's face," said Jade between gritted teeth.

"Where's Lao, Kwan-Sook?" asked Mei-li.

"Managing another shop," said Kwan-Sook, her nose in the air.

The Triplets yelled at the young girls, "Scabs!"

The fresh-off-the-boats looked dazed. They have no idea what is going on, Suyin thought. She remembered her own shock and disappointment when she'd first arrived. She pitied those poor girls, could not bring herself to call them that horrible name.

A scab was a strikebreaker, but it was also a crust that formed over a wound. And now she understood that they were all wounded—the illegal immigrants—the faceless ones without a country to call their own. Only a few would be lucky enough to climb Gold Mountain. The rest would languish at the bottom, pushing shopping carts full of broken dreams.

"Congratulations on your *promotion*, Kwan-Sook," said Jade sarcastically.

"Why, thank you, Jade," replied Kwan-Sook with mock sweetness.

A bedraggled little girl dressed in rags lagged behind the others. Kwan-Sook grabbed the girl by the collar and yanked her inside.

"Hurry up, you laggard," she barked. "We've got a quota to meet."

Through the open window of the shop, above the roar of the machines, Kwan-Sook's high-pitched yelps drifted into the street.

"Faster! Faster, stupid! Time is money!"

When Pang stopped by the picket line that evening, Wing called him aside. Shortly after, the two disappeared. When Wing returned, her eyes were puffy and swollen.

"Pang bought me a phone card to telephone my father," said Wing. "I thought he would be happy to hear my voice . . . but all he talked about was money."

She burst into tears.

"What did he say to you?" asked Jade, stroking her back.

"He said he gave Lao his life savings and wants a return on his investment. I told Father I was broke, that Sister had withheld our wages. He didn't believe me. He thinks I spent the money on nice clothes and a good time." Tears streamed down her cheeks.

"Oh, Wing," said Suyin, hugging her.

"He said he'll disown me if I don't send him his money by next week." She grabbed Suyin's hands, squeezing her fingers. "What am I going to do?"

Suyin shook her head, unable to offer her consolation. She thought about Wing's father, how the snakeheads had cheated him of his life savings. The Snake was too powerful to fight, so he blamed his daughter.

Wing buried her face in her hands. "I asked to speak to my mother, but my father refused. He called me a bad person, too selfish to live."

The rain continued. It fell so hard that their cardboard picket signs grew soft and the lettering was impossible to read.

Suyin walked the picket line as if she were in a trance. Watching the replacement workers take her job was the last straw. Even if a miracle happened and she and her friends received their back pay, they would be saddled with Kwan-Sook for a boss.

The following morning, Mr. Lee warned them that a young seamstress from the Pearl River shop had been badly beaten.

"Two of Sister's thugs broke her arm," said Mr. Lee.

Wing gasped.

"As long as you stay together," said Mr. Lee, "there's no need to worry."

Liar.

When night fell, they spotted Mr. Leung staggering toward them.

"Here comes the dirty old man," said Jade. His hair was slicked back with oil and his clothes were rumpled. He smelled of alcohol, cigarettes, and sweat.

"Good evening, girls," Mr. Leung mumbled in awkward English. "I need more girls at the Lotus Flower. Get out of rain. Pay off your debt fast. In two year."

Jade placed her hands on her hips, scowling. "We're—not—interested!"

Mr. Leung pointed a yellow nicotine-stained finger at Jade. "Not you. You too plain. Her!" A sly grin crept slowly across the old man's face. "The delicate one, like flower. Men like nice girl. Pay good money." He took a pretty jade necklace from his pocket and held it out to Wing. "White jade. It will change your fortune, little girl. Here! You keep! It's kindness only. Heart present."

"Don't take it, Wing," warned Jade.

Wing reached out for the necklace, her eyes bright. She held it up to the light.

"White jade is lucky," she said, fastening the necklace around her neck. "I'm in need of some luck. Thank you, Mr. Leung."

"Now you owe that disgusting old codger," said Jade.

Wing's eyes flashed. "I owe him nothing. Why would you begrudge me such a small pleasure?"

"There's blood on that necklace," said Jade. "Blood and tears."

Suyin thought of how wolves or feral dogs attack the weakest member of the flock. Like a predator smelling blood, Mr. Leung sensed Wing's vulnerability. If Wing's father hadn't been so blind to his daughter's nature, he would have kept her home, where surrounded by family, she would have blossomed.

On the tenth day of the strike, Pang came riding up the street, waving a newspaper. Suyin's heart lifted. If it hadn't been for Pang's donations to their strike fund and Mrs. Wong's noodles, she and her friends would have starved.

"Suyin!" he called, beaming. He hopped off his bike, breathing hard. He had grown more handsome over the last few months. Dark eyes with thick girlish lashes. Perfect teeth. A smile that melted the hearts of old ladies and young girls alike. Mrs. Wong and Nancy spoke highly of him.

"A good boy," said Mrs. Wong.

"Looks like a movie star," said Nancy. "All the girls in the neighborhood have a crush on him," she joked. "Me too!"

She had also noticed he'd grown taller and more muscular. His pants were patched and too short. She could see his bare ankles, and the buttons of his faded shirt pulled against his chest. Yet even his worn and ugly clothes couldn't hide his beauty.

"Is business going well?" she asked nonchalantly. "You look like you're celebrating."

"Which business?" he asked, teasing.

She frowned. "The rat catching."

"Business is booming!" cried Pang. "Gold Mountain is teeming with rats. Except for the Noodle House! I'm working for Mr. Ng, the owner of the grocery. Mrs. Wong recommended me. But never mind me. I have good news for you!"

"You do?"

He thrust the newspaper into her hands. "I couldn't wait to show you." He was so excited he stumbled over his words. "I could only read a few words of English, but I recognized your embroidery."

She stared down at the newspaper. There was a colored photograph of her *hebao* and another of Mrs. Tang modeling her embroidered shawl.

"You're famous!" said Pang. He picked her up and whirled her around. She laughed uncertainly. A small fluttering of hope soared in her chest.

She read the article slowly, trying to digest every word.

New York socialite Helen Tang, known for her charity work in Chinatown, recently opened a second fashion outlet on Fifth Avenue. One of the more interesting features of Tang's store is the embroidered evening bags, scarves, and shawls. These one-of-a-kind items are gorgeous, but pricey. An embroidered evening purse sells for $500, a scarf for $800, and a shawl for $1500. But for those who can afford it, these works of art are worth every penny.

She felt as if she'd been struck.

"What's the matter?" asked Pang. "What does it say?"

"Lao and Mrs. Tang cheated me!" said Suyin. "You were right all along. Mrs. Tang is charging a fortune for my work and paying me a pittance!"

"Maybe Lao lied to you," said Pang.

"Now you're standing up for her?"

"No," protested Pang. "But maybe I was wrong."

Suyin shook her head sadly. "Mrs. Tang's been in the business a long time. She must have known what Lao was like. If she cared about me, she would have made sure I was paid fairly. No, Pang. Mrs. Tang, Lao, and Sister are cut from the same cloth!"

Pang stared at her helplessly.

Suyin folded her arms. If Mrs. Tang had known anything about embroidery, she would know how precious a *hebao* was to a girl. That woman had stolen her pride and her heritage. She had broken her heart. Suyin dropped her picket sign.

"Where are you going?" asked Pang. He rode after her, apologizing.

"It's not your fault, Pang, but I want to be alone now."

She was tired of the lying and cheating. She was tired of marching in the rain and cold. She was tired of holding up those pointless picket signs. She and her friends would never win against the likes of Sister Fang-chou. She wanted to escape. She wanted her mother.

At Columbus Park, she sat on a bench and counted her broken dreams. Her people sending her away, Lao's and Sister's betrayals, and now Mrs. Tang's. She took out the imperial tapestry from her jacket and stared at it until her eyes swam with tears.

A longing, deep and consuming, clutched at her chest, a yearning too long denied. Did every orphan yearn for a mother, she wondered? Did they long to feel a mother's embrace or to be touched by her tender words? Was Suyin's need so different from Pang's or Kwan-Sook's?

The cranes had warned her that a hasty transformation carried great risk, but they had also told her that a queen (and surely a princess) had to chart her own course. Maybe this meant setting out to save her mother sooner rather than later? If she could restore the queen to the sisterhood and the world, surely she would be forgiven.

She wondered if she would miss her human body. Would her heart be the same heart? Would her mind be the same mind? Would transformation hurt?

Wind rocked the trees above her. She looked up at the sky. The clouds were gathering again. Now that the moment had finally come, she felt an icy terror run through her body, but her longing dampened her fear. She tucked the tapestry into her pocket. She closed her eyes and took a deep breath.

With trembling fingers, she clutched her heart feather, felt the shaft against her skin. Concentrating with every inch of her being, she thought *wings* and *flight* and *mother*. She gave a quick hard tug on the feather. Something ancient and wild rose up in her.

"Now," she whispered. "Give me wings."

She heard a wild thrumming. Spots danced before her eyes like stars exploding. Surges of energy like mild electric shocks flowed through her limbs. Her breath quickened. Her heart pounded like a drum. The ground shifted under her feet. The sky spun. The bones in her neck were lengthening and growing hollow. In her pectoral and pelvic girdle and her spinal column, the fusion occurred in one short rapid burst. Blood and marrow flowed through the narrow cavities of her bones. Pockets of air filled the spongy hollows of each new vertebra. Her humerus grew longer. The radial of her wrists became a lovely hinge. Her fingers grew together at the outer edges. Her arms became wings. She felt her teeth dissolving. Her mouth became fluid, flowing outward like a stream that suddenly hardened and then split into two distinct parts to form her beak. Her voice box lengthened, hollowed, and coiled. Feathers sprouted from her skin like mushrooms after a rain: the small downies, the body contour feathers, the tertials, the primaries and secondaries.

Her heart was breaking. Two chambers became four. Blood rushed into her new body, as familiar as it was strange. Fear and wonderment like two currents flowing in opposite directions pushed and pulled against each other, then crashed, leaving her breathless. She was coming home to herself. *Bird,* she said to herself. *I am bird.* Her first utterance was like the cry of a newborn. The sound rose from her long convoluted throat, the ancient cry of crane.

And then suddenly, miraculously, she was flying! She felt light and free, until it suddenly occurred to her that she had no idea where she was or where she was going! She saw the park below her, a small square of green in a maze of streets and buildings. She flapped her wings and felt herself lifted up and over the building tops. She flew higher and higher until the cars and buildings looked like dots on a map.

She blinked, suddenly aware that she had three eyelids—a top, a bottom, and a transparent membrane like the windshield wipers of a car. She felt a wild burst of happiness, fraught with uncertainty. She rode the wind like a kite, twisting and turning, experimenting with her wings. She cut through the air with her primaries, propelled her body forward, and executed a dazzling pirouette in midair. Oh joy! Oh terror!

Her new body enchanted her. She loved her grayish white wings and her sleek black head and neck. She loved her razor-sharp beak and her long slender legs.

I am a lovely black-necked crane. She soared past cloudbanks infused with sunlight. She tucked her heart feather inside the down of her breast feathers, so it pressed against her tiny heart. She breathed two quick bird breaths for every human breath, felt the rapid pulse of blood pumping through her arteries, into the hollow spaces of her slender bird bones.

Fear and excitement rose and fell in her chest with every breath. How high could she fly without falling? She rose higher and higher into the light. She gazed down on the distant landscape below: snow-covered mountains, bright green valleys, cities of concrete and steel, rivers winding through farmland. She remembered riding on Li-Wen's back, seeing a similar landscape, but now she was alone and lost. Emerging from a thick bank of clouds, she blinked into the fiery brightness of the sun. She opened her beak to sing, pushing the air through her coiled windpipe, experimenting with sound: trumpeting, croaking, trilling, ratcheting, rattling, and whooping. She was every instrument in her own orchestra.

She was lost in the pleasure of her own music—so lost that she almost missed hearing the background chorus. A flock of cranes were answering her calls, folding their voices into hers. *The unison call. The symbol of unity.*

She continued calling until the flock joined her—black-necked cranes, whoopers, demoiselles, hooded cranes, blue cranes and sandhills. They surrounded her like a protective squadron. She recognized Grandmother and Mulaba, Hazrat, and Demi, and leading the flock, Li-Wen, beating her wings in syncopation.

A sudden burst of light filtered through the clouds. The flock responded with wild cries and clamorous rattles.

Below her, the land shimmered in riotous shades of blues and yellows and greens. She shivered with delight. And the smells! The scent of roses and damp feathers, raindrops, sun-baked meadows, musk and pine and cedar!

The cranes landed in the meadow. Even before she began her descent, Suyin sensed that something was wrong. The cranes seemed nervous. Some paced stiff-legged, plucking at their feathers or scratching the ground. Others rooted quietly, avoiding her eyes. The atmosphere was somber, unlike the happy welcoming she'd received when she first arrived on He Shan.

Lowering her legs, she spread her wings and landed

with a gentle bounce. Li-Wen, Hazrat, and Grandmother were waiting for her. The remaining flock surrounded her in silence.

"Princess Suyin," said Grandmother. Although the crane's voice was tender, her rheumy eyes looked troubled. She could see the same barely disguised disappointment in the eyes of the others.

"What's wrong?" Suyin asked, though in her heart she knew.

Hazrat placed her wing mitt gently on Suyin's head.

"It is unwise to transform out of hurt . . . or anger."

"The risk was to myself," said Suyin. "It's my life to lose."

"*Your* life," said Hazrat. "*Your* risk. A princess must think of *others* before herself."

"But don't you see?" pleaded Suyin. "I transformed to save my mother—your queen!"

"You transformed for selfish reasons," said Mulaba bluntly. "Against the advice of older and wiser sisters."

"How is a quest to save my mother selfish?" asked Suyin.

"Suyin," said Hazrat gently. "What about your friends on earth?"

Suyin felt the blood drain from her cheeks. "I didn't think," she whispered. She had broken their pact. She had betrayed her friends.

Regret crept into her heart, but she hid it. She had too much pride to admit that she was wrong, especially after Mulaba's condemnation.

She lifted her chin, her eyes stubborn. "I'm going to save my mother with or without your help."

Hazrat placed her wing on Suyin's crest. "Come with me."

When they reached the wild turnip patch, Suyin thought about how Auntie Huishan and Hazrat both loved turnip cakes. And they both had green eyes.

Hazrat offered Suyin a root. Suyin shook her head. She was too upset to eat.

"Will you help me?" asked Suyin. "I need directions to the Gray World."

"Be patient," said Hazrat the Wise. "You've barely fledged. You'll need to build up your strength before you leave.

"Mulaba presented a strong case against your going," said the crane.

"She never liked me."

"It's not that," replied Hazrat, lowering her voice. "Her daughter tried to save your mother. She traveled to the netherworld, but she never returned. Her name was Mudiwa. It means *beloved*. She lacked your imperial heritage and she possessed no heart feather to guide her, only compassion and a burning desire to save the clan."

Suyin felt a lump form in her throat. Now she understood why Mulaba saw the world through a dark lens.

When the light faded, Suyin flew to the wetland to think. There was a dank smell of fish and waterlogged roots.

She stared at the thin sliver of moon and felt loneliness envelop her like a shroud.

The tension in the air was palpable. The crane sisters had been debating for hours. There were two opposing camps. Mulaba and her supporters argued that Suyin's mission was doomed to fail and that the sisterhood would lose her like they'd lost Mulaba's daughter. They had accepted the fact that their days of transformation were numbered and they believed that their only hope, a slim one at best, was that Suyin might discover the key to the Mysteries in the tapestry. They believed that embroidery was the road to their salvation, and they were determined to teach their princess every stitch they knew.

Li-Wen's camp argued that the clan should support Suyin's quest to save the queen no matter how grave the risks. The problem for both groups was that Suyin had failed to prove herself worthy. The cranes had expressed their disappointment in her. Someone had said cruelly, "The apple doesn't fall far from the tree."

The cranes' words felt like knives in her heart. Tucking her head under her wing, she tried to drown out the sound of desperation in the birds' voices. She slept fitfully, plagued with nightmares. She dreamed that the cranes were so disappointed in her that they clipped her wings. She dreamed she'd flown to the Gray World to find her mother dead, her body frozen like her father's. Sometime during the night, she woke to find the cranes around her, the warmth of their bodies a soft blanket of feathers, the low hum of their breathing like a lullaby.

At dawn, the cranes announced their plans for her. In the mornings, Grandmother would give her flying lessons. In the afternoons, she would join the cranes' sewing circle for embroidery lessons. A compromise between the two camps.

"But I want to leave today," said Suyin. *Before I lose my courage.*

"You are young and strong, but you are not invincible," said Mulaba.

"Mulaba's right," said Grandmother. "The journey to the Gray World is long and arduous. Unless you build up your strength, you'll never make it."

Reluctantly, Suyin agreed.

After a trip to the turnip patch with Hazrat, Grandmother took her flying. The old crane taught her how to fly into headwinds and ride the updrafts. She taught her how to read clouds, rain, and mist. These were survival skills, not tricks, stressed Grandmother.

After a rest, Suyin joined the cranes' sewing circle. When she spotted the Australian crane, Suyin rolled out the imperial tapestry and asked the brolga for help.

The brolga looked pleased. She placed her stitching aside and waited.

"The embroidery style stitched by the fourth queen looks a lot like yours," said Suyin. She pointed to a yellow circle with the two inverted arcs inside. "What does that motif mean?"

The crane answered without hesitation. "It means to forget."

"And the green circle with the squiggly lines?"

"A bush tree."

Suyin's excitement was growing. "And that twisted mark under the tree?"

"A root . . ." The brolga gave Suyin a sly look. "But there's a line through the middle that negates the meaning."

"What about that line of small red dots?"

"Our ancestors."

"*Tree, root, ancestors, forget,*" Suyin whispered. It hit her like a flash of lightning.

"To forget one's ancestors is to be a tree without a root." The saying was as familiar to her as sticky rice.

"I wondered how long it would take you to figure it out," chortled the brolga.

"You knew all along?" asked Suyin, taken aback.

The crane shrugged.

"Why didn't you tell me? I've spent hours puzzling over it."

"A future queen must learn to ask for advice from her elders," said the brolga. "You've taken an important step, Princess Suyin."

The cranes nodded in agreement.

Suyin's eyes brightened. She was beginning to understand.

"A princess who asks for help reveals humility," said Hazrat the Wise. "The core of the Chinese word *humility* or *integrity* is *unity*. Not the merging of *many* into *one* but one of holding *many* closely together. That is the role of a princess and a future queen."

"All these needlewomen were queens, weren't they?"

"Every one of them," said the brolga. "Each queen usually passes on the tapestry to her daughter for study and safekeeping. The tapestry is a history book and advice manual for a princess-in-waiting."

Suyin pondered her words. "If the queen passes the tapestry on to her daughter, why are some of the queens from different parts of the world?"

"All the women in the world are from one family," answered the brolga. "Your father's people were Han Chinese. Your mother's ancestors were originally from Thailand."

Suyin was surprised. "I didn't know that."

"In the earliest times, our ancestors were nomads. The women traded embroidery stitches like silks and spices."

The next afternoon, as Li-Wen showed Suyin how to stitch a good fortune pattern, Suyin caught the scent of thorn-apples clinging to the crane's feathers. The perfume reminded her of Auntie Cho-Ye. The shaman had always carried the dried petals to use in her healing potions. Even in the dead winter, the fragrance of flowers trailed her like a sweet summer breeze.

Suyin gave Li-Wen a questioning look, but she held her

tongue. She didn't want the crane to think her weak or immature. There was something else bothering her. After the initial euphoria of flight, she had yet to experience the wild joy that the sisterhood described.

Since Little Sister was a younger initiate, she approached her.

"I've transformed," said Suyin, "but something is missing."

"That's because you transformed for the wrong reasons," said Little Sister sadly. "You wanted your mother. You placed your own needs before those of others." Suyin saw pity in Little Sister's eyes.

"I hope you don't mind my honesty," said Little Sister, "but when you answer the call of your feather, you will feel the difference."

Suyin felt the sting of the young crane's words. Her gentle forthrightness reminded her of Shan-Shan. Was this possible? Since Shan-Shan was a year older than Suyin, could she have earned her wings a year ago?

"Tell me, Little Sister, are crane sisters allowed to confide in each other when they're in their human form?"

Little Sister touched Suyin's crown with her wingtip.

"In their human form," said Little Sister softly, "crane sisters can share their deepest feelings. They can sing and gossip and write poems as they stitch. They can promise each other eternal love, loyalty, and friendship."

Suyin's heart leaped. She wrapped her wings around Little Sister and laid her bird head on the young crane's breast. She could feel Little Sister's heart beating against hers and she wanted more than anything in the world to believe that she was embracing her best friend. Even if this was wishful thinking, she didn't want to know for certain because soon she would leave for the Gray World, and if she were to die, she wanted the memory of Shan-Shan's last embrace to remain with her.

Her nightmares were growing worse. Visions of her mother's half-formed wing, the malformed bones, the sparse feathers held her in their thrall. She woke gasping for air. These visions were like seeds taking root inside her, until she could think of nothing else but tending her dark garden of despair.

It was her fourth night on He Shan. She was afraid. If she didn't act soon, she would lose her courage. Unable to sleep, she rose from her nest. The moon was full and the sky was dotted with stars. She imagined her mother waiting for her. She held that image in her mind until her doubts disappeared. She would leave at daybreak. It was her destiny to mend what was broken—a promise, a wing, a heart.

In the distance, she saw a bird moving toward her. It was Little Sister.

"I need to know how to get to the portal between worlds," said Suyin. "Will you help me?"

The young crane hesitated. Her eyes looked sad. Finally she gave Suyin a small nod.

"You have to fly north to Yin Shan," said Little Sister. "It's that tall mountain over there. The crosswinds over Yin Shan are perilous, so you must take every precaution. The Cave of Yin Shan is located in a deep valley. Inside the cave is a dark underground labyrinth. The labyrinth descends to the netherworld. That's where you'll find the portal to the Gray World. It is said that the spirits of the netherworld will try and lull a seeker to sleep. Whatever you do, don't go to sleep! If you do, you might never wake up. I cannot tell you more than that. No one has ventured that far and returned."

"Thank you, Little Sister."

When dawn broke, the flock met Suyin in the meadow. Little Sister had told the others of her plans.

"You mustn't go," said Mulaba. "It's too dangerous."

"Her mind is clear now," said Li-Wen. "We must help her."

Mulaba's wings slumped in defeat.

Suyin bowed before the sisterhood. She felt humility and gratitude. She felt an aching love for her sisters, even for Mulaba, who wanted to protect her so fiercely. This might be the last time she saw her family.

"Tell me what to do," said Suyin.

"You must pierce your mother's heart with the shaft of your feather," said Li-Wen.

Suyin was incredulous. "What?"

"It is the only way you can transfer your life force to hers," said Li-Wen. *"Heart to heart.* If you succeed, your mother's wing will be made whole. You and your mother could fly to He Shan together. However, the risk to you is great because you have only your own transformative power to draw from. If you had proven yourself worthy, you would have enjoyed the collective power of the sisterhood. We could have helped you."

A shiver worked its way down Suyin's neck and into her chest.

"But we acknowledge the depth of your sacrifice, Princess Suyin," said Hazrat, bowing. "Your life has barely begun."

The fears she'd held at bay came rushing back, snapping at her like a pack of snarling wolves.

"Could I—?" She couldn't say it.

Li-Wen read her eyes. "Yes, Suyin. You could die. Your mother too. You could lose your transformative power. We all could. You could be trapped in the Gray World. We don't know." Li-Wen's voice shook with emotion. "And then we would have to live with ourselves for *allowing*, even *encouraging* you to sacrifice your own life to try and save us." The crane struggled for composure. "If you change your mind about going, we will understand."

Was Li-Wen testing her strength, Suyin wondered. The task ahead of her seemed insurmountable. She felt small and weak, a piece of flotsam on a stormy sea.

"I haven't changed my mind."

"You are our hope," said Li-Wen.

Hazrat touched Suyin's heart feather. "When you

pierce her heart, do not falter," she said. "Your intention must be pure. It is the purity of your heart that will save her."

"What do you mean?" Suyin asked helplessly.

"Love," said Hazrat. "I mean love."

18
The Gray World

Doubt knocked against her heart like a pendulum. She felt its force as a dull pain radiating through her body. She spent the first day gliding on the thermals, circling in larger and larger spirals, slowly gaining altitude until she spotted the peak of He Shan far below. When night fell, the temperature dropped, but her coat of feathers kept her warm. She used the stars to guide her. She tried to close her mind to the dangers that lay ahead by concentrating on each breath and wing beat.

As the sun rose, she caught the first glimpse of Yin Shan, its jagged peaks glistening with snow. The sight filled her with a sharp sense of foreboding. She beat her wings rapidly, concentrating on the shifting light to keep her terror at bay. At midday, she flew over the highest peak. Forests of coniferous trees lined the slopes. Between the peaks, she saw a ravine bathed in strange blue shadows, exactly as the cranes had described it. Circling the ravine, she searched for the cave's entrance, but she saw only a few patches of green in a vast expanse of white.

Snow was falling. She shivered and puffed up her feathers, trying to keep warm. She descended into the ravine and landed wing deep in a snowdrift. Using her wing mitts to hoist herself up, she slid on a slick layer of ice beneath the freshly fallen snow.

A deep silence hung in the air. Except for the tracks she'd made, she saw no other signs of life. As the wind picked up, swirling snow stung her eyes. She took long stiff steps in the deep snowdrifts, moving her head from side to side, watching for movement. The loneliness of the place terrified her.

She walked until she was exhausted and then she took flight again, scanning the ravine from above. The shadows gradually deepened. The snow covered her footprints. When she'd almost given up, she spotted a flicker of light through the drifting snow and flew toward it. Two torches marked the cave's entrance. She brushed the snowdrifts aside with her wings, lowered her head and entered the cave. The light seemed to glow from within the cave's high ceilings and sharp sloping walls. Cone-shaped stalactites of bloodred and burnt orange hung from the dome. From the floor, stalagmites rose in twisted shapes like the sculptures of a madman. She stood awestruck at the cavern's eerie beauty. She tapped the wall of the limestone cave with her beak. The air smelled of mold and decay.

"Hello! Anyone there?"

"Hello! Anyone there?" echoed her voice.

The light inside was like sunlight through mist, yet she could see no light source. At the back of the cavern, she spotted a narrow tunnel. She followed the tunnel downward, walking for what seemed like hours. As she descended into the darkness, the air grew bitterly cold. She followed the tunnel until she came to a fork. She decided to turn right each time the tunnel forked so she could find her way back. However, she soon discovered that the passage was full of switchbacks. Eventually she became disoriented.

Her legs were growing weaker, but she pressed on. She felt her way in the darkness, using her beak and her wingtips. Her eyes grew heavy with fatigue. She closed her eyes, twitched, and shook her wings, forgetting for a moment where she was. She reminded herself of Little Sister's warning: If she went to sleep, she might never wake up.

She staggered to her feet, shook her feather bustle, and set out again. The bottoms of her claws hurt. She curled them up to relieve the pain.

Gradually, the passageway grew smaller, until it was no wider than a foxhole. She was forced to bend her neck to push her body forward. Chunks of glutinous clay glommed on to her feathers, destroying the insulation of her feather coat. Shivering from the cold, she began to snuffle.

"Help me!" she called as she collapsed, her limp head resting on the floor.

A deep loneliness washed over her. She'd once asked Li-Wen if a bird could be lonely. The crane had told her that loneliness was a human trait, but that once a sister had transformed, she could never be entirely bird or entirely human again. It wasn't physiological, she'd explained. It was memory. Once you'd experienced another form of yourself, you carried the memory of your other self like an old suitcase. Now she felt that burden.

Her head felt like a dead weight. She lifted it and pulled herself forward using her claws. To fight her growing claustrophobia, she imagined open fields of moving grasses, a glassy sea stretching to a distant horizon, a vast expanse of sky on a clear day. But she could only hold those pictures in her mind for a moment.

Sometime later, the tunnel dipped sharply downward and she slid into a thick sludge. Exhaustion took hold of her. She closed her eyes and fought sleep. Something brushed against her wing. Her eyes flew open. Her body jerked. Something or someone seemed to be pulling her along.

"Who's there?" she whispered.

She felt a presence in the darkness, heard a voice calling her name. And then a low moaning sound like wind. *There had to be an opening ahead!* She inched forward, suddenly energized. A rush of icy air buffeted her wings. Bits of mud flew into her eyes. Lifting a wing in the darkness, she suddenly realized that the passageway had widened and she could stand. She took two tentative steps, but the force of the wind blew her off balance. Her bird legs collapsed and folded beneath her. The wind moaned like a woman crying. She fluffed up her feathers against the cold. She began to shiver. Her feathers were coated with ice. It would be hard if not impossible to fly. Turning her tail to the wind, she took small tentative steps into the maelstrom. If only she could see! Her claw felt the edge of the precipice, but it was too late. She slipped and fell. She landed on a narrow ledge below.

She pressed her tail feathers against the steep escarpment. It was thick with tangled roots. If she used her beak and claws, she might be able to climb back up, but nothing lay behind her but failure. A pebble skittered past her foot and slid over the ledge. She pricked up her ears. There was no sound. This was more than a drop-off. It was space itself.

So it had come to this. She had to leap or retrace her steps. She pondered her fate, sitting on her tail feathers. She thought of her Cao Hai aunties and Shan-Shan, Pang and Jade and Wing and Mrs. Chin and the Triplets. She thought of her mother and the sisterhood. She had never been so afraid. She didn't want to die. Life had never seemed so important as it was now.

How strange, that the darkness of the lower world

would bring her such clarity. She had always felt alone, but she realized, suddenly, that she hadn't been alone in Chinatown. She'd had good friends, but she'd abandoned them.

But here in the lower world, she was alone of her own making. What had she done? Even if her life would soon be over, she had been loved. Her friends in Gold Mountain had loved her, and in their own way, her people back home had too. They had fed her and clothed her and sent her to school. Her heart swelled as she thought of her mother and the crane sisterhood who had placed such trust in her.

"You are our hope."

She leaped.

She fell, head over claws into a whirlwind of light and air. Using her wings and beak, she threw her body against the torrent, only to be flung backward, twisting helplessly in the swirling eddy. The voice kept calling. She leaned toward the sound, pushing outward, and found herself propelled through the spinning air like a pebble in a slingshot.

She was in darkness, floating, almost weightless, blindly trusting her instincts.

In the far-flung distance, a shooting star burst into flame. It lit up the sky and spiraled downward. She followed its wake, moving her wings in slow motion.

A shimmering object spun slowly past her. Her breath caught in her throat.

It was the vision she'd seen in her dream! A twisted neck drooping over the right wing, pinions tinged with frost, a thin layer of ice coating a beak. Her bird mother's eyes were vacant, staring. Whirling above her crown was an aura of stars.

The air stilled. Suyin spread her wings, buoyed and held in place by the swirling stars.

Her mother was a perfectly formed crane except for her left wing—not really a wing, nor a human arm, but a skeletal bone rack from which strips of flesh and feathers hung like a set of beggar's rags.

She breathed warm air on her mother's beak until the ice melted, dampening her feathers. She wrapped her wing mitts around her mother's body and wiped the frost from her pinions. She pressed her ear against her mother's breast, listening for a heartbeat. Its faint thumping sent a shiver of joy through her body.

Her mother's pupils widened.

"Mother, it is I, Suyin. I have come for you at last."

A spark of recognition lit up her mother's golden eyes.

"My daughter! Suyin! My precious!"

Suyin's eyes welled up. Her heart opened to a room that had never been entered before. The room held happiness and light and warmth.

"You're so beautiful," said her mother, touching Suyin's crown with her wing mitt.

As their eyes met, Suyin's heart almost burst with joy. "Mother!"

She felt the backward folding of time. And all she had forgotten returned to her.

She was sitting on her mother's knee. She was wearing a festival outfit, an embroidered blouse of deep blue, a little red vest, and a starched pleated Miao skirt of white cotton. On her feet were two tiny silk slippers stitched with graceful birds and pear flowers. She kicked up her legs so she could see the pretty birds her mother had embroidered for her. On the sewing table by the window sat her mother's needlework. Her mother turned to her and smiled. She was beautiful.

She traced her mother's face with her tiny finger. She looked into her mother's dark expressive eyes, at her small nose, her high cheekbones, and rosebud mouth. She touched her mother's thick black hair piled high on her head in a topknot. She placed her fingers inside her mother's long silver earrings and gently tugged. She pulled on her mother's thick silver neck rings hung with silver coins. Her mother was wearing her people's wealth around her neck in the way of the Miao. She looked regal, like an empress.

Her mother planted a kiss on her cheek. The kiss tickled and she giggled in response. Her mother carried her to the window. They looked out at the lake. She perched her feet on the windowsill like a sparrow.

"There's your father!" cried her mother. "In that fishing boat on the lake! Look!"

Her father waved to her. His eyes had the mark of love.

"Soon it will be spring, precious daughter," whispered her mother. "I must leave you soon, but I will return with the first snowfall."

Her mother's lips pressed against her cheek. "How hard it will be to leave you." Her mother hugged her tightly, closing her eyes.

Another memory returned unbidden. This was the memory she'd tucked away in the darkest corner of her heart, the hiding place for whispers and secrets. The terrible day when everything changed.

She locked her tiny arms around her mother's neck, because her mother was leaving. Over her shoulder, she saw her father's grief-stricken face.

"They call you the crane wife," said her father. "The men in the village laugh at me. Why must you go away?"

Old Auntie Dou held her small hand tightly as her mother walked toward the lake. In the distance she could hear the cranes' clamorous calls.

Later, she heard her father's cries. She pulled her hand from her auntie's grip and ran toward the sound.

"An-Lan! Forgive me," sobbed her father. He was staring up at the circle of cranes bearing one of their sisters skyward.

Suyin felt herself pulled back to the present. Only now did she realize the immensity of what she had lost.

She rested her crown against her mother's breast. Her mother wrapped her inside her wings and she was carried along in her mother's orbit. She wanted this moment to last forever. *Mother and daughter. Bird to bird.* Her mother began to sing to her. It was a song about a wild green marsh and a fisherman who fell in love with a crane.

Her heart feather brushed against her mother's beak. Her mother started.

Suyin sensed her mother's distress.

"You must go now, beautiful daughter," said her mother.

Her mother knows what she has come to do.

"I have come for you, Mother. We will fly home together."

Her mother's eyes were full of pain. Her wing began to quiver. She pushed Suyin away with a strangled cry.

"No, my precious. My heart is a house divided. It has been my weakness as queen. I was deaf to the advice of my sisters and it has led me to this. Ask the sisterhood to forgive me, but I cannot allow you to trade your life for mine. I am a mother before a queen."

Suyin gazed deeply into her mother's eyes. The love she felt was pure and deep and miraculous.

Now, she thought. Before it's too late. She gripped her heart feather in her beak and mustering all her power, she plunged it into her mother's breast. And in that moment, she surrendered all she was and all she would ever be to the woman who had given her life.

She drove the shaft without flinching, but the membrane of her mother's heart refused to give. Using the last of her strength, she pushed the shaft deeper until the heart sac burst and the feather broke. She felt the rupture in her own chest, a sharp river of pain, as her mother's body, an empty carapace of bones and blood and feathers, slowly slipped from her grasp.

19

Return to Earth

When she woke, she was lying in an alley. A March wind blew her hair around her face and stung her skin. The light was too bright. Dazed and confused, she crawled behind a pile of cardboard boxes and buried her face in her hands.

Li-Wen's words echoed in her ears. "If you succeed, your mother's wing will be made whole. You and your mother could fly to He Shan together."

Where was her mother?

Her memories returned with sickening clarity—her descent into the Lower World, her last desperate act, then her mother slipping away. In transforming before she had proven herself, she had destroyed her mother and failed the sisterhood.

What remained of her heart feather lay on the pavement. When she reached for it, the feather crumbled. Only the cord remained, a reminder of what she once was—Princess Suyin, daughter of Queen An-Lan. She began to cry. She cried until her throat was hoarse and her chest ached. She knew now that her mother had loved her, but the knowledge had exacted a terrible cost.

She still had the tapestry. But what good would it do her now? Without the queen to perform the Mysteries or help Suyin unlock its secrets, the sisterhood had no future.

She pressed the tapestry to her chest, her eyes brimming with tears. If only the crane sisters would come to her, she would ask them for forgiveness. If she had been more patient, if she had somehow found a way to open her heart to others, maybe history would have told a different tale.

She gazed at the sky, her longing for flight so sharp and intense that people passing her on the street stepped away from her as if she were crazy.

Catching her reflection in a shop window, she was shocked to see how wretched she looked. Her eyes were haunted, her clothes ragged, her skin caked with dirt. She wasn't crazy, she told herself; she was drunk with grief, a girl who'd lost her mother and her wings.

And then for the first time since she'd fallen to earth, she thought about her friends.

When she reached the corner of East Broadway, she spotted Jade, Mrs. Chin, and the Triplets walking the picket line, but no Wing. Something was wrong. Wing would have never gone anywhere alone. Not with Sister's thugs roaming the streets. As Suyin approached the picket line, she saw Kwan-Sook and Lao leave the building. When Suyin reached them, she stopped to ask about Wing.

Lao snickered, but made no reply.

"She's working at Mr. Leung's beauty parlor," said Kwan-Sook with a smirk, "but she's not doing hair."

Suyin stared at her in shock. "You're lying."

"See for yourself if you don't believe me." Kwan-Sook snorted. "It's only a matter of time before you'll all be working there too."

Suyin ran until she reached her friends. Their weary faces registered disapproval.

"Where have you been?" asked Jade. "Everyone's been worried sick."

"You left without telling anyone," accused Mrs. Chin.

Cousin Jin scrutinized her. "You look like you've been rolling in the mud."

"Your hair's all matted," said Mei-li and Mei-Xia, tugging at the knots with their fingers. "What's that chalky stuff in it?"

"A relative died," said Suyin. "I've been grieving." Her friends looked at her in disbelief.

"Kwan-Sook told me Wing is working for Mr. Leung," said Suyin.

"That's right," said Jade coldly. "She thought you'd abandoned us. I didn't know where you were. No one did."

A sinking feeling settled in her chest. She'd been so wrapped up in herself that she'd shut out her friends.

Suyin touched Jade's arm. "I'm sorry, Jade."

Jade pulled away as if she'd been burned.

"Sorry isn't enough," she spat. "Working for that horrible man will kill her. If you hadn't left, she'd probably still be here."

"Please forgive me," said Suyin, staring at her feet. She had broken her friends' trust.

Jade's lips quivered as she tried to contain her tears. "Wing was desperate. Your leaving was the last straw."

"She'll have no friends at Mr. Leung's," said Mei-li sadly.

Suyin nodded. Wing would be lost without friends.

"Sister was charged with labor infractions," interrupted Mrs. Chin. "The police raided three of her shops. They broke down the doors and took her to jail. Mr. Lee said she'll get off with a fine, but it's a sign the city is cracking down on sweatshops." Mrs. Chin shook her head. "I never thought I'd see the day. Sister charged!"

Suyin barely listened. She was grieving her mother's death and the loss of a friend. She felt like a ghost as she trudged past the Waloy Bakery, past the AVC store where the televisions and boom boxes played Chinese music, past the fishmonger and the herbalist and then back to the strikers again.

If a loved one died back home, grief was shared among the villagers. There would be funeral songs and rituals, traditional foods and comfort, but when her mother died, she was bound to secrecy. Secrecy could be a bond for those who shared it, but a wall for those left out. Now she felt the wall between herself and her friends, one of her own making.

She had always felt set apart. In her village, she was the crane wife's daughter, a girl forbidden to stitch. In He Shan, she'd felt separated by secrecy. When the cranes had tried to help her, she had turned her back on them. She had destroyed her mother's life and the future of the sisterhood to feed her own need. The walls she'd built had become a prison.

When Pang spotted her, he dropped his bike on the sidewalk.

"Where were you?" he said, scowling. "How could you leave your friends like that? Wing was beside herself. So was I. I thought Xiaoli might have hurt you."

She gave him a puzzled look. "Xiaoli?"

"He joined the Flying Dragons gang after his sister was killed. The factory bosses hired him to do their dirty work."

"No one hurt me, Pang."

His face softened. "I've been worried about you. I've hardly slept since you disappeared."

"Pang!" yelled Jade. She pointed to Kwan-Sook, returning from her errand. She was marching toward Pang. When she reached him, she glared at him, crooked her finger, and the two disappeared inside the building.

Snatches of Kwan-Sook's angry voice drifted into the

street. When Pang finally emerged, after Kwan-Sook had torn a strip off him, he said wearily, "Kwan-Sook kept saying I didn't care about her. I told her I loved her like a sister and she slapped me across the face." He shrugged. "I don't understand girls."

Jade and Mrs. Chin exchanged looks.

"You're smart in some ways, but dumb in others, Pang," said Jade.

"What do you mean?"

Suyin touched Pang's arm. "Kwan-Sook doesn't want to be your sister, Pang. She wants to be your girlfriend."

Pang flushed.

When Pang left, Jade turned to her. "He cares about you," she said angrily. "But you're too wrapped up in yourself to notice."

"I care about Pang too," said Suyin quietly. She watched him as he sped down the street to deliver his takeout order. "He still thinks he's the Chinese version of Robin Hood."

"He's loyal and true," snapped Jade. "He's been supporting us. He and the Wongs."

"I know," said Suyin. "But one of these days he's going to be caught and he'll lose everything he's worked for."

She walked the picket line in silence, her remorse growing with every step.

"I'm going to Mr. Leung's," said Suyin. "Please come with me, Jade."

Jade nodded her head wearily.

The door of the Lotus Flower Beauty Parlor was locked,

so Suyin rang the buzzer. Wing opened the door a crack.

"I'm sorry, my friends," she said, her eyes filling with tears. "I need the money."

"Forgive me, Wing," said Suyin.

"You shouldn't be here," whispered Wing. "You'll get me in trouble."

Jade reached for Wing's hand. "Come back, please."

Wing shook her head sadly. "It's too late."

"No it's not," said Suyin. "Tell Mr. Leung you've changed your mind. We're going to win the strike. You'll see."

Wing laughed bitterly. "Win? You won't win. And even if you did, Sister will always find an excuse to cheat you. Lao is no better either. He told me he'd sent a hundred dollars to my father, but my father never got it. Lao stole it to pay his gambling debts. He bragged about it to Mr. Leung. He's probably stealing from you too."

Suyin tried to hold her composure. "Things are going to change, Wing," she pleaded. "Mr. Lee told us the Labor Department has hired more investigators. It will be harder for our bosses to cheat us."

She didn't believe her own words, but she would have spouted a thousand lies to persuade Wing to leave that dreadful place.

"The money's good here," said Wing, "Two years and I'll have my debt paid off." She glanced nervously over her shoulder. "I'd better get back to work."

Out on the street, Jade bit her lip, trying not to cry. "I should have done more—"

258

"It's not your fault," said Suyin dully. "It's no one's."

Jade's voice was angry, her eyes accusing. "It's *somebody's* fault."

Her friend's words hit her like a punch. Jade blamed her for Wing's fate as much as she blamed herself.

Suyin walked away, blinking back tears. Somewhere in an alley, she sank to the pavement and curled up in a little ball. If it was possible, she would have left her body and become a dust mote or a pebble, but the shell that contained who she was and whom she'd come to hate, had survived the catastrophe.

It was dusk when Pang found her. He parked his bike and sat on the ground beside her, wrapping her in his arms.

"My mother's dead," she said, bursting into tears.

"Oh Suyin, I'm sorry," he said, stroking her hair.

She felt herself letting go. There was no need to protect herself any longer. She'd been holding on too tightly to things. The world was an awful place and she'd made it even more so with her selfishness.

"Where are your crane friends?" he asked.

"I don't know," she said. "I failed them. I've been childish and selfish."

"Don't forget stubborn," said Pang, smiling a little. "You are all those things, but you are also loving and kind and brave." He leaned over and kissed her on the cheek. She turned to him, lifting her face, and he leaned down and kissed her on the lips. Her heart opened like a flower.

And when they broke apart, a sudden shyness overtook them both. A kiss could change everything, she thought. It could make the world a little more bearable. Maybe it could help heal a broken heart.

"The first time I saw you, I thought you were a beautiful creature from another world," said Pang. "I told Kwan-Sook."

Suyin smiled sadly. "That was dumb, Pang."

"I know that now," said Pang. "She's hated you ever since."

The night was clear and the air still.

"Have you ever dreamed of flying, Pang?"

Pang gave her a surprised look. "All the time. I dream I'm a bird and I'm flying over the treetops, and it's such a beautiful feeling that when I wake I'm disappointed that I don't have wings. Isn't that crazy?"

She shook her head. "No. Maybe you have a bird heart."

Pang grinned. "Is that good?"

"It's the best thing imaginable."

The moon had risen. They sat together silently watching the stars. He reached for her hand. His skin was soft. His fingers were long and graceful. She loved his hands. It was one of the first things she noticed about him. She was afraid to speak, afraid to spoil that magical moment with something ordinary. Every emotion she felt was close to the surface, grief and loss and love.

After a while she began to worry. "Shouldn't you be at work?" she asked. "I don't want you to get fired."

"My friend's got me covered," said Pang, smiling broadly. "Besides, I earn as much with my rat-catching business as I do as a delivery boy. Mr. Ng recommended me to three more businesses. The word's spreading." Pang's expression suddenly turned serious. "I have something for you." He opened his palm.

"My needle!" she said, her hand flying to her heart. *My mother's needle.*

"Wing stole it," he said, grimacing.

"What?" She stared at him with shock and disbelief.

"Kwan-Sook saw her trying to stitch with it."

"Maybe Kwan-Sook lied."

Pang shook his head. "I confronted Wing and she admitted it. She returned it to me and said to tell you she was sorry. She wanted to stitch piecework for Mrs. Tang. She figured the needle would help her, but whenever she used it, her stitches became a mess of tangled threads."

20

A Clarion Call

April arrived carrying flowers: cherry blossoms raining pink petals along the avenues, tulips waving red and yellow heads in Columbus Park, lilacs releasing their fragrance into the newly awakened spring air. Despite the loveliness of the season, Suyin felt blind to everything except her own grief. A week had passed since she'd lost her wings, but it seemed like a lifetime. The image of her mother's broken body haunted her. Walking the picket line, she gazed at the sky, searching for the cranes. A thousand unanswered questions crowded her mind. Would she ever see the cranes again? Would their feathers crumble and turn to dust? Would the secrets in the tapestry be lost forever?

She had lost her mother but found her memories: her mother's smile, her voice filled with tenderness, her bittersweet heart, torn between duty and love. She had caught a glimpse of her father too. And in that briefest of moments, she knew she had been loved.

Jade had once loved her too, but they were no longer close. Although the two still shared the basement in Mrs. Wong's building (Mrs. Wong had promised them a safe place to stay until they went back to work), they seldom talked. When Suyin told her that Wing had admitted stealing Suyin's needle, Jade refused to believe it.

"Kwan-Sook lied," shouted Jade. "Wing was a loyal friend." *Unlike you.*

It was hard to imagine Wing stealing from her, and at first she was angry, but she understood Wing's selfishness. She had been selfish too—perhaps more so. She and Wing had both yearned for a family. They had both acted out of desperation, and in doing so, betrayed their loved ones. It was easier to forgive Wing than to forgive herself.

Every evening after picket duty, she and Jade trudged back to Mrs. Wong's basement in silence. In the warmth of the old furnace, Jade stitched baby bibs and hair ribbons, and Suyin stitched a *hebao* using her mother's needle.

This *hebao* would never be sold. The embroidery would express Suyin's true nature, a girl who had made mistakes but was trying to make up for them. She used the royal tapestry as inspiration, copying the motifs and arranging the colors and threads in a way that pleased her. Embroidery had become her happiness. She lost herself in the beauty of art. In this way, she had become her mother's daughter.

One evening, she deciphered the missive of the nineteenth queen and she felt the needlewoman's voice travel across the years. "Patience and wisdom are twin sisters." As she recorded the missive in her Nu Shu notebook, she felt her understanding deepen. Her impatience had caused her mother's death. Her sisters had warned her, but she had been too foolish to listen. Her teachers had been Tragedy and Sorrow, but it was too late to turn back the clock.

On a cold and rainy morning, twenty-five days after the Good Fortune seamstresses had walked off the job, Sister Fang-chou sent Lao to the picket line to deliver an ultimatum. The workers were to go back to work or their smuggling fee would be due, in full, in one week's time. If they failed to meet that deadline, Sister's thugs would pay them a visit.

Suyin felt her chest tighten. "What are we going to do, Mrs. Chin?" she asked, clutching the tiny woman's wrinkly arm.

Mrs. Chin pushed her spectacles up with her thumb. "I'm not going to sugar-coat our options, girls. If we return to work . . ."

"That's not an option, Mrs. Chin," said Jade, her eyes flashing.

Mrs. Chin looked relieved. "Glad to hear that. We've sacrificed too much already to give up now. Our other two options would be to borrow from Toothless Li at twenty percent interest. If you girls do that, you'll be working off your debt until your hair's gray and your teeth fall out. If you don't pay, you'll have to face Sister's enforcers."

Two days later, as the sun was rising over the city, Mr. Lee raced up East Broadway, waving his arms and smiling. When he reached the Good Fortune picket line, he was breathing hard.

"Ten more shops are striking," he said excitedly. "The Chinese Staff Workers Association has organized a march to Seward Park. Be ready at ten this morning."

"Why today?" asked Mrs. Chin, surprised.

"Timing," said Mr. Lee. "The newly appointed head of the Labor Apparel Industry Fair Wages Task Force is anxious to show the community she means business. The task force is investigating labor violations in five of Sister's shops. Garment workers have to strike now when the iron is hot."

"Sister's been investigated before," said Mrs. Chin doubtfully, "but she cooks the books."

"The Labor Department's becoming more aggressive in ensuring the suppliers obey the law," said Mr. Lee. "And the business community is putting pressure on the factory bosses too. A man named Edward Tang is leading the charge. He and his associates are concerned about loss of revenue to the city if there's a prolonged garment workers' strike."

"He's probably as phony as his wife," muttered Suyin under her breath.

As the seamstresses marched down East Broadway that morning, the traffic slowed to a halt. The April day was unseasonably mild. Pushcart vendors pulled their carts off the sidewalks. Impatient cabbies, stuck in the traffic jam, leaned on their horns.

Suyin carried a picket sign saying, *On Strike for Unpaid Wages*. As she passed the Golden Palace, she saw Pang race toward the marchers on his bike. He parked his bike and joined the onlookers lining the streets. When he spotted her, he smiled. She waved, her heart fluttering in her chest. She felt her cheeks redden as she remembered his kiss.

Yesterday when Pang had come to see her at the picket line, he seemed like a stranger. Suddenly he was tongue-tied around her, stumbling over his words and blushing every time she looked his way.

"Stop daydreaming, Suyin!" croaked Mrs. Chin. "You're dragging your sign."

"She's staring at Pang," laughed Mei-Xia.

Mei-li giggled. Suyin hurried ahead to escape their teasing.

Mrs. Chin carried a homemade sign—*Stop Factory Bosses From Swindling Old People!*

A photographer took Mrs. Chin's picture, her sign raised in one hand, her cane in the other. It was the photograph that would appear in *The New York Times* the next day, the photo that was said to capture the mood of the strike. *David against Goliath.*

As they passed the Lucky Eight Tea Parlor, the Flying Dragons harassed them.

"Ingrates!" hissed a tough in a black bomber jacket.

"Piggies!" sneered another, amusing himself by swinging a bat at their legs. When the seamstresses gave them a wide berth, the men roared with laughter. By the time the procession reached Seward Park, Suyin's stomach was in knots.

In the park, a television crew from the local Chinese station had set up cameras below a makeshift stage. Leaning against the stage with folded arms, glaring back at the strikers, were two angry factory bosses dressed in shiny green suits.

Mr. Lee pushed his way through the crowd. His brow was knit with worry.

"Five hundred workers walked out today," he said, chewing a wad of gum. "I've visited every picket line and not a single seamstress is willing to speak out."

"They're scared," said Jade. "It's suicide to speak out."

Suyin's heart beat furiously. She could smell fear in the crowd, and anger. If only she had the courage, she thought, she would tell the world what she and her sisters had suffered. But she was afraid.

"I thought you were going to speak, Mr. Lee," said Mrs. Chin.

"I am," said Mr. Lee. "But I've never worked in a garment factory. Your bosses will say our association is trying to stir up labor trouble. If you girls won't speak for yourselves, your silence will speak for you."

"The INS could deport us if we complain," said Mrs. Chin. "We could be thrown in prison back home and still owe our smuggling fee."

Mr. Lee rolled his eyes. "The INS turns a blind eye. If they deported every illegal seamstress in the city, the apparel industry would grind to a halt."

"Leave the girls alone," scolded Mrs. Chin. "They're kids."

"They're *working* kids," said Mr. Lee.

"I will speak," said Suyin.

Jade looked surprised. "Don't do it," she warned. "I've already lost one friend. I don't want to lose another."

Did Jade's words mean that she had forgiven her?

A clarion horn call drew Suyin's attention skyward. A flock of cranes was circling overhead. The sky seemed to open up, turning from a dull slate gray to a bright bejeweled blue. The cranes called down to the crowd, trumpeting a greeting.

Suyin felt her heart ache with longing as the birds performed a graceful aerial ballet. People bent their necks, pointing and nudging their neighbors. Their mouths fell open in awe. Their blood spoke to the cranes' presence, their pulses wakened the way babies waken to a new world on the day they are born.

It was always like that when the Birds of Heaven neared the earth. Humans sensed some distant connection to a time when people could become a wolf, a deer, or a bird, and every living creature could move between worlds.

She wondered if the cranes belong to the sisterhood. Or if they were crane birds that had flown off course. Watching the birds spiraling in the updrafts, growing smaller and smaller until they were specks in a vast expanse of blue, she remembered how it felt to be lifted up by the warmth of the air, to glide like a ship over a sea of clouds.

It would be a lie to say she was content to be rooted to the ground like a turnip. But standing among the crowd, she felt a part of the human sisterhood. She had failed her mother and the clan, but perhaps she could help her sisters here on earth. She would be their voice and their truth.

She felt the same mind-numbing fear as when she stood on the ledge of the precipice in the nether world. Or when she sank her feather into her mother's heart. She knew more than most that not all acts of courage are rewarded. But finding her voice was the greatest risk, for she had to open her heart to all the women in the world, her family, the one in which she truly belonged. At last she understood that her life mattered, that every life mattered, not just to herself, but to the world, and that losing her life would not just be a loss to herself, but to everyone.

If she could do some good, her mother wouldn't have died in vain.

Climbing the steps to the podium, she spotted Pang in the crowd. He shook his head in warning. He was afraid for her as she, so often, had been afraid for him.

As she gazed at the sea of faces before her, she felt a sudden calm. These are my sisters, she thought. I will speak to *them*, not the factory bosses who were glowering at her, their mouths pinched with rage. The crowd grew quiet as she began to speak.

"My name is Zhu Suyin. I am a seamstress at the Good Fortune Garment Shop. I am fourteen years old. Most days I work the same number of hours as my age with no days off. Sometimes I have to sleep in the shop to finish my piecework. If my coworkers and I are too slow, our boss beats or curses us. Our long workdays make it hard to stay awake. That's when it's easy to make mistakes. If we miss a loose thread or sew a crooked seam, our boss docks us a day's pay. It's an excuse to cheat us."

Her sisters nodded with approval.

"We walked off the job because our boss hadn't paid us in six and a half months. Others shops haven't been paid for eight months. Why should anyone work for free? If there are labor laws in America, why are they not enforced?"

"Enforce labor laws!" shouted Mr. Lee

"Enforce labor laws," echoed the seamstresses.

"Many of us have been threatened by the factory bosses," said Suyin. "They've threatened to fire us or have us beaten."

"She's lying," shouted a factory boss. A vein in the man's forehead pulsed with anger. "No threats were made to anyone!" He cupped his hand, whispered in the ear of a man in a rumpled green silk suit. The man gave a quick nod, and pushed his way through the crowd.

As she stared into the eyes of her sisters, the weight on her chest lifted. Despite her fear, she felt wonderment, as if her two selves, her bird self and her human self had become one.

"She's telling the truth," shouted a young seamstress.

"Our bosses threatened to beat us!" cried a woman, hugging her daughter.

"They threatened to blacklist us!" added the daughter.

The man in the green suit began cuffing the girl on the head. The girl screamed. Three garment workers jumped on the man, knocking him to the ground. A television crew began filming the fracas until Lao knocked the cameraman down and stomped on his camera.

"Suyin, get off the stage," yelled a worried-looking Mr. Lee.

"Look behind you!" screamed Pang.

Rough hands pulled her backward into the melee. She screamed for help, but her cries were drowned out by the shouts of the crowd. *Enforce labor laws! Enforce labor laws!*

"Make a sound and you're dead," rasped a voice. Something hard dug into her side. Baldy Chun and Fat Wu grabbed her arms and pushed her through the throng. She scanned the crowd for her friends, but they had disappeared. Someone was calling for calm over a megaphone, but the crowd's chants grew louder.

Minutes later, she found herself in an alley. Lao stepped out of the shadows. He held a cigarette between his lips and a steel baseball bat in his hands.

She was terrified.

Fat Wu pulled her arms behind her back. White Tiger stared at her with a look of amusement.

There was no use struggling, she told herself. She was outnumbered and the thugs had weapons.

"The little upstart needs to be taught a lesson," sneered Lao.

"Blacken her eye," urged Baldy Chun.

White Tiger raised his fist. Steeling herself, Suyin closed her eyes. She felt a dull pain in her head, then dizziness. The flesh around her eye began to swell. A second blow grazed her cheek. Through muddied vision, she saw drops of blood staining her shoes. White Tiger punched her in the stomach, knocking the wind out of her. She doubled over, choking back tears. The pain rose and fell in waves.

"My turn, brother," spat Lao. He threw his cigarette on the ground and stomped on it.

Laughter. Fat Wu loosened his hold. She swayed on

her feet, searching desperately for escape, but the men had her cornered.

Lao swung the bat, aiming for her knees. She moved quickly, avoiding the blow. Lao chortled, showing off. "Watch the monkey dance, brothers!"

"Stop!" cried a woman.

The snap sounded like a twig breaking. The pain was hot and piercing. Her knee buckled. She lay on the ground, her cheek against the dirt. Above her, the sky spun like a toy windmill. She heard the whoosh of wings and faint rattling cries.

Heels clicking across the pavement. The scent of ylang ylang.

"Leave her alone," said a familiar voice.

Lao drew back. His face flattened. "It's Big Shot Tang. Let's go, brothers."

Suyin felt a gentle hand on her shoulder. Mrs. Tang knelt beside her. "They're gone now."

"My knee," she said, her eyes flooding with tears.

21

Two Birds. One Stone.

Mrs. Tang lived in a tall brick building uptown. A doorman in uniform brought a wheelchair out to the taxicab. Despite her throbbing knee, Suyin was awestruck by the fineness of the surroundings: the crystal chandeliers and gold-trimmed mirrors, the white carpets and elegant furnishings. At first, Mrs. Tang had insisted on taking her to the hospital, but Suyin had begged her to change her mind. She had no papers! She risked being deported.

Finally Mrs. Tang asked her doctor to make a house call.

"Don't worry, Suyin," said Mrs. Tang, patting her hand. "Dr. Lu is discreet. Besides, he owes Mr. Tang and me a favor."

Mrs. Tang propped Suyin's leg on a chair and iced her

swollen knee while they waited for the doctor to arrive. Her leg felt as if a thousand jackhammers were drilling into it. She tried not to be a baby, but she almost screamed when the doctor examined her bruised and swollen knee-cap. He cleaned up her cuts, ordered an X-ray and a pre-scription for pain.

"Will I be crippled?" she asked.

"It's too soon to tell," said the doctor gravely. Later, Suyin heard the doctor and Mrs. Tang speaking in low tones.

". . . stay off her feet."

". . . crutches. . . . a wheelchair . . ."

After the doctor left, Mrs. Tang brought a pot of tea. "Those thugs could have killed you."

Suyin stared at her rescuer with mixed feelings. The woman who had cheated her had saved her life. "How did you—"

Mrs. Tang broke in. "I knew you were in danger the moment you spoke out. When you left the stage, I followed you, but I lost you in the crowd. I searched the back alleys near the park." She shook her head sadly. "If only I'd found you a moment sooner . . ."

"Thank you for saving my life," said Suyin. "I'm grateful."

"Once someone saved mine," said Mrs. Tang softly. "The last time I saw you in the shop, I felt so guilty. I knew the factory bosses were taking advantage of girls like you. And when I heard you speak, I felt disgusted with myself. I had spoken against smugglers myself, so I couldn't pretend I didn't know what was going on." She took Suyin's hand. "You were brave today. Much braver than I have ever been."

"I'm not brave at all," said Suyin. "I'm scared most of the time."

"That's what being brave is," said Mrs. Tang. "It's doing the right thing, even when you're scared. When you stood up on that stage and told the truth about the working conditions in the factories, that was the bravest thing I've ever seen. I was so proud of you and so ashamed of myself. You showed me what I should have done and didn't have the courage to do."

"Cheating people doesn't take courage, Mrs. Tang," she said, her eyes flashing. "It's cowardly."

Mrs. Tang was taken aback. "Why would you think I cheated you?"

Suyin dug into her pocket, whipped out the newspaper clipping, and waved it under Mrs. Tang's nose. "Were you worried I might see this?"

"Of course not," said Mrs. Tang, looking bewildered. She opened her purse and handed her the same carefully folded newspaper clipping. "I was going to surprise you with it. Mr. Tang and I flew in from Beijing late yesterday evening. My assistant left the article on my desk."

"I received one hundred and forty dollars for work that you sell for thousands! I trusted you and you cheated me in the worst way imaginable."

Mrs. Tang froze. "I didn't cheat you, Suyin."

"Yes, you did, Mrs. Tang," said Suyin firmly.

"Suyin, our contract called for forty percent of the final selling price for you, forty percent for Tang's Fashion, and twenty percent for Sister. Lao assured me he had discussed the terms of agreement with you. I paid him in full and I assumed he'd paid you."

"I was paid a flat rate per piece, not a percentage," fumed Suyin. "For every piece I slaved over, Sister received forty dollars and I received twenty for a *hebao* that you'll sell for five hundred! Lao said my earnings would be delivered to my people back home, but I doubt he even did that."

"Lao lied to you."

"I saw your signature on the contract," said Suyin.

Mrs. Tang turned pale. "That scoundrel must have drawn up a different contract and forged my signature. I thought a written contract would protect you. I should have known better than to trust him." Mrs. Tang shook her head. "I knew the system was corrupt. You see, I was once a seamstress too."

Suyin gasped. "You?" She couldn't imagine Mrs. Tang as a seamstress.

"Yes me, and my mother too. I come from a long line of seamstresses. I sat at my mother's knee in a garment factory. When I went into business years later, I told myself that the industry had improved since then, but I realize now that I didn't want to know the truth. If I knew, how could I live with myself?" Mrs. Tang reached over and took Suyin's hand. "I'm so sorry, Suyin. Please forgive me. I'll make it up to you, I promise. You'll be paid every cent you're owed."

Suyin nodded. It would take time to forgive Mrs. Tang, but she knew that even the most loving people sometimes acted selfishly.

Suddenly Mrs. Tang pulled back her hand. "Goodness gracious!" she exclaimed.

A small white feather had sprouted on Suyin's wrist.

"Your natal feather marks the beginning of a life of service," said Mrs. Tang solemnly. "It is the true measure of your worth."

Suyin couldn't believe her ears. "Do you belong to the sisterhood?"

"I did once," said Mrs. Tang. Her voice was wistful.

"After I spoke at the rally," said Suyin, "I noticed that my chest suddenly felt lighter and I felt . . ."

"Worthy?" offered Mrs. Tang.

"Yes! I felt *worthy.*"

"You risked your life to be the voice of your sisters," said Mrs. Tang. "You've proven yourself."

"You said you *once* belonged to the sisterhood," said Suyin, lowering her voice to a whisper. "What happened?"

"I'm one of the fallen ones," said Mrs. Tang quietly. "I turned my back on the clan. I was young and foolish. Knowledge, riches, and power meant more to me than my sisters. I lost the will to transform." Mrs. Tang looked deeply into Suyin's eyes. "But I still have my feather."

Mrs. Tang opened an old tin box with hieroglyphs of two birds on the lid.

She placed the small black feather in Suyin's palm.

"What kind is it, Mrs. Tang?" asked Suyin in a hushed voice.

"It's a head feather," said Mrs. Tang. "I followed my head, not my heart. But something shifted when I met you."

"I lost my feather," said Suyin, trying not to cry. Her grief was too raw to talk about that fateful day. "Do you think I could use my natal feather to transform?"

Mrs. Tang shook her head sadly. "A natal feather is as temporal as a dream. By tomorrow it will have turned to dust."

All my dreams have turned to dust, thought Suyin. What good was proving herself worthy, when her mother was dead and the sisterhood was dying?

"There's something else I wish to show you," said Mrs. Tang. She pulled a carved wooden trunk next to the sofa where Suyin sat propped up with pillows. Inside the trunk were layers of embroidered clothing: a high-collared embroidered jacket appliquéd in red, blue, white, and yellow, a pleated accordion skirt, leg wrappings, a wide apron and belt, a baby carrier, perfume bags and tapestries.

"The embroidery is beautiful," Suyin said, examining the heavily couched stitching on the panels. "Who stitched it?"

"I did," said Mrs. Tang. "That's my festival dress. Edward took me back to my home village to retrieve it many years after we were married. It means everything to me."

"Why didn't you tell me you were Miao?"

Mrs. Tang lowered her eyes. "I was ashamed."

Suyin started, aghast. "Ashamed of being Miao?"

"No—of being poor, of being illegal, of working in a garment factory. I was born in Langde Village near Kaeli. My mother brought me here when I was ten. We came in a smuggler's ship like you."

Suyin's mouth fell open.

"When I left that life," said Mrs. Tang, "I never wanted to look back. I wanted to start with a blank slate as the wife of a wealthy and influential man and the owner of a successful business that caters to the rich. I wanted a clean break from my past. I didn't want to be reminded of my humble roots, so I kept my head in the sand. It was wrong. I know that now."

The pain in Suyin's knee began to throb. It ran up her leg and into her groin. It was a burning, aching sensation. She felt like crying, but she was afraid that if she broke down, Mrs. Tang might stop talking.

"I was unbelievably lucky," said Mrs. Tang. "I had worked in garment factories since I was three years old, sitting at my mother's feet. When I was sixteen, something wonderful happened. A young man named Edward Tang walked into the shop and fell in love with me. Edward was from a prominent family in New York, second-generation Chinese American. I told this young man, this stranger, that I would marry him in two years if he paid a living allowance for my mother and me, and my schooling. To my surprise he agreed. I wasn't in love with him then. I fell in love with him later. Edward's mother taught me all I needed to know to fit into high society. I went on to university and studied textile art and in particular Chinese embroidery and a few years later, I opened Tang's House of Fashion. When I met you in the Good Fortune shop, a poor but talented seamstress, you reminded me of my younger self."

As Suyin studied the embroidery pattern on the apron, the Nu Shu characters lifted from the background like birds taking flight.

All women are sisters.

"You know Nu Shu, Mrs. Tang!"

And once again Mrs. Tang became a living, breathing dream, a beautiful Miao woman who loved embroidery as much as she did.

As Mrs. Tang reminisced about her early years in Langde, she confessed that sometimes she missed the old ways. Suyin hung on to every word. When her friend was done, the two sat together without speaking.

What will become of me now? Suyin wondered. She had no money. She was injured, maybe crippled. She thought of Jade, then, alone and friendless. Lao might try to hurt her too.

"I have to go."

"Don't be silly," said Mrs. Tang. "You still need an X-ray,

you can hardly walk, and you're in pain. Dr. Lu is going to meet us at the hospital in an hour."

Suyin shook her head. "It's too risky, Mrs. Tang."

"That leg needs attention," insisted Mrs. Tang, placing her hand on Suyin's. "I'll take care of your paperwork. After the hospital visit, you'll stay here."

"I can't leave Jade," said Suyin anxiously.

"She can stay too—until things are settled with Sister," said Mrs. Tang.

Suyin went cold. "Sister?"

"Don't worry," said Mrs. Tang, her eyes suddenly steely. "I drove a hard bargain with Mr. Tang. I can drive a harder bargain with Sister Fang-chou."

"What kind of bargain?"

"Sister is rich but she has no *guanxi,* except with the criminal element. She's desperate to move up in society. My husband's family is influential. I could offer Sister a carrot to change her ways."

"A leopard doesn't change its spots, Mrs. Tang."

Mrs. Tang laughed. "I know. Sister's a crook, but sometimes you have to dirty your hands to find the tiniest speck of gold in the mud."

"Even if Sister *did* change," said Suyin, "Lao or Kwan-Sook would find a way to cheat us. Lao is even cheating Sister!"

Mrs. Tang's eyes lit up with interest. "Is that so?"

*　　*　　*

"Maybe I should have used my crutches," said Suyin as Mrs. Tang wheeled her into the entrance of the Golden Palace restaurant. She had butterflies in her stomach at the thought of facing Sister, but Mrs. Tang's calm confidence helped.

"Oh, no, a wheelchair's better," insisted Mrs. Tang.

Suyin caught a glimpse of herself in a mirror on the restaurant wall. Black eye. Swollen face. Bandaged knee. *Kill the monkey to scare the chickens.* She was the monkey, like Xiaoli's sister. Only she was still alive.

Sister's restaurant was like a palace: thick red carpets, gold silk drapes, and a giant mural of a fire-breathing dragon. Businessmen and families sat around circular tables eating and chatting while elderly pushcart ladies moved from table to table serving delicacies from steaming trays.

A cacophony of sounds filled the room: dishes clattering, waiters shouting orders, swinging doors swooshing, the buzz of conversation and laughter.

"Are you scared?" whispered Suyin.

"A little, but I'm a good actress," said Mrs. Tang, under her breath. "And I'm wearing my feather for fortitude."

"I see her, Mrs. Tang. She's sitting in the far corner." Suddenly her nervousness turned to terror. "Lao's with her."

Lao was a smooth talker, a liar and a bully. He'd find a way to blame Suyin for what happened. She gripped the wheelchair to stop her hands from shaking.

"All the better," said Mrs. Tang grimly. "Two birds. One stone."

Suyin didn't know what was worse, the pain in her knee or the sick feeling in her stomach as Mrs. Tang wheeled her toward the two people in the world she feared most.

Sister's brow furrowed when she spotted them. Her eyes slid from Mrs. Tang to Suyin like a snake sizing up its next meal.

"Why, Mrs. Tang!" said Sister in a voice as sweet as rice syrup. She smiled, baring her fangs. "What a surprise! You must join us."

Mrs. Tang's face gave away nothing. She pulled up a chair.

"Who's the little handicapped girl?" sneered Sister, feigning innocence.

"One of your employees," replied Mrs. Tang coldly. "From the Good Fortune shop."

"You mean one of the strikers," bristled Sister. "Hmm, yes. The ungrateful *yazi* who spoke at the rally."

Lao rose to leave.

"Stay, Mr. Lao," said Mrs. Tang. "What I have to say involves you too."

Sister was taken aback. "Sit, Lao," she barked, snapping her fingers at a waiter. "Feng! Send over tea for my guests."

Mrs. Tang began. "Sister Fang-chou, there's a rumor—"

"Pshaw to rumors," interrupted Sister.

"As I was saying, there's a rumor you're going to declare bankruptcy and close your shops," said Mrs. Tang. "Is this true?"

"No . . . well, yes," said Sister. Her cheek twitched.

"Then I'm returning your donation to the Chinese Benevolent Fund," said Mrs. Tang, sliding a check across the table. "And the obligation it implied when I accepted it on behalf of our board of directors."

The check was for twenty-five thousand dollars. *Guanxi.*

Sister flushed. "Let's not be hasty, Mrs. Tang. Think of the unfortunates."

"That's precisely who I'm thinking of, Sister. The unfortunates like my friend Suyin, who will lose their jobs when you close your shops and move them to Brooklyn."

"I might *not* have to close," said Sister slyly. "It depends on my business partners. If they pay me . . ."

Suyin felt her hackles rise. "Don't believe her, Mrs. Tang."

"Get to the point, Mrs. Tang," sighed Sister.

"Lao and your hired thugs beat this child," said Mrs. Tang fiercely. "They beat her because she spoke out against labor practices in *your* sweatshop." Mrs. Tang lowered her voice to a growl. "Something has to be made right. And if it isn't, I will make it my life's work, using all my money and influence, to find justice for girls like Suyin."

Sister sniffed. "*If* Lao beat the girl, he'll answer for it."

Lao bolted up, indignant. "I'll what?"

Sister gave him a murderous look. She lowered her voice to a whisper. "If you say another word, Mr. Lao, it could well be your last."

"There's no *if*," said Suyin. "Lao did this." She pointed to her knee, staring him down.

"There's another matter I'd like cleared up, Sister," said Mrs. Tang. "As I'm sure you know, I hired Suyin to stitch some high-end garments through the Good Fortune shop. I paid Mr. Lao a considerable amount of cash for her work, but Suyin hasn't seen a cent of it and I'd like to know if *you* received payment from Mr. Lao."

Sister leaped up, her eyes flashing. She reached across the table and smacked Lao across the face.

"Scoundrel!" shrieked Sister. "Thief! Stealing my money. Skimming the cream off the top!"

Murmurs of dismay drifted through the restaurant. Stares.

As Sister turned her fury on Lao, he seemed to shrink before Suyin's eyes. Now she watched, terrified and fascinated, as her boss's thick sausage fingers grasped Lao's wrist.

"Where's my money?" Sister rasped, her face red with rage.

"I only b-b-borrowed it," Lao stammered.

Sister cackled. "Do you take me for a fool?"

"I used it to pay my gambling debts," said Lao, his voice ragged. "I was going to pay you back. I was desperate. The loan sharks are after me. They've threatened . . ."

"To cripple you?" interjected Mrs. Tang.

Lao paled.

"You're fired, Lao," said Sister. "But I want the money you stole in three days. All of it, plus interest."

Lao's face turned from fear to anger. "I deserved that money. You've been paying me peanuts. Everyone knows you're the biggest skinflint in the city. Except when it comes to buying *guanxi*."

Sister's eyes were black with rage. "Get out of my sight, you sleazy little cockroach, or you'll wish you'd never been born."

Lao hurried off, muttering curses under his breath.

Sister's face glistened with sweat. She picked up a linen napkin and wiped her brow.

"Feng!" she thundered. "Send over a platter of food!"

Shocked into silence, Suyin and Mrs. Tang exchanged glances. *What now?*

At last Sister spoke. "Mrs. Tang, you and I need to talk in private . . . without the *yazi*."

"This little duck's not leaving my sight," said Mrs. Tang, smiling sweetly.

Sister suddenly lowered her voice. "I have a proposal . . ."

As the two women talked, Suyin felt herself drifting off. The medication the doctor had given her had taken effect. It masked the pain, but it made her drowsy.

"I can't afford it . . .

". . . I'd lose big face . . .

". . . I'll go bankrupt . . ."

Laughter from Mrs. Tang. "Now really, Sister."

Between periods of sleep and wakefulness, Suyin watched as the check was passed back and forth across the tablecloth.

Mrs. Tang's persuasive voice.

". . . the business community would be grateful . . .

"Two tickets to the charity ball at the Waldorf Astoria . . ."

"The charity ball?" asked Sister, her eyes widening, a smile of understanding spreading over her oily fat-cheeked face.

So Mrs. Tang had guessed right, thought Suyin. Sister was as trustworthy as a pit viper, but Mrs. Tang had sensed her adversary's weakness—a desire for glamour and the veneer of respectability.

Their voices faded as Suyin slipped in and out of sleep. Suyin dreamed that the queen was dead and the sisterhood was in mourning. The future would be a world where the bond between humans and the natural world would be completely undone.

When she woke, her forehead was damp with sweat.

Mrs. Tang and Sister were shaking hands, so she knew they had struck a deal, but as to what or how it might affect her, she had no idea. Nor would Mrs. Tang say. But Mrs. Tang looked satisfied as she wheeled Suyin out of the Golden Palace into the brightness of the afternoon sunshine.

22

Hope

The garment workers strike was settled on April seventeenth, a week after the seamstresses' rally. The Good Fortune strikers had been off the job for thirty-four days, although other shops had struck for even longer. Sister Fang-chou was the first to welcome her staff back to work. She announced that since her business partners had finally paid her the money they owed, she was able to pay her workers their back wages. She blamed the strike on bad apples like her ex-manager, Lao, a bloodthirsty cockroach who had cheated workers and management alike. She also promised to pay her staff minimum wage, to shorten their work hours, and to close her shops on Sundays. Mr. Lee was skeptical of Sister's promises—she'd sung the same tune for years—but that the seamstresses had wrung their back pay from the grasp of that wily old skinflint was something to celebrate.

When the business leaders got the news that Sister Fang-chou had settled, they breathed a collective sigh of relief. They pressured the other factory bosses to follow Sister's example. There were rumors that a prominent business leader, Edward Tang, was particularly anxious to see the wheels of industry run smoothly again.

Mrs. Tang told Suyin that the Fair Wage Task Force investigators were keeping an eye on Sister and they were becoming savvier. They planned to conduct surveillance on shops more frequently and interview seamstresses away from their workplaces so bosses like Sister had less power to intimidate workers. But Sister's thugs still roamed the streets threatening the fresh-off-the-boats, so things were far from perfect.

For Suyin and her friends, victory was sweet and sour. They were happy to return to work and grateful to collect the wages owed to them, but the thought of kowtowing to that wretched Kwan-Sook sickened them. Jade especially dug in her heels.

"I won't work for that back-stabber," she said firmly.

Suyin saw she meant it; Jade was as stubborn as she was kind.

"Then I won't either," Suyin said.

"Me neither," said Mrs. Chin. She pointed her forefinger at her shoe. "I'd rather shoot myself in the foot than listen to that donkey braying at me all day."

"I'd rather be boiled in oil," said Cousin Jin quietly.

"Or have my fingernails pulled off with pliers," said Mei-Xia, determined not to be outdone.

"Now all we need is a plan," said Suyin.

On her first day back on the job, Suyin's challenge was to make her way up six floors on crutches. Despite Mrs. Tang's pleas for her to rest for a few more days, she was anxious to start earning money again.

"If Mrs. Chin can climb those stairs with a bad hip," said Suyin, "I can do it on crutches."

As she climbed the stairs, she thought of her lost self, her broad elegant wings, slender legs, and velvet black neck. She mourned that physical other as much as she mourned her mother and the sisterhood. As she swung her body up the last step, she was breathing hard.

Manager Kwan-Sook had hurried the six replacement workers ahead, muttering about wasted time. The young girls stole curious glances at "the troublemakers" (as Kwan-Sook had dubbed them) as they passed them on the stairs.

It felt strange, thought Suyin, to be back at work after the long days on the picket line. But today would be no ordinary day. If their plan was successful, she hoped to persuade Wing to return to work.

The troublemakers took their usual places in the shop. The sparrow that had often stopped by to visit landed on the windowsill to welcome the girls back.

At Jade's signal, Mrs. Chin and the girls silently folded their arms.

The six little replacement workers, sensing that something was up, began to titter.

"What's going on?" demanded Kwan-Sook, her heels clicking on the plywood floor. "The strike's over. Get back to work!"

No one moved. Not even the replacement workers. They stared at the sparrow, who had begun to sing.

"Stupid *yazi!*" screamed Kwan-Sook. "Get to work!"

The little girls blinked. They looked at the troublemakers, then at Kwan-Sook.

Jade cocked her head to one side, motioning to the girls to join them. A girl with a jaunty ponytail slowly folded her arms. A second girl did the same, then a third, until all six little girls sat as primly as students at school, folding their arms and watching the sparrow as it fluttered around the room, chirping.

Kwan-Sook flew into a rage. She cuffed the ponytail girl and pushed her head against the sewing machine. The girl began to sob.

"Get to work!" Kwan-Sook shrieked.

"Don't hit her again," said Suyin firmly, struggling to her feet.

Kwan-Sook's eyes narrowed. A look of hatred crossed her face.

"I'm calling Sister!" snapped Kwan-Sook, whipping out her cell phone. When she'd finished telling Sister her woes, she leaned over Suyin, cupped her hand, and whispered in her ear, "I'm going to enjoy firing you."

Kwan-Sook paced, checking her watch every few minutes. The shop was deadly quiet except for the humming of the ceiling fan, Kwan-Sook's grunts, and the nervous foot tapping of the ponytail girl.

The youngest seamstresses sat with stiff backs, stealing quick frightened glances around the room.

Suyin smiled at the ponytail girl, who offered a shy smile in return.

As the minutes passed, Suyin grew more anxious. If their plan failed, they could be out on the street. They were tempting fate to try such a stunt. Their sit-down strike was a gamble, but the thought of having to grovel to Kwan-Sook was more than any of them could bear.

They heard a key turn in the lock and the clump of Sister's shoes.

"What's going on here?" Sister thundered.

"They refuse to work!" whined Kwan-Sook.

Sister rolled her eyes and groaned. "Not again!"

"We won't work under Kwan-Sook," said Jade. "She can't be trusted."

Sister turned to the fresh-off-the-boats. "What's your excuse?"

"She hits us," said the girl with the ponytail.

Sister twisted her mouth, raising her hands, palms up. "So?"

"Sister Fang-chou, production will suffer under Kwan-

Sook," said Suyin. "Mrs. Chin deserves the job. She's experienced, she speaks English, and we respect her. We'll work hard for her. Maybe you could find a place for Kwan-Sook in one of your other shops?"

Sister sighed wearily. "I can't afford any more work stoppages. It's costing me too much money. Mrs. Chin, you've got the job—temporarily." She turned to Kwan-Sook. "They need another seamstress over at the Pink Peony. Tell Mrs. Wang I sent you over."

"You mean I'm no longer manager?" shrieked Kwan-Sook. "After all my hard work?"

"No," said Sister. "I don't want any more headaches. Leave the cell phone when you go."

"I quit!" screamed Kwan-Sook. She slapped the cell phone on the table and threw her manager's pin at Mrs. Chin, who ducked just in time. Kwan-Sook stomped out, slamming the door behind her.

Sister Fang-chou gave Mrs. Chin a sly look.

"I didn't know you spoke English, Mrs. Chin. It appears you've been hiding your light under a bushel all these years."

"A manager who speaks English will sell more to the *lao fan* buyers," said Mrs. Chin. "According to Mrs. Tang."

Sister snorted. "That's why I hired you."

Mrs. Chin is a wily old bird, thought Suyin.

When Sister left, the seamstresses congratulated Mrs. Chin. After thirty years of drudgery, Mrs. Chin had finally begun her climb up Gold Mountain.

*　　*　　*

Late that evening, after their first day back at work, Suyin and Jade headed to the Lotus Flower. Jade walked patiently beside Suyin as she hobbled along on her crutches, and Pang, Suyin's protector, rode behind her on his bike. The girls had tried to see Wing twice before, but Mr. Leung told them that Wing was busy. Tonight they would insist. Finally they had something concrete to offer, a respectable job and a nice manager.

Suyin had forgiven Wing as Jade had forgiven Suyin. She understood that Wing had stolen her needle out of desperation, and that friends deserved compassion, even if they let you down.

Now standing at the door of the Lotus Flower, Suyin's heart was buoyant with hope. When she rang the buzzer, a wrinkled face with dyed black hair and bright red lipstick appeared. The woman was dressed in a crimson see-through negligee. She wore high-heeled slippers with tiny feathers over the toes. She gave them a suspicious look.

"What do you want?" she snarled.

"We're here to see Wing," said Suyin.

"She's working," said the woman, slamming the door.

"We're not leaving until we talk to her!" shouted Jade, pounding on the door.

Finally, Mr. Leung pulled back a curtain.

"Go away!" he barked. "Your friend doesn't want to talk to you."

"We're not leaving this time!" said Jade.

Mr. Leung's eyes hardened. "Wait here." Moments passed. The door opened slowly.

"Wing," Suyin called softly. "Wing?"

Wing's eyes were distant moons, cold and vacant. She was wearing a rumpled black silk kimono, kohl eyeliner, and smeared lipstick. Her feet were bare.

"Wing, come back to work," pleaded Suyin. "We won the strike! We're getting our back pay and Mrs. Chin's our new manager!"

"We miss you, Wing," said Jade. "Please come back to work."

"I have to go," said Wing with a strangled laugh. Her smile faded and for an instant Suyin glimpsed tenderness beneath her tough exterior. "Time is money, remember?"

"Please, Wing," said Suyin.

"Hurry," called a gruff male voice from inside. "I haven't got all day."

"Don't come here again," Wing said, her eyes brimming with tears. "I have become a lowlife."

23
An Uneasy Alliance

On a balmy evening in June, Suyin sat stitching by the open window of the rental apartment she shared with Jade and their six younger coworkers. An apartment in Gold Mountain was as scarce as hen's teeth and very expensive, but the owner was a business associate of Mrs. Tang's who owed her a favor. Every time Suyin turned her key in the lock, she felt overwhelmed with gratitude. Though the apartment was small, it was clean and bright. It was home.

Once they had settled in, she and Jade went to Mr. Leung's to ask Wing to move in with them. When Wing opened the door, Suyin's heart sank. Wing's cheeks were gaunt. She had dark circles under her eyes. She was weaving on high heels, holding on to the door to steady herself.

A grizzled old man poked his head through the opening of the door and pulled her away.

"Leave me alone," said Wing, and she closed the door on them before they could tell her why they'd come.

Suyin tried to push away the images that rose in her mind unbidden. The grizzled old man. Mr. Leung feeding her drugs. Wing, fragile as a porcelain cup.

Her friend's absence had left a hole in her heart that couldn't be mended. On nights like this when her mistakes haunted her like ghosts, she reminded herself that she had been brave and that perhaps by speaking out, she had helped improve the lives of her sisters.

Above the tenement buildings across the street, Suyin saw a brilliant scattering of stars. It struck her that all the people she loved—her Cao Hai aunties and Shan-Shan and Uncle Pei-Pei—might be watching those very same stars at that moment. She wondered if the cranes were stargazing too. She tried to imagine them lifting their long slender necks from their feathercoats, struck by wonder at the miracle of the world. Thinking about the cranes, her heart ached. Would she ever see them again, now she was unable to transform? Had they already lost their feathers? Did they blame her for her mother's death?

Loneliness trailed her like a comet, shining in its purity. And yet she had so much to be thankful for. She had gotten a promotion. She spent mornings machine-stitching and afternoons embroidering for Mrs. Tang, her dear friend and mentor. Mrs. Tang had offered to adopt her, but Suyin had come too far to accept her offer. A princess had to chart her own course. Even if she never saw the cranes again, she had royal blood, and with that came responsibility, not only to her people back home, but to her friends in Chinatown. Never again would she abandon a sister or break a promise.

Suyin glanced at the imperial tapestry for a moment before returning to her work. She was embroidering a cross-stitched pattern of flowers and birds inspired by the fifteenth queen. It was strange calling the queens by number, but she had yet to discover their names. Earlier that week, she had deciphered another missive. *Endurance in the face of adversity.*

In the bedroom off the kitchenette, she could hear the sounds of breathing and the occasional snore. Jade and the girls were sleeping after a busy workday at the shop. Both she and Jade had grown to love the brave little girls since the day the girls had dared to join their sit-down strike. The girls had come without their parents, so she and Jade mothered them. They felt like a family.

Suyin had been teaching the girls English since they'd moved in together. She loved to see the look of pleasure and excitement on the girls' faces as they learned to speak the language of their new country. She had also offered to teach them embroidery. Jade's ambitions lay in becoming a manager, and Suyin wished with all her heart that her friend's dream would come true.

After the strike, when Mrs. Chin had finally found

time to clean out Lao's office desk, she'd found a stack of letters stuffed in the back of a drawer. Among them was a bundle of letters from Suyin's aunties written in Nu Shu. Suyin recognized Shan-Shan's handwriting on the envelopes. Her aunties told her how much they loved and missed her and asked her to write.

Reading her aunties' letters, she'd cried with happiness. Yet, knowing they cared made her feel more homesick. She felt guilty too because she had doubted them. When they told her that they had yet to receive any overseas money, she was furious with Lao. He must have stolen the seamstresses' mail to hide his swindling.

But Sister Fang-chou's thugs persuaded him to repay every penny he owed her, although he did so by borrowing even more money from Toothless Li.

Last week, the Labor Department investigators paid a visit to the shop. Before they came, Sister had coached the seamstresses to play dumb.

"What's past is past, loyal workers," she said slyly.

It felt wrong to keep quiet, especially since they knew that their boss still cooked the books. But if they told the truth, they could be deported. Reluctantly, they accepted Sister's terms. It was an uneasy alliance, one that was aided by the watchful eyes of the Labor Department investigators (Sister called them a pack of wolves) and Mrs. Tang's social calendar.

On Sundays, Suyin went to Central Park to talk to the birds. Sometimes she found herself standing in the open meadow, searching the lonely skies for the cranes.

Would she ever see them again, she wondered, now that she'd lost her feather? Her grief over her mother's death was like an underground spring that bubbled up when she was least expecting it. The sight of a woman holding her daughter's hand could bring tears to her eyes.

Whenever her sorrow threatened to overwhelm her, she turned to her embroidery. She visited the library for books on needlework and studied photographs of world embroideries. Unlocking the secrets of the ancient tapestry was like climbing Gold Mountain. It required the head and the heart.

Using her mother's special needle was a guide and a comfort, but not a necessity. Sometimes she felt as if the cranes' wingtips were guiding her fingers. If she listened hard enough, she could hear the cranes whispering ancient secrets.

The square is the garden in which the ancestors lived and were forced to leave. The red line within the square is the fish; the curved lines are the trees; the horse hoof patterns are the wanderings of a people cast from the places they loved. These are the memorable patterns: the ones that must never be forgotten.

She worked ellipses, whirls, and triangles into patterns once stitched by shamans in clay-baked huts on windy plains. She listened to the voices from the past, but like her sisters before her, she combined the ancient patterns with those that sprung from her own heart.

Li-Wen used to tell her that only when we are ready

would we discover why we were born. After she'd lost her mother, she found herself stitching with greater purpose, as a means to something else, something she couldn't define, yet was present and waiting.

It had begun as a dream many years ago, the vision of a Western school she'd seen in her English textbook. The school was beautiful. It had glass windows, rows of wooden desks, and shelves of books. After the strike was settled, she had written to the village chief asking that a quarter of the overseas money be earmarked for a new school. It would be a school for girls and boys both. She imagined the pleased faces of her aunties. She imagined rows of Miao girls bent over books. She imagined a village of educated girls who would send their daughters to school so the seed of hope she'd sown across time and distance would flower a world away.

She paused to rub her aching knee. It was still swollen. Though it caused her discomfort at times, she no longer needed her crutches. She walked with a slight limp. But considering how well her life had turned out, she didn't dwell on it. It wasn't the life of her dreams, but one she could endure.

Recently Mrs. Tang had designed a one-of-a-kind line of clothing inspired by the traditional Miao festival dresses. It was called East Meets West. Each item in the collection featured Suyin's signature embroidery. Sometimes this was as little as an embroidered pear flower on the shoulder of a peasant blouse or a pair of cranes dancing down the skirt of a sundress. Sometimes it was a Nu

Shu poem stitched in a leafy pattern around the sleeves of a blouse. The clothes had sold well.

A noise in the hallway pulled Suyin from her thoughts. Her heart lurched. It was past midnight, too late for Mrs. Tang or Nancy to visit. She tiptoed to the door and pressed her eye against the peephole.

"Pang!" She flung open the door. He had been badly beaten. There were deep bruises on his forearms. His cheek was swollen. A trickle of blood streamed from his mouth. He took two steps toward her and slid to the floor. She dragged him inside. She ran to the sink, moistened a cloth, and kneeling on the floor, wiped the blood from his face. He flinched with pain. Tears flooded his eyes.

"White Tiger and Xiaoli stole my money," he said, coughing up blood. "All my savings. Five thousand dollars. All these months . . . scrimping and saving. I've lost everything."

"I'm so sorry, Pang," she said, gently touching his arm.

"Kwan-Sook betrayed me," he said in a whisper.

She shook her head in disbelief. "Kwan-Sook? Are you sure? You were the only person she cared about."

"She cared about my money more." Pang began to cry softly. "She told White Tiger that I picked Mr. Chu's pocket and that I hid my money in a secret compartment in my coat. Kwan-Sook was the only person who knew where it was."

"Maybe the gangsters *guessed* where your money was." She couldn't stand to see him cry.

"No. Kwan-Sook planned the whole thing. She was angry at losing her management position. She was angry with me for helping you girls. She said I took your side. The three of them split the money. Kwan-Sook said she needed it more than me because she was out of work." He wiped his nose with his hand, staring up at her with tear-stained eyes. "How could she do that to me? I loved her."

Suyin wrapped her arm around his shoulder and hugged him. She kissed his cheek and stroked his hair. "One day you will climb the mountain of gold. You will be the finest rat catcher in the city. You will own your own takeout. You will have big face."

Pang didn't answer. He buried his head in his hands and wept.

24
Missing the Root

When Suyin entered the factory on a bright July morning, Mrs. Chin pointed to a parcel.

"You've got mail, Suyin. From home. You too, Jade." It had been more than a year since Suyin had left her village. It was so good to hear from home.

Jade grabbed her letter and tore it open. A photograph fell out. Jade held it to the light, beaming.

"My mother sent my little brother's school picture," said Jade, proudly showing the photo to her workmates, who had gathered around her. "That's his school uniform. Look how tall he's grown. Such a handsome boy." Happy tears came to her eyes. She held the photograph to her chest. "This is a good day for me."

"Aren't you going to open your parcel?" asked Mrs. Chin, who was dying of curiosity.

"Not now," Suyin said. *Later. When I'm alone.* She returned to her stitching, a pale yellow Indian cotton skirt with a butterfly pattern embroidered along the hem. Fatima, the sarus crane, had once asked Suyin if she knew what the butterfly pattern meant.

"It means missing the root," Suyin had replied. "The root symbolizes an ancestor." And then she'd asked if it was possible to forget an ancestor after they've passed on and Fatima had replied, "The deepest part of you never forgets."

Still, she was afraid she might no longer be able to call up her mother's face. Those brief moments in the Gray World seemed like a dream. Sometimes she wondered if she had imagined the whole thing.

Yet the grief she felt was real. She found herself writing more and more Nu Shu poems, scribbling missives in her notebook (*The saddest death is that of the heart*) and later embroidering them in Nu Shu on the clothing she stitched. She was working on a decorative pattern of the Chinese sweet gum tree, hiding the characters, in plain sight, among the leafy patterns. As with the women and girls before her, Nu Shu remained an act of resistance against a life over which they had little control.

When lunchtime rolled around, Pang, the reformed pickpocket, and Mrs. Wong's recently hired busboy and waiter, dropped by the shop. Mrs. Wong had hired Pang on a promise that he would stop stealing. His new boss was a church lady and couldn't abide thievery.

"Mrs. Wong sent this soup over for Suyin," said Pang,

blushing. "It's wonton, Suyin, your favorite. It's on the house."

He stood before her, shifting his weight from foot to foot, holding out his humble offering. He looked so awkward and sweet, her heart melted a little.

"Please thank Mrs. Wong for me, Pang," said Suyin. "It smells delicious."

Jade laughed. "Come on, Pang. We weren't born yesterday. It's from you, not Mrs. Wong. Everyone knows you're sweet on Suyin."

Pang stammered. "Uh . . . well . . . the soup's from *both* of us."

"You're embarrassing Pang," Suyin scolded. "Stop it right now, Jade. Pang and I are good friends. Like you and me."

"You two are such lovebirds," teased Jade.

It was true that she loved Pang, especially now that he no longer had Kwan-Sook anchored around his neck, but she wasn't ready to think of him as a suitor. *Not yet.* She carried the weight of a village on her shoulders, and for now, that was enough.

Mrs. Chin crooked her finger to Pang. He gave her an affectionate pat on her head.

"Is it true that Sister had a conniption when you quit the Golden Palace to work for the So Good Noodle House?" asked Mrs. Chin.

Pang shrugged. "Pah! She squawked a lot, but Mrs. Tang smoothed her ruffled feathers. As long as I pay back my debt, Sister doesn't care. She's already hired a replacement. Have you seen my business card, Mrs. Chin?" asked Pang, pulling the card from his sleeve.

Mrs. Chin pushed back her spectacles with her thumb. "Read it to me, Suyin."

"Rat Catcher Pang," said Suyin. *"Rat-free or no fee! Phone 212-555-TRAP"*

"Congratulations on your success!" said Mrs. Chin. "Mrs. Wong told me that hiring you was a stroke of good luck. She says her customers love you—especially the little kids. They beg their parents to go to 'Noodle' to watch the magic boy do tricks."

"You should see him, Mrs. Chin," joked Jade. "He's a waiter and magic act rolled into one. He makes chopsticks disappear and coins fall out of his pockets and fortune cookies show up in kids' pockets."

"I'm a tourist attraction," said Pang. "I was mentioned in *New York Magazine*."

"You're a peacock," laughed Suyin.

As the day wore on, Suyin stole anxious glances at the package from home, willing the time to go faster.

It was midnight when the staff switched off their sewing machines.

"You're not coming home now?" asked Jade.

"Not yet," said Suyin. "I'm going to work a little later."

"Let's go, girls," said Jade, turning to her new charges. "Save some of your energy for tomorrow."

When Suyin heard the door close, she reached for the parcel. Her fingers trembled as she unwrapped the layers of brown paper. The parcel contained perfumed pouches, embroidered by her Cao Hai aunties and Shan-Shan. She lifted each *hebao* and inspected it for the quality of its workmanship: the clarity and harmony of its colors, yellow, blue, and red silk on black fabric, the fineness of its needling and the delicacy of its artistry.

Her sworn sisters of Cao Hai had stitched the memorable patterns: birds and butterflies, pear flowers and centipedes, pomegranates and spirals, yet the composition and arrangement of the patterns were unique. What pleased her most was the down of a crane feather lovingly stitched into the wings of a pair of embroidered birds.

She smiled, relieved. The perfume bags were far lovelier than she had imagined. They would more than meet Mrs. Tang's standards. Mrs. Tang planned to sell each bag for five hundred American dollars; a third of the money would go to her sisters back home, a third to pay off her debt, and a third to Tang's House of Fashion. When she had worried that the price tag might be too high, Mrs. Tang had laughed.

"On Fifth Avenue, women pay five thousand dollars for a handbag. They'll sell like rice cakes." Suyin hoped she was right.

In the tradition of her people, a *hebao* was a treasured object, never to be sold. Yet the sale of a single *hebao* in

Gold Mountain could transform the life of a Cao Hai family; the sale of ten could transform a village.

She arranged the *hebao* carefully on the table. Each one was lovely, but her favorite was a deep blue, exquisitely stitched in pale yellow and silver silk. Opening the bag, she found sprigs of mugwort and perfumed grass.

She carried the perfume bag to the open window. Glancing up at the sky, she saw that the breeze had parted the clouds. The full moon looked like a dragon festival lantern. She picked up the posy of mugwort and perfumed grass and rubbed the aromatic leaves between her thumb and forefinger. She brought her fingers to her nose and breathed in deeply, a habit from childhood. The scent of camphor and lemon released a flood of homesickness. Tears filled her eyes.

"That was my first perfume bag," said a voice.

Perched on the railing of the balcony was her mother in feathered regalia, her pale gray wings spread open, a nimbus of stars whirling above her crown. She flew into the open window and landed on the floor of the shop. Her beautiful bird mother was almost perfectly formed, except for an almost imperceptible crook in her left wing.

Suyin blinked, unable to believe her eyes.

"I thought you died."

Tears of confusion flowed down her cheeks. Anger, relief, joy. Why had her mother not come to her? She had been grief-stricken.

"I wanted to come sooner," said her mother softly. "But

I have been performing the sacred ceremonies for the sisterhood."

"The Mysteries?" asked Suyin, still in shock.

"Yes, my daughter, and not a moment too soon. The clan's connection to the natural world was as tenuous as a spider's thread. The ceremonies required the collective energy of every sister in the realm."

Every sister but her. She felt left out and hurt, though she understood. She had lost her wings and her power. How could she have helped the sisterhood? Still, despite everything, her mother had survived. Wiping away her tears, Suyin felt her hurt fall away and she began to laugh.

"You're alive, Mother! You're alive!"

"Yes, my daughter," said her mother, ushering Suyin inside her feathercoat.

"We just returned from Cao Hai," said a familiar voice. Suyin looked up to see Grandmother, Li-Wen, Hazrat, and Little Sister.

Grandmother cackled, Li-Wen's eyes danced, Hazrat gave Suyin a wise look, and Little Sister wrapped her wings around Suyin in a hug.

"Shan-Shan," said Suyin, closing her eyes, her suspicions at last confirmed.

"Shh," whispered Little Sister, looking embarrassed. Suyin smiled knowingly, remembering that in bird form a sister who spoke about her human counterpart was considered weak. She didn't mind. The heart had its own language for happiness.

A wild whoop made Suyin start. Moments later the garment factory was full of cranes. Suyin clasped her hands with happiness.

There were cranes perching on sewing machines, lighting on cupboard tops, walking along the tables, sitting in canvas carts stuffed with fabric, whooping and rattling, chortling and snorting, snuffling and growling and puttering in a dizzying display of joy and celebration. She saw the haughty whoopers, the beautiful blues, the delicate demoiselles, the prickly sarus and the gorgeous gray crowned and red-crowned cranes. She saw the white-naped cranes, the black crowned cranes, the sandhills, the Eurasians, the brolgas, the Siberians, the wattled cranes, the hooded cranes and the black-necked cranes—the world sisterhood.

Suyin whispered in her mother's ear. She wished to address her family.

Queen An-Lan raised her right wing. "Princess Suyin wishes to speak."

The shop grew quiet. Suyin's hands grew clammy. Her heart raced in her chest.

"Please forgive me, sisters," said Suyin. "I was impatient and selfish. I deserted my friends in their darkest hour. I transformed before I was worthy. You warned me, but I didn't listen. I am sorry."

To Suyin's surprise, Mulaba stepped toward her. "I too must ask for forgiveness, Princess Suyin," she said.

"I feared for your safety and doubted your strength. I was wrong. It is true that you were headstrong, but your heart was true and you were brave. The future of the sisterhood looks bright because of you."

Queen An-Lan nodded.

"You saved my life and the lives of your sisters," said her mother. "I will never be human again, but I will remain queen until you are ready to take my place."

Suyin felt her heart plummet. "But I can't become queen! I lost my feather!"

"You lost your feather saving my life," said her mother. "In that act of sacrifice, your heart was pure. You made a mistake and you paid the price. But the sisterhood believes you deserve a second chance."

Suyin's heart filled with joy. "I can choose another feather?"

"Yes," said her mother. "But this time you will choose your feather from my feathercoat."

The cranes drew closer, their wingtips forming an unbroken circle. During her first feather ceremony, Suyin had little understanding of the significance of her choice. She had a child's heart, but now her heart was that of a careworn soldier, tired of warring with herself. Whatever feather was fated to be hers, she would accept it with humility. These lovely beings had given her a second chance and she would do her best to honor them.

"The feather you choose is a symbol of the power

within you," said Grandmother. "It will inform the path you must follow to earn your wings. Are you ready to choose, Princess Suyin?"

"I am."

As her mother spread her wings, turning slowly, Suyin opened her heart. She chose a feather beneath her mother's wing. To her surprise, it came away easily but it looked strange. It was encased in a thin wax-like sheath. When her mother removed the casing, the feather unfurled.

A silence fell over the flock.

"What kind of feather is it, Mother?" asked Suyin in a worried voice.

"It is the most delicate of feathers—a pin feather," replied her mother. "Each time we lose a feather, we grow a new one. A pin feather is not yet fully developed."

"But what does it mean?" asked Suyin anxiously.

"The call of your feather is patience," said her mother tenderly. "It means perseverance in the face of adversity. It means waiting and hoping."

"For what?" Suyin asked, still confused.

"Transformation."

"But I've already proven myself worthy," said Suyin, almost in tears.

"You are worthy of a place in the sisterhood," said her mother. "But to become the queen requires more of you. When you transform, we will fly to He Shan together. I will sing you the songs that your foremothers sang and you will remember them. You will be by my side when I perform the Mysteries until they become part of you and when you have deciphered every missive and memorized every embroidery stitch in the imperial tapestry, you will take my place as queen of the birds."

Suyin swallowed hard. "But the missives are hidden, Mother. Who will help me discover their secrets?"

"The needle and the tapestry will guide you. Your sisters too. Every princess-in-waiting before you spent years studying the tapestry stitched by her foremothers. It is the patient quest for knowledge that will prepare you to become queen."

"Nature's secret is patience," added Mulaba. "The most beautiful flowers take several seasons before they bloom."

And then with a short length of cord, her mother fastened the delicate pin feather around Suyin's neck.

The orbs of her mother's eyes looked fierce and proud. Her crimson crown pulsed with life as she opened her wings.

"Come here, Suyin," said her mother.

When Suyin stepped into that cave of feathers, she closed her eyes and sank into the warm down of her mother's breast.

She wanted time to stop. She wanted to make the moment last forever.

A troop of black-necked cranes began a slow ceremonial dance. The cranes moved their heads in an arc as they two-stepped in a circle, bowing on every fourth beat. As the birds danced, accompanied by Li-Wen's haunting song, Suyin felt her heart grow lighter. The air seemed to move in concert, the clouds slid across the sky, the floors of the tenement shifted, creaking and groaning. Outside, traffic lights blinked and pavements moved like escalators. Someone was singing in the street. She heard shoes tapping a rhythm on the sidewalk below the tenement. Everything was stirring: the towers of the city, the trees in the park, the stars and moon, her own heart and blood and bones. All was happiness.

But the celebration had just begun. The Australian brolgas formed a wild chorus line, shaking their feather bustles as Grandmother stomped in the circle. The old crane motioned to Suyin to join in. As Suyin danced, giggling as she stomped her feet, her mother nodded her head with approval.

The dancing was joyous. Legs high-kicking, fabric scraps tossed into the air like confetti, yelps and whoops and plumes flying. As the night wore on, the cranes taught Suyin the ancient dances of her ancestors and somehow her body remembered.

Toward morning, the queen of the birds and their princess danced together slowly, lovingly, mother and daughter, while Hazrat and a choir of hooded cranes sang a melody so beautiful that Suyin felt weepy again.

"Soon we must leave," said her mother, "but not before I make one more request of you."

"Anything you ask."

"You must return to our village. That is where you will truly find yourself."

"I will, Mother."

As the dawn light poured into the sewing room, her mother turned to the open window. She began to beat her wings in preparation for flight.

"Can't you stay a little longer?" pleaded Suyin, trying to be brave.

But her mother's eyes were full of longing.

She is bird, not human, Suyin reminded herself, remembering the overwhelming pull toward flight. It was like downing a magic potion that rendered you helpless with yearning. Air. Cloud. Sky. That was all you wanted. Hunger, thirst, pleasure paled in comparison. Only love remained.

"One day I will return, my precious," said her mother, brushing Suyin's cheek with her wing.

Suyin willed herself not to ask when. She willed herself not to cry.

The crane sisters arched their wings and bowed in reverence to their queen and then to their princess. Suyin bowed in return. Grandmother and Li-Wen flew through the open window and perched on the balcony railing. In the sunlight, the crimson crowns of the cranes glistened as if dipped in dew. And then her mother joined them and the three cranes took wing, followed by the others. As Suyin waved good-bye at the window, her crane sisters flew across a tapestry of red and orange and purple light, their white and gray wings weaving a graceful arc over the towers of the city.

Part Three

CAO HAI,
GUIZHOU, CHINA
Four Years Later

25

Home

As the boatman set the flat-bottomed boat in motion, Suyin fixed her eyes on the end of Cao Hai Lake. Even from a distance, she could see there was no one waiting on the shore to greet her. She felt a growing apprehension, even though she told herself that the postal system in China was unreliable; her letter might not have arrived.

Halfway across the lake, a wind sprang up, blowing swirls of snow into her face. Its icy blast took her back to the harsh winters in the stone houses of the village when she'd shivered under a thin blanket, without fuel to heat the kang, her stomach aching with hunger. Life in the village was still hard, but there were improvements too. The roof of the Ancestral Hall had been replaced and recently the villagers had brought electricity to the village.

She had paid off her debt in record time, three and a half years, thanks to Mrs. Tang and her Cao Hai sisters, who were sending their embroidery to America to be sold in Mrs. Tang's shop. Despite the odds stacked against her, she had kept her promise to her people. She had carried them with her as she climbed the steep and arduous path up the mountain of gold.

Before she left, Mrs. Tang threw a party to celebrate the success of Mrs. Tang's East Meets West clothing line. She'd invited the Good Fortune staff, Pang, and the Wong family to help her celebrate. In five more years, Pang would have paid off his smuggling debt, and he was saving his money in the Bank of America so lowlifes like White Tiger and Xiaoli couldn't rob him. His plans to save enough money to go into partnership with Mrs. Wong on a new takeout restaurant no longer seemed like such a pipe dream. But best of all, he'd kept his promise to Mrs. Wong—no more thieving. He'd become the son she'd always wanted, charming Mr. and Mrs. Wong as he did everyone he'd ever met (including Suyin). She knew now that she loved Pang and in that knowing she'd finally understood the power of love and the sacrifice her mother had made for it. She had rescued her mother out of that same longing and in acting before she was ready, she had lost her feather and her wings.

Since that joyful reunion with her mother, Suyin had kept the tapestry close at all times. It was her hope and consolation. And with her crane sisters' help, she was slowly unraveling its secrets. If sometimes she felt as if she were following a string in a maze, she no longer felt so impatient. If she persevered, maybe one day she would fly again. In the meantime, she would enjoy the journey, not just the destination.

From Suyin's vantage point in the boat, she could see wisps of smoke rising from the villagers' stone houses, but the shoreline was still deserted. She swallowed a tiny pebble of disappointment. If no one showed up to meet her, she would walk to the Ancestral Hall. It was the likeliest place to find the village chief. After showing her respect, she would visit her aunties, each in turn.

The closer the boat came to shore, the more anxious she became. She searched the skies for the cranes, but she saw only clouds and a few patches of blue. Perhaps the cranes had gathered in the fen, where it had all begun, where she'd pulled the crane chick from the mud and Li-Wen had offered her a ride to He Shan. She reflected on all she'd been through: the horrific journey on the migrant ship, the realization that she'd been tricked, the months of drudgery in the shop, the bitterness of the strike, and the year she had grown up in Gold Mountain.

She thought of the time she'd spent as a lovely black-necked crane. She thought of the ecstasy of flight, the joyful celebration with the crane sisters and the reunion with her mother. And she thought about that night in the alley when Lao had crushed her knee, leaving her with a limp—a small price to pay for a life of privilege.

An injured knee. A crooked wing. The uncanny consequences of impetuous hearts. Her mother's too open, hers too closed. She liked to think that they had learned from each other.

Wing's death, a year ago, had deeply affected her. When Jade broke the news to her, they had both cried. Jade thought it was the drugs that killed her, but Suyin thought the real killer was the loss of her home and family.

Lao was in jail awaiting trial for human trafficking. She was happy to be rid of him, but she knew there would be a hundred Laos to replace him. Sister Fang-chou was as big a scoundrel as ever, though the Good Fortune shop was operating within the labor laws. Sister was still in the smuggling business, but so far the INS hadn't gathered enough evidence to arrest her.

The boatman hummed a Miao song as he pushed his long pole through a patch of wild onions. Alongside the boat, a diving duck held out a tiny fish in its beak as an offering.

A high-pitched cry cut through the air. "She's here!"

The boatman hopped into the muddy water and pulled the boat onto the shoreline. After he unloaded her boxes, he pushed off, leaving her standing alone.

A tall slender girl wearing a festival dress ran up the grassy slope to the crest of a hill. The girl was waving her arms with excitement. Moments later, a welcoming party appeared. She spotted Cho-Ye first. How could she miss her in her elaborately carved silver crown, her five silver neck rings, her embroidered jacket, and brightly embroidered accordion pleated skirt? Old Auntie Dou and Auntie Huishan appeared next, decked out in their festival dresses. Only then did she realize that the tall girl was Shan-Shan. The youngest children in the village peeked out at her, from behind their mothers' skirts. Bringing up the rear strode Uncle Yong, Uncle Li, and Uncle Pei-Pei wearing their colorful linen jackets, wide trousers, and their puttees, the cloth wrap-around leggings. Farmer Wu, the village chief, arrived last, looking very official.

As Suyin raced toward them, Shan-Shan and her aunties ran to meet her, one hand clasping their silver crowns, the other hitching their skirts. She felt their tears on her cheeks as they embraced her one by one.

"Grandmother," she whispered, bending down to embrace Old Auntie Dou's tiny frame. Auntie Dou gave a soft snort.

"Hazrat," Suyin said as Auntie Huishan planted a kiss on both her cheeks.

Even before Auntie Cho-Ye reached her, Suyin felt enveloped in a cloud of perfume and she knew then that *home* was captured in the scent of thorn-apple flowers, in the touch of her aunties' wrinkled skin and the sound of Shan-Shan's voice. And before she could even utter "Li-Wen," Auntie Cho-Ye's secret name, the village shaman wrapped Suyin in her arms and held her so tightly she could barely breathe. Then her stalwart auntie began to cry and that started everyone crying, her three aunties and Shan-Shan and herself, and they hugged each other for a long time while Suyin's uncles shifted nervously in the background waiting their turn for hugs until Chief Wu cleared his throat and began his official speech.

"Welcome, Esteemed Benefactress Zhu Suyin. We are honored at your presence." When the chief was finished speaking, the men in the village played "Song of Happiness Overflowing" on their lusheng pipes as the high, clear voices of the women filled the air with sweetness. The music brought tears to her eyes and bittersweet memories, how she'd spoken out at the seamstresses' rally, how Mrs. Tang had rescued her from the thugs, and how she and her sisters had won the strike against all odds.

The journey back to her birthplace was just a beginning. She would leave and return many times, torn between the country of her birth and the country that had shaped her dreams.

When the men placed their lusheng pipes aside, Old Auntie Dou and Auntie Huishan held out an embroidered coat so stunning in its beauty that Suyin's breath caught in her throat. The coat was richly decorated in hundreds of embroidered birds, but there were also butterflies and centipedes and pear flowers. Along the hem of the coat hung tassels of crane feathers and tiny silver beads to protect her from evil spirits. Inside the Mandarin square at the front of the jacket were two dancing cranes and hidden in the intricate patterned border, the Nu Shu missive leapt out at her. *Neither time nor distance nor death will separate sworn sisters.*

"A hundred-bird coat!" Suyin exclaimed, overwhelmed by the significance of the gift.

Cho-Ye nodded. "A hundred-bird coat is reserved for auspicious events and must only be worn by a woman of the highest rank. Your aunties and I, and Shan-Shan, have been stitching this coat since the day you left home. You were never far from our hearts."

As her sworn sisters helped her don the marvelous coat, she tried to thank them, but she choked on tears.

"Later, we have another surprise for you," her aunties told her, assuring her with secret smiles and muffled laughter that the welcoming ceremony was far from over. As the chief led the procession past her ancestral home, she looked back wistfully, knowing there would be time to claim the only inheritance that mattered—her mother's needles, spools and sewing box. The boy would be glad to be rid of them for he thought them cursed. But she knew they were blessed. They belonged to the warrior bird of He Shan, Queen An-Lan of the Crane Women Clan.

When the villagers reached the crest of the hill, Suyin saw a newly constructed building. It had a red tile roof, walls of stone, and windows of glass. She gave the villagers a questioning look. *Could it really be? Had her dream actually come true?*

"It's our new school," Chief Wu announced proudly, "built with your overseas money. Go ahead, look."

She broke away from her aunties, holding up her skirt, the openings of her hundred-bird coat flapping like wings.

Her heart was beating so wildly, she thought it might burst. She ran up the steps, her happiness too big to contain. Before she could knock, the door opened.

"Welcome, Suyin," said Teacher Zhang, smiling broadly. Her teacher bent down and hugged her. "Come inside and look around. The village elders have worked hard to complete the school in time for your visit."

As she stepped inside, the room seemed bathed in light. Two electric lights hung from the ceiling. There was a wooden floor, a potbellied stove and rows of desks, a chalkboard, and a small shelf of books. But best of all, there were as many girls in the class as boys.

"Does it please you?" asked Teacher Zhang uncertainly.

"It's perfect," she said, struggling for words to express the happiness of a dream realized. Perhaps her people had been right all along, thought Suyin. Perhaps she was a girl truly blessed with luck.

"Your aunties paid for the students' tuition with the money they earn with the embroidery they send you," said Teacher Zhang.

Suyin turned to see her aunties nodding proudly.

Each girl presented Suyin with a small square of embroidery. Suyin knelt beside them, admiring their Peking knots and cross-stitches and their lovely patterns of cranes, flowers, and butterflies.

"I have brought gifts too," said Suyin.

"The books are from me," explained Suyin, "and the school supplies are from my friend Nancy Wong, an

American-born Chinese. Nancy collected money from her classmates in Gold Mountain."

Later, the village elders accompanied Suyin and her family to the Ancestral Hall so she could see the new roof and pay respects to her ancestors. On the altar sat portraits of her father and Grandfather Chen. The absence of her mother's portrait was like a splinter in an old wound.

Auntie Cho-Ye touched her arm and murmured, "The Ancestral Hall honors those who have passed on, not those who remain. Your mother's absence is not a slight, but a question of faith."

As her auntie placed an arm around her shoulder, their eyes met. An understanding passed between them.

Her homecoming celebration continued with more music, singing and dancing, and bowls of rice wine for the adults. There was a feast of oxen, red rice, sweet potatoes, cabbage soup, and Auntie Huishan's wonderful turnip cakes, followed by more merriment.

At dusk, she listened for the call of the cranes, but the lake was quiet. She and Shan-Shan went for a walk.

"Are you betrothed yet, Shan-Shan?" asked Suyin.

Shan-Shan shook her head. "No, I don't want to marry young. My father's not happy about it. He doesn't realize that things have changed for women in the village. We're no longer content to let the men do our thinking for us. We are earning our own money." Shan-Shan's eyes danced. "You've inspired us."

"Did you give a rice ball to a boy at the sisters' rice festival?"

Shan-Shan smiled. "I gave two."

Suyin's eyes grew wide. "Two! Did you put a love token inside?" she asked excitedly.

"I put a pine needle in one because the boy seemed nice."

"That's a love token!" said Suyin. "It means *Give me embroidery needles!*"

Shan-Shan nodded. "Embroidery needles, not marriage. I'm not ready to put a thorn inside a rice ball yet."

"What was your second token?"

Shan-Shan giggled. "There's a boy with big ears and a foul mouth who likes me. I put a chili pepper inside."

Suyin giggled. *"Find someone else!"*

"Do you still like the same boy?" asked Shan-Shan.

Suyin blushed. "I love him, but he's too handsome. You know what Old Auntie Dou would say."

"Long on looks, short on character," they said together.

Hooking her arm around Shan-Shan's, Suyin checked to see that no one was following them.

"Show me your feather," Suyin whispered.

Shan-Shan lifted her heavy neck-ring and pulled out a black cord. At the end of the cord was a tiny black feather.

Suyin examined it closely. "Let me guess. It's a throat feather."

"No," said Shan-Shan. "Why a throat feather?"

"Because you are gifted as an orator."

Shan-Shan laughed. "No, this is an ear feather. I had to learn to listen. It is still a challenge. You know how much I love to talk."

Suyin giggled. "That's true, but I love the sound of your voice, Shan-Shan."

"There's a rumor going around among the crane sisters," said Shan-Shan, lowering her voice, "that soon you'll be ready to transform." Shan-Shan's eyes shone with excitement. "And then you'll be queen."

"I still have much to learn, Shan-Shan," said Suyin. "There are embroidery stitches to master and missives to decipher and songs to sing." She met Shan-Shan's gaze. "I'm scared. There's so much responsibility."

"Remember you are not alone," said Shan-Shan. "Your mother will be by your side and your sisters will be at your back."

As the girls walked along the shore, they could hear the brass drums and the lusheng pipes.

"Let's go back," said Shan-Shan, pulling her by the hand. "They've started the dancing."

Shortly after midnight, Cho-Ye announced that Suyin's aunties and Shan-Shan were going to have a sleepover with their special guest, at Cho-Ye's place.

"We women have a lot to catch up on." Cho-Ye winked.

"Catch up on drinking," teased Uncle Pei-Pei. "Cho-Ye made a fine batch of rice wine especially for this occasion."

"Pshaw!" said Auntie Huishan. "We're going to teach her some new stitches."

Everyone laughed.

Uncle Pei-Pei was partially right. Her aunties drank rice wine, but they also sang and stitched and reminisced.

"There's a boy I like in Gold Mountain," began Suyin hesitantly.

"That pickpocket with a face like a film star," croaked Old Auntie Dou.

Suyin's face fell. "Reformed pickpocket," she said quickly.

Old Auntie Dou's suddenly reached out and grasped Suyin's hand with her gnarled fingers. "He's a good boy."

Suyin beamed. "Really? How do you know that, Auntie?"

"We saw him pull you from the sea," said Old Auntie Dou. Auntie Cho-Ye nodded. "He was born with a bird heart."

"They make good husbands," said Auntie Huishan with a knowing smile.

Happy tears flooded Suyin's eyes. She'd wanted so badly for her aunties to approve of the boy she loved, but she'd never dreamed that such a miracle was possible.

As the night wore on, Suyin finally gathered enough courage to ask her aunties the question that had burned in her mind for so long.

"Why did none of you ever want to adopt me?"

Auntie Cho-Ye placed her arm around Suyin's shoulder. "I'll always remember the day you wandered off," she said. "It was the dead of winter. You were only three years old, just a little tyke. We found your body by the lake, blue with cold. When we carried you to the Ancestral Hall, we were full of shame. You had lost your parents, and your grandfather had neglected you. We lit joss sticks and prayed for a miracle. And we promised the spirits that if you lived, you would have as many parents as families in the village. We pledged that each family would love you as they would their own son or daughter. And when your heart began to beat again, we rejoiced. From that moment on you became the daughter of our hearts."

All at once Suyin saw everything clearly: the dishes placed on her step, the invitations to eat at many houses, the gifts of rice and mulberry tea. All these years she'd thought her people had pitied her. She had thought of herself as a burden, when they had thought of her as a daughter. She had not just one family—but many.

That night she slept on the warm kang, surrounded by three snoring aunties and her best friend.

Sometime toward morning, she woke to a haunting horn note. She sat up in bed, a song rising in her throat. She lifted her arms, as if to take flight, believing for the briefest of moments that she was a bird.

Suyin pushed her feet into her boots, grabbed her jacket, and crept outside. The calls had come from the fen side of the lake. She ran to the lakeshore and waited, her heart wild with hope. Through the gray light of early dawn, she watched as a flock of black-necks wheeled above her. One by one, the cranes descended in a winding spiral, calling out to her. She stood transfixed, one hand reaching skyward, willing them to stay. As the sun rose, the flock began their ascent, except for a lone crane that lingered, circling above her. Suddenly, Suyin noticed the crook in the crane's wing.

"Mother!" she cried.

As her mother landed, Suyin held out her hand. Her mother touched her fingers with her wingtips. Suyin's eyes welled up as she gazed into her mother's golden eyes and saw her own reflection. Her mother raised one wing and removed a small silver object from her sewing pouch with her beak. It was her mother's embroidery scissors— the scissors that had been lost at sea.

"I pass these on to you, my precious daughter," said her mother. "Your inheritance for a future queen."

Suyin bent down and wrapped her arms around her mother's body. She felt the faint beating of her mother's heart.

And then all too soon, her mother flapped her wings and rose into the sky.

Suyin pressed the embroidery scissors to her chest. They were a reminder of everything she had lost then found—her heritage, her membership in the clan, and the love of her sworn sisters across time.

She raised her hand in a wave as the flock flew across the lake and beyond the Wushan Mountains. She stood watching until the lake was quiet again, then she crept inside to join her human family.

Glossary

cheongsam—traditional Chinese silk dress, usually long and slit at the sides

dim sum—traditional Chinese dishes served in small portions as a meal

face—an expression that means to have prestige or high status: "Don't break my face" or "I've got big face today"

fen—a low-lying grassy wetland

fresh-off-the-boat—newly arrived immigrants

gong si fong—usually a small one-bedroom apartment that has been divided into compartments by plywood partitions so ten to fifteen people can share the rent

green card—the card that permits a worker to be legally employed in the United States

grus—Latin word for crane

guanxi—connections, influence

Gung Hay Fat Choy—Cantonese expression meaning "Wishing you prosperity!" An expression used on Chinese or Lunar New Year.

He Shan—English translation is Crane Mountain

hebao—embroidery pouch; young girls stitch this pouch to practice their embroidery and show their skill

illegal—an immigrant who has come to a country without papers

INS—an abbreviation for Immigration and Naturalization Service, a branch of the U.S. government responsible for immigration

jiaozi—Chinese dumpling in Mandarin; ground meat or vegetable filling wrapped into a thinly rolled piece of dough

kang—a sleeping platform of masonry, heated with a fire underneath

lao fan—barbarian or a white person, used matter-of-factly to mean non-Chinese or as an insult

li—a Chinese unit of measure equivalent to approximately one third of a mile

lusheng—a reed-pine wind musical instrument used by the Miao minority people

mahjongg—game using tiles, played by four players; often used for gambling

Mandarin square—also called a rank badge, a large embroidered badge stitched onto a jacket or vest of an official or royalty in Imperial China. The badge indicated the rank of the person wearing it (the crane was the highest rank).

merrow operators—workers that run the sewing machines that sew seams

Miao—also referred to as the Hmong; population of 8.9 million

Miao hundred-bird coat—a coat embroidered with hundreds of birds as well as frogs, butterflies, dragons, and insects; this wonderful coat was only worn on auspicious occasions by a person of high rank to honor their worship of their ancestors

migrant—a person who moves from one region or country to another, often in search of work; the term often refers to undocumented people

missive—a written or stitched message

naturalization—acquiring citizenship by somebody who was not a citizen of that country when he or she was born

Nu Shu—a secret women's script invented by a small group of women in rural China

piggies—a derogatory name the snakeheads call illegal migrants

pig's bones work—tricky garments that take time to sew and pay little

snake—the human smuggling pipeline

snakeheads—smugglers who transport undocumented people, illegally, into different countries

soy sauce chicken—piecework that is quick, easy to sew, and pays well

strike—a temporary work stoppage by workers to express grievances or to resist demands from their bosses

sweatshop—a factory that violates labor laws such as child labor, minimum wages, unemployment, fire safety, or workers' compensation

ren-qing—personal favor by means of guanxi or connections; once a favor is bestowed, the receiver is obligated to repay the favor

thorn-apple—a large fragrant trumpet-like flower belonging to the datura family, used in love potions and witches' brews; although it is medicinal, it is also poisonous.

thread cutters—lowest paid workers who cut threads in a garment factory

yazi—literal translation: little ducks, illegal migrants

ylang ylang—(pronounced ee-lang-ee-lang) an evergreen tree growing in Asia with fragrant greenish-yellow flowers that yields an oil used to make perfumes

Author's Note

....

C ircle of Cranes is a work of fiction inspired by real life events: the interception of a number of migrant ships off the west coast of British Columbia, Canada, between 1999 and 2000, the horrific conditions in the hold of these ships, and the intimidation methods used by human smugglers toward undocumented garment workers in the sweatshops of Chinatown, New York.

The villages around Cao Hai Lake are among the poorest in China. In an effort to protect the flock of eight hundred black-necked cranes that winter on the lake and help the villagers, the International Crane Foundation (ICF) and the Trickle Up program of New York City provided farmers with micro-credit of one hundred U.S. dollars. ICF has also set up a sponsorship program for the education of girls called One Helps One. This program enables a sponsor to pay a twenty-dollar tuition fee to send a girl to school for a year. There is no administration fee. Interested readers may contact Li Fengshan at fengshan@savingcranes or log onto the ICF website (www.savingcranes.org/one-helps-one-program.html).

For simplicity's sake, I have used the term Miao, the Chinese term, rather than the self-referenced names of the various sub-groups, which include the Hmong, the Hmu, the A-Hmao and the Ko Xiong. Of the fifty-six ethnic groups in China, the Han makes up approximately 92 percent of the population, while the fifty-five minorities, including the Miao, make up the rest. There are 8,940,116 Miao in China, the largest group of the minorities.

Although Nu Shu, the secret women's script, has been used for centuries, it was unknown until recent years. Scholars believe that it was written, sung, and embroidered by women in the southwestern corner of Hunan province by the Yao minority people. Since Suyin was a Miao girl from Guizhou province, her sworn sisters' usage of Nu Shu was imagined. That said, some evidence exists that Nu Shu may have been wider spread. In Guizhou province, Nu Shu was discovered on a tombstone and in Jiangsu a copper coin was discovered with the Nu Shu script "all women are sisters." Professor Xie Zhimin (South China Ethnology Academy and South-Center University for Ethnic Minorities) and Professor Ye Xumin theorize that Nu Shu was created more than three thousand years ago and that the characters were derived from bird worship. However, scholars differ on the age and origin of the women's script, leaving Nu Shu still shrouded in mystery.

Circle of Cranes was inspired by a variation of an ancient folktale called "The Crane Wife." While the story is traditionally recognized as Japanese, it has roots in many Asian cultures.

Acknowledgments

Heartfelt thanks to Alisha Niehaus, who acquired *Circle of Cranes* and whose generous and wise advice guided me through the big structural changes required to make this novel fly; and an extra-special thanks to Heather Alexander, whose sensitive and thoughtful suggestions, gentle prodding, and encouragement helped me stitch the threads of Suyin's story into a unified whole.

Gratitude to Steven Chudney, agent extraordinaire, for his insightful advice on my first draft, for his faith in Suyin's story, and for cheering me on through the years I've worked on this novel. Thanks also to the readers of early drafts: Michael Sather, Leah Lindsay, Joan and Jerry Domer, and Anne Laurel Carter.

In China, appreciation to cadre Li Ming-Jun for treating me as an honored guest during my visit to Cao Hai Lake; to my friend Li Ming-Xia, for accompanying me on my journey to the remote mountain villages near Kaeli to research the Miao minority people; and in British Columbia, to the Canadian immigration officer (who prefers to remain anonymous) who not only gave me an interview about the conditions on the smugglers' ship, but also read and vetted the manuscript for accuracy. In New York City, appreciation to the expert in illegal Chinese immigrants and American labor who pointed out the locations of the sweatshops in Chinatown and to the garment workers who allowed me a glimpse of their world.

Thanks also to the Saskatchewan Writers and Artists Colony at St. Peter's Abbey for providing me with a quiet and meditative place to write.

And not least, thanks to my wonderful husband, Michael Sather, and my family: Sara Bates Rowe, Mike Rowe, Charly Rowe, Christian Bates, and Erin Pierson.